Blue Flag Beaches

This book presents a comprehensive study of the role that the Blue Flag beach program has played around the world, considering economic, social and environmental perspectives.

Since its creation in the 1980s, The Blue Flag program awards the management of beaches and marinas based on sustainability, services and quality of their management. To date there are currently close to five thousand awards around the world. Forty years on from the program's creation, this book provides a thorough evaluation of the program, to understand how it has evolved over time, the successes it has enjoyed and the challenges it has overcome, and may face in the future. As an international program, this book reflects the global nature of this program and actively discusses, examines and assesses the different realities and challenges faced by different countries around the world, drawing on case studies from across Europe, North America, Latin America, Africa and Asia. It examines the impact of the award on economic growth, from local to national, environmental protection and education, the development of sustainable tourism, and the sustainable management of beaches. The volume also contributes to emerging debates surrounding the certification of natural resources, where the Blue Flag program has been a pioneer in this field.

This book will be of great interest to students and scholars of sustainable tourism, environmental economics, coastal and beach management, environmental conservation and sustainable development.

María A. Prats is Professor of Applied Economics at Universidad de Murcia, Spain, and Visiting Senior Fellow at the European Institute, London School of Economics and Political Science, United Kingdom.

Fernando Merino is Professor of Applied Economics at Universidad de Murcia, Spain.

Earthscan Studies in Natural Resource Management

Participatory Governance of UNESCO Biosphere Reserves in Canada and Israel
Resolving Natural Resource Conflicts
Natasha Donevska

Balancing the Commons in Switzerland
Institutional Transformations and Sustainable Innovations
Edited by Tobias Haller, Karina Liechti, Martin Stuber, François-Xavier Viallon and Rahel Wunderli

Natural Resource Sovereignty and the Right to Development in Africa
Edited by Carol Chi Ngang and Serges Djoyou Kamga

Reindeer Husbandry and Global Environmental Change
Pastoralism in Fennoscandia
Edited by Tim Horstkotte, Øystein Holand, Jouko Kumpula and Jon Moen

The Bioeconomy and Non-timber Forest Products
Edited by Carsten Smith-Hall and James Chamberlain

Drylands Facing Change
Interventions, Investments and Identities
Edited by Angela Kronenburg García, Tobias Haller, Han van Dijk, Cyrus Samimi, and Jeroen Warner

Blue Flag Beaches
Economic Growth, Tourism and Sustainable Management
Edited by María A. Prats and Fernando Merino

For more information about this series, please visit: www.routledge.com/books/series/ECNRM/

Blue Flag Beaches
Economic Growth, Tourism
and Sustainable Management

**Edited by
María A. Prats and Fernando Merino**

First published 2024
by Routledge
4 Park Square, Milton Park, Abingdon, Oxon OX14 4RN

and by Routledge
605 Third Avenue, New York, NY 10158

Routledge is an imprint of the Taylor & Francis Group, an informa business

© 2024 selection and editorial matter, María A. Prats and Fernando Merino;
individual chapters, the contributors

The right of María A. Prats and Fernando Merino to be identified as the
authors of the editorial material, and of the authors for their individual
chapters, has been asserted in accordance with sections 77 and 78 of the
Copyright, Designs and Patents Act 1988.

All rights reserved. No part of this book may be reprinted or reproduced or
utilised in any form or by any electronic, mechanical, or other means, now
known or hereafter invented, including photocopying and recording, or in
any information storage or retrieval system, without permission in writing
from the publishers.

Trademark notice: Product or corporate names may be trademarks or
registered trademarks, and are used only for identification and explanation
without intent to infringe.

British Library Cataloguing-in-Publication Data
A catalogue record for this book is available from the British Library

Library of Congress Cataloging-in-Publication Data
Names: Prats, María A., editor. | Merino, Fernando (Economist), editor.
Title: Blue Flag beaches : economic growth, tourism and sustainable
management / María A. Prats, Fernando Merino.
Description: New York, NY : Routledge, 2024. | Includes bibliographical
references and index.
Identifiers: LCCN 2023008085 (print) | LCCN 2023008086 (ebook) |
ISBN 9781032347349 (hardback) | ISBN 9781032347356 (paperback) |
ISBN 9781003323570 (ebook)
Subjects: LCSH: Foundation for Environmental Education. | Coastal zone
management. | Sustainable development. | Environmental economics.
Classification: LCC HT391 .B523 2024 (print) | LCC HT391 (ebook) |
DDC 333.91/7—dc23/eng/20230412
LC record available at https://lccn.loc.gov/2023008085
LC ebook record available at https://lccn.loc.gov/2023008086

ISBN: 978-1-032-34734-9 (hbk)
ISBN: 978-1-032-34735-6 (pbk)
ISBN: 978-1-003-32357-0 (ebk)

DOI: 10.4324/9781003323570

Typeset in Times New Roman
by codeMantra

Contents

List of contributors	*ix*
List of tables and figures	*xiii*

General introduction   1
MARÍA A. PRATS AND FERNANDO MERINO

1 Origin, first steps and forthcoming challenges to the Blue Flag   9
JOSÉ R. SÁNCHEZ MORO

**2 The Blue Flag programme, at national and international
levels: What, why, how and where to?**   24
NIKOS PETROU AND JOHANN DURAND

3 Blue Flags in the world: A bibliometric analysis   43
FERNANDO MERINO AND MARÍA A. PRATS

**4 Social, political and managerial perspectives on Blue Flag
beach certification**   58
SEWERYN ZIELINSKI AND CAMILO M. BOTERO

**5 Does the Blue Flag program contribute to the achievement of
the Sustainable Development Goals?**   69
JOSÉ A. ALBALADEJO-GARCÍA AND JOSÉ A. ZABALA

6 Dive in Blue Flags: A historical evolution in Europe   85
MARÍA ESCRIVÁ-BELTRÁN AND ROSA CURRÁS-MÓSTOLES

**7 The path of Blue Flag in Latin America and the Caribbean:
History, challenges and learnings**   97
CAMILO M. BOTERO, PALOMA ARIAS AND LOURDES DIAZ

vi *Contents*

8 Impact of Blue Flags on local economy in Spain 108
ANA B. RAMÓN-RODRÍGUEZ, TERESA TORREGROSA, LUIS MORENO-
IZQUIERDO AND JOSÉ F. PERLES-RIBES

**9 Blue Flag supporting implementation of environmental
policies and nature conservation: The case of Greece** 122
NIKOS PETROU, DAREIA-NEFELI VOURDOUMPA AND CHARA AGAOGLOU

10 Blue Flag and tourism destination efficiency: The French case 133
AURÉLIE CORNE, OLGA GONCALVES AND NICOLAS PEYPOCH

**11 The challenge of sustainability in territorial development:
The impact of Blue Flag on tourism – the Italian context** 144
FRANCESCO MANTA, GIULIO FUSCO AND PIERLUIGI TOMA

12 Blue Flags on islands in the Republic of Croatia 156
KRISTINA BUČAR, IZIDORA MARKOVIĆ VUKADIN
AND ZVJEZDANA HENDIJA

**13 The impact on the local economy of having coastal areas with
Blue Flag: The Turkish case** 171
ZELIHA ESER AND SELAY ILGAZ SÜMER

14 Blue Flag South Africa: Reflections on a decade of progress 184
SERENA LUCREZI AND PEET VAN DER MERWE

**15 Challenges and opportunities of the Blue Flag certification
in Canada** 199
RACHEL DODDS AND MARK HOLMES

**16 Managing paradise: Reflections on the management of
Mexican beaches with the Blue Flag label** 209
OMAR CERVANTES, ARAMIS OLIVOS-ORTIZ, JERÓNIMO RAMOS SÁENZ
PARDO, DORA MARÍA CASTRO-LINARES AND ITZEL SOSA-ARGÁEZ

17 Blue Flag in Brazil: Beginning and growth 219
MARINEZ SCHERER, LEANA BERNARDI, ISABELA KEREN GREGORIO
KERBER AND ALESSANDRA PFUETZENREUTER

18 Blue Flag in India: Beacons for sustainable coastal management 230
SUJEETKUMAR M. DONGRE, SHRIJI KURUP AND SANSKRITI MENON

Contents vii

**19 The status of Blue Flag in Japan: Can Blue Flag be used for
beach community development as a sustainable tourist destination?** 241
NORIE HIRATA AND SUSUMU KAWAHARA

General conclusions 253
MARÍA A. PRATS AND FERNANDO MERINO

Index *257*

Contributors

Chara Agaoglou EU projects officer, Hellenic Society for the Protection of Nature (HSPN), Athens, Greece

José A. Albaladejo-García Departamento de Economía Aplicada, Universidad de Murcia, Murcia, Spain. Member of Proplayas Network

Paloma Arias Instituto Escola do Mar, Pero, Rio de Janeiro, Brazil. Member of Proplayas Network

Leana Bernardi Instituto Ambientes em Rede. Florianópolis – SC, Brazil

Camilo M. Botero Coastal Systems Research Group, CIF-Playas, Panama City, Panama and Rowe School of Business, Faculty of Management, Dalhousie University, Halifax, Canada, Member of Proplayas Network

Kristina Bučar Faculty of Economics and Business, University of Zagreb, Zagreb, Croatia

Dora Maria Castro-Linares Consultoría Especializada en Calidad y Certificación Turística. Ciudad de México, México

Omar Cervantes Facultad de Ciencias Marinas, Universidad de Colima, Manzanillo, México. Member of Proplayas Network

Aurélie Corne CRESEM, University of Perpignan, Perpignan, France

Rosa Currás-Móstoles Departament de Lingüística Aplicada, Universitat Politècnica de València, València, Spain

Lourdes Diaz Foundation for Environmental Education, Copenhagen, Denmark

Rachel Dodds Ted Rogers School of Management, Toronto Metropolitan University, Toronto, Ontario, Canada

Sujeetkumar M. Dongre Centre for Environment Education, Ahmedabad, India

Johann Durand International Blue Flag Director, Foundation for Environmental Education, Copenhagen, Denmark x *Contributors*

María Escrivá-Beltrán Departament de Comptabilitat, Universitat de València, València, Spain

Zeliha Eser Department of Business Administration, Başkent Üniversitesi, Ankara, Turkey

Giulio Fusco Department of Economic Sciences, University of Salento, Lecce, Italy

Olga Goncalves MRM, University of Perpignan, Perpignan, France

Zvjezdana Hendija Faculty of Economics and Business, University of Zagreb, Zagreb, Croatia

Norie Hirata Department of Tourism Science, Tokyo Metropolitan University, Tokyo, Japan

Mark Holmes School of Hospitality, Food and Tourism Management, Gordon S. Lang School of Business and Economics, University of Guelph, Guelph, Ontario, Canada

Selay Ilgaz Sümer Department of Business Administration Başkent Üniversitesi, Ankara, Turkey

Susumu Kawahara Department of Tourism Science, Tokyo Metropolitan University, Tokyo, Japan

Isabela Keren Gregorio Kerber Instituto Ambientes em Rede. Florianópolis – SC, Brazil

Shriji Kurup Centre for Environment Education, Ahmedabad, India

Serena Lucrezi Tourism Research in Economics, Environs and Society (TREES), North-West University, Potchefstroom, South Africa

Francesco Manta Department of Economic Sciences, University of Salento, Lecce, Italy

Izidora Marković Vukadin Institute for Tourism, Zagreb, Croatia

Sanskriti Menon Centre for Environment Education, Ahmedabad, India

Fernando Merino Departamento de Economía Aplicada, Universidad de Murcia, Murcia, Spain, Member of Proplayas Network

Peet van der Merwe Tourism Research in Economics, Environs and Society (TREES), North-West University, Potchefstroom, South Africa

Luis Moreno-Izquierdo Departamento de Análisis Económico Aplicada, Universidad de Alicante, Alicante, Spain

Aramis Olivos-Ortiz Centro Universitario de Investigaciones Oceanológicas, Universidad de Colima, Manzanillo, México

Contributors xi

José F. Perles-Ribes Departamento de Análisis Económico Aplicada, Universidad de Alicante, Alicante, Spain

Nikos Petrou Vice-President of the Foundation for Environmental Education and President of Hellenic Society for the Protection of Nature (HSPN), Athens, Greece

Nicolas Peypoch CRESEM, University of Perpignan, Perpignan, France

Alessandra Pfuetzenreuter Instituto Ambientes em Rede. Jaraguá do Sul – SC, Brazil

María A. Prats Departamento de Economía Aplicada, Universidad de Murcia, Murcia, Spain, and European Institute, London School of Economics and Political Science, United Kingdom. Member of Proplayas Network

Ana B. Ramón-Rodríguez Departamento de Análisis Económico Aplicada, Universidad de Alicante, Alicante, Spain

Jerónimo Ramos Sáenz Pardo Escuela Superior de Turismo – Instituto Politécnico Nacional (IPN). Unidad Zacatenco. Ciudad de México, México

José R. Sánchez Moro Cofounder and Honorary Member of the Foundation for Environmental Education (FEE), Spain

Marinez Scherer Federal University of Santa Catarina and Instituto Ambientes em Rede. Florianópolis, Brazil. Member of Proplayas Network

Itzel Sosa-Argáez Facultad de Turismo y Gastronomía, Universidad de Colima. Manzanillo, México

Pierluigi Toma Department of Economic Sciences, University of Salento, Lecce, Italy

Teresa Torregrosa Departamento de Análisis Económico Aplicada, Universidad de Alicante, Alicante, Spain

Dareia-Nefeli Vourdoumpa Blue Flag Program Coordinator, Hellenic Society for the Protection of Nature (HSPN), Athens, Greece

José A. Zabala Departamento de Economía de la Empresa, Universidad Politécnica de Cartagena, Cartagena, Spain, Member of Proplayas Network

Seweryn Zielinski Department of Hospitality and Tourism Management, Sejong University, Seoul, Republic of Korea, Member of Proplayas Network

Tables and figures

Tables

1.1	GAIA 20:30 strategy: Together, we can change the world	22
2.1	Criteria for getting a Blue Flag (2022)	31
3.1	Academic research on BF: Main results	44
3.2	Academic research on BF: Most global cited documents	46
3.3	Academic research on BF: Most influential authors	48
3.4	Academic research on BF: Analysis on keywords	54
5.1	Direct and indirect contributions of BFs to SDGs	71
5.2	Proposal of key BF indicators for meeting each SDG	80
6.1	Evolution of BF awarded by year by continents	89
6.2	Main data of Blue Flags in EU countries	91
7.1	Evolution and national operators of Blue Flag in Latin America and the Caribbean	100
8.1	Literature review on studies of the impact of BF in Spain	112
8.2	PLS-SEM analysis on the impact of BF in Spain: Variables	114
8.3	PLS-SEM analysis on the impact of BF in Spain: Descriptive analysis	115
8.4	PLS-SEM analysis on the impact of BF in Spain: Correlation analysis	116
8.5	PLS-SEM analysis on the impact of BF in Spain: Path coefficients and bootstrap p-values (basic bootstrapping 500 reps)	117
8.6	Dynamic panel data model on the impact of BF in Spain: Results	118
10.1	Analysis on the impact of BF in efficiency in the French touristic sector: Descriptive statistics	138
10.2	Analysis on the impact of BF in efficiency in the French touristic sector: Efficiency scores of French regions	139
11.1	Analysis on the impact of BF in Italy: Descriptive analysis	151
11.2	Panel data model on the impact of BF in Italy: Results	152
12.1	Most visited islands in Croatia (2019)	160
14.1	Assessment of the status quo related to Blue Flag in South Africa	192
19.1	Basic information on six BF Beaches in Japan	242

xiv *Tables and figures*

Figures

1.1	Diagram of Blue Flag's signs of identity and lasting success and expansion	19
3.1	Number of research publications on Blue Flag per year	45
3.2	Academic research on Blue Flags. Co-occurrence authors	49
3.3	Number of published research articles on Blue Flags by journal	51
3.4	Number of citations on Blue Flags by journal	52
3.5	Word cloud relative to research in the Blue Flag topic	53
3.6	Co-occurrence keywords in research articles on Blue Flags	55
6.1	Evolution of the number of BFs obtained by the top 5 countries by year	92
8.1	PLS-SEM: Results of the exploratory analysis in Spain	117
11.1	Blue Flag sites around the world	147
11.2	Blue Flag sites in Italy	148
12.1	Spatial distribution of beaches and marinas with Blue Flag in Croatia	163
14.1	Map of Blue Flag beaches in South Africa in 2021–2022	185
14.2	Information boards found on Blue Flag beaches in South Africa	188
14.3	Education boards found on Blue Flag beaches in South Africa	189
14.4	Regulation boards found on Blue Flag beaches in South Africa	190
16.1	Blue Flag beaches in Mexico (2022–2023 season)	215
17.1	Blue Flag Programme timeline in Brazil	220
17.2	Blue Flag sites in Brazil for 2022/2023	221
17.3	Blue Flag's growth in Brazil since its implementation	222
17.4	Blue Flag certified sites across the years 2006–2022 in Brazil	223
19.1	Maps of Japan's BF beach location and around Yuigahama Beach	243
19.2	Community development that takes advantage of the sea	246

General introduction

María A. Prats and Fernando Merino

Tourism is an important factor in the economic growth of a country, region or town. According to World Travel & Tourism Council, before the pandemic in 2019, the Travel & Tourism sector contributed 10.3% to global gross domestic product (GDP), one in ten jobs created belonged to this sector, and between 2014 and 2019, 25% of the net jobs generated globally were created in this sector.

That is why, worldwide, tourism is one of the most prominent and fastest growing sectors and has the greatest capacity to boost a country's economy. An increase in the flow of tourism can generate positive economic results for nations, especially in GDP and employment opportunities. But also, at regional or local level, tourism has an important capacity to transform, renovate and promote growth. This aspect is essential to structure disadvantaged territories, and boost developing economies or areas in decline due to problems such as depopulation. The tourist product constitutes one of the backbones of any tourism planning strategy of a territory. An adequate strategy will guarantee, on the one hand, the integration of tourism with the economic, social, cultural and environmental dimensions and, on the other, the adequate satisfaction of tourist demand.

Among the different motivations for tourism, the use and enjoyment of beaches attract large numbers of people. Beach tourism is inextricably linked to the start of the development of mass tourism. This is related, to a large extent, to the changes that occurred in industrial societies in the second half of the 20th century. Beach tourism, especially mass tourism, has had a significantly negative impact on the environment. The expansion of this type of tourism, and its public support and promotion, generated countless negative impacts during its most acute growth stages. These additional areas saw noticeable alterations to landscape and ecosystems, loss of natural and cultural heritage, intensive requirements of water and energy, and increased waste and urbanization.

Since the beginning of the 1990s, there has been a change in perspective to the tourism sector that has substantially altered its evolution. During this time a new and growing public consensus has been generated worldwide that has imposed a change of model in the sector. Local communities, and societies in general, demand that tourist areas, and especially beaches and coasts, be used and managed sustainably to ensure that their use by a large number of visitors is compatible with the protection of the environment.

DOI: 10.4324/9781003323570-1

2   María A. Prats and Fernando Merino

If we focus on the marine environment, which is what interests us in this book, this new international consensus has forced policy makers to create a legal framework that leads to managing coastal resources in a responsible, sustainable manner; one that is compatible with the economic development of the involved territories. New international policies for the management of seas and coasts emphasize the need to develop sustainability strategies that incorporate the principles of ecosystem management, whose objective is based on adequately harmonizing the relationships between human societies and the ecosystems that sustain them. In 1992, recognizing the socioeconomic importance of the coastal zone, the United Nations Conference on Environment and Development (UNCED) included integrated management of coastal and marine zones in Agenda 21. The European Commission defines Integrated Coastal Zone Management (ICZM) as "a dynamic, multidisciplinary and iterative process to promote sustainable management of coastal zones". Despite the difficulty of implementing integrated coastal management, all countries have assumed that this is the framework in which they must move.

This constituted the starting point for developing environmental quality certifications, beach certification schemes (with standards of excellence such as the Blue Flag) and environmental management systems to manage the recreational uses of the beaches.

Since then, the objective of developing the tourism industry can no longer be to exploit the existence of "sea, sun and beach". The need to implement actions that add value to the mere existence of these resources has emerged as a fundamental strategy. Among these strategies, the Beach Certification Schemes (BCSs) stand out. The BCSs are, above all, a recognition given to a beach for achieving a management that ensures its good environmental performance, while maintaining the social and economic function of the tourist activity located on and around the certified beach. The objective of the BCSs is to establish an objective system for the assignment of an environmental ecolabel that guarantees the balance between recreation and conservation. In this sense, the BCSs are a strong asset to achieve the objectives of ICZM.

The BCS make it possible to guarantee compliance with a set of standards in six categories: (1) environmental, (2) services, (3) security, (4) management, (5) information and education, and (6) others. Certification, by analyzing these standards, helps to distinguish those beaches that offer high quality, in terms of services, management, education and security, while local authorities protect the natural environment and cultural integrity. Beach certification schemes are based on sustainability principles, which means they give equal importance to economic, social, cultural and environmental aspects.

Quality certifications in maritime, environmental or tourist beaches are a relatively modern tool. In the mid-1980s, the first certification of beaches in the world with the name of Blue Flag was created in France. This environmental ecolabel for tourist beaches quickly spread throughout Europe and from there to the rest of the continents. At the same time, other certifications emerged such as the Seaside Award and the Good Beach Guide in the United Kingdom, or Playa Ambiental, Ecological Blue Flag, Playa Natural or Ecoplayas in Latin America. The adoption of an ecolabel scheme is a way of introducing economic, social, reputational and environmental benefits into a country. However, the use of ecolabels also has detractors who criticize different aspects, such as the labels either not encouraging the preservation of beaches or coastal resources in their wild state or including elements that are more related to the services available at the beach.

Despite the controversy, the importance of ecolabel schemes is deeply rooted today as a strategy for both differentiating locations and promoting more sustainable and environmentally respectful management. Today, ecolabeling schemes for tourist attractions are common among developed countries because they allow the development of sustainable tourism promotion strategies at local, national and international levels. On the one hand, the objective of ecolabels is not only to maintain but also to enhance the physical elements, encouraging the emergence of products and services compatible with sustainable environmental development in both the short and the long term. On the other hand, ecolabels are good for the tourism industry, tourist companies and tourists. The use of ecolabels is extremely beneficial in three respects: (1) it reverses the negative impact of tourism enterprises on the environment by requiring compliance with the ecolabel criteria, which are usually more demanding than are those established by national/regional law; (2) it increases the sensitivity and responsibility of tourists towards the environment of the visited places; and (3) it favors the appearance of new products and services compatible with a sustainable environmental development.

Among all the ecolabeling systems, the one with the Blue Flag stands out above all the others. Blue Flag, promoted by the Foundation for Environmental Education (FEE), is the oldest ecolabeling system. In 2023 it marks 35 years of operation, and during this time, it has spread from Europe to Africa, America, Oceania and Asia, reaching almost 50 countries.

It is a program of high international recognition that has consistently been able to maintain its commitment to excellence in beach certification. The selection of beaches to be awarded a Blue Flag is made annually. This selection is based on quality criteria that are constantly updated and rigorously analyzed by a solid accreditation body thereby guaranteeing the award's reputation. Subsequently, this ecolabel scheme can also be a driver for the economic development of the locality of the awarded beaches. The reputation of this program acts as a focus for tourist attraction and, consequently, as the driver for economic development and job creation in the locality.

This book has three fundamental objectives. Firstly, it tries to delve into the role of the Blue Flag program in the economies in which it currently operates, and demonstrates that this beach certification program and the award that comes with meeting the criteria for obtaining the Blue Flag have acted as a catalyst for the growth of the tourism sector, and therefore economic growth and job creation in the countries where it has been established. Secondly, this book aims to demonstrate that the adoption of the Blue Flag program in a country can be an important strategy not only for the sustainable management of beaches, but also for the sustainable development of the environment in which it is framed. This objective is especially important since its effects will positively result in a greater contribution

4 *María A. Prats and Fernando Merino*

to the fulfillment of the Sustainable Development Goals (SDGs) in the countries where the program is adopted.

Finally, the book attempts to fill a gap in the literature on a subject of growing importance. To the best of our knowledge, there is no publication that provides a global and international overview of the important work of the Foundation of Environmental Education and its Blue Flag program, and its impact on economic growth, the tourism sector, employment and environmental sustainability, among many other benefits, in the countries where it has been adopted.

The book is the collective work of 49 authors from 28 institutions spread across 16 countries, all of them recognized as experts in this area. This set of authors combines the personal experience of one of the promoters of the program with managers of the FEE and academic researchers with previous published articles in academic journals on the topic. As usual in scientific publications, the chapters have been peer-reviewed by 11 experts to minimize mistakes or errors as well as endorse the quality of the publication. We want to express our gratitude to them for this work.

Undoubtedly, the Blue Flag program is not the only existing certification system, nor is it without criticism. However, its undoubted effects on the economy of the countries that have obtained recognition and the demanding, continuous and committed role that the program has played over the past 35 years have made it an international benchmark with a solid reputation and, therefore, deserving of the analysis offered in this book.

To meet its objectives, the book is divided into three fundamental parts.

The first part of the book presents an overview of the Blue Flag program and its development over time. This first part is made up of two complementary chapters, written by representatives of the FEE. The involvement of the FEE, as well as academics, in contributing to this book has allowed us to outline, in first person, the details of the program from its origins to its future development. In **Chapter 1** Mr. J. M. Sánchez Moro, co-founder and honorary member of the FEE, outlines the history and intra-history of the growth of the FEE, the Blue Flag program and the Blue Flag award. This chapter describes the origins of the Foundation for Environmental Education, first as a European foundation that, over the years has developed into an international foundation with over 100 members in 81 countries. The author entertainingly analyzes the steps and vicissitudes experienced during the process of creation, implementation, first steps and consolidation of both the FEE and the Blue Flag award; as well as the support received from a multitude of international institutions such as the European Commission and the United Nations World Tourism Organization, among others. The chapter ends with an assessment of the future challenges included in the GAIA 20:30 strategy of the FEE, closely aligned with the United Nations Sustainable Development Goals, as well as personal reflections.

In **Chapter 2** Mr. Nikos Petrou, Vice-President of the Foundation for Environmental Education and President of the Hellenic Society for the Protection of Nature (HSPN) and Johann Durand, International Blue Flag Director, analyze the Blue Flag program and the process and criteria required to obtain recognition. In addition, the chapter analyzes some of its impacts and future strategic planning.

General introduction 5

The second part of the book includes five chapters (Chapters 3–7), which aim to present the general framework of recent research on Blue Flags and its prospects for the coming years. This section is based on three fundamental elements that seek to conceptualize and lay the foundations of Blue Flag research over time, analyze its relationship with sustainability and its contribution to the SDGs, and obtain an overview of implementation of the Blue Flag program. It also looks to draw future lessons from the two continents where the program is more established.

To that aim, **Chapter 3** looks at state-of-the-art academic research on the impacts and consequences of Blue Flags across the world. Through a bibliometric analysis, this chapter traces the evolution of published research about the Blue Flag, providing an overview of scientific research developments in this field. It includes the most relevant authors and their impact, the leading international journals that have published research on this area, as well as the evolution of issues that have caused the most concern in this area over time.

Regarding sustainability, **Chapter 4** centers on the growing scientific research that demonstrates the effectiveness of Blue Flag certification as a tool for sustainable tourism. The chapter addresses the limitations of Blue Flag as a tool for sustainable development measured through a set of common sustainability indicators. It also explains the disparity between academics' expectations of Blue Flag's effectiveness and the actual role beach certifications play in promoting sustainability.

As it has been said, the criteria to get a Blue Flag for a beach cover a wide array of factors. Several of them are addressed directly to a sustainable use of these natural areas, such as cleanliness of the water (that will require an adequate treatment of sewage of nearby cities, for example), or even educational activities supporting local awareness. Meanwhile, others may enhance the local economy or involve certain stakeholders in their use and management. **Chapter 5** reviews how the requirements to get a Blue Flag for a local beach, the inherent policies to achieve them, and the dynamics that a Blue Flag generate in a locality are all factors that contribute to the achievement of the United Nations' SDGs. The examples provided, from a large array of countries and different types of beaches, provide a valuable study of this factor as well as serve as examples of good practice for beach managers to incorporate SDGs into their goals.

Chapters 6 and 7 provide a perspective on how the Blue Flag program was developed in the two continents where it is most widely spread: Europe and Latin America and the Caribbean. In **Chapter 6** there is an exhaustive review on where and when the Blue Flags were awarded in European coasts from the 1980s to date. **Chapter 7** explains the expansion of the Blue Flag program in Latin America and the Caribbean (LAC) since it started in 2004 with the incorporation of Puerto Rico and the Dominican Republic. Since 2022 the program has been activated in six other countries (Brazil, Virgin Islands, Mexico, Trinidad and Tobago, Colombia and Chile) and two more (Argentina and Ecuador) are in their pilot phase, with the expectation of their first flags in 2023. This chapter reviews almost 20 years of Blue Flags in LAC and focuses not only on the successes achieved, which are common to all these countries, but also the multiple differences that identify them individually.

6   *María A. Prats and Fernando Merino*

The third part of the book comprises a series of 12 case studies of highly representative countries within the Blue Flag program that are presented from Chapters 8 to 19. These chapters delve into the impact that the Blue Flag program has had on local economies, challenges posed by this program and some specific aspects related to its management and the policies implemented to achieve them. The case studies are grouped by continents, starting with Europe (where the Blue Flag program was initiated), followed by Africa (some of their countries incorporated in 2001), the Americas, both North and South, and finally Asia.

Chapter 8 studies the relationship between the number of Blue Flags a destination has, its degree of tourism development and the standard of living of its residents. The authors analyze this relation using a PLS-Structural Equation Model that allows them to identify the existing relations in a case of special interest: the Valencian Community. This region has the highest number of Blue Flags in Spain and welcomes a large number of tourists that are mainly looking to enjoy the beaches and coasts, as well as all the tourist industry that has developed around them.

Chapter 9 develops the Greek case, highlighting the leadership role that the Hellenic Society for the Protection of Nature (HSPN), national Blue Flag Operator in Greece since 1992, is exercising on national and international networks of Blue Flag to carry out a project to protect *Posidonia Oceanica*, an endemic Mediterranean Sea grass that provides a multitude of benefits for the coastal zone. Based on the results of the project, HSPN proposes an update of the relevant Blue Flag criteria.

The aim of **Chapter 10** is to reveal whether achieving a Blue Flag is a goal for beach managers to be more efficient with the resources they have. Using a DEA model, the authors study a French case to illustrate whether the Blue Flag award becomes a tool that leads to a better use of the available resources and not only the reason to do a larger investment of the available ones. In a world where sustainability is a requirement to manage most activities, efficiency in the use of the available resources becomes a duty, not only towards the citizens that are defraying the costs, but also on future generations.

In many cases, a kind of trade-off seems to emerge between a larger economic development and more environmentally conscious policies and measures, while other approaches highlight that there are possible economic growth paths that are not contradictory to sustainability. **Chapter 11** studies this trade-off focusing on whether the Blue Flag program, and the necessary policies to achieve it, allow both kind of targets in the case of Italian coastal localities.

In many parts of the world, the islands have oriented their economies towards the tourism sector despite the fact that access to the islands has an additional cost of transport. In addition, the islands face two further challenges: first, they have to compete with the vast coastal areas of the mainland with valuable resources both from its beaches and from its marinas; second, they encounter more restrictions for economic growth since, in general, their smaller size means that their tourist attraction is more limited to a territory with a smaller network of cities or areas of economic support. **Chapter 12** studies whether the Blue Flag program enhances other sustainability strategies as well as supports socioeconomic growth in these cases, analyzing the Croatian islands where tourism plays a crucial role. However, the limitations of the lack of continuity with the rest of the national territory become a disadvantage, both for its development, as well as the wider possibilities that the territory may offer to their inhabitants.

Chapter 13 also focuses on the impact of the Blue Flag program on the local economy but from the perspective of an emerging economy where coastal tourism has quickly developed in the past few years. The growth of the tourism sector in Turkey has gone hand in hand with its incorporation to the Blue Flag program. The perspective of this question is further developed by studying cases where beach tourism has a longer tradition and the sector had a major economic impact, before the Blue Flag program was launched. In this sense, the fact that Turkey has become one of the countries with the most Blue Flags in the world gives an idea of how important this strategy has acquire in the development of coastal tourism in the country.

Chapter 14 discusses the important role that the Blue Flag program has played in South Africa. Twenty years ago, the country was the first outside Europe to adopt the program for beach management, becoming the forerunner of many other African countries. The authors highlight in the chapter how in this country, the Blue Flag program has triggered a growing commitment of all the involved groups and at all levels of administration (national, provincial and local) to improve the standards of environmental management, security, education and water quality in coastal areas and the tourism sector in order to promote the sustainable growth of coastal tourism in South Africa.

In **Chapter 15** the authors outline the importance of beach and recreation tourism and then discuss their impact within Canada and more specifically the province of Ontario. Maximizing the opportunities that Blue Flag offers to destinations and beachgoers requires a clearer articulation of the benefits of using such a program, especially in a post-Covid era where there is an increasing transition towards net zero emissions, a green strategy and the fulfillment of the commitments, such as the SDGs and the Paris Agreement. The authors consider that the Blue Flag program should take a broader approach in the future to address all these challenges in order to protect beaches, preserve the environment, include communities and also provide a good tourism experience.

Chapter 16 presents a dissertation on the Blue Flag scheme outlined from the perspective of the socio-environmental and cultural complexities of Mexico. In this context, the scope, benefits, problems and pending issues of the evolution of this recognized ecolabel in the context of Mexican recreational and tourist beaches are described and compared with other beach certification schemes that present a strategic social perspective that does not present the Blue Flag program.

In some countries, the Blue Flag program has been developed hand in hand with a national public project that seeks to articulate different policies to influence the coast with effective measures that balance economic development and environmental and heritage protection as well as aspects of urban occupation, conservation and leisure, among others. This is the case of Brazil, which is discussed in **Chapter 17**. The authors explain how the Orla Project and the Blue Flag program

8 *María A. Prats and Fernando Merino*

complement and support each other to achieve better results. On the one hand, the Orla Project develops a strategy to resolve conflicts, ordering the coastline and beaches, and paving the way for the beach to receive the Blue Flag. On the other hand, municipalities that want recognition for their efforts in coastal management can develop the Orla Project and request a reward through Blue Flag.

The incorporation and attainment of the requirements to get a Blue Flag is a complex issue and many challenges are faced by those countries/regions that wish to use this ecolabel as reference. Besides, in most of the countries, the participation in the Blue Flag program departs from local authorities or stakeholders that aim to increase the value of their coastal areas and ensure that their management is on track from a quality and sustainability perspective. However, this is not always the case, as **Chapter 18** shows. In India, national authorities launched a program to protect and develop their coastal areas and Blue Flags played an important role within this. In this chapter, a review of the challenges to implement the program and how they were dealt with by local and national authorities is carefully studied, providing a valuable reference for all those regions in the world that aim to use this strategy to develop its tourism sector and use of their beaches in a sustainable manner. This Indian example incorporates a perspective (from the highest levels of the government towards the lowest ones) that is different to the one most commonly adopted.

The Blue Flag program, as expected from a recognition that aims to promote and improve the quality of beaches, generates significant economies of scale: the more locations obtain a Blue Flag, the more benefits for the municipalities in which they are located in terms of both an increase in tourists and an increase in employment and economic growth. In countries where the tourism industry, or more specifically the part linked to beaches, is an important factor, it can have a more significant effect. These factors, in turn, may become a barrier to participation for the first locations of a country, as well as those countries where coastal tourism does not play a key economic part. **Chapter 19** deals with examples of these cases, providing a study of the societal impact of Blue Flags in one country where the program has a reduced presence and where the tourism economy is relatively small: Japan.

As can be seen, with all these topics, an exhaustive vision of the Blue Flag program is provided to the reader: from its inception and characteristics to a set of research results concerning its impact on the local economy, the tourism sector, sustainability strategies as well as challenges concerning its implementation. Many of the questions that a reader may have concerning the Blue Flag program will be answered, and we will highlight areas for future research topics related to this ecolabel that marks beaches in 50 countries across the world.

1 Origin, first steps and forthcoming challenges to the Blue Flag

José R. Sánchez Moro

1.1 Introduction

I am grateful for the opportunity to contribute to this comprehensive and thrilling initiative, as a co-founder of the Foundation for Environmental Education in Europe (FEEE) and later the Foundation for Environmental Education (FEE), with the present reflection of its origin, initial steps and some forthcoming challenges for the Blue Flag award, in relation to the 2020–2030 GAIA strategy and the United Nations Sustainable Development Goals (SDGs).

I also congratulate and thank all those who, with their work, have shown that even in times of global crisis, such as the current one, the values and programs of FEE remain valid and, more importantly, have improved their social value and wider acceptance.

This gratitude extends to those who are not yet here and will take over from us, as well as those who are no longer here, but who, with their efforts and examples, made our dreams real and helped us to reach this point.

I wanted to begin with the same words with which I addressed the whole of the FEE on its 40th anniversary. The motives of those invitations and the audience were similar to those of FEE, as they were still a sign of our "evolutive continuity". The FEEE, which we created in 1982, within the European cultures and borders, no longer exists, nor would it maintain today its original opportunity and social usefulness. So let us proclaim: "Our glorious European FEEE is dead. Long live our hopeful global FEE!" Moreover, how can we continue to recognize in this FEE the best of our original DNA and culture?

I believe that we can because of the existence of, and capacity to anticipate, the signs of identity, which will be thoroughly described later. We need to change but still maintain the DNA and "style", the objectives and social utility, that have justified our creation and permanence.

This chapter and the next one are complementary, attempting to avoid repetitions and maintaining our own styles and functions. What they present is the official vision of what FEE currently is and aspires to be and do in the future, as well as with and for whom. In my case, it is simply a personal testimony of who we were as co-founders, and why and for what purpose we acted as we did. When I suggest reflecting on my proposal of a diagram, or I make some suggestions for the future,

DOI: 10.4324/9781003323570-2

10   *José R. Sánchez Moro*

these correspond to my own vision, or if I speak on behalf of all the co-founders, including those who can no longer do so, I try to adhere to what we agreed on.

In my examples I refer to the *Asociacion de Educacion Ambiental y del Consumidor* (ADEAC)/FEE; this is because, after 40 years, it is what I know best and what responds to my vision. In addition, it is because of the difficulty for the ADEAC, a small entity created in 1984 as the FEE's Spanish branch, to play a key role in Blue Flag's first steps and in Spain's global leadership, as well as in the number of Blue Flags, in addition to its contribution in terms of inclusiveness, public/private cooperation and new initiatives. These include the network of 80 blue trials, the thematic distinctions and excellence on one criterion, as well as its exemplary aspects in terms of lifeguarding and the public health system.

1.2 Antecedents

In terms of its origins, FEEE did not appear suddenly and out of nowhere in 1982. In that "birth" FEEE was assisted, in the delivery and long gestation, by our small group of "co-founders". We had been working together in the Committee for Environmental Education of the Council of Europe since the mid-1970s. This entitled a triple requirement for people to be faithful to their principles, defenders of the interest of the countries we represented and, lastly, "neutral" bureaucrats and promoters of international actions by a multilateral organization.

All this involved a long learning process regarding how to harmonize the local and global dimensions, the public and private interest and values, and interdisciplinary and inter-administrative collaboration. In addition, we had to balance urgency and importance at the local and global level, including respect for the past and openness to the future, or when and how to centralize or decentralize our actions or decisions. Many of these issues are recognizable among the attributes of the current FEE's identity, which we will examine later for their interdependence and contribution to the Blue Flag's success and global extension.

Our progressive awareness of the importance and limits of our work demonstrated the need to create a parallel entity, one more agile, independent and equitable, that would use the advantages and avoid the inconveniences of the different forms and areas of proven collaboration. All this, without being the only reason or circumstances, notably contributed to the subsequent FEEE's creation. Since then, we have all been co-founders and we are helping to reinvent the FEE's and Blue Flag's future.

1.2.1 *When and why the Blue Flag was created*

Jean Baptiste de Vilmorin, another co-founder of the FEEE, had been advisor to the French Ministry for the Environment since its creation in 1971. The minister, Mrs. Hugette, asked him, in August 1985, to accompany her to Port Camargue, and to propose a campaign idea involving an environmental protection association.

To this end, Jean Baptiste asked his Belgian friend Marcel Clébant, creator of the Message to the Sea's campaign, to lend him his logo, but without the bottle

Origin, first steps and forthcoming challenges to the Blue Flag 11

containing the messages which floats on the three waves. He would thus make one of his visionary dreams come true: "You who love the sea, let others know it, hold up a sign that, from afar, testifies: I love you and I protect you. At that moment I already conceived the principle that would eventually become the Blue Flag".

Harry Wals, co-founder and first president of the FEEE, invited the first four member countries, the Netherlands, Germany, Denmark and Spain, to ratify this agreement, and extend it within the FEEE. Having turned this brilliant idea into a symbol to express it into one of the three official international programs sponsored by the EU, our next dedicated collective task was to reach a consensus for some common objectives, criteria, methods and required resources.

1.3 Launch and first Blue Flag steps

It is not easy to imagine, today, the inherent difficulties involved in the launching and introduction into the market, in 1987, of a new mark for the environmental quality of the coast, by an unknown non-governmental organization without any previous experience in the subject. This mark, with the ambition of becoming an international reference, proposed to grant its distinction based on objective and known criteria, with independence, transparency and fairness, regardless of any political, economic or territorial influences.

It was required that the award be renewed every year with an inspection "in situ" that could withdraw the Blue Flag in cases of non-compliance. Finally, the right to hoist the Blue Flag did not give entry into any Olympus of beaches, or for beaches to be classified in any ranking or top 10. It only assured the fulfillment of some minimum and easily known requirements during the following bathing season. But the real difficulty lay in the fact that the Blue Flag was, even timidly, orienting its evaluation criteria toward a delicate theme: "The negative environmental and social impact, of traditional tourism on the coast, among other factors, in recent decades".

This was a growing and urgent problem that was well known, but no one ventured to be the first to set limits or remedies, given the potential conflicts of interest, or their economic and political consequences.

In this regard, hardly anyone could oppose the objective of the Commission, through the Blue Flag, to raise the level of environmental quality of its beaches and ports. But this exercise of objective clarification could, and in fact did, show that some classic or famous destinations, despite their long-standing reputation and media image, did not reach that "supposed excellence" in their sanitary, environmental and social conditions.

Some of these destinations, aware of this, do not present themselves for the Blue Flag, and instead question the aims and methods or deny their own need for improvement. Some of them even urge the creation of a more benevolent award that would estimate "other" variables. Thus, for example, they suggest the European Community's minimum exigence of "water quality suitable for bathing" is sufficient instead of the recommended "excellent in all its sampling points, throughout the bathing season", which is promoted by the Blue Flag.

How can one avoid evoking Ibsen's Dr. Stockman in *An Enemy of the People*, or *An Enemy Among Us*, where the official doctor of the spa, which is essential to the town's economy, discovers and risks revealing that the spa's waters were seriously polluted? Even more so, the real problem is not this fact, but the tolerance or connivance of a society that puts short-term economic interests before the health of their whole population.

In addition, one main value and obstacle is that Blue Flag is the oldest ecolabel in this field, as it dates from 1985, and has thus become a model for and precursor of all others. Whether the Blue Flag was an isolated precedent without continuity, or whether it was consolidated as a new and more exigent scale of "environmental quality", different from the traditional, so-called "total quality" or "quality of services", was therefore of crucial importance.

Consequently, the Blue Flag award was able to become, as it is now, a new criterion to be considered in the choice of vacation destination for millions of tourists.

On the other hand, positively, the Blue Flag award also revealed many unknown destinations, which are modest and have limited means, that demonstrate an exemplary and admirable desire for improvement.

1.3.1 The European Commission's support

In 1987, the European Year of the Environment, the European Commission co-sponsored this idea, agreeing with the FEE to extend its scope and objectives to the beaches and marinas of the 12 member states, as well as including new criteria, such as the fulfillment of the European Directive on Bathing Waters.

The remarkable and unexpected media coverage and social repercussions of the Blue Flag, in promoting and distinguishing the improvement of European beaches, motivated the European Commission to extend its support during the following years, in which the criteria and their control were extended and strengthened.

Throughout these 11 years, in which the European Commission supported and co-sponsored the Blue Flag, they faced different economic, social and political situations. Logically, this affected the problems and priorities of the Commission, as well as its expectations and demands on the Blue Flag. To illustrate this evolution and differences, we will transcribe the official statements of the two first supportive Commissioners for the Environment, from Brussels' annual ceremonies and press conferences, to publicize the Blue Flag's results at the European level.

Somewhat later, when discussing the 10th anniversary of the Blue Flag, we include a third commissioner's testimony, from Ritt Bjerregaard. I propose the following question: Why, for each of these three commissioners, is it more important to promote or to thank Blue Flag?

1.3.2 Every year is a European Year of the Environment

The Blue Flag campaign has been one of the most successful actions at European level, among those carried out, on the occasion of the European Year of the Environment, increasing the degree of awareness of local authorities, users of the sea and the population in general, about the environmental state of the coast and the responsibility, that each one of us, has in its protection.

It is also a means of stimulating international concern for the quality of the environment and the need for close cooperation, in the struggle for a cleaner, safer and healthier world. Proudly fly a Blue Flag as a symbol, of environmental quality and commitment, to the European environmental ideals.

(Stanley Clinton Davies, member of the Commission of the European Communities for the Environment during the 1987–1988 campaigns)

1.3.3 A sign of solidarity and a contribution to European citizenship

For his part, the Commissioner for the Environment, Carlo Rippa di Meana (1989–1992), stated that:

The millions of Europeans, who spend their holidays in other countries, did not need to wait, until 1992, to perceive the whole of Europe as one country. … The Blue Flag campaign, with its goal of clean and safe beaches, everywhere and for everyone, is a real sign of solidarity and a practical contribution, to a citizens' Europe. … I congratulate the Blue Flag, for having subjected its award to strict rules, in the respect of bathing water regulations, where the Commission had to confront, several Member State governments.

In fact, this was the main reason for the Commission's initial support, and where the Blue Flag achieved a dramatic positive change, in the widespread non-compliance with this Bathing Waters Directive, ten years after its adoption. Finally, he claims to: "Particularly welcome, the importance given to information and education, in order to make holidaymakers, feel responsible for the beaches they visit".

1.4 First decade of Blue Flag 1987–1998

In this first decade between 1987 and 1998, the main task was to better define this brand and its signs of identity and to introduce it into the market, with the necessary social, political and economic support, to achieve its credibility, diffusion and verifiable results.

14   *José R. Sánchez Moro*

In the analysis of needs and priorities, the focus was on the local municipal level and its possible problems, such as inertia or shortcomings, with respect to the required criteria. More specifically, the focus was on:

- Compliance with legislation on the quality of bathing waters, discharges or waste and on the littoral management or planning.
- Improvements in the accessibility, cleanliness and maintenance of facilities and services, especially the staff, equipment and organization of lifeguard services.
- Absences or deficiencies in environmental information and education.

In terms of methodology, the following actions were focused on:

- Stimulating, accompanying and rewarding the fulfillment of objective criteria, which were known and equal for all, as well as progressively more demanding.
- Raising awareness of the existence, aims and identity of the Blue Flag, as well as its contribution to a network for permanent cooperative advantages, rather than temporary competitive ones.
- Setting up and strengthening the structures and mechanisms for public/private participation and cooperation, at different levels, as well as the coordination at national and international levels.
- Obtaining the necessary social and financial support, especially after the end of the European Union's contribution.

1.4.1 Ten years of Blue Flag campaigns

Tourism clearly demonstrates the need to reconcile environmental conservation with economic development. Increasingly, the characteristics of a healthy environment stand out, along with recreational services and facilities, as its main attraction.

Tourism thus obviously requires a sustainable development-oriented approach. This is particularly urgent and important for European coastal areas, which are highly vulnerable and under increasing pressure.

The merit of the Blue Flag campaign is that it stimulates this necessary process. It is an excellent example of the application of, the principles of subsidiarity and shared responsibility, central components of the European Union's environmental policy.

The increase in the number of award-winning candidates shows that local stakeholders feel committed to playing their part in protecting the environment. The positive response of tourists to Blue Flag education and awareness programs also underlines the value of this voluntary approach.

I would like to warmly commend the Blue Flag campaign and all its operators and partners for their contribution to the conservation of Europe's natural heritage.

(Ritt Bjerregaard, member of the Commission of the European Union,
responsible for the environment, 1995–1999)

Origin, first steps and forthcoming challenges to the Blue Flag 15

By the end of the 1990s, the number of candidates and the administrative requirements had multiplied, and an increased number of non-EU members, and even non-European countries, had joined the Blue Flag program. Consequently, the European Commission was relieved of its main global institutional support of the Blue Flag by the United Nations World Tourism Organization (WTO), together with other global partners, such as the United Nations Environment Programme (UNEP), International Union for Conservation of Nature (IUCN) or International Life Saving Federation of Europe (ILSE). Hereinafter, the FEE strengthened its global and inclusive character.

During this period, the Blue Flag has enriched and consolidated its criteria and convergent initiatives with partners, as well as its methodology, international coordination, and corporate image and social reputation. The focus has moved, step by step, from local and regional to national and FEE levels, and from environmental and technical problems to a more social and holistic approach, as well as long-term and global sustainable solutions.

1.4.2 Awards for improving the coastal environment

An official publication by UNEP, WTO and FEE that globally promotes the Blue Flag includes the following priorities and demands:

a) Coastal regions are, among the most densely populated and environmentally vulnerable, due to industrial urban pressure, exploitation of marine resources and tourism. There is therefore an urgent need to integrate the various possible uses of coastal resources, so that they can be developed in harmony, with each other and with the environment.
b) The Blue Flag has contributed, at the European level, and we hope that it can serve as an inspiration, for actions to be undertaken with this objective, in other geographical areas, with different geographical and socio-economic conditions.

In 2007, with 3,300 flags in 37 countries, Blue Flag still modestly self-defines as: "An international ecolabel, awarded to the beaches and marinas of the world that meet a specific set of criteria, within the areas of water quality, environmental education, information or management and safety and services".

In the same year, Ian Eriksen, as FEE's president, signed a memorandum of understanding with Francesco Frangialli, Secretary General of the UNWTO, which includes other innovative aspects, such as that it: "Recognizes the work done by FEE in tourism certification... specially the definition and implementation of the Blue Flag and Green Key,... and their joint efforts towards more sustainability in tourism... and promoting carbo offsetting mechanisms, through the FEE CO_2 Fund".

Once again, we have been given an expectation, a new undertaking and higher responsibility, from the outside, beyond our modest objectives: to move from European to global beaches and ports, from beaches to the whole coastline, and from

16 *José R. Sánchez Moro*

ecological factors, and services, to a more holistic concept that includes new social factors of sustainability.

On the other hand, that is a clear sign that our "promises" have been surpassed, rather than unfulfilled, as well as that the outside perception is often more benevolent than our own evaluation, or perceives collateral positive aspects outside of our assessment.

All this has already translated in 2020 to more than eight million visitors and some 20,000 environmental educational activities, per year, at the 4,671 Blue Flag sites, in 47 countries. In addition, the Blue Flag has been confirmed by the UN-WTO as the most valuable, oldest, widespread, and globally recognized award for sustainable beaches and marinas.

1.5 Public–private cooperation

The Blue Flag initiated and consolidated an unprecedented type of public–social initiative of "critical and loyal cooperation". It goes beyond a simple convergence of objectives or an economic contribution, in exchange for carrying out certain tasks of common interest.

The difference does not lie in the chosen legal formula, which is no different from the usual ones of a contract service, grant or agreement. Thus, to varying degrees, and countries, that cooperation is distinguished by the fact that:

- It is global and covers all levels, from multilateral, state or regional to local. It ranges from collaboration with a small town council, to joint participation, on equal footing and under our presidency, in the national or international jury.
- It favors inter-administrative cooperation, between the different levels of the administrations involved: local, supra-municipal and state, and between their different departments, with their political bias, or converging competences, which are not always perfectly delimited or free of controversy.
- It implies the pooling of ideas and human and technical resources, as well as possible mutual support in the other convergent initiatives of each of the parties.
- It has maintained its uninterrupted continuity over almost 40 years, regardless of political changes and crises at all levels.
- In addition to bilateral agreements or cooperation, it also takes place jointly in juries and meetings, not only to exchange opinions, but to deliberate and take decisions, searching for consensus on sensitive issues, where interests, competencies or political positions may meet without converging.

1.6 In search of excellence

1.6.1 From total quality to sustainable global quality

The concept of "ideal quality" and its methodologies have been evolving. The markets, which are increasingly globalized and informed, demand a growing variety,

Origin, first steps and forthcoming challenges to the Blue Flag 17

accessibility, reliability and convenience in the use of products and services, without renouncing the price and savings factors, and with a minimum but growing threshold of respect for the environment and human rights. Depending on the hierarchy of these attributes, we will have one quality model or another, and this concept of total quality or "quality of services" has now become inadequate for the Blue Flag's purposes.

The European Union, international agreements, and consumer pressure have introduced new social and environmental variables, according to current global threats. The world of quality reacted with certain shifts in savings and efficiency procedures, or some attitude and behavioral changes, but in no case do they include education, or a change of values, as an objective. All of this may have been and perhaps still is useful in some industries or services.

But a beach or a national park is not a company, nor a commodity or a simple "opportunity cost". Consequently, their managers cannot act, like any other businessman, in the evaluation of their needs and priorities or in the analysis of their costs and benefits. In any case, there is no single, ideal quality improvement or certification system that is applicable to all situations, including the Blue Flag. They do not differ in their methods or their costs/benefits, but in their own distinct underlying vision and mission.

1.6.2 Our search of excellence

The Blue Flag's search for excellence is not only a hope or a promise as part of its utopia or vision and those values which it tries to educate about or exemplify, such as truthfulness, equity or transparency. Nor does it correspond to some current meanings of excellence: superior, pre-eminent or prime, as opposed to inferior, or to something or someone beyond the reach of the majority that is exquisite or precious, or of closer meaning, worthy, or even unusual.

We do not strive to improve, or to contemplate ourselves in the mirror, like Snow White's stepmother. Rather, we aim to follow that medieval knight who had a well on his shield, with the motto: "The more I give, the more I have".

I believe that "our excellence" does not pretend that we are or we must be more or better than all the others. I could define it thus: "Among all of us, we strive to be and do the best we know and can, according to our capabilities and opportunities, to become more helpful, beneficial or serviceable".

It is not a single and difficult goal, like reaching Everest, but is instead a never-ending story, like the conquest of oneself or outer space. It is a process, and it brings our expectations closer to the reality, here and now, through some principles and concrete exigences:

a) The requirement of legality, whether it is related to the environment, health, labor, or land use planning. There is no quality or excellence without legality, and it would be close to complicity to excuse or reward such an absence.

b) The selection of minimum criteria that are well known and equal for all, scientifically based and responding to real and perceived needs, demanding and

18   *José R. Sánchez Moro*

achievable, so as to leave no one behind, and evolutionary, that are periodically reviewed, and expanded by consensus. The ADEAC's Thematic Awards for Excellence, in one specific criterium or the voluntary exigence of some additional criteria, constitute an inventory of excellent practices.

c) The Blue Flag is not an annual competition with an award, but a continuous process, throughout the year and over time, that involves suggestions and requirements for improvement, and a personalized "accompaniment".

d) Quality control is not exercised alone, through application dossiers or on-site inspections. Each user is invited to submit suggestions for improvement or complaints of non-compliance. In some cases, there is also an exchange of data with the official inspection services.

e) It seeks to give permanent cooperative advantages, rather than temporary competitive ones. There are no winners, no rankings, and no material prizes. It is a team competition, a sort of Ryder Cup, where the triumph or failure of one or an occasional couple is the triumph or failure of all. This means that Blue Flag beneficiaries can emulate, help and learn from each other's successes or failures. The elitist concept of "The more we are, the less we touch" is replaced by "The more we are, the more prestige and notoriety we share".

f) We care for your life and for your beach. Concern for health and saving lives is the Blue Flag's main objective, of which the ADEAC has been an example. We benefited from previous work regarding the prevention of vital risks, with approximately 35,000 workshop participants, and the training and improvement of their social consideration of more than 3,000 lifeguards, as the "beachhead" of the public health system or the emergency brigades. Rescue teams have saved a thousand people's lives, and a further 10,000 deaths were prevented in time. But the unique fact is that out of approximately a hundred total cardiorespiratory arrests, 49 people (52%) were "resuscitated" with a defibrillator, within five minutes and in the sand itself. Only 60 persons, 34 of them on the water, were unfortunately dead in 2021, within a daily peak average of 3,000,000 users, on the 610 Spanish Blue Flag beaches.

The three religions of the book agree that "whoever saves a life saves the whole of humanity". All those lives saved or recovered, in one summer, in a single country, constitute our most precious contribution to this excellence to which we aspire.

1.7 Blue Flag's signs of identity and lasting success and expansion

This diagram (Figure 1.1) summarizes some truisms, many proven experiences, and several intuitions and dreams, not always fulfilled. What I have tried to synthesize and visualize in it is a big picture of the Blue Flag and FEE's hallmarks or signs of identity which justified its creation and current validity, as well as its social usefulness, independence, credibility and effectiveness, to achieve verifiable benefits, and its global success and uninterrupted consistent expansion.

The necessary interdependence of these signs of identity is a part of their differentiating, not excluding, character. On the contrary, they stimulate the search for potential confluences and synergies, with other public or private, local or global entities.

Origin, first steps and forthcoming challenges to the Blue Flag 19

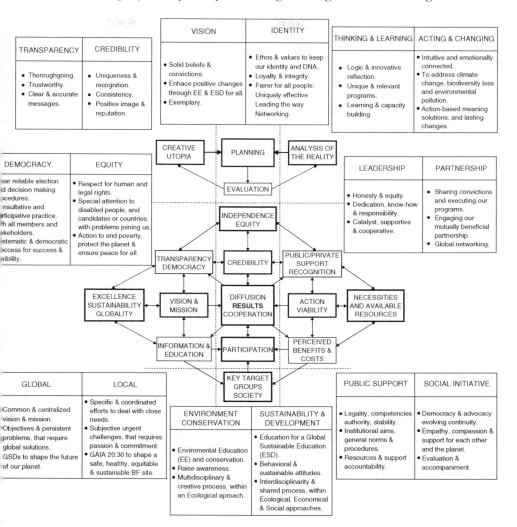

Figure 1.1 Diagram of Blue Flag's signs of identity and lasting success and expansion

The upper part of the central diagram shows the existence of our *creative utopia*, which is always unattainable and, therefore, even more motivating. It represents an ideal project involving people, society and the planet, which points out and stimulates us to reach that destination, "where we want to arrive". This ideal must be confronted, dialectically, with the *analysis of our reality*, or in other words, "where we are starting from". In what aspects, to what extent or at what pace do our situation and available means allow us to advance in the desired direction? The result of this synthesis is a *plan*, which requires prioritizing goals, means and deadlines, according to their importance or urgency, at the local or global level. Its final *evaluation* will allow us to know to what extent we have achieved these objectives. Likewise, it enables us to offer feedback, not only for future *planning*, but also for the revision of our creative utopia and of that "new reality" resulting from the changes achieved. Next, the diagram outlines on its sides why and for

20 *José R. Sánchez Moro*

what reasons we undertook this hazardous journey, including how, with whom and with what results, costs and benefits.

The central part of the diagram answers these essential questions: Is the Blue Flag vision and mission maintaining its attractiveness and usefulness on a personal and social level? Is it credible and viable, economically, ecologically and socially? Does it have the necessary support and resources, and a favorable cost/benefit ratio, to guarantee its viability and progressiveness? Do its proclaimed independence and equity, transparency and democracy, reputation and support guarantee its credibility? Do the three axes of its vision and mission, including the search for excellence, sustainability and globality, which they defend and disseminate, remain true and valid, as we asserted? Do the information and education provided by the Blue Flag ensure a level and quality of open and inclusive participation? As far as the proclaimed network cooperation is concerned, is it global and effective? Do the same information, education or verifiable benefits raise the curiosity or awareness of society on this issue? Does it encourage its recipients and potential beneficiaries to participate in obtaining, maintaining and/or improving "their" Blue Flag?

Finally, the lower part of the diagram refers to the *key target groups*, which are potential Blue Flag participants and cooperators. These addressees, in addition to the local authorities and technicians or beach users and workers, include the society as a whole, encompassing both locals and visitors, regardless of their status, with special attention paid to disabled people or those with special needs.

The interdisciplinary nature of the Blue Flag involves its different axes: education, health or sustainability, as well as its direct or collateral economic effects, not only in their "passive" condition as recipients and/or beneficiaries, but also in their "active" "condition" as necessary cooperants. Let us not forget that the Blue Flag requires changes in attitudes and behaviors, and a correlative exercise of rights and duties, on the part of its managers, as well as its local users and visitors. So, the sporadic irresponsibility of a few can hinder or spoil the continuous efforts of the majority.

In synthesis, the key to the successful results of Blue Flag, obtained in a cooperative way, and awarded in an equitable way, requires the confluence of four elements: vision and mission, credibility, viability and participation. In turn, these variables are the result of the quality and interdependence, of all the other signs of identity, as mentioned above. I leave it to the reader to analyze the interactions and potential meaning of the direction and sense of the arrows, or the absence or suppression of some of the mentioned factors.

1.7.1 Much more than a diagram

In the spirit of FEE, I have tried, when addressing my students, readers or collaborators, to emphasize the importance of the story, the word's meaning, the examples and evocative quotes and the personal and emotional dimension, not only the rational one, of the messages. As Socrates said: "Questions are more important than answers". His maieutic method helps, through dialogue, to give birth to ideas, so that the other discovers the truth for himself by answering his questions and raising new ones, rather than through repeated and reassuring answers. These include new hypotheses that are still unproven and voluntary "homework" for checking or turning them into theses.

In this case, I have already suggested analyzing one's own position, before starting to evaluate the FEE's one. Discovering what each one considers, as well as what is left or missing in the diagram, in addition to what relationships are certain or doubtful or what it shows or hides, can be a useful exercise for knowing yourself and enriching your assessment.

Moreover, a diagram is like the outline of a body, with its anatomy and physiology, organs and functions. Where can one find the soul or what is called "the spirit of the foundation"? What is the role of inspiration, which Picasso claimed should find us at work, or intuition, now revalued by neuroscience? Where should we place loyalty and fidelity or the hidden reasons for adhesion and commitment?

To facilitate this task, without further explanation, I propose to the reader, in addition to the central diagram, some pairs of complementary words and brief statements. All of these represent one aspect or period of the "Blue Flag's body and spirit". They could be added to or placed inside one other in the diagram. This will permit you to clarify or hint at the ideal of the Blue Flag and/or its daily reality in order to create your own diagram. So, I invite you to reflect on what should or should not be the presence or importance of those words, pairs or concepts, either in mine or in your own diagram.

What does all this have to do with the Blue Flag? For me, it is very relevant, starting with the Blue Flag being a flag and not a trophy cup, and being blue, rather than black or white, for we are not pirates and we do not use it to give up.

1.8 The FEE's GAIA 20:30 strategy

Our common legacy of 40 years in environmental education and action is thoughtfully reflected in our GAIA 2020–2030 strategy to shape a safe, healthy, equitable and sustainable future for our planet, which is aligned with the SDGs' objectives and strategies.

Working with our members, we educate and empower a great variety of audiences of all ages and cultures to take actions and implement solutions, to mitigate effects, locally, nationally and globally, in over 100 countries, across six continents, and involving 20 million young people per year.

In this regard, we have redefined our goals, subgoals and priorities, at a global level, according to the mentioned United Nations SDGs. We need to reinvent ourselves to cope and to give priority to current and global problems, as well as to provide solutions to an unknown future and unexpected situations.

This outline presented in Table 1.1 seeks to provide a brief and dynamic overview of the GAIA 20:30 strategy, presenting in parallel its initial objectives and its intended final outcomes. Thus, three basic goals have been chosen, around the *climate crisis*, *environmental pollution* and *biodiversity loss*, each subdivided into four subgoals, with 12 in total.

22　*José R. Sánchez Moro*

Table 1.1 GAIA 20:30 strategy: Together, we can change the world

GAIA 20:30 strategy	*Specific strategic goals and subgoals*	*What we envision as a success by 2030*
Empower climate action		
	• Ensure FEE's policies and programs meet its environmental goals. • Increase climate change knowledge to drive impactful action. • Support actions for climate resiliency. • Accelerate the transition to climate neutrality.	• A minimal carbon footprint for FEE. • Climate-literate citizens taking action. • Resilient and knowledgeable community. • Many achieving net zero CO_2 emissions.
Protect global biodiversity		
	• Preserve existing and create new forests/natural areas. • Promote sustainable management of the coastal zone. • Combat pollinator and insect loss. • Raise awareness of and support actions to remove invasive alien species.	• Healthy ecosystems, with flourishing native flora and fauna. • Thriving and balanced coastal zones. • Robust and growing pollinator populations. • Improved global Green Infrastructure.
Reduce environmental pollution		
	• Reduce litter and waste. • Promote responsible production and consumption. • Increase knowledge and take action to reduce invisible pollutants. • Promote the circular economy model	• People doing more and better with less. • Restorative and regenerative economies. • Cleaner land, air and water resources. • Responsible actions and sustainable lifestyles.

Any stakeholder supporting our vision, mission and strategy may emphasize some of the SDGs or GAIA's subgoals, sharing the consensus with the common objective:

To improve the sustainability of the coastline and local tourism, as a destination, capable of attracting responsible travelers, who cooperate in the joint effort of the local population, its authorities and its tourism sector, to maintain and improve, those standards of sustainability, environmental and social excellency, already achieved.

Origin, first steps and forthcoming challenges to the Blue Flag 23

1.9 Conclusions: The forthcoming challenges of the Blue Flag

Blue Flag sites, in my opinion, should be characterized by the fact that they constitute a common space, which is multi-purpose, creative and participatory, offering areas for meeting, resting, learning and activities. This could require specialized sections or spaces: smoke and/or noise-free corners; free areas for rented or sold items; or delimited locations for workshops, cultural and environmental resources or activities, with specialized staff to cope with the specific needs of beach users. They should aim to be:

- Open and accessible, without physical, economic or cultural barriers.
- Inclusive for the access and participation of people with disabilities or special needs.
- Protected, biodiverse, informative and awareness-raising.
- Safe, responsible, foresighted and healthy, as public spaces that promote health.
- Informative, educational and awareness-raising, as public spaces and promoters of culture.
- Intelligent (smart) and connected, as public spaces promoting a greener and more equitable digitization.
- Reflective of the best environmental practices of their municipalities and an appropriate place for testing and innovating new initiatives, as public spaces and promoters of sustainability within their communities.
- Exemplary, in their respect for the rules and their solidarity and responsibility and in their attitudes and behaviors, as public spaces that promote civic-mindedness and the knowledge and exercise of the rights and duties implied by the Blue Flag.

2 The Blue Flag programme, at national and international levels

What, why, how and where to?

Nikos Petrou and Johann Durand

2.1 Introduction

The Blue Flag programme is, in essence, a catalyst that enables local actors to engage in the decision-making process and implement actions to sustain their local environment, following the vision, the mission, and the values of the Foundation for Environmental Education (FEE). As one of the first eco-labels launched worldwide, the Blue Flag paved the way for many others in existence today. Focusing on the tourism sector, the programme, recognised internationally by its award, had to be holistic, bound by time and location, with strong sets of criteria to fulfil its mission of excellence, while being appealing to local tourism actors.

In 1987, the two first sets of criteria were launched in Europe: The Blue Flag for Beaches and the Blue Flag for Marinas. A third set of criteria – the Blue Flag for Tourism Boats – was launched 29 years later, in 2016. All sets of criteria are divided into overall categories, including Bathing Water Quality (only applicable for beaches), Information and Education to Sustainable Development, Environmental Management, Safety, Services and Accessibility. New categories were added in the Blue Flag for Tourism Boats: Social Responsibility and Responsible Operations around Wildlife. Since 1987, the sets of criteria have been revised continuously to ensure consistency with the latest scientific findings, national or international regulations and evolving needs of the Blue Flag-awarded sites network. These sets of criteria are the minimum requirements across all countries flying the Blue Flag. Participation has grown from the original five countries running the Blue Flag programme in 1987, to 50 countries as of early 2023.

2.2 The role of the Foundation for Environmental Education

The Foundation for Environmental Education manages the programme at the global level as Blue Flag International. It also coordinates its network of members that are implementing the programme at national level (National Operators). These members may add to or strengthen the existing criteria to follow national needs or regulations, or to support a specific agenda regarding the coastal or inland environment, safety, services, accessibility, etc. These global sets of criteria must remain challenging but achievable for all. They are an excellent entry-point to implement

DOI: 10.4324/9781003323570-3

The Blue Flag programme, at national and international levels   25

a compelling action plan to achieve the Blue Flag, while national additions keep challenging the awarded sites year after year.

The sets of criteria, designed by FEE, with the cooperation of its member organisations and capitalising on the expertise of its external partners, represent the holistic approach as intended from the very beginning. As a matter of principle, all criteria must be backed up by science-based evidence, and answer real needs on-site for the local communities and tourists alike. The FEE network of institutional partners supporting the Blue Flag programme is rich and diverse in expertise and knowledge, including the United Nations World Tourism Organization (UN-WTO), United Nations Environment Programme (UNEP), United Nations Educational, Scientific and Cultural Organization (UNESCO), International Lifesaving Federation (ILS International), European Environment Agency (EEA), World Cetacean Alliance (WCA), European Network for Accessible Tourism (ENAT), the Coastal and Marine Union (EUCC), the International Council of Marine Industry Associations (ICOMIA), and ICLEI - Local Governments for Sustainability.

To ensure quality outcomes on the ground, a strong administrative process and mandatory on-site visits have been set up by FEE and its members, all abiding by the same rules of procedure. The Blue Flag award is currently available only in countries where FEE has an official member running the programme. To receive the Blue Flag award, every site, a beach, marina or tourism boat, must apply for it. This is the first step of a voluntary approach towards sustainability. The completed application form and its annexes are then reviewed by the national Blue Flag team and presented to a National Jury. The multi-stakeholder approach of the international level is replicated at the national level. National Juries represent the holistic approach and all the specific expertise required to implement the Blue Flag. They are usually composed of representatives of different relevant ministries, e.g. education, environment, health, tourism or others, national lifesaving associations, national associations of municipalities, national marina associations, national associations for accessibility, and so on. This National Jury is not the final awarding body, and its responsibility is to ensure compliance with the criteria at the national level and confirm that the Blue Flag applicants can be presented to the International Jury. A second review and evaluation of applications is completed at the FEE level, and only then the applications are forwarded to the Blue Flag International Jury, which decides on the final awards. The International Jury is composed of the international equivalent of those stakeholders present at national level, representing a global consensus of knowledge in their respective fields. The members of the International Jury are the institutional partners of FEE mentioned above. The Blue Flag award is valid for one touristic season and must be renewed every year.

The Blue Flag administration process extends well beyond document review. During the touristic period, every Blue Flag awarded site is visited by a controller from the National Operator at the very least once per season. These on-site control visits ensure compliance with the programme criteria. In cases of non-compliance, and depending on its severity, remedial measures are taken, from temporary withdrawal of the flag until rectification, to a full withdrawal of the flag for the season in cases of serious problems. In addition to the mandatory national control visits,

FEE has a team of trained controllers that perform international control visits every year, usually unannounced, as a complementary verification.

In order to provide a strong administration system, on-site visits, partnership developments and representation, the national FEE member organisations, in most cases, charge an application fee. This fee covers the National Operator expenses to run the Blue Flag programme and is paid upon application, regardless of the applicant being awarded the Blue Flag or not.

Since its founding in 1981, FEE, one of the largest environmental education organisations globally, has been continually striving to create a sustainable world through education. Together with its more than 100 member organisations in 81 countries, FEE uses education to engage and empower people in order to achieve positive change for all.

At the core of FEE's five programmes, working towards excellence in Environmental Education (EE) and Education for Sustainable Development (ESD), are eight educational principles. They ensure that participants are: actively engaged in the teaching/learning process; empowered to make informed decisions and act accordingly; encouraged to collaborate and involve their communities in finding solutions; supported in developing critical thinking, and accepting change; encouraged to respect cultural practices as integral to sustainability issues; encouraged to share inspirational stories of their achievements, failures and values, learning from them, and to support each other, continuously exploring, testing, and sharing innovative approaches, methodologies, and techniques. Continuous monitoring and evaluation ensure that the programmes are adapted and improved in response to changing conditions.

The Blue Flag is one of the two FEE programmes focusing on the tourism sector, the other being The Green Key. In addition to water quality, management and safety criteria, Blue Flag encompasses the abovementioned educational principles, aiming to connect visitors and users, site managers, administrators at the local and regional level, and the local communities with their surroundings, providing knowledge and information, and encouraging them to respect and care for their environment. Blue Flag sites attract large numbers of visitors, in the case of many beaches reaching hundreds of thousands every season. They are, therefore, ideal points to broadly disseminate information, share good practices and promote changes in behaviour and lifestyle. With more than 5,000 awarded sites in 50 countries currently, the Blue Flag is a powerful tool for implementing FEE's GAIA 20:30 strategic plan, aiming to reduce the environmental footprint of touristic activities, support the achievement of the Sustainable Development Goals (SDGs) and contribute towards holistic management of the coastal zone.

2.3 The Blue Flag Programe and the Sustainable Development Goals

In September 2015, the General Assembly of the United Nations agreed upon the 17 Sustainable Development Goals, meant as "a shared blueprint for peace and prosperity for people and the planet, now and into the future". The SDGs were further reinforced with specific targets for each goal, and with indicators to measure progress towards their achievement. The end date for achieving them is usually between 2020 and 2030, but no end date is given to some of them. The SDGs seek to address economic, social and environmental challenges: poverty, hunger, disease, fear and violence, education, healthcare, social protection, sanitation, safety, ecosystem and habitat health, and climate change. In this sense, the criteria that Blue Flag establishes for the management of beaches and coastal areas as well as the effects that they have on the local communities and the promotion of environmental education for visitors, have clear positive effects to achieve the SDGs.

2.4 The contribution of the Blue Flag programme to the objectives of Integrated Coastal Zone Management

In the course of its history, humanity has always had a close relationship with the coast. The coastal zone provided space for settlement, trade, migration, conquest and defence, and for building cultural and spiritual identity. Coastal zones are still of crucial importance today: they are home to the bulk of the population, and account for a considerable share of the economic activities in coastal countries, also providing highly valued ecosystem services.

A wide range of human activities take place in the coastal zones (industry, tourism, fishing, aquaculture, etc). Among them, tourism creates strong anthropogenic pressures through the expansion of infrastructures, degradation on habitats, decline of biodiversity, overexploitation of resources, pollution, and often has social and cultural impacts. The continuing growth in tourism will increase human pressure on natural, rural and urban environments, exacerbated by the effects of climate change.

The highly dynamical interactions at the interface of land and sea, both of natural and social processes, make coastal zones vulnerable and, therefore, necessitate careful management that takes into account the many interdependencies and developments in the short and long term.

Integrated Coastal Zone Management (ICZM) is aimed at promoting sustainable development of the coastal zone, preventing disasters or reducing their impact, while taking into account diverse interests and possible futures. The concept was born at the Earth Summit of Rio de Janeiro in 1992. ICZM is defined as "a dynamic, multidisciplinary and iterative process to promote sustainable management of coastal zones". It covers the full cycle of planning, decision making, management and monitoring of implementation. It uses the informed participation and cooperation of all stakeholders to assess the societal goals in a given coastal area, and to take actions towards meeting these objectives, endeavouring to balance environmental, economic, social, cultural and recreational objectives, all within the limits set by natural dynamics. "Integrated" in ICZM refers to the integration of objectives, of the many instruments needed to meet these objectives, of relevant policy areas, sectors, and levels of administration, and of the terrestrial and marine components of the target territory, in both time and space.

28 *Nikos Petrou and Johann Durand*

The Blue Flag programme fosters this inclusive cooperation between stakeholders and authorities at many levels and touches upon almost all elements of sustainable growth and development in coastal areas. It can, consequently, be a strong asset towards achieving the goals of Integrated Coastal Zone Management.

2.5 Blue Flag as an asset on the path towards sustainable tourism development

In the last two decades, the ease of travel and the advent of new tourist segments and destinations have introduced deep changes in the tourism sector. Concurrently, the level of environmental awareness has increased significantly, and with it the demand for environmentally friendly services and products, which has become one of the important determinants in purchasing decisions. Tourists who are aware of global environmental issues want to travel responsibly and are interested in green products. Awards like the Blue Flag contribute towards balancing the needs of all stakeholders in tourism –government, the tourism industry, local community and visitors – while reducing environmental risks and degradation.

In addition to increasing environmental consciousness and having a tangible effect on a site's environmental footprint, the Blue Flag can be an invaluable asset on the path towards sustainable touristic development. It offers economic benefits, it can influence consumer choice, encourage market development, create a positive image and brand, and enhance job fulfilment for employees. In fact, the Blue Flag is often perceived more as a tourism promotional tool than an environmental management or protection tool (Klein & Dodds, 2018).

Direct economic benefits arise from lower usage of resources such as water and energy, leading to reduced operating costs. Research indicates that eco-labels attract environmentally conscious tourists that have higher income and higher conservational anticipations and are, therefore, willing to pay up to 5% higher premiums for eco-friendly service delivery (Chan, 2013). In Costa Rica, it was shown that awards could increase hotel-anticipated profits by improving the environmental quality as well as the corporate environment in a coastal community, and that they had an economically substantial influence on new hotel investment (Blackman et al., 2014). A study in Italy offered clear evidence about the effectiveness of the Blue Flag in attracting seaside foreign tourists (Capacci et al., 2015). Results such as those are of great relevance for policymakers and tourism stakeholders, who plan promotional strategies at the national or local level, and who will bear the costs, financial and non-financial, required to fulfil the award criteria.

Eco-labels provide visitors with information concerning environmental performance and actions of tourism businesses, thus assisting them in making informed selections on sustainable products and services. Because of its global recognition and credibility, the Blue Flag can play a key role as a marketing tool, nationally and internationally, and is an important factor in consumer choice. The number of tourists inquiring about Blue Flag beaches before deciding on their holiday destination has been steadily growing, already from 20 years ago (Aliraja & Rughooputh, 2004), and the Blue Flag is now included as a criterion in destination search engines. Findings from Canada (Dodds & Holmes, 2020) show that knowledge of the Blue Flag award increased the importance that beachgoers attributed to future destinations, and resulted in higher levels of overall satisfaction, satisfaction with water quality, water cleanliness and beach cleanliness.

As the tourism trade depends significantly on the continued attractiveness and sociability of the destinations and societies it functions in, encouragement of sustainable practices at site level, but also in the surrounding community, promotes market development and accrues added value for coastal destinations.

Widely recognisable and trusted, the Blue Flag award enhances a site's image and brand amongst consumers and can serve as a marketing and promotion tool and a way to ensure a competitive advantage. It can also function as safeguard against potential unfavourable publicity. Additionally, it has been claimed that tourism businesses acquiring a sustainability eco-label are in fact co-branding their products or services; this is especially significant for small businesses or destinations that lack international market recognition, where the label can be used as a symbol of quality and dependability (Font & Harris, 2004).

In recent years, employees are becoming increasingly more environmentally conscious and, consequently, expect employers to conduct business according to higher environmental and social standards. Studies indicate that employees of an enterprise committed to sustainability and environmental management may experience greater job satisfaction possibly leading to increased productivity and profitability, while favourably separating themselves from enterprises that are not environmentally conscious (Wagner, 2015).

2.6 The uniqueness of the Blue Flag programme compared to other eco-labels

A crucial difference, one that sets Blue Flag apart from all other similar eco-labels, is its educational component. It is mandatory for site managers to organise environmental education activities, according to their goals and capacities. These engage learners, visitors and users, staff and local stakeholders of all ages, connect them with nature, encourage them to ask questions about the environment and support behavioural change. In this way, educational activities enhance learner understanding, urging them to address environmental problems and take action for change in pursuit of sustainable development.

As the number of tourism eco-labels continues to grow globally, the Blue Flag faces various challenges including competition from inconsistent and poorly structured eco-labels, maintaining quality and trustworthiness of the award and ensuring a sustained positive environmental impact.

The decisive issue in any certification scheme is its credibility. Many programmes are poorly designed, lack reliable standards and do not conduct audits, in some cases amounting to nothing more than a means of "greenwashing". Such cases may undermine the overall integrity of eco-labels, resulting in unfavourable public views and doubt among consumers. Coinciding and opposing labels create much confusion among the public, consequently hindering the effective function

30 *Nikos Petrou and Johann Durand*

of all. Related to this is the challenge of sustaining excellence and consistency over time and space. In the highly competitive environment of the global tourism industry, eco-labels that are recognized internationally and provide criteria that are adaptable to issues faced within a specific host destination are far more effective in their mission. Equally important is the continued relevance as local and/or global circumstances change. Appropriate standards, uninterrupted monitoring, and improvement and synchronization of criteria at the international level by a strong accrediting body are required to ensure the growth and effectiveness of the award.

The structure of the programme as administered by Blue Flag International addresses all these challenges. As described in the programme structure, the criteria in all categories are periodically revised, adapted and expanded with the participation of all National Operators, so that they remain relevant and effective. The multiple control levels –National and International Juries, audits of all sites by national controllers, unannounced audits by FEE's international controllers, and the ability of users to submit complaints – ensure fulfilment of the criteria; indeed, numerous Blue Flags are withdrawn every season, temporarily or permanently, in cases where sites fail to comply. In fact, it has been stated that Blue Flag has more transparent procedures that guarantee the thoroughness of the scheme in comparison to other eco-labels (Hughes et al., 2015). The steady growth of the programme throughout the world highlights the commitment of existing National Operators in maintaining its high standards, as well as the appeal it has for new applicants.

2.7 The criteria of the Blue Flag programme over time

In 35 years of operation, the Blue Flag programme has seen its criteria revised and its geographical dimension extended from a European to a truly global award scheme, with the Blue Flag flying on all continents. The last major update was the addition, in 2016, of the new set of criteria dedicated to boats taking tourists to sea or lake for environmental, educational, and/or recreational activities. These criteria are organized in four main axes: i) environmental education and information, ii) water quality, iii) environmental management, and iv) safety and services, as can be seen in Table 2.1, in its 2022 edition. In the case of marinas and tourism boats some additional elements are included, given their specific features. Besides, it must be remarked that while some criteria are imperative (indicated with an (i) in the table) in order to obtain a Blue Flag, other ones are established as guidelines (indicated with a (g) in the table) on the management of the places.

2.8 Plans for the future

In 2021, the member organisations ratified FEE's new GAIA 20:30 strategy built around three pillars: Empowering Climate Action, Protecting Global Biodiversity and Reducing Environmental Pollution. This strategy, supported by all FEE members and aligned with the latest scientific findings in its three pillars, is a game changer for the Blue Flag. From a governance perspective, all FEE members have approved the implementation of the strategy within the Blue Flag programme,

Table 2.1 Criteria for getting a Blue Flag (2022)

	Beaches	*Marinas*	*Tourism boats*
Environmental education and information	6 (i)	4 (i) 2 (g)	8 (i)
Water quality	5 (i)	1 (i)	
Environmental management	13 (i) 2 (g)	10 (i) 12 (g)	19 (i) 3 (g)
Safety and services	5 (i) 1 (g)	4 (i) 1 (g)	6 (i) 1 (g)
Corporate social responsibility		1 (g)	2 (i) 3 (g)
Social community involvement		1 (g)	
Responsible operation around wild animals			8 (i) 1 (g)
Additional			For bird watching: 5 (i) For cage diving: 7 (i) For recreational diving: 11 (i) For fishing: 9 (i) For seal watching: 6 (i) For whale watching: 8 (i)

Note: See the annex for the details of all the criteria.

opening the door for a major revision of its sets of criteria and the development of new initiatives based on awareness raising, capacity building, partnership projects and behavioural change.

The Blue Flag programme has always been a bridge between global science and frameworks and a comprehensive action plan for local communities and tourists. The principle of Blue Flag should remain unchanged. From a global perspective, the programme will capitalise on existing robust frameworks, designed and validated by the scientific community and international organisations, including the global institutional partnerships of FEE. These frameworks, such as the Paris Agreement, the Glasgow Declaration, the Global Biodiversity Framework, and others, will be used for inspiration for the new Blue Flag sets of criteria, aiming to achieve state-of-the-art sustainability. By providing a clear path to engage stakeholders at the local and regional level and helping to achieve the objectives of these global frameworks, the Blue Flag does not only provide a holistic approach to implementing actions, but also a purpose and an understanding of doing the right thing that scientists desperately call for, and national politics have difficulties to attain. These frameworks won't be the only source of information. As mentioned previously, some FEE member organisations have been implementing stricter and wider criteria, corresponding to the needs of their national context. This work will be assimilated and projected at the international level, thus capitalising on best practices worldwide. This revision will continue to look at a seasonal timeframe and a demarcated zone, but will also go over and beyond to a more holistic approach at the municipality level, through action plans targeting various sectors, aiming at consistent results year after year. Capitalising on its decades of

32 *Nikos Petrou and Johann Durand*

experience, the programme will push for change and better management beyond the zones awarded the Blue Flag, providing best practices and relevant action plans along whole coastal areas, under the responsibility of the Blue Flag applicants.

Through its institutional partners, Blue Flag will revise all its other components and ensure that sustainability remains consistently at the core of its environmental, economic and social pillars. Safety, accessibility, information and education criteria will be revitalised to fit the latest developments in these fields.

This revision is not the only challenge the Blue Flag is facing for the future. As part of the mission of FEE, the programme must continue its geographical expansion and grow in terms of delivering quantifiable impact in diverse ways and sectors. The Blue Flag is a successful programme, and every year new organisations show interest in joining and implementing it within their national boundaries. With its broader vision under the GAIA 20:30 strategy, the Blue Flag can certainly help local and regional authorities tackle the major environmental issues of our time by providing a decision-making framework, a management tool and adaptation and mitigation solutions in countries where they are the most needed. The implementation of the programme will become more challenging at the national level, dependent on the FEE member organisation's capacity to build and sustain strong relationships with national stakeholders, and its capacity to move freely in all corners of the country to meet with local authorities. Successful implementation at the national level will also rely on existing conditions, such as strong and democratic legal frameworks, the public's will to create a positive change, and available, sustainable finances to support such initiatives.

In India, full implementation of the Blue Flag programme has been added as a Key Performance Indicator (KPI) for the success of the national ICZM plan, funded by the World Bank. In the Jeddah Convention, recommendations were made to signatories "to facilitate and encourage delivery of Blue Flag certified beaches so as to improve the State of the Marine Environment (SOMER) of beaches and associated habitats specifically and the SOMER of the Red Sea and Guld of Aden generally".

In some parts of the world, the success in expanding the Blue Flag programme and, in a broader perspective, the success of local implementation of global frameworks, may rely on supranational conventions and zone managements. FEE will also endeavour to develop further synergies between its members, to share best practices and to build capacities in order to ensure the efficient and effective implementation of the revised Blue Flag criteria, striving for a wider and greater impact towards the urgent environmental problems our blue planet faces.

2.9 References

Aliraja, S. & Rughooputh, S. D. (2004). Towards introducing the Blue Flag eco-label in SIDS: The case of Mauritius. In: Proceedings of *IRFD World Forum on Small Island Developing States: Challenges, Prospects and International Cooperation for Sustainable Management.* Virtual Conference at www.irfd.org, 2004. Mauritius: University of Mauritius, 1–15.

Blackman, A., Naranjo, M. A., Robalino, J., Alpízar, F. & Rivera, J. (2014). Does Tourism Eco-Certification Pay? Costa Rica's Blue Flag Program. *World Development*, 58, 41–52.

The Blue Flag programme, at national and international levels 33

Capacci, S., Scorcu, A. & Vivi, L., (2015). Seaside tourism and eco-labels: The economic impact of Blue Flags. *Tourism Management*, 47, 88–96.

Chan, E. S. W. (2013). Gap analysis of green hotel marketing. *International Journal of Contemporary Hospitality Management*, 25(7), 1017–1048.

Dodds, R. & Holmes, M. (2020). Is Blue Flag certification a means of destination competitiveness? A Canadian context. *Ocean & Coastal Management*, 192, 105192.

Font, X. & Harris, C. (2004). Rethinking standards from green to sustainable. *Annals of Tourism Research*, 31(4), 986–1007.

Hughes, M., Weaver, D. & Pforr, C. (2015). *The Practice of Sustainable Tourism: Resolving the Paradox*. Oxon: Routledge.

Klein, L. & Dodds, R. (2018). Blue Flag beach certification: An environmental management tool or tourism promotional tool. *Tourism Recreation Research*, 43(1), 39–51.

Wagner, M. (2015). A European perspective on country moderation effects: Environmental management systems and sustainability-related human resource benefits. *Journal of World Business*, 50(2), 379–388.

Annex: Detail of the criteria to obtain a Blue Flag

The criteria can be imperative or guidelines for management. This is indicated with an (i) or (g) respectively.

A) For beaches

A.1. Environmental education and information

1. Information about the Blue Flag programme and other FEE eco-label must be displayed. (i)
2. Environmental education activities must be offered and promoted to beach users. (i)
3. Information about bathing water quality must be displayed. (i)
4. Information relating to local eco-systems and environmental phenomena must be displayed. (i)
5. A map of the beach indicating different facilities must be displayed. (i)
6. A code of conduct that reflects appropriate laws governing the use of the beach and surrounding areas must be displayed. (i)

A.2. Water quality

7. The beach must fully comply with the water quality sampling and frequency requirements. (i)
8. The beach must fully comply with the standards and requirements for water quality analysis. (i)
9. No industrial, waste-water or sewage-related discharges should affect the beach area. (i)
10. The beach must comply with the Blue Flag requirements for the microbiological parameter Escherichia coli (faecal coli bacteria) and intestinal enterococci (streptococci). (i)

34 *Nikos Petrou and Johann Durand*

11. The beach must comply with the Blue Flag requirements for the following physical parameters. (i)

A.3. Environmental management

12. The local authority/beach operator should establish a beach management committee. (g)
13. The local authority/beach operator must comply with all regulations affecting the location and operation of the beach. (i)
14. Sensitive area management. (i)
15. The beach must be clean. (i)
16. Algae vegetation or natural debris should be left on the beach. (i)
17. Waste disposal bins/containers must be available at the beach in adequate numbers and they must be regularly maintained. (i)
18. Facilities for the separation of recyclable waste materials should be available at the beach. (i)
19. An adequate number of toilet or restroom facilities must be provided. (i)
20. The toilet or restroom facilities must be kept clean. (i)
21. The toilet or restroom facilities must have controlled sewage disposal. (i)
22. On the beach there will be no unauthorised camping or driving and no dumping. (i)
23. Access to the beach by dogs and other domestic animals must be strictly controlled. (i)
24. All buildings and beach equipment must be properly maintained (i)
25. Marine and freshwater sensitive habitats (such as coral reefs or sea grass beds) in the vicinity of the beach must be monitored. (i)
26. A sustainable means of transportation should be promoted in the beach area. (g)

A.4. Safety and services

27. Appropriate public safety control measures must be implemented. (i)
28. First aid equipment must be available on the beach. (i)
29. Emergency plans to cope with pollution risks must be in place. (i)
30. There must be management of different users and uses of the beach so as to prevent conflicts and accidents. (i)
31. There must be safety measures in place to protect users of the beach. (i)
32. A supply of drinking water should be available at the beach. (g)
33. At least one Blue Flag beach in each municipality must have access and facilities provided for the physically disabled. (i)

B) For marinas
B.1. Environmental education and information

1. Information relating to local eco-systems and environmental phenomena must be available to marina users. (i)

The Blue Flag programme, at national and international levels 35

2. A code of conduct that reflects appropriate laws governing the use of the marina and surrounding areas must be displayed at the marina. (i)
3. Information about the Blue Flag marina programme and/or the Blue Flag marina criteria and other FEE eco-label must be displayed in the marina. (i)
4. The marina is responsible for offering at least three environmental education activities to the users and staff of the marina. (i)
5. The individual Blue Flag for boat owners is offered through the marina. (i)
6. Twice a year there is a meeting with the staff about Blue Flag measurements/ environment/sustainability. (g)
7. Every employee knows about Blue Flag and can communicate about Blue Flag with the guests. (g)

B.2. Environmental management

8. A marina management committee should be established to be in charge of instituting environmental management systems and conducting regular environmental audits of the marina facility. (g)
9. The marina must have an environmental policy and an environmental plan. The plan should include references to water management, waste and energy consumption, health and safety issues, and the use of environmentally friendly products wherever possible. (i)
10. Sensitive area management. (i)
11. Adequate and properly identified, segregated containers must be in place for the storage of hazardous wastes. The wastes have to be handled by a licensed contractor and disposed of at a licensed facility for hazardous wastes. (i)
12. Adequate and well-managed litterbins and/or garbage containers must be place. The wastes are handled by a licensed contractor and disposed of at a licensed facility. (i)
13. The marina must have facilities for receiving recyclable waste materials, such as bottles, cans, paper, plastic, organic material, etc. (i)
14. Bilge water pumping facilities should be available at the marina. (g)
15. Toilet tank waste reception facilities must be present in the marina. (i)
16. All buildings and equipment must be properly maintained and be in compliance with national legislation. The marina must be well integrated into the surrounding natural and built environment. (i)
17. Adequate, clean and well sign-posted sanitary facilities, including washing facilities, must be in place and provide drinking water. Sewage disposal is controlled and directed to a licensed sewage treatment. (i)
18. If the marina has boat repairing and washing areas, no pollution must enter the sewage system, marina land and water or the natural surroundings. (i)
19. Sustainable transportation should be promoted. (g)
20. Parking/driving is not permitted in the marina, unless in specific designated areas. (i)
21. The water consumption in the sanitary facilities and showers must be controlled. (g)

36 Nikos Petrou and Johann Durand

22. There must be an environmental policy and an environmental plan for the marina. The plan should include references to water management, waste and energy consumption, health and safety issues as well as the use of environmentally friendly products wherever possible. All employees must be informed and educated about these issues. (g)
23. Only environmentally friendly cleaning products must be used for the cleaning of the facilities in the marina. (g)
24. Only environmentally friendly toiletries, paper towels and toilet papers must be provided in the sanitary facilities of the marina. Soap and other personal care products must be provided in dispensers with a dosing system. (g)
25. Only energy efficient lighting must be used. Sensors which regulate the use of the light should be installed wherever considered as being useful. (g)
26. The energy supply of the marina should be based on renewable energies. (g)
27. The marina should aim at being climate neutral. (g)
28. Artificially/Man-made green areas and gardens in the marina must be maintained sustainably. (g)
29. The facilities in the marina must be made of environmentally friendly materials. Local suppliers should be preferably used when equipping the marina with new buildings, infrastructure or furniture. (g)

B.3. Safety and services

30. Adequate and well signposted lifesaving, first-aid equipment and fire-fighting equipment must be present. Equipment must be approved by national authorities. (i)
31. Emergency plans in case of pollution, fire or other accidents must be produced. (i)
32. Safety precautions and information must be posted at the marina. (i)
33. Electricity and water is available at the berths; installations must be approved according to national legislation. (i)
34. Facilities for disabled people should be in place. (g)
35. A Map indicating the location of the different facilities must be posted at the marina. (i)

B.4. Water quality

36. The water in the marina must be visually clean without any evidence of pollution, e.g. oil, litter, sewage or other evidence of pollution. (i)

B.5. Corporate social responsibility

37. The marina management has a CSR policy, covering the areas of Human Rights, Labour Equity Environmental Education and Anti-corruption. (g)

The Blue Flag programme, at national and international levels 37

B.6. Social/Community involvement

38. The marina management takes at least two measures to encourage sustainable relationships in the immediate environment and to fulfil its commitment to perform better on social fields. (g)

C) For tourism boats
C.1. Environmental education and information

1. Information relating to local ecosystems and environmental phenomena must be available to tourists. The tour operator must also provide a map and information about the area of operation and, if applicable, about the protected area they are operating in. (i)
2. A code of conduct for tourists that reflects appropriate rules governing the use of the boat must be displayed. The tour operator must also provide relevant information about the appropriate behaviour in the harbour area. (i)
3. Information about the Blue Flag programme and the Blue Flag for tourism boats must be displayed on the boat and in the boat office. (i)
4. The boating operator is responsible for offering at least one environmental education activity to the tourists, employees or local community within the Blue Flag awarded year. (i)
5. All staff must be trained on the environmental undertakings of the operator. (i)
6. The staff of the tour operator must receive training on the local environment and/or other environmental and sustainability issues at least once a year. (i)
7. The tour operator must provide a qualified guide who is in charge of the safety instructions and the environmental education on board for each tour. (i)
8. Tour operators that transfer tourists to land-based excursions, or that offer ferry services next to other tourism activities must provide information about the environment at the destination and inform tourists about their possible impact on the local ecosystems. (i for all boating operators that transfer tourists to land-based excursions.)

C.2. Environmental management

9. A management committee should be established, with responsibility for instituting environmental management systems and conducting regular environmental audits of the tourism boat, the buildings of the tour operator and the tours. (g)
10. Each boating operator must have an environmental policy and an environmental plan which includes concrete environmental goals. All employees must be informed and educated about the plan. (i)
11. The boating operator must comply with all regulations pertaining to the location and operation of the tourism boat and offered services. All buildings must be properly maintained and be in compliance with national legislation. (i)

12. Hazardous waste generated on the tourism boat and in the buildings must be stored and disposed of responsibly. (i)
13. Adequate and well-managed litter bins and/or garbage containers must be in place on the boats and in the buildings of the tour operator. The wastes must be disposed of at a licensed facility that is handled by a licensed contractor. This can be done through the harbour. (i)
14. Facilities for receiving recyclable waste materials such as bottles, cans, paper, plastic and organic material must be in place on the tourism boat and in the tour operator's buildings. (i)
15. Single-use products used in connection with food and beverages must be avoided. If single-use products are used, recyclable products and products made of biodegradable materials must be used. (i)
16. 50% of food and beverages offered to tourists must be or contain local products, organic products, eco-labelled products or fair-trade products. (g)
17. In EU countries, paper towels, facial tissues and toilet paper must be made of nonchlorine bleached paper or awarded with an eco-label. Tour operators operating in non-EU countries are strongly encouraged to follow this criterion. (i)
18. Smoking should be prohibited on the tourism boat. If smoking is allowed on the boat, it must have special facilities for the disposal of cigarette butts. (i)
19. If bilge water pumping facilities are available in the harbour, the tour operator should make use of them. Untreated bilge water must not be released into the water. (i)
20. Sewage disposal must be controlled and directed to a licensed sewage treatment facility. Untreated water from toilets must not be released into the sea or freshwater bodies, nor close to sensitive areas. (i)
21. When selecting products such as paints, paint remover, detergents, cleaning products etc., the tour operator must source environmentally friendly versions, where available and effective. Special precautions must be taken when using detergents on the outside sections of the tourism boat. Cleaning products that enter the grey water produced on the boat must be biodegradable. (i)
22. Repair and painting works on the tourism boat must be limited to specifically designated areas in the harbour or locations where there is no danger that toxic substances might enter the water or the ground. (i)
23. The tour operator must provide to employees and tourists only environmentally friendly toiletries. All toiletries on the tourism boat must be biodegradable. (i)
24. Sustainable means of transportation must be promoted whenever advising tourists and staff as to how to get to the tourism boat or the ticket office. (i)
25. The relevant authorities must be notified immediately regarding accidents that might cause environmental damage. (i)
26. Speed and engine maintenance must be aimed at maximising energy efficiency and minimising pollution. (i)
27. Anchoring restrictions must be respected. If available, mooring buoys must be used to protect the seabed. If no mooring buoys are available, the tourism boat must only anchor in insensitive grounds. (i)

The Blue Flag programme, at national and international levels 39

28. After the life service of a tourism boat has been reached, it must be disposed of in accordance with national regulations. (i)
29. Noise pollution from the tourism boat must be minimised. (i)
30. Best environmental practice should also be adopted in the tour operator's buildings and facilities that are not open to the public. (g)

C.3. Safety and services

31. Adequate and well signposted lifesaving, first-aid and fire-fighting equipment must be present on the tourism boat. This equipment must be approved by relevant national authorities. (i)
32. Emergency plans for different possible kinds of accidents must be produced. The crew must be trained on these emergency plans on a regular basis. (i)
33. Safety precautions and information must be presented on the tourism boat. (i)
34. If the tour operator offers alcohol on its tourism boats, it has to be done in a responsible manner. (i)
35. Sanitary facilities must be available to the tourists. They must be clean, well signposted and the access must be safe. Drinking water must be provided on the tourism boat. (i)
36. Facilities for people with disabilities should be in place. (g)
37. Adequate signage indicating the location of the different facilities must be posted on the tourism boat. (i)

C.4. Social responsibility

38. Discrimination based on gender, sexual orientation, disabilities, origin or religious affiliation should not be accepted within the tour operator. (i)
39. The tour operator is in compliance with international and national labour legislation. (i)
40. The tour operator should support the local economy by choosing to buy and use local products. (g)
41. The tour operator actively supports local sustainability activities or initiatives of environmental/social organisations or of other groups in the local community. (g)
42. Materials, equipment and furniture that are no longer used are collected and donated to charitable organisations. (g)

C.5. Responsible operation around wild animals

43. Vulnerable and protected areas must be respected. (i)
44. Any wildlife must be approached at a slow speed and in a manner that allows the wild animal(s) to evaluate the situation. They must not be encircled, trapped or chased. (i)
45. Special precaution must be taken in the vicinity of breeding wild animals. Young animals must not be separated from their group. (i)

40 *Nikos Petrou and Johann Durand*

46. When in the direct vicinity of any wildlife, noise must be reduced to a minimum and the engine should be put into neutral whenever appropriate. (i)
47. The tour operator is responsible for advising tourists not to touch or collect living wild animals and plants. (i)
48. Tourists and employees must not feed wild animals. (i)
49. If there are any signs of disturbance, the boat must increase its distance to the wild animals. (i)
50. The tour operator should be open to cooperation with research institutions. The company's boats might function as a research platform, and collected data of wildlife sightings should be made available to researchers. (g)
51. Injured, entangled, stranded or dead wild animals must be reported to the local authorities. (i)

C.6. Additional criteria for specific purpose boats
    C.6.a. For bird watching boats

52. Boats must not drive through clusters of birds. (i)
53. It is not allowed to use playbacks of bird calls to attract them. (i)
54. Flash photography must be avoided. (i)
55. Birds must not be spotlighted with torches or other illuminants. (i)
56. It is not allowed to flash birds to get a better view on them. (i)

C.6.b. For cage diving boats

57. The cage used for cage diving must be designed in such a way that it neither poses a danger to the people in the cage nor to the sharks outside the cage. The gaps between the railings must be so narrow that no shark of any size is able to enter the cage. (i)
58. It must be secured that the cage is properly attached to the boat. (i)
59. All entry points to the cage must be lockable with a door or portal. The access to the cage must be safe. (i)
60. All entry points to the cage must be lockable with a door or portal. The access to the cage must be safe. (i)
61. Decoys used for attracting sharks have to be designed in such a way that they do not pose a danger to the wild animals. (i)
62. In a predation situation, the boat must not cut off the path of the prey. It is not allowed to approach any predation closer than 50m. No more than two boats are allowed to be within 100m of a predation. (i)
63. If there is more than one cage diving boat within a radius of 300m of a shark, the boat has to slow down to a speed which should not exceed 10 knots. (i)

C.6.c. For recreational diving boats

64. Only qualified dive masters with a valid certification must be hired to conduct diving tours. (i)

The Blue Flag programme, at national and international levels 41

65. Prior to the dive, the divers have to be briefed on the dive site and about environmentally friendly diving techniques. (i)
66. All divers must prove their level of experience with a valid diving certification and have to complete the appropriate liability and medical statement documents before going on a dive trip. (i)
67. The size of the diving group must be limited and diver's level of experience must be considered when choosing the dive site and when forming the diving groups. (i)
68. Dive sites must be switched on a regular basis to prevent their overuse. Dive operators should choose their diving spots in cooperation with the local authorities and local environmental experts. (i)
69. Water entry points must not be located above sensitive sea beds. (i)
70. The diving equipment has to be fully operative and must be inspected regularly. (i)
71. A risk assessment has to be conducted for every dive site. Dive masters have to brief the divers on possible risks prior to every dive trip. (i)
72. The dive master and the crew on board must be able to administer first aid in case of an emergency. First aid training and refresher courses should be repeated at least once a month. (i)
73. The boat must be equipped with suitable oxygen units and surface signalling devices according to national regulations. The oxygen and signalling equipment must be accessible at any time and the crew on board must be familiar with the use of the equipment. (i)
74. Diver propulsion vehicles must only be used by divers who carry a respective certification. (i)

C.6.d. For recreational fishing boats

75. All international and national regulations for recreational fishing practices have to be respected. (i)
76. Endangered and protected species must not be caught. (i)
77. No-take zones in marine protected areas and nursery grounds have to be respected. (i)
78. No more aquatic animals than needed for the private use must be caught. (i)
79. The choice of bait must not pose a danger to the local ecosystems. (i)
80. Caught aquatic animals must be handled in a humane way. (i)
81. Fishing equipment must not be abandoned at the fishing sites. Defective fishing equipment must be recycled. (i)
82. Fish waste must be disposed of responsibly. (i)
83. Artisanal, subsistence and commercial fisheries must be respected. (i)

C.6.e. For bird seal watching boats

84. Personal watercrafts are not permissible for seal watching. (i)

85. Seals must not be approached closer than 50m. If a seal voluntarily approaches the boat any closer the engine should be put into neutral until the seal leaves the vicinity of the boat. (i)
86. The boat must always approach seals which are in the water from an oblique angle. They shouldn't approach them directly from the back or the front. (i)
87. Within a radius of 300m haul-out sites must be approached at a no wake speed. (i)
88. Flash photography must be avoided in the vicinity of seals. (i)
89. Decoys to attract seals are not permitted. (i)

C.6.f. For whale watching boats

90. Personal watercrafts are not permissible for whale watching. (i)
91. Cetaceans must be approached from an oblique angle. They must not be approached directly from the back or the front. (i)
92. Within a radius of 300m of the cetaceans, whale watching boats must slow to a no wake speed, which should not exceed 5 knots. (i)
93. When approaching cetaceans, the recommended distance to leave between the boat and the individual(s) is 100m. When safe to do so, the engine should be put into neutral during such an encounter. Irrespective of this recommendation, the national legislation concerning the allowed approach distance to cetaceans stands above this recommendation and must be respected. No boat, however, is permitted to approach a cetacean closer than 50m. (i)
94. No more than two boats must be present within an observation radius of 300 to 100m. Boat must be in contact with one another via radio to coordinate their movements. Additionally, they should stay on the same side of the cetacean or group of cetaceans to prevent them from feeling encircled. (i)
95. Time spent with one individual or group of cetaceans must be kept to a maximum of 30 minutes per boat, per tour. If more than one boat is within the observation radius (300–100m), this time must be reduced to 15 minutes per boat, per tour. (i)
96. In the case of bow-riding dolphins, the whale watching boat must not change its direction or speed abruptly. If the boat has to stop or change its course, speed must be slowed down gradually. (i)
97. It is not permissible to use sonar to detect cetaceans. (i)

3 Blue Flags in the world

A bibliometric analysis

Fernando Merino and María A. Prats

3.1 Introduction

Recognition of the Blue Flag as an important and distinctive award throughout the world has been increasing in recent years. Consequently, academic research has paid attention to the certification, as well as its impacts and consequences. This research is heterogeneous in terms of the topics covered, the researchers involved and the outlets where it is published. However, a bibliometric analysis that synthesizes the research literature generated in this field is lacking. To fill this gap, this chapter traces the evolution of published studies on the Blue Flag topic, providing an overall perspective of developments in research on the Blue Flag.

To do so, we examine the published documents collected in the Web of Science™ (WoS) Core Collection (CC), the most important database of academic studies, which includes only those books, conference proceedings and journals that adhere to strict quality criteria. For example, with respect to journals, we consider only those whose publications are peer-reviewed, with a publicly known editorial board, etc. Although the results seem to be biased toward works in the English language (and substantially less toward non-European languages), this does not seem to be a major shortfall in this field and, in any case, WoS is recognized by the academic community as the reference database for quality publications in most areas. We have restricted the search to those citation indexes within WoS related to the topic, including the Social Sciences Citation Index (SSCI), Social Citation Index Expanded, Emerging Sources Citation Index (ESCI), Institute for Scientific Information (ISI) Proceedings – Social Sciences & Humanities Edition (ISSHP) and the Book Citation Index.

The search for documents in WoS has been carried out using the topic "Blue Flag". It has been extended from the beginning of the databases to May 2022 and the search has been restricted to those citation indexes within WoS related to the Blue Flag, i.e. Social Sciences Citation Index (SSCI), Science Citation Index Expanded (SCIE), Emerging Sources Citation Index (ESCI), ISI Proceedings – Social Sciences & Humanities Edition (ISSHP) and the Book Citation Index. We have excluded some documents whose subject, although it contained the search term, was not related to the award. We finally obtained 71 documents. In this chapter we present a bibliometric analysis based on them, including the main conclusions

DOI: 10.4324/9781003323570-4

44   *Fernando Merino and María A. Prats*

regarding the temporal evolution of these publications, the main authors, and their impact, as well as the journals where these works were published. Finally, we present an analysis of the keywords that characterize each of these studies to provide information on the topics considered the most important over time.

In the following section, the results of the bibliometric analysis are presented. The paper ends with the main conclusions.

3.2 Results of the bibliometric analysis

3.2.1 General results

This study identifies 61 articles, six book chapters and three proceedings. This constitutes a total of 70 documents retrieved from the WoS CC by 194 different authors affiliated with 89 institutions in 17 countries and published in 38 source titles, including 30 journals. These publications included 2,525 references as the basis for research on the subject and were cited by 1,171 studies (see Table 3.1).

Table 3.1 Academic research on BF: Main results

Criteria	Quantity
Documents (articles)	70 (61)
Authors	194
Total sources (different journals)	38 (30)
Countries (corresponding author)	17
Institutions	87
Total references	2,525

Source: Own elaboration based on WoS data

3.2.2 Number of publications per year

The growing pattern of Blue Flag research and the chronological distribution between 1985 and 2022 show three stages in the publication trend (see Figure 3.1). The first period comprises years up to 2005, in which the publications are very scarce. In subsequent years, 2006–2013, the number of works increases notably, with a total of 18. After 2014, the interest in research on topics related to Blue Flag flourishes, with over 45 papers published (note that the figure for 2022 only covers the studies published in the first five months of the year).

3.2.3 Most globally cited documents

The most used indicator of the impact of a piece of research is the number of other publications that cite it, since this indicates that it acts as a basis for further research. In order to know which publications have had the largest impact, we have calculated all the citations that each one of the studied publications has generated from all the other scientific works registered in WoS. The set of papers identified

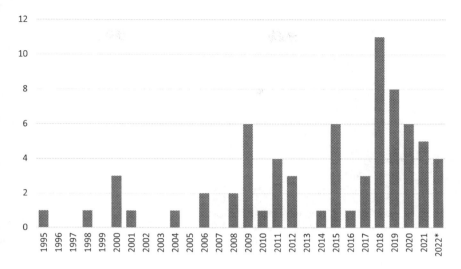

Figure 3.1 Number of research publications on Blue Flag per year
* Dates from January to May
Source: Own elaboration based on WoS data

in the field of Blue Flag research presents an average citation rate of 16.7 citations per article. However, 11.4% of the documents have not been cited in the analyzed period, and 41.4% have been referenced between one and ten times. In Table 3.2 we present those publications with the highest number of citations (over 12).

The article "Users' perception analysis for sustainable beach management in Italy" (Marin et al., 2009) is the most cited article of all, with 92 citations. This paper's aim is to obtain a clear image of the user's profile, perception, awareness and attitude on issues related to beach management (fundamentally the Blue Flag award). The results reveal, regarding this last aspect, that although the Blue Flag award was more recognized than others, these management tools were still not known and correctly perceived by beach users when the research was carried out. This outcome highlights the need to increase public awareness through environmental education and information campaigns. The authors note that a higher level of public awareness can lead to greater efficiency of local environmentally sound management efforts (p.275).

Rigall-i-Torrent et al. (2011) is the second most cited document, entitled "The effects of beach characteristics and location with respect to hotel prices". This paper accounts for 81 citations. In their study, the authors measure the effect that both the characteristics of the beach and the location of the hotel have on the price of hotels using hedonic estimations. The main results indicate that, after controlling for the relevant variables, both a beachfront location and the fact that the beach has a Blue Flag have a positive effect on the price of the rooms.

The third most cited paper is "Beach awards and management", by Nelson et al. (2000). They investigate the importance of beach awards (the Blue Flag, Seaside

46 Fernando Merino and María A. Prats

Table 3.2 Academic research on BF: Most global cited documents

Rank	Document	Citations
1	Users' perception analysis for sustainable beach management in Italy (Marin et al., 2009)	92
2	The effects of beach characteristics and location with respect to hotel prices (Rigall-i-Torrent et al., 2011)	81
3	Beach awards and management (Nelson et al., 2000)	72
4	A rationale for beach selection by the public on the coast of Wales, UK (Tudor & Williams, 2006)	69
5	Blue Flag or Red Herring: Do beach awards encourage the public to visit beaches? (McKenna, Williams & Cooper, 2011)	68
6	Does tourism eco-certification pay? Costa Rica's Blue Flag program (Blackman et al., 2014)	51
7	Determinants of willingness to pay for coastal zone quality improvement (Halkos & Matsiori, 2012)	50
8	Managing beaches and beachgoers: Lessons from and for the Blue Flag award (Lucrezi, Saayman & Van der Merwe, 2015)	44
9	To clean or not to clean? A critical review of beach cleaning methods and impacts (Zielinski, Botero & Yanes, 2019)	44
10	Beyond performance assessment measurements for beach management: Application to Spanish Mediterranean beaches (Ariza et al., 2007)	43
11	Towards a new integrated beach management system: The ecosystem-based management system for beaches (Sardá et al., 2015)	36
12	A critical view of the Blue Flag beaches in Spain using environmental variables (Mir-Gual et al., 2015)	34
13	Microbiological epidemiologic-study of selected marine beaches in Malaga (Spain) (Marino et al., 1995)	28
14	Mechanical grooming and beach award status are associated with low strandline biodiversity in Scotland (Gilburn, 2012)	26
15	Assessing the utility of beach ecolabels for use by local management (Boevers, 2008)	24
16	After over 25 years of accrediting beaches, has Blue Flag contributed to sustainable management? (Fraguell et al., 2016)	23
17	Education and certification for beach management: Is there a difference between residents versus visitors? (Dodds & Holmes, 2018)	21
18	Persistent marine litter: Small plastics and cigarette butts remain on beaches after organized beach clean-ups (Loizidou, Loizides & Orthodoxou, 2018)	19
19	Blue Flag beach certification: An environmental management tool or tourism promotional tool? (Klein & Dodds, 2018)	18
20	Assessing users' expectations and perceptions on different beach types and the need for diverse management frameworks along the Western Mediterranean (Cabezas-Rabadán et al., 2019)	16
21	Beachgoers' demands vs. Blue Flag aims in South Africa (Lucrezi & Saayman, 2015)	15
22	Awards for the sustainable management of coastal tourism destinations: The example of the Blue Flag program (Creo & Fraboni, 2011)	15
23	Education and certification for beach management: Is there a difference between residents versus visitors? (Dodds & Holmes, 2018)	15
24	Microbiological analysis of selected coastal bathing waters in the UK, Greece, Italy and Spain (Rees et al., 1998)	15

(Continued)

Table 3.2 (Continued)

Rank	Document	Citations
25	The impact of water quality changes on the socio-economic system of the Guadiana Estuary: An assessment of management options (Guimarães et al., 2012)	15
26	The influence of polystyrene microspheres abundance on development and feeding behavior of Artemia salina (Linnaeus, 1758) (Albano et al., 2021)	14
27	Perceived effectiveness of Blue Flag certification as an environmental management tool along Ontario's Great Lakes beaches (Klein & Dodds, 2017)	13
28	Geochemical beach sediments studies – a contribution to a standard definition useful for public health (Vidinha et al., 2009)	13
29	Metals and their ecological impact on beach sediments near the marine protected sites of Sodwana Bay and St. Lucia, South Africa (Vetrimurugan et al., 2018)	13
30	Is beach scenic quality a function of habitat diversity? (Duck et al., 2009)	12

Award and Good Beach Guide) for beach users and the level of knowledge they have of these awards and their implications. The authors conclude that nearly three quarters of beach users stated that recognition of the beach was an important basis for their choice. However, the results suggest that users had little information and a high level of ignorance regarding what the awards imply.

3.2.4 Most relevant authors

Another element to highlight is the most influential authors in this field. To establish this, we focus on three elements: the number of publications per author in this field, the number of citations that each author's contribution has received from other publications and the h-index. The h-index measures the number of publications published (productivity), as well as how often they are cited. For example, an h-index of 3 means that the author has published at least three articles, of which each has been cited at least three times, and to obtain an h-index of 4 implies not only that those publications have more citations, but that it is necessary that a fourth document also attains this number of citations. It is a commonly used indication of the impact an author's publications has on the academic community.

This study identifies the top-ranking influential authors (see Table 3.3). The number of documents published by each author on the subject, the number of citations each possesses in WoS and the h-index of each author describe the impact of the most productive authors.

Concerning the number of publications that each author has generated, we can see that approximately 80.9% of the authors in the sample have produced one paper, and 14.4% have published two or three documents. Only 4.6% have a number of publications between four and six. R. Dodds is the author who has published the most (six documents), followed by C. M. Botero, A. T. Williams and E. Ariza with five each.

Regarding the number of citations per author, as we can see, there is only one author with more than 50. The most cited author is A. T. Williams (author of five

48 *Fernando Merino and María A. Prats*

documents) with 69 citations. The fact that 47.4% of the authors have not received any citation by the end of the analysis period is also remarkable, but it is important to note that recently published papers will have few registered citations, since it takes time for publications to become known by other researchers and for their conclusions to be incorporated in further research that will also need time to be published.

If we analyze the relationship between the number of publications per author and the number of citations, we can establish a measure of the impact ranking of the authors. The analysis includes authors with at least two papers and six citations (see Table 3.3). According to the data, A. T. Williams is the most influential author, with an average number of citations per document of 13.8, followed by J. Cooper and J. Mckenna with 13 and only two papers, and S. Lucrezi with 10.3 and three published papers. In contrast, despite having a high number of publications, the works of R. Dodds, C. M. Botero, E. Ariza, S. Zielinsky and M. R. Holmes have been cited less on average.

If we consider the h-index of each author, based on the number of citations for each article on the subject, we find that the most influential authors are A. T. Williams and R. Dodds with an h-index of 5, followed by E. Ariza and M. R. Holmes with 4 and S. Lucrezi, M. Saayman, C. Botero and S. Zielinsky with 3. Let us remember that this measure is a more accurate indicator of the impact of an author

Table 3.3 Academic research on BF: Most influential authors

Rank	Authors	Documents	Citations	Average citation per document	H index
1	Williams, A. T.	5	69	13.8	5
2	Cooper, J.	2	26	13.0	1
3	Mckenna, J.	2	26	13.0	1
4	Lucrezi, S.	3	31	10.3	3
5	Van Der Merwe, P.	2	20	10.0	2
6	Saayman, M.	3	28	9.3	3
7	Martin-Prieto, J. A.	2	17	8.5	1
8	Rodriguez-Perea, A.	2	17	8.5	1
9	Morgan, R.	3	24	8.0	2
10	Jimenez, J. A.	2	16	8.0	2
11	Sardá, R.	2	16	8.0	2
12	Fraguell, R. M.	2	15	7.5	2
13	Marti, C.	2	15	7.5	2
14	Klein, L.	2	13	6.5	2
15	Ariza, E.	5	21	4.2	4
16	Dodds, R.	6	22	3.7	5
17	Zielinsky, S.	4	10	2.5	3
18	Botero, C. M.	5	11	2.2	3
19	Holmes, M. R.	4	9	2.3	4

Source: Own elaboration based on WoS data

than the previous one (average citations per published document) and it is the most widely used to evaluate the impact of a researcher.

A final element to consider concerning the researchers in this field is the collaborative relationships among them. This can also be used to discover the influential research groups in the field of Blue Flag research. Figure 3.2 presents the results of a network analysis that determines different clusters based on the co-authored publications; the size of each of the circles refers to the occurrence of each author and the thickness of the lines that joins them to the number of collaborations.

It must be noted that this kind of analysis can be more revealing when the number of publications is larger, but in any case, we can see that there appear to be 11 different research groups, but they do not collaborate with each other. The most important group (presented at the top of the figure) is made up of seven authors, with two of them playing a central role (P. D. Roy and M. P. Jonathan). There is another group around E. Ariza and another group of five authors, none of whom

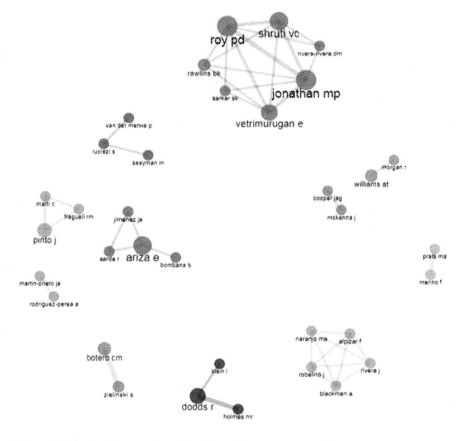

Figure 3.2 Academic research on Blue Flags. Co-occurrence authors

Source: Own elaboration based on WoS data

50   *Fernando Merino and María A. Prats*

has a central role. The other groups are smaller and reflect collaboration among their members.

3.2.5 Most cited journals

To highlight which academic journals are the most influential in this field, we analyze the 30 peer-reviewed journals where the 61 articles have been published. We will focus on the number of published articles in this area that each journal has published as well as the number of citations that their publications have received as a measure of the impact that each journal has on the research on this field.

As we can see in Figure 3.3, research in this field includes a large number of journals that are not specifically concerned with it: 71.9% of the journals have published only one article in this area, and 15.6% two or three. In contrast, there are two journals (*Ocean & Coastal Management* and the *Journal of Coastal Research*) that have published ten or more articles each, indicating that this topic fits clearly within their aims.

We will use the number of citations received by the document as an indicator of the impact each journal has. Considering that there are a large number of journals with only one or two published articles related to the Blue Flag, it is not surprising that a large number of journals receive very few citations. Thus, to better determine the impact, we will focus on those journals with at least three publications in this field that have received at least 50 citations from publications on this topic (Figure 3.4).

The data presented in Figure 3.4 reveal that the journals with the highest number of citations from publications that deal with the Blue Flag are *Ocean & Coastal Management*, with 310 citations, followed by *Tourism Management* (193) and the *Journal of Coastal Research* (94). On the other hand, if we relate the citations to the number of publications per journal, we find that *Tourism Management* is the most influential journal, with 64.3 citations per article. *Ocean & Coastal Management* (28.8), *Coastal Research* (25), *Marine Pollution* (14.7) and the *Journal of Coastal Research* (9.4) are the next most cited journals.

3.2.6 Keyword analysis

The bibliometric analysis of the publications in the field of Blue Flag research allows us not only to detect the most important authors, journals and their evolution, but also the topics treated. To do this, we analyze the keywords that WoS identifies in each of the documents to characterize the publications. There are more than 200 different keywords, 65 of them with two or more appearances and one of them (quality) featuring in 15 of the 71 publications. Figure 3.5 displays the different keywords (which appear in at least two publications) with a larger size according to the number of times each of them appears.

The results displayed in Figure 3.5 show that publications in the Blue Flag field are highly related to themes such as "quality", "tourism", "management" and "awards". Different topics related to pollution (from the word "pollution" itself to others such as "heavy metals", "debris" and "contamination") are also quite

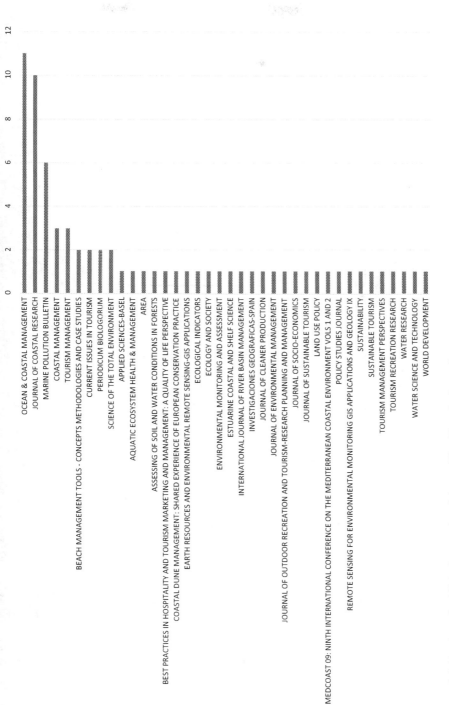

Figure 3.3 Number of published research articles on Blue Flags by journal

Source: Own elaboration based on WoS data

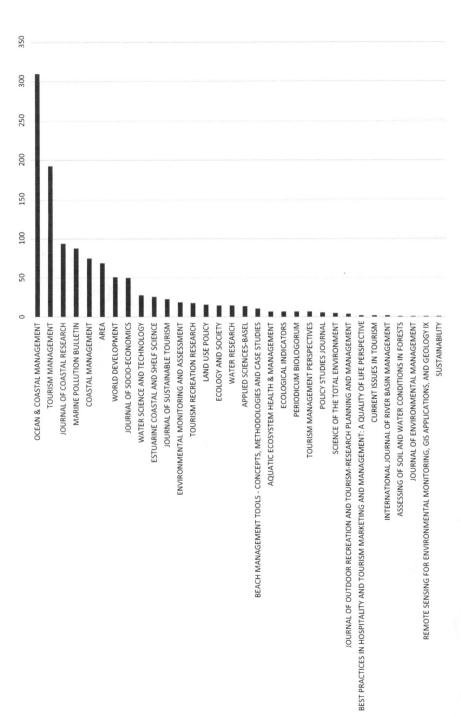

Figure 3.4 Number of citations on Blue Flags by journal
Source: Own elaboration based on WoS data

Figure 3.5 Word cloud relative to research in the Blue Flag topic
Source: Own elaboration based on WoS data

common. Therefore, we can conclude that research related to the Blue Flag has a clear relationship with topics associated with the quality of the beaches, as well as strategies related to their management and the impact on tourism. There is also another set of papers whose keywords are connected to pollution. To a certain extent, it is a little surprising that the keywords related to the authorities in charge of beach/coast management (municipalities, city councils and governments) do not appear in this set. The lack of these terms indicates that the role of local authorities has not yet attracted specific research, and scholars have instead focused more on management strategies without concentrating on the agents that must design and implement them.

The evolution of the appearance of the different keywords in the publications reveals how the topics studied have evolved over time. In Table 3.4, we present the top 39 keywords and the periods in which the publications that include them appeared.

The top ten keywords show how Blue Flag research topics have changed over time to consider the issues from different points of view. In 2009, four topics in particular emerge. These are "quality", "tourism", "management" and "award", which have remained recurring subjects ever since. Around 2015, two new topics appear in the publications alongside the previous ones. These are "certification", "cost" and "pollution". In the late 20th and early 21st century, "ecolabel", "heavy metals" and "perception" were also important issues in the field of Blue Flag research.

This analysis can be complemented with the co-occurrence of these keywords. To undertake this, we develop a network analysis that displays which of them are

54 Fernando Merino and María A. Prats

Table 3.4 Academic research on BF: Analysis on keywords

Keywords	Number of articles	Begin–End
quality	15	2006 2022
tourism	12	2009 2020
management	11	2000 2019
award	10	2009 2020
certification	9	2016 2022
coast	9	2011 2020
pollution	7	2011 2020
ecolabels	5	2018 2022
heavy metals	5	2009 2022
perception	5	2006 2019
coastal	4	2017 2919
contamination	4	2006 2019
debris	4	2018 2021
destination	4	2017 2020
escherichia-coli	4	2015 2022
impact	4	2019 2022
marine	4	2012 2022
public perception	4	2015 2019
spatial distribution	4	2018 2019
system	4	2017 2019
tool	4	2018 2020
users	4	2000 2019
bay	3	2015 2021
beach	3	2015 2022
beach management	3	2019 2021
beaches	3	2015 2019
Blue Flag beaches	3	2019 2019
environ. manag.tool	3	2019 2020
estuarine sediments	3	2018 2019
indicators	3	2018 2019
surface sediments	3	2018 2019
tourist beaches	3	2018 2020
attitudes	2	2009 2018
climate-change	2	2018 2021
coastal scenery	2	2009 2019
coastal zone	2	2009 2016
communities	2	2008 2012
competitiveness	2	2021 2022
conservation	2	2015 2016

Source: Own elaboration based on WoS data

Figure 3.6 Co-occurrence keywords in research articles on Blue Flags
Source: Own elaboration based on WoS data

jointly identified in the studied documents. The results, presented in Figure 3.6, show that there is an important co-occurrence between "quality", "awards", "management" and "tourism". There is also another group related to "certification", "ecolabels" and "management". The other important groups involve one that includes all those keywords related to pollution and another where "perception" and "users" are important terms.

3.3 Conclusions

In this chapter we have explored the development of Blue Flag research between 1995 and 2022 by employing a bibliometric analysis. To do so, we analyzed the published documents collected in Web of Science™ (WoS) Core Collection (CC), restricting the search to Social Sciences Citation Index (SSCI), Science Citation Index Expanded (SCIE), Emerging Sources Citation Index (ESCI), ISI Proceedings – Social Sciences & Humanities Edition (ISSHP) and Book Citation Index. This study identifies 70 documents: 61 articles, six book chapters and three proceedings.

The chronological distribution of publications indicates three different stages with a growing pattern, especially from 2014. The results of the citation analysis do not suggest any correlation among the most cited articles and the most eminent authors. The most cited article is "Users' perception analysis for sustainable beach management in Italy" (Marin et al., 2009) and the second is "The effects of beach characteristics and location with respect to hotel prices" (Rigall-i-Torrent et al., 2011).

56 *Fernando Merino and María A. Prats*

This study identifies the most eminent authors by analyzing the number of publications per author in this field, the number of citations that each author's contribution has received from other publications and the h-index. Considering the last one, which is a more accurate indicator of the impact of an author, we find that the most influential authors are A. T. Williams, R. Dodds, E. Ariza, M. R. Holmes, S. Lucrezi, M. Saayman, C. M. Botero and S. Zielinsky. After analyzing the collaborative relationships among the authors, we have detected 11 influential research groups in the field of Blue Flag research.

The most influential journals in the field, in terms of the number of articles and citations, are *Tourism Management, Ocean & Coastal Management, Coastal Research, Marine Pollution* and the *Journal of Coastal Research.*

The evolution of the appearance of the different keywords in the publications reveals how the topics studied have evolved over time, with "quality", "tourism", "management" and "award" being recurring subjects during the entire period, while other important issues have been "certification", "cost", "pollution" and "ecolabel".

3.4 References

Albano, M., Panarello, G., Di Paola, D., Capparucci, F., Crupi, R., Gugliandolo, E.,... & Savoca, S. (2021). The influence of polystyrene microspheres abundance on development and feeding behavior of Artemia salina (Linnaeus, 1758). *Applied Sciences, 11*(8), 3352.

Ariza, E., Sardá, R., Jiménez, J. A., Mora, J., & Ávila, C. (2007). Beyond performance assessment measurements for beach management: Application to Spanish Mediterranean beaches. *Coastal Management, 36*(1), 47–66.

Blackman, A., Naranjo, M. A., Robalino, J., Alpízar, F., & Rivera, J. (2014). Does tourism eco-certification pay? Costa Rica's Blue Flag program. *World Development, 58*, 41–52.

Boevers, J. (2008). Assessing the utility of beach ecolabels for use by local management. *Coastal Management, 36*(5), 524–531.

Cabezas-Rabadán, C., Rodilla, M., Pardo-Pascual, J. E., & Herrera-Racionero, P. (2019). Assessing users' expectations and perceptions on different beach types and the need for diverse management frameworks along the Western Mediterranean. *Land Use Policy, 81*, 219–231.

Creo, C., & Fraboni, C. (2011). Awards for the sustainable management of coastal tourism destinations: The example of the Blue Flag program. *Journal of Coastal Research, 61*(10061), 378–381.

Dodds, R., & Holmes, M. R. (2018). Education and certification for beach management: Is there a difference between residents versus visitors? *Ocean & Coastal Management, 160*, 124–132.

Duck, R. W., Phillips, M. R., Williams, A. T., & Wadham, T. (2009). Is beach scenic quality a function of habitat diversity? *Journal of Coastal Research*, 415–418.

Fraguell, R. M., Martí, C., Pintó, J., & Coenders, G. (2016). After over 25 years of accrediting beaches, has Blue Flag contributed to sustainable management? *Journal of Sustainable Tourism, 24*(6), 882–903.

Gilburn, A. S. (2012). Mechanical grooming and beach award status are associated with low strandline biodiversity in Scotland. *Estuarine, Coastal and Shelf Science, 107*, 81–88.

Guimarães, M. H. E., Mascarenhas, A., Sousa, C., Boski, T., & Dentinho, T. P. (2012). The impact of water quality changes on the socio-economic system of the Guadiana Estuary: An assessment of management options. *Ecology and Society, 17*(3).

Blue Flags in the world: A bibliometric analysis 57

Halkos, G., & Matsiori, S. (2012). Determinants of willingness to pay for coastal zone quality improvement. *The Journal of Socio-Economics*, *41*(4), 391–399.

Klein, L., & Dodds, R. (2017). Perceived effectiveness of Blue Flag certification as an environmental management tool along Ontario's Great Lakes beaches. *Ocean & Coastal Management*, *141*, 107–117.

Klein, L., & Dodds, R. (2018). Blue Flag beach certification: An environmental management tool or tourism promotional tool? *Tourism Recreation Research*, *43*(1), 39–51.

Loizidou, X. I., Loizides, M. I., & Orthodoxou, D. L. (2018). Persistent marine litter: Small plastics and cigarette butts remain on beaches after organized beach cleanups. *Environmental monitoring and assessment*, *190*(7), 1–10.

Lucrezi, S., & Saayman, M. (2015). Beachgoers' demands vs. Blue Flag aims in South Africa. *Journal of Coastal Research*, *31*(6), 1478–1488.

Lucrezi, S., Saayman, M., & Van der Merwe, P. (2015). Managing beaches and beachgoers: Lessons from and for the Blue Flag award. *Tourism Management*, *48*, 211–230.

Lucrezi, S., & Van der Merwe, P. (2015). Beachgoers' awareness and evaluation of the Blue Flag award in South Africa. *Journal of Coastal Research*, *31*(5), 1129–1140.

Marin, V., Palmisani, F., Ivaldi, R., Dursi, R., & Fabiano, M. (2009). Users' perception analysis for sustainable beach management in Italy. *Ocean & Coastal Management*, *52*(5), 268–277.

Marino, F. J., Morinigo, M. A., Martinez-Manzanares, E., & Borrego, J. J. (1995). Microbiological-epidemiological study of selected marine beaches in Malaga (Spain). *Water Science and Technology*, *31*(5–6), 5–9.

McKenna, J., Williams, A. T., & Cooper, J. A. G. (2011). Blue Flag or Red Herring: Do beach awards encourage the public to visit beaches? *Tourism Management*, *32*(3), 576–588.

Mir-Gual, M., Pons, G. X., Martín-Prieto, J. A., & Rodríguez-Perea, A. (2015). A critical view of the Blue Flag beaches in Spain using environmental variables. *Ocean & Coastal Management*, *105*, 106–115.

Nelson, C., Morgan, R., Williams, A. T., & Wood, J. (2000). Beach awards and management. *Ocean & coastal management*, *43*(1), 87–98.

Rees, G., Pond, K., Johal, K., Pedley, S., & Rickards, A. (1998). Microbiological analysis of selected coastal bathing waters in the UK, Greece, Italy and Spain. *Water Research*, *32*(8), 2335–2340.

Rigall-i-Torrent, R., Fluvià, M., Ballester, R., Saló, A., Ariza, E., & Espinet, J. M. (2011). The effects of beach characteristics and location with respect to hotel prices. *Tourism Management*, *32*(5), 1150–1158.

Sardá, R., Valls, J. F., Pintó, J., Ariza, E., Lozoya, J. P., Fraguell, R. M.,... & Jimenez, J. A. (2015). Towards a new integrated beach management system: The ecosystem-based management system for beaches. *Ocean & Coastal Management*, *118*, 167–177.

Tudor, D. T., & Williams, A. T. (2006). A rationale for beach selection by the public on the coast of Wales, UK. *Area*, *38*(2), 153–164.

Vetrimurugan, E., Shruti, V. C., Jonathan, M. P., Roy, P. D., Rawlins, B. K., & Rivera-Rivera, D. M. (2018). Metals and their ecological impact on beach sediments near the marine protected sites of Sodwana Bay and St. Lucia, South Africa. *Marine Pollution Bulletin*, *127*, 568–575.

Vidinha, J. M., Rocha, F., Silva, E., Patinha, C., & Andrade, C. (2009). Geochemical beach sediments studies – a contribution to a standard definition useful for public health. *Journal of Coastal Research*, *56*, 905–908.

Zielinski, S., Botero, C. M., & Yanes, A. (2019). To clean or not to clean? A critical review of beach cleaning methods and impacts. *Marine pollution bulletin*, *139*, 390–401.

4 Social, political and managerial perspectives on Blue Flag beach certification

Seweryn Zielinski and Camilo M. Botero

4.1 Introduction

Beach certification schemes (BCS) include awards, ecolabels or management systems, which are based on the constant improvement in performance, and which evaluate the characteristics of a particular beach by using measurable compliance criteria (Botero et al., 2015). Blue Flag (BF) Campaign is the first beach certification and one of the first ecolabels in general operation since 1987 (Zielinski & Botero, 2015). Based on the number of certified beaches (5,042 in 2022) and its wide geographic coverage (49 countries on five continents), the BF has been considered to be a global leader.

Despite an increasing body of research, the academic literature has always been divided on the value and significance of beach certifications, including the BF (McKenna et al., 2011; Zielinski & Botero, 2019; Botero & Zielinski, 2020). Most of the early analyses of BF, many of which were carried out in Wales, criticized its limited utility for environmental conservation and lack of recognition by beachgoers (Nelson & Botterill, 2002; McKenna et al., 2011; Nelson et al., 2000; Phillips & House, 2009; Tudor & Williams, 2006). On the contrary, more recent studies have demonstrated BF's ability to generate economic benefits and attract visitors. Capacci et al. (2015) carried out a quantitative study on the economic effect of BF in 56 coastal provinces of Italy to conclude that the BF had a positive effect on the current inbound flow of tourists. On the other hand, Cerqua (2017) estimated the signaling impact of the BF in 145 territorial units in Italy between 2008 and 2012, and concluded that BF alone does not encourage tourists to choose a particular destination, but it does so when combined with a clear sustainability policy. Castillo-Manzano et al. (2021) evaluated BF's effectiveness in attracting international tourists to Spanish provinces between 2000 and 2019 to find that BFs are effective at promoting international tourism, but not domestic. A study carried out by Merino and Prats (2020) determined that Blue Flag recognition has a positive impact on the economic development of the tourism sector in those Spanish municipalities in Comunitat Valenciana that have opted for BF, in comparison to those that did not. Research on four Canadian beaches carried out by Dodds and Holmes (2020) demonstrated that BF certification does influence the consumer when choosing a destination, which indicates that BF is a signal of indirect

DOI: 10.4324/9781003323570-5

competitiveness. The few available economic valuation studies also show BF in a rather positive light. Researchers calculated that the loss of the Blue Flag status at a beach in KwaZulu-Natal in South Africa would cost between £1.5 million and £2 million per year with a visitor drop of just 6% (Nahman & Rigby, 2008). The study by Rigall-i-Torrent et al. (2011) on the economic effect of BF on nearby accommodation prices reported that the BF status increases them by around 11.5%.

It is clear that the existing literature is skewed towards environmental and economic evaluation of the effectiveness of beach certifications. It can be argued that for a long time beach certifications were promoted as tools to improve environmental management of beaches and at the same time to increase their commercial value. The latter argument was perhaps made in the past to encourage the uptake of the certification by public and private stakeholders who would have to bear the financial weight of implementing and maintaining it. The research followed to test these two assumptions about environmental and economic impacts of BF. Despite the growing body of research, there is little evidence showing high effectiveness of certifications in achieving overall tourism sustainability with all the three key dimensions (Esparon et al., 2014; Zielinski & Botero, 2015). While much of the debate about the utility of BF is about its commercial and conservation values, its social, political and managerial benefits have not been discussed as widely. These aspects are rarely evaluated (Font, 2005; Mason, 2007), perhaps because social, political and managerial benefits are difficult to define and measure. Hence, this chapter gathers evidence from available bodies of literature on the topic to demonstrate that the true advantage of BF lies in those areas.

4.2 Social perspectives

Tourism certification schemes have been criticized in the past for focusing too much on environmental benefits (Font, 2002; Font & Buckley, 2001) and ignoring sociocultural issues (Bien, 2007; Font & Harris, 2004; Tepelus & Cordoba, 2005). This is also true in 2022. As such, a great deal of criticism has been focused on the lack of certification criteria that address sociocultural sustainability in areas such as participative management and the inclusion of community values and stakeholder perceptions (Boevers, 2008; Cagilaba & Rennie, 2005; Nelson et al., 2000). Research carried out by Zielinski and Botero (2015) on sustainability of various beach certifications, including Blue Flag, found that all but one certification scored low on social sustainability measured through sustainable tourism and sustainable development indicators. Wider sociocultural benefits are especially affected by exclusion of human settlements from the area of certification, which prevents the certification from ensuring equal distribution of benefits, maintenance of cultural integrity, control and resolution of sociocultural conflicts, and application of other social principles of sustainable development. In order to achieve wider social benefits, BF would need to extend its area of influence beyond the physical limits of the beach, taking on a broader perspective on beaches as tourism destinations. This limited influence decreases BF's effectiveness as tools for achieving sustainability (Zielinski & Botero, 2015).

On the other hand, one should ask whether it should even be an objective of any beach certification to fulfill wider social sustainability criteria described previously. Due to the commercial nature of beach certifications, their management jurisdiction to ensure compliance with social objectives outside the area of the beach is relatively limited. Although Blue Flag, or any other beach certification for that matter, does not require participative management or distribution of benefits, the requirement to create a beach management body composed of relevant stakeholders offers a possibility for inclusion of local citizen organizations in decision making, control and resolution of sociocultural conflicts, and creation of arrangements with local people to operate businesses in the beach area.

Naturally, these social considerations could be imposed by a certification to meet stricter sociocultural criteria. However, research shows that beach certifications have reached the point where adding new requirements to comply with higher environmental and social standards is just not economically feasible. Zielinski and Botero (2015) measured through indicators whether nine beach certifications in Latin America are sustainable to conclude that BF meet 37% of sustainability indicators, which is close the average of 39%. However, the authors also concluded that those certifications that met over 50% of all indicators and hence were more rigorous in terms of social and environmental standards were also the ones that were not implemented by private operators and required substantial subsidies from the governmental bodies that designed the certification. In reality, it is unrealistic to design an implementable beach certification that is exceptionally good in all aspects and at the same time commercially viable and attractive (Zielinski & Botero, 2019). The commercial viability of improving social standards may seem like a secondary issue given that globally most Blue Flags are implemented and maintained in Europe by local governments whose objectives are clearly aimed at providing social values. But even governments have to deal with limited budget and the experience shows that additional requirements would require considerably larger investments to extend BF's area of influence to meet stricter social standards.

Destinations that implement the BF show a high level of loyalty for the award, using it as a guarantee of compliance with current legislation, and generally good quality standards (Fraguell et al., 2015). Some of these quality standards provide significant social benefits that come from the primary objectives that the certification was designed to meet: free public access to the beach, public security and safety in a recreational area, and environmental education. Every BF beach must provide free access for everyone and at least one certified beach in a municipality must be fully inclusive, providing not only facilities, but also water access and equipment (e.g., floating beach chairs) for people with physical disabilities. In this context, Santana-Santana et al. (2021) analyzed the reliability of certificates/ awards, including BF, for 90 urban and semi-urban beaches in 35 Spanish municipalities in terms of ensuring universal accessibility. Although the BF was not the top scorer, it followed other certifications closely; including accessibility UNE 170001 (Universal Accessibility Certification), complying with evaluation criteria such as reserved parking spaces for persons with reduced mobility close to adapted access points, adapted access points, pedestrian paths accessible to the beach, ramp access to the beach, adapted walkways to the sand, and adapted toilets and showers. Public safety refers to the presence of authorities, lifeguards, lifesaving equipment, designated safe areas on the beach and in the water, dangerous zones, separation of different activities to avoid accidents, water quality monitoring and regular removal of litter.

While no one can argue against the lifesaving services and strategies implemented to ensure safety of beachgoers, the cleaning requirements of the BF have been criticized for allowing the common practice of mechanical grooming and removal of natural debris for their impact on the environment (Boevers, 2008; Fraguell et al., 2015; Mir-Gual et al., 2015; Roig-Munar et al., 2018). Although neither the usage of machinery for cleaning nor the removal of natural debris are required by BF, certified beaches are usually urbanized and the high numbers of visitors make it difficult to deal with litter without mechanical cleaning as there is a strong correlation between beach visitor density and litter generation (Ariza et al., 2008; Becherucci et al., 2017; Martinez-Ribes et al., 2007; Santos et al., 2005), as well as between the proximity to an urban center and the contamination of beaches (Araujo et al., 2018; Leite et al., 2014; Poeta et al., 2016).

The guidelines from BF recommend that not all of the seaweed should be removed, indicating the need for consulting environmental specialists regarding management of algal vegetation washed on to the beach. From a strictly environmental perspective, the mechanical cleaning and removal of natural wrack have negative effects on a beach ecosystem, although it is arguable to what extent it affects highly urbanized and already degraded beaches (Zielinski et al., 2019). But from the social perspective of beach safety, cleaning machinery moves the upper sand layer exposing potentially contaminated sand to sunlight that kills harmful bacteria. Similarly, accumulation of seaweed on the shore may reduce access to the beach for recreational activities or for disabled users (FEE, 2008, 2018), the algal mats pose a health hazard by sheltering Escherichia coli and enterococci (Byappanahalli et al., 2003; Whitman et al., 2014), and decaying organic matter produces odors that attract flies and their larvae (Alves et al., 2014; Davenport & Davenport, 2006; McLachlan & Brown, 2006). Finally, natural debris and litter are more likely to pose a greater risk or injury on intensively used beaches as compared to relatively natural and regularly cleaned beaches (Campbell et al., 2016), especially accumulated, rotting seaweed that could also be slippery and therefore become a hazard for people walking on the shoreline.

Finally, environmental education has been one of the key objectives for creation of BF in the 1980s. BF requires a beach to have an environmental education plan and to offer a range of educational activities to beach users or local communities. A number of studies revealed that beach managers value the BF program for its activities for citizens and students (Pencarelli et al., 2016; Ulme et al., 2018). The environmental education requirement, present in all BCS, provides a platform for integration of activities with municipal environmental education strategies and supporting partnerships with local environmental initiatives, NGOs, schools, and media (Ulme et al., 2018). Without the BF framework, many of these actions would not be realized as the capacity of local governments increase substantially through partnership with educational, environmental, civil society and other governmental organizations working together to obtain and maintain the certification.

Environmental education can be very effective in reduction of beach littering and litter generation by beach users. It includes staff training and user education, and adequate provision of waste receptacles (bins) (Ballance et al., 2000; Campbell et al., 2016; Eastman et al., 2013). Environmental education and disposal facilities are not only considered effective by managers and the BF program, but they are also highly supported by beach users (Campbell et al., 2016). The positive social impact of all the above-mentioned benefits is especially significant on beaches that receive large number of visitors such as those certified by Blue Flag, which has traditionally provided guidelines for frequently used developed beaches (Ariza et al., 2008; Cervantes and Espejel, 2008; Fraguell et al., 2015; Lucrezi & Saayman, 2015; Williams and Micallef, 2009).

Another social benefit of BF is that the certification gives local communities the ability to pressure governmental agencies into taking specific actions of general interest (Cagilaba & Rennie, 2005). Once a certification has been implemented, meeting specific environmental, security and safety criteria, its maintenance becomes an obligation for local authorities. Loss of certification is perceived to damage the image and prestige (Fraguell et al., 2015), and cause local criticism, which is negatively received among local politicians. Hence, BF maintenance can be used by local authorities as leverage for competing for public resources (McKenna et al., 2011). Contrary to shifting priorities, each time a new government is in power, certifications allow for a level of continuity in terms of funds and management of beaches (Botero & Zielinski, 2020), which without any doubt has a significant social benefit.

4.3 Managerial perspectives

The BF was designed to raise environmental awareness and increase good environmental practices among tourists, local populations and beach management staff (FEE, 2018). Hence, management requirements make up an important part of all requirements found in BF (Zielinski & Botero, 2015). This fact is based on the assumption that proper management will lead to social or environmental benefits. Although there is still little hard evidence to support it, it is safe to assume that management actions such as beach cleaning, water quality monitoring, access limitation to sensitive areas (dunes, coral reefs, seagrass meadows) will have noticeable positive effects on beachgoers and the environment. However, beach management is a complex task that challenges local authorities and private beach operators to achieve good standards that have to meet the needs of the environment and visitors, which lie on opposite sides of the spectrum and require very specific knowledge from managers.

Unfortunately, few beach managers have the academic knowledge or technical capacity to understand and use the variety of tools to make educated decisions (Esteves, 2018). Therefore, one of the most prominent roles that BF can play is to act as a blueprint for the management of beaches (Marchese et al., 2021; McKenna et al., 2011; Williams & Micallef, 2009; Zielinski & Botero, 2015; Botero & Zielinski, 2020). This role may be insignificant in countries or localities where beaches have historically been managed by capable authorities and where there is clear legislation in place that supports beach management. In this context, Klein and Dodds (2017) reported that interviewed managers in Ontario, Canada stated that their beaches had already been meeting high standards, and the BF certification did not provide any further benefits. In such cases, the argument that the only role of BF is commercial image building and marketing is valid. On the other hand, there are also reports of beach managers appreciating the BF standards as a clear guideline for management (Creo & Fraboni, 2011; Pencarelli et al., 2016). This is especially valuable for less experienced beach managers without the scientific expertise to manage their beach according to integrated beach management tools and principles (Esteves, 2018). BF provides targets that should be achievable by a nonscientific group of managers with some expertise from environmental authorities (Zielinski & Botero, 2019). This has been confirmed in a study in Colombia (Botero & Zielinski, 2020), and it is likely to be the case for many beaches worldwide, especially in many low- and middle-income countries (Kolhoff et al., 2018).

4.4 Political and institutional perspectives

Another area where BF certification really shines is political and institutional. According to the research on the effectiveness of beach certifications for integrated coastal management (sustainable development of coastal areas), most schemes are strongest in the biophysical sphere with a substantial number of requirements (37 on average) focused on environmental management (Zielinski & Botero, 2015). However, when the same research used an expert panel to identify those requirements that are the most crucial to beach management, it was found that while the strengths of most beach certifications are still biophysical, the BF's forte is institutional. According to the results of the research, BF's requirements met a number of institutional objectives extracted from various sets of sustainability indicators, such as: 1) strengthen and ensure coordination of authorities and administrative policies; 2) support integrated management through appropriate legislation and regulations; 3) increase public awareness about sociocultural and environmental sustainability in the coastal areas; and 4) resolve conflicts over coastal space and resources. It should be noted that these indicators used in the study apply best to a large coastal area and therefore they may not be fully compatible with beach certifications applicable to a much smaller area.

The first objective is met by BF through the requirement to clearly define and adopt administrative authorities (beach management authorities) and beach management goals and objectives. In the study of Zielinski and Botero (2015), the expert panel identified the creation of a beach management authority (BMA) as the most important aspect of beach certifications that support beach management. The objective of a BMA is to regulate the interrelations between different elements in a coastal system. BMAs are internal beach authorities that have direct responsibility for the adjustments that are needed to maintain the stability of the entire coastal system, and which assume the roles of central decision-making centers (Vallega, 1999). An important aspect of a BMA is its coordination of the often discordant interests of stakeholders, and its role as a conflict resolution mediator.

The second objective is met by BF through the requirement to set management structures and strategies are in line with current legislation and coastal management plans that include the beach within their jurisdiction. In other words, the BF requires enforcing compliance with legal and local agreements, and recognizing local authorities, ensuring compatibility between legal (formal) and local (informal) agreements. BF also requires creation and enforcement of a beach management plan (Marchese et al., 2021).

The third objective is met by BF through the requirements to provide to the public information on the environmental situation of the beach, periodically hold media events at the beach that cover coastal issues and the key importance of the environment, and provide information on integrated beach management, sustainable tourism and certifications (costs/benefits) through informational and educational public activities.

Finally, the fourth objective about conflict resolution is partially met by BF through the requirements to organize and separate different uses of the beach, preventing conflicts that could arise from engaging in different activities, and through a code of conduct for visitors and beach personnel. One aspect that has been neglected by most beach certifications, including the BF, is the lack of formal requirement for a conflict resolution mechanism with its own tribunal and sanctions. Although BF's BMA may take up the task to coordinate conflicting interests of local stakeholders and mediate conflicts, which would be in the best interest for the management of a beach, it is not a formal requirement.

Meeting all four of the above-mentioned objectives brings tangible benefits to the coastal areas where the certified beaches are located. More importantly, they perfectly align with various policy objectives specific to coastal areas. For public sector officials, BF ensures compliance with regulations and high standards through a ready-to-implement blueprint (Fraguell et al., 2015; Marchese et al, 2021; Pencarelli et al., 2016) without the need for troublesome administrative control and inspection by public authorities. Hence, in this way BF acts as a tool for achieving public policy objectives centered on meeting health and safety standards, environmental management and education, coastal zoning and the integration of stakeholders. At the same time, certifications are believed to provide commercial value in terms of a comparative advantage and direct and indirect economic benefits for the destination, stimulating the tourism industry (Boevers, 2008). This is not inherent to BF, but is a general characteristic of tourism ecolabels as noted by Buckley (2002, p.23): "ecolabels can be used as instruments of government policy as well as mechanisms for consumer choice", which can encourage involvement of stakeholders in the pursuit of BF and support from the general public, following the logic of collective action (Olson, 1965).

This political power of Blue Flag is often overlooked by debates centered on the effectiveness of environmental requirements for nature conservation. The political value of BF implementation is evident even before the formal decision about pursuing the certification is made, when local stakeholders are gathering around the common purpose of defining standards for improving local recreation and tourism (Font, 2005). There is evidence, albeit limited, that once there is a consensus among stakeholders, and the local government politically supports the idea of pursuing a beach certification, local stakeholders on their own accord implement management actions directed toward reaching BF criteria (Botero & Zielinski, 2020). These "improvements" may range from facilities that increase the safety of beach users to environmental management actions, wastewater treatment and environmental education activities.

In this context, BF is a catalyst for agreements between managers, funders and beneficiaries that can form partnerships and work together towards common goals and priorities (Zielinski & Botero, 2015). The evidence shows that many key partnerships among local stakeholders were signed specifically because of the Blue Flag campaign (e.g., Botero & Zielinski, 2020; Cerqua, 2017; Klein & Dodds, 2017, 2018; Ulme et al., 2018). In this way, even the local governments that have limited scientific expertise can take advantage from collaboration with other stakeholders that pursue the shared goal of obtaining the certification. Examples from case studies include infrastructural improvements such as toilets, access roads, wastewater treatment plants or solid waste management (Botero & Zielinski, 2020; Creo & Fraboni, 2011; Pencarelli et al., 2016). According to the respondents, if it was not for the BF, most of them would not have been implemented. The adherence to BF criteria also opens doors for other certifications or recognition awards such as ISO or EMAS that are often pursued as they do not require additional investments.

4.5 Conclusion

Despite a large portion of BF debate centered on criticizing its focus on amenities and visitor satisfaction and its effectiveness for nature conservation, this chapter argues that the BF program play a much wider social and political role, offering a set of key benefits for beach managers and local governments responsible for the implementation and maintenance of the certification. This role is largely overlooked in the literature on beach certifications despite its critical importance. At the managerial level, BF provides a clear and ready-to-use blueprint that can be understood and implemented even by a team without expertise in this area. One of the key requirements of BF is to establish a beach management authority that has a central role in coordinating among local stakeholders' decision making. BF can also secure initial funding for beaches that might not be able to secure it otherwise. At the political level, BF can be used as a policy tool to adhere to and/ or exceed environmental and safety standards, at the same time providing environmental educational activities to citizens. The public character of beaches and a fear of public criticism if a beach loses the status of BF demand steady political support for certification, which is usually continued irrespective of which government is currently in power. These aspects of BF make it a very powerful management tool, especially in many developing countries that only recently started paying attention to the management of their beaches.

4.6 References

Alves, B., Benavente, J., & Ferreira, O. (2014). Beach users' profile, perceptions and willingness to pay for beach management in Cadiz (SW Spain). *Journal of Coastal Research*, SI70, 521–526.

Araujo, M.C.B., Silva-Cavalcanti, J.S., & Costa, M.F. (2018). Anthropogenic litter on beaches with different levels of development and use: A snapshot of a coast in Pernambuco (Brazil). *Frontiers in Marine Science*, 5(233).

Ariza, E., Sarda, R., Jiménez, J.A., Mora, J., & Avila, C. (2008). Beyond performance assessment measurement for beach management: Application to Spanish Mediterranean beaches. *Coastal Management*, 36(1), 47–66.

Ballance, A., Ryan, P.G., & Turpie, J.K. (2000). How much is a clean beach worth? The impact of litter on beach users in the Cape Peninsula, South Africa. *South African Journal of Science*, 96(5), 210–213.

Becherucci, M.E., Rosenthal, A.F., & Pon, J.P.S. (2017). Marine debris in beaches of the Southwestern Atlantic: An assessment of their abundance and mass at different spatial scales in northern coastal Argentina. *Marine Pollution Bulletin*, 119(1), 299–306.

Bien, A. (2007). A simple user's guide to certification for sustainable tourism and ecotourism. Washington, DC: The International Ecotourism Society.

Boevers J. (2008). Assessing the utility of beach eco-labels for use by local management. *Coastal Management*, 36(5), 524–531.

Botero, C.M., Williams, A.T., & Cabrera, J.A. (2015). Advances in beach management in Latin America: Overview from certification schemes. In C.W. Finkl, C. Makowski (Eds.), *Environmental Management and Governance: Advances in Coastal and Marine Resources* (pp.33–63). Coastal Research Library 8. Springer International Publishing.

Botero, C.M., & Zielinski, S. (2020). The implementation of a world-famous tourism ecolabel triggers political support for beach management. *Tourism Management Perspectives*, 35, 1006912.

Buckley, R. (2002). Tourism eco-labels. *Annals of Tourism Research*, 29(1), 188–208.

Byappanahalli, M.N., Shively, D.A., Nevers, M.B., Sadowsky, M.J., & Whitman, R.L. (2003). Growth and survival of Escherichia coli and enterococci populations in the macro-alga Cladophora (Chlorophyta). *FEMS Microbiology Ecology*, 46(2), 203–211.

Cagilaba, V., & Rennie, H. (2005). *Literature review of beach awards and rating systems* (Report No. 2005/24). Hamilton: Environmental Waikato.

Campbell, M.L., Slavin, C., Grage, A., & Kinslow, A. (2016). Human health impacts from litter on beaches and associated perceptions: A case study of "clean" Tasmanian beaches. *Ocean & Coastal Management*, 126, 22–30.

Capacci, S., Scorcu, A.E., & Vici, L. (2015). Seaside tourism and eco-labels: The economic impact of Blue Flags. *Tourism Management*, 47, 88–96.

Castillo-Manzano, J.I., Castro-Nuño, M., López-Valpuesta, L., & Zarzoso, Á. (2021). Measuring the role of Blue Flags in attracting sustainable "sun-and-sand" tourism. *Current Issues in Tourism*, 24(15), 2204–2222.

Cerqua, A. (2017). The signalling effect of eco-labels in modern coastal tourism. *Journal of Sustainable Tourism*, 25(8), 1159–1180.

Cervantes, O., & Espejel, L. (2008). Design of an integrated evaluation index for recreational beaches. *Ocean & Coastal Management*, 51(5), 410–419.

Creo, C., & Fraboni, C. (2011). Awards for the sustainable management of coastal tourism destinations: The example of the blue flag program. *Journal of Coastal Research*, SI61, 378–381.

Davenport, J., & Davenport, J.L. (2006). The impact of tourism and personal leisure transport on coastal environments: A review. *Estuarine, Coastal and Shelf Science*, 67(1–2), 280–292.

Dodds, R., & Holmes, M.R. (2020). Is Blue Flag certification a means of destination competitiveness? A Canadian context. *Ocean & Coastal Management*, 192, 105192.

Eastman, L.B., Nunez, P., Crettier, B., & Thiel, M. (2013). Identification of self-reported user behavior, education level, and preferences to reduce littering on beaches – a survey from the SE Pacific. *Ocean & Coastal Management*, 78, 18–24.

Esparon, M., Gyuris, E., & Stoeckl, N. (2014). Does ECO certification deliver benefits? An empirical investigation of visitors' perceptions of the importance of ECO certification's attributes and of operators' performance. *Journal of Sustainable Tourism*, 22(1), 148–169.

Esteves, L.S. (2018). Beach management tools: Concepts, methodologies and case studies. *Journal of Coastal Research*, 34(5), 1270

Font, X. (2002). Environmental certification in tourism and hospitality: Progress, process and prospects. *Tourism Management*, 23(3), 197–205.

Font, X. (2005). Critical review of certification and accreditation in sustainable tourism governance. Retrieved from: https://www.crrconference.org/Previous_conferences/downloads/font.pdf

Font, X., & Buckley, R.C. (2001). *Tourism eco-labelling: Certification and promotion of sustainable management*. CABI.

Font, X., & Harris, C. (2004). Rethinking standards from green to sustainable. *Annals of Tourism Research*, 31(4), 986–1007.

FEE – Foundation for Environmental Education (2008, 2018). *Blue Flag Beach Criteria and Explanatory Notes*. FEE.

Fraguell, R.M., Martí, C., Pintó, J., & Coenders, G. (2015). After over 25 years of accrediting beaches, has Blue Flag contributed to sustainable management? *Journal of Sustainable Tourism*, 24(6), 882–903.

Klein, L., & Dodds, R. (2018). Blue Flag beach certification: An environmental management tool or tourism promotional tool? *Tourism Recreation Research*, 43(1), 39–51.

Kolhoff, A.J., Driessen, P.P.J., & Runhaar, H.A.C. (2018). Overcoming low EIA performance – a diagnostic tool for the deliberate development of EIA system capacities in low and middle income countries. *Environmental Impact Assessment Review*, 68, 98–108.

Leite, A.S., Santos, L.L., Costa, Y., & Hatje, V. (2014). Influence of proximity to an urban center in the pattern of contamination by marine debris. *Marine Pollution Bulletin*, 81(1), 242–247.

Lucrezi, S., & Saayman, M. (2015). Beachgoers' demands vs. Blue Flag aims in South Africa. *Journal of Coastal Research*, 31(6), 1478–1488.

Marchese, L., Botero, C.M., Zielinski, S., Anfuso, G., Polette, M., & Correa, I.C.S. (2021). Beach certification schemes in Latin America: Are they applicable to the Brazilian context? *Sustainability*, 13, 934.

Martinez-Ribes, L., Basterretxea, G., Palmer, M., & Tintore, J. (2007). Origin and abundance of beach debris in the Balearic Islands. *Scientia Marina*, 71(2), 305–314.

Mason, P. (2007). "No better than a Band-Aid for a bullet wound!" The effectiveness of tourism codes of conduct. In R. Black & A. Crabtree (Eds.), *Quality assurance and certification in ecotourism* (pp.46–64). CAB.

McKenna, J., Williams, A.T., & Cooper, J.A.G. (2011). Blue Flag or Red Herring: Do beach awards encourage the public to visit beaches? *Tourism Management*, 32(3), 576588.

McLachlan, A., & Brown, A.C. (2006). *The ecology of sandy shores* (2nd ed.). Academic Press.

Merino, F., & Prats, M.A. (2020). Sustainable beach management and promotion of the local tourist industry: Can Blue Flags be a good driver of this balance? *Ocean & Coastal Management*, 198, 105359.

Mir-Gual, M., Pons, G.X., Martín-Prieto, J.A., & Rodríguez-Perea, A. (2015). A critical view of the Blue Flag beaches in Spain using environmental variables. *Ocean & Coastal Management*, 105, 106–115.

Nahman, A., & Rigby, D. (2008). Valuing blue flag status and estuarine water quality in Margate, South Africa. *South African Journal of Economics*, 76(4), 721–737.

Nelson, C., & Botterill, D. (2002). Evaluating the contribution of beach quality awards to the local tourism industry in Wales – the Green Coast Award. *Ocean & Coastal Management*, 45(2), 157–170.

Nelson, C., Morgan, R., Williams, A.T., & Wood, J. (2000). Beach awards and management. *Ocean & Coastal Management*, 43(1), 87–98.

Olson, M. (1965). *The Logic of Collective Action*. Harvard University Press.

Pencarelli, T., Splendiani, S., & Fraboni, C. (2016). Enhancement of the "Blue Flag" eco-label in Italy: An empirical analysis. Anatolia, 27(1), 28–37.

Phillips, M.R., & House, C. (2009). An evaluation of priorities for beach tourism: Case studies from South Wales, UK. *Tourism Management*, 30(2), 176–183.

Poeta, G., Conti, L., Malavasi, M., Battisti, C., & Acosta, A.T.R. (2016). Beach litter occurrence in sandy littorals: The potential role of urban areas, rivers and beach users in central Italy. *Estuarine, Coastal and Shelf Science*, 181, 231–237.

Rigall-i-Torrent, R., Fluvia, M., Ballester, R., Salo, A., Ariza, E., & Espinet, J.M. (2011). The effects of beach characteristics and location with respect to hotel prices. *Tourism Management*, 32, 1150–1158.

Roig-Munar, F.X., Fraile-Jurado, P., & Peña-Alonso, C. (2018). Analysis of Blue Flag beaches compared with natural beaches in the Balearic Islands and Canary Islands, Spain. In C.M. Botero, O. Cervantes, & C.W. Finkl (Eds.), *Beach management tools – concepts, methodologies and case studies* (pp.545–559). Coastal Research Library 24. Springer International Publishing.

Santana-Santana, S.B., Peña-Alonso, C., & Pérez-Chacón Espino, E. (2021). Assessing universal accessibility in Spanish beaches. *Ocean & Coastal Management*, 201, 105486.

Santos, I.R., Friedrich, A.C., Wallner-Kersanach, M., & Fillmann, G. (2005). Influence of socio-economic characteristics of beach users on litter generation. *Ocean & Coastal Management*, 48 (9–10), 742–752.

Tepelus, C.M., & Córdoba, R.C. (2005). Recognition schemes in tourism from "eco" to "sustainability"? *Journal of Cleaner Production*, 13(2), 135–140.

Tudor, D.T., & Williams, A.T. (2006). A rationale for beach selection by the public on the coast of Wales, UK. *Area*, 38(2), 153–164.

Ulme, J., Graudiņa-Bombiza, S., & Ernsteins, R. (2018). The Blue Flag programme as proenvironmental behaviour instrument for coastal destinations: Towards municipal coastal governance and communication. *Regional Formation and Development Studies*, 24(1), 120–132.

Vallega, A. (1999). *Fundamentals of integrated coastal management*. Kluwer.

Whitman, R.L., Harwood, V.J., Edge, T.A., Nevers, M.B., Byappanahalli, M., Vijayavel, K.,... & Solo-Gabriele, H.M. (2014). Microbes in beach sands: Integrating environment, ecology and public health. *Reviews in Environmental Science and Bio/Technology*, 13(3), 329–368.

Williams, A., & Micallef, A. (2009). *Beach management: Principles and practice* (1st ed.) Earthscan.

Zielinski, S., & Botero, C.M. (2015). Are eco-labels sustainable? Beach certification schemes in Latin America and the Caribbean. *Journal of Sustainable Tourism*, 23(10), 1550–1572.

Zielinski, S., & Botero, C.M. (2019). Myths, misconceptions and the true value of Blue Flag. *Ocean & Coastal Management*, 174, 15–24.

Zielinski, S., Botero, C.M., & Yanes, A. (2019). To clean or not to clean? A critical review of beach cleaning methods and impacts. *Marine Pollution Bulletin*, 139, 390–401.

5 Does the Blue Flag program contribute to the achievement of the Sustainable Development Goals?

José A. Albaladejo-García and José A. Zabala

5.1 Introduction

Over the years, beach quality criteria have been established as a tool for beach managers to monitor and respond to the negative impacts of human pressures on beaches, including increased land and water pollution (Lucrezi et al., 2015). Eco-labels, such as the Blue Flag (BF) program, have been introduced to assess the state of beaches and whether quality criteria are met (Williams & Micallef, 2009).

In particular, the BF program, developed by the independent and non-profit Foundation for Environmental Education, seeks to promote the sustainable development of coastal areas, employing a year-by-year accomplishment of high-quality standards and criteria regarding: (1) environmental information and education, (2) water quality, (3) environmental management, and (4) safety and services. It provides an accredited distinction of quality for beaches that encompass environmental, social, and economic benefits, not only for the beaches themselves but also for the local communities and regions where they are embedded. This kind of eco-labelling is also highlighted for being able to attract more responsible beachgoers, improving pro-environmental behavior among beach users, and leading beach managers and stakeholders to work together in the compliance and maintenance of required BF criteria. Recent studies (Merino & Prats, 2020; Castillo-Manzano et al., 2021) have demonstrated the role of BFs in promoting sustainability in the tourism sector, being in line with the Sustainable Development Goals (SDGs) for the period 2015–2030.

The United Nations (UN) 2030 Agenda for Sustainable Development is a holistic strategy that encompasses a set of 17 integrated and indivisible SDGs (UN, 2015). Utilizing these 17 SDGs, and 169 specific targets, the 2030 Agenda addresses the worldwide development that meets the needs of the present without compromising the ability of future generations to meet their own needs. SDGs become a tool for embodying the global concept of sustainability into concrete and measurable actions to be pursued. The economic, social, and environmental dimensions of SDGs seek to address poverty, hunger, disease, fear and violence, health and well-being, education, social protection, sanitation, security, sustainable habitats, and energy (Boluk et al., 2019).

Specifically for the tourism sector, targets in SDGs 8, 12, and 14 focus on promoting sustainable tourism for the creation of jobs, the promotion of local economies,

DOI: 10.4324/9781003323570-6

and the sustainable management of marine resources. As shown, coastal sustainable tourism, which is at the heart of the BF program, is also one of the priorities for the 2030 Agenda for Sustainable Development, revealing therefore a narrow and direct link between both.

Global implementation of the SDGs will be led by countries' own sustainable development policies, plans, and programs (UN, 2015). Success in the achievement of the SDGs will require a good understanding of the impact of such policies, plans, and programs on the SDGs. Similarly, monitoring their implementation and development will be only pursued if appropriate indicators link the actions undertaken by the plans and programs to the SDGs. This is particularly of high importance for the BF program.

Although BFs work closely with the SDGs in promoting sustainable coastal tourism development, there is limited comprehensive assessment of their contribution to achieving the SDGs. Hence, given the holistic and interrelated nature of the SDGs, which address a wide range of goals, it is vital to understand the impact of the BFs on the achievement of the SDGs. In this sense, this work aims to assess the contribution of BF-certified beaches to the achievement of the SDGs. For this purpose, each of the 17 SDGs has been linked to the BF beach criteria and are represented by specific case studies around the world to show the direct contribution of BFs. Besides this, the empirical literature has been reviewed to understand the indirect contribution of BF beaches to the achievement of the SDGs. By using this information, specific indicators have been proposed and discussed to better monitor such contributions. This will support decision-makers, managers, and communities in implementing policies to deliver environmental and social benefits, as well as address sustainability challenges and potential trade-offs between goals (Gissi et al., 2022). Through these 17 goals, many countries are making an effort toward more sustainable tourism. However, while sustainable tourism measures can be effective as tools to drive greater sensitivity, they are not easy to implement in the tourism sector, demonstrating the need for deeper research and innovation in the sector (Sipic, 2017).

5.2 Blue Flags and their contributions to the Sustainable Development Goals

The benefits that the BF program can provide for local economies and coastal areas derive from: (1) all the management actions required to positively verified the award BF criteria, as well as their yearly renovations; (2) the specific campaigns and projects that national operators develop in the BF-awarded beaches; (3) the knock-on effect that the BF award might generate in the local economies in the medium and long term through the tourism promotion, stakeholder cooperation, water quality improvement, or new capital investments. In consequence, the contribution of the BF program to the attainment of the SDGs might be direct (1, 2) and indirect (3).

This section presents the SDGs and the revised contributions from the BF program, together with their specific initiatives and plans developed in concrete case studies, as well as the indirect contributions evinced from the revision of empirical literature. Table 5.1 shows a summary of such contributions and embodying instruments. Some of these SDGs have been grouped under the same heading for better understanding.

Table 5.1 Direct and indirect contributions of BFs to SDGs

SDG	Direct contributions			Indirect contributions	
	Criteria for BF award	Actions, plans, and programs developed	Case Studies	Knock-on effects	Empirical evidence
1. Ending poverty		Job opportunities for disadvantaged communities	South Africa | Dominican Republic	BF award encourages employment	Guadiana Estuary – Portugal and Spain (Guimarães et al. 2012)
2. Zero hunger		Facilities to make the most of fish offcuts for local fishers and fight food waste	New Zealand		
3. Well-being	27. Appropriate public safety control measures 28. First aid equipment available on the beach 29. Emergency plans to cope with pollution risks 30. Beach management to prevent conflicts 31. Safety measures to protect beach users and grant free access	Prevention of accidents and promotion of healthy habits at beaches | Teaching lifesaving techniques | Walking activities for elderly and lonely people | Swimming to deal with mental health	Spain | England	BF sites promote a higher quality of life	Portugal and Spain (Chamorro-Mera et al., 2019)
4. Quality education	1. Information about the BF program 2. Environmental education activities for beach users 3. Information about bathing water quality 4. Information about local ecosystems, environmental elements, and cultural sites 5. A map of the beach indicating facilities	Summer libraries, book loans for free to beachgoers, and public readings on beaches | Educational trips about local conservation and restoration	Slovenia | New Zealand	Education for sustainable development | Environmental education activities promote pro-environmental behaviour	Ireland (Ryan-Fogarty et al. 2016) | Canada (Dodds & Holmes. 2018) | Cyprus (Leonidou et al. 2015)

(Continued)

Table 5.1 (Continued)

SDG	Direct contributions		Case Studies	Indirect contributions	
	Criteria for BF award	Actions, plans, and programs developed		Knock-on effects	Empirical evidence
5. Gender equality		Awareness-raising activities on sexual harassment and violence | Same opportunities and wages for beach-related jobs	Mexico | Spain | Portugal | Italy		
6. Water quality	7. Water quality sampling requirements 8. Standards and requirements for water quality analysis 9. Discharges must not affect the beach area 10. Requirements for the microbiological parameter Escherichia coli and intestinal enterococci 11. Requirements for physical parameters 21. Controlled sewage disposals for toilets and restrooms	Support for improved wastewater treatment plants | Support to implement wastewater management systems	Spain | Slovenia	BF award drives wastewater treatment efficiency | BF beaches have cleaner waters | Water quality reduction and BF withdrawal provide nonmarket economic costs	Guadiana Estuary – Portugal and Spain (Guimarães et al., 2012) | Western Mediterranean basin (Merino & Prats, 2022) | South Africa (Nahman & Rigby, 2008)
7. Clean energy		Electric charging stations for vehicles are promoted in parking lots	Sweden		
8. Economic growth		Promotion of events and hospitality sector to attract tourism	Northern Ireland	BF award spurs new hospitality investments | BF's as a sign of competitiveness and price premium	Costa Rica (Blackman et al., 2014) | Canada (Klein & Dodds, 2018) | Croatia (Sipic, 2017)

Does Blue Flag contribute to the achievement of the SDGs? 73

SDG	Direct contributions			Indirect contributions	
	Criteria for BF award	Actions, plans, and programs developed	Case Studies	Knock-on effects	Empirical evidence
9. Sustainable infrastructure	24. Properly maintained buildings and beach equipment	Promotion of affordable public transport and footpaths | Innovative ways to treat seaweed for compost or fertilizer	Cyprus	BF sites as a guide of design for sustainable behavior	Israel (Portman et al., 2019)
10. Reduce inequalities	33. Access and facilities for the physically disabled	Public and accessible spaces for everyone | Beach cleaning by mentally disabled people	Spain | Greece | Dominican Republic		Spain (Santana-Santana et al., 2021)
11. Sustainable cities	26. Sustainable means of transportation	Only sustainable means of transport are allowed | Training in environmental education for local communities	Bulgaria | South Africa		
12. Responsible consumption/ production	32. Available drinking water	Installation of water taps near beaches | Single-use plastics are forbidden	Netherlands | Virgin Islands	BFs promote sustainable tourism	Spain (Merino & Prats, 2020; Castillo-Manzano et al., 2021)
13. Climate action		Reforestation to mitigate the effects of climate change	Puerto Rico	BF sites are slightly adapted for climate change effects	Greece (Tzoraki et al., 2018)
14. Life below water	16. Algal vegetation or natural debris left on the beach | 25. Monitored marine and freshwater sensitive habitats (such as coral reefs or seagrass beds)	Turtle-release activities and monitoring of coral reefs are developed | Code of conduct on how to navigate around protected marine spaces | Support of the marine investigation	Dominican Republic | Spain		

(Continued)

Table 5.1 (Continued)

SDG	Direct contributions		Indirect contributions		
	Criteria for BF award	Actions, plans, and programs developed	Case Studies	Knock-on effects	Empirical evidence
15. Life on land	15. Cleaned beaches 17. Available and regularly maintained waste disposal bins/containers 18. Available facilities for the separation of recyclable waste materials 19. Adequate number of toilets and restrooms 20. Clean toilet and restroom facilities 22. No unauthorized camping or driving and no dumping on the beach 23. Controlled access to domestic animals	Ocean bins to remove large pieces of marine waste	Development of biodiversity monitoring and conservation programs	Denmark	Italy	BF sites are quite clean	Cyprus (Loizidou et al., 2018)
16. Peace and justice	6. A displayed code of conduct 12. An established beach management committee 13. Compliance with laws and regulations by local authority/beach operator 14. Management of sensitive areas	Cooperation between the public and private sector and NGOs to foster peace and social justice	Turkey	Slovenia		
17. Partnership for the goals		Engagement of public authorities, stakeholders, and society	Enhancement of the cooperation between governments, organizations, and municipalities	Cooperation with research institutions	Cyprus	Japan	New Zealand	BF awards increase cooperation among stakeholders in local communities and raise political will	Colombia (Botero & Zielinski, 2020)

Source: Own elaboration based on FEE (2020) and cited references

5.2.1 The Blue Flag program contributes to ending poverty (SDG 1) and achieving zero hunger (SDG 2)

Although there are currently no specific criteria for the BF award covering these two first SDGs, there are many socioeconomic areas in which the BF program can exert its influence to overcome poverty and hunger. One of the main economic opportunities for the BF program is the creation of jobs related to beach maintenance and management, which can support local communities through increased tourism, hospitality, and commercial activities. Promoting the sustainability of tourism activities ensures that communities traditionally dependent on the ecosystem services provided by beaches continue to enjoy the benefits they bring.

Thanks to the "Blue Flag for Tourism" program, paid jobs are offered in less developed countries, such as South Africa, in a variety of functions such as lifeguarding, beach cleaning, tourism support, and environmental education to people from disadvantaged communities (FEE, 2020). Other BF sites, such as the beaches of the Dominican Republic, contribute significantly to the tourism sector, creating jobs and reducing poverty among the local population. Indeed, the BF award is considered one of the main drivers for stimulating employment generation and fixing the population in the territory where BF beaches are located (Guimarães et al., 2012).

In addition, the BF program promotes food security through activities such as supporting sustainable fishing communities, protecting fish nursery habitats, and disseminating sustainable agricultural practices. New Zealand is a clear example of how BF contributes to zero hunger (FEE, 2020). At the Outboard Boating Club Marina in Auckland, boat owners can clean and fillet their fish. Thanks to the Kai Ika project, fish offcuts that would normally have been discarded are now stored and delivered daily to Papatūānuku Kokiri Marae. This initiative helps to reduce hunger and revitalize Maori cultural tradition.

5.2.2 The Blue Flag program contributes to well-being (SDG 3), quality education (SDG 4), and gender equality (SDG 5)

It is evident that the BF program directly contributes to well-being and quality education. Ten criteria for a beach to be BF-awarded cover such SDGs (FEE, 2020). BF beaches require appropriate public safety measures, first aid equipment, emergency plans, and free access to guarantee, and even increase, beachgoers' well-being. Furthermore, environmental education activities, together with the provision of information about water quality, local ecosystems, and cultural places need to be publicly displaced to ensure a BF is awarded.

The BF program has a positive effect on health where sites with these flags support healthy lifestyles, create clean environments that minimize disease, and promote active lifestyles. In this way, BF-awarded beaches in Spain prevent accidents and promote social interactions related to sunbathing, swimming, and cycling, which ultimately displays a higher quality of life for such areas (Chamorro-Mera et al., 2019). It is also common to find environmental education workshops on safety and anti-drowning issues. On some English beaches, for instance, the NHS offers swimming-related services for people with mental health issues, and even for lonely elderly people (FEE, 2020).

To cite some direct actions from case studies, in Slovenia, summer libraries offering free book loans are provided to beachgoers. This promotes inclusive learning opportunities for beach users. In New Zealand, a sustainable tourism boat operator educates its passengers on each trip about the restoration and conservation project for the islands of the Eastern Bay of Islands (FEE, 2020). In Ireland, the BF actions towards environmental education on beaches evolved in the Eco-Schools program and ensures both environmental education and education for sustainable development reach all students across the country. The success of such a program enabled it to evolve into the Green-Campus program by teaching work that continues throughout all stages of the Irish educational system (Ryan-Fogarty et al., 2016).

Besides this, the role of education in the frame of BFs becomes a significant driver, together with environmental awareness, of pro-environmental behaviour. Environmental education activities developed in BF beaches may entail a positive contribution to pro-environmental behaviour, which will revert into better beach conservation in the medium and longterm. As such, in Cyprus, individuals with positive environmental attitudes are characterized by traits such as morality, respect for the law, and political activity; therefore, positive environmental attitudes are key to forming pro-environmental behavior towards beaches (Leonidou et al., 2015). Similarly, in Canada, it has been evinced the close relationship between environmental education within BF activities and the social support for maintaining beaches' certification, and so contribute to their protection and conservation (Dodds & Holmes, 2018). In this regard, beach managers are provided with information and educational tools on beach conservation to attract sustainable tourism.

Despite it not being included as a concrete criterion, the BF program involves both men and women in its projects, regardless of age, religion, or ethnicity, to foster their participation in society. Thus, Mexico's BF beaches promote activities that ensure gender equality and reduce violence against women. This is the case of the "Orange Days" initiative to raise awareness of harassment and gender-based violence on Isla Mujeres (FEE, 2020). It should also be noted that in most BF countries, such as Spain, Portugal, and Italy, there is no gender discrimination and both genders are employed as lifeguards with equal pay.

5.2.3 The Blue Flag program contributes to water quality (SDG 6) and affordable and clean energy (SDG 7)

The BF program pursues the sustainable development of freshwater and marine areas, encouraging public authorities to achieve high standards of water quality and to improve water efficiency, minimizing the environmental footprint and promoting good practices. In this way, 6 out of 33 criteria for beaches to be BF-awarded refer to water quality. There is high concern about the water's physical and microbiological parameters, and the control of discharges to seawater.

Wastewater treatment has led to major improvements in water quality in Spain thanks to the BF program. It is not only given direct support to improve treatment plants but also an indirect contribution that drives treatment efficiency (Guimarães et al., 2012). Good water management practices have also been developed in Slovenia, where the BF program has played a crucial role in wastewater management and the sharing of water quality data (FEE, 2020). This is ultimately reflected in cleaner waters in BF beaches across the western Mediterranean basin (Merino & Prats, 2022), which may even provide socioeconomic nonmarket benefits (Nahman & Rigby, 2008; Guimarães et al., 2012).

On the other hand, the BF program also promotes energy savings and the application of good energy practices in marinas and on boats with solar panels, wind turbines, or energy-saving light bulbs. Examples of the use of such low-energy systems can be found in countries such as Sweden, where the use of electric vehicles is promoted on most beaches, where charging stations are installed (FEE, 2020).

5.2.4 The Blue Flag program contributes to economic growth (SDG 8), sustainable infrastructure (SDG 9), and the reduction of inequalities (SDG 10)

The BF program contributes to the creation of new jobs, promotes personal commitment and fair employment, and fosters full employment while minimizing the environmental footprint. In this way, economic growth is decoupled from environmental degradation on BF beaches. The hospitality sector directly benefits from the BF program due to the increase of tourists during the sunny beach season in most countries. To illustrate this, Northern Ireland is used as an example. Here, many BF beaches have become popular in recent years for their stunning landscapes and the promotion of a wide range of events and services (FEE, 2020). Hence, in the medium and long term, the BF award is revealed to be responsible for fostering new hospitality investments and increasing the competitiveness and prices in the tourism sector of the awarded areas (Blackman et al., 2014; Sipic, 2017).

BFs not only contribute to economic growth but also support environmental innovation, encouraging the use of ecological resources. In countries such as Cyprus, public transport and the use of bicycles are being promoted, and environmentally friendly seaweed removal is carried out through composting (FEE, 2020). The indirect contribution of BFs to resilient and sustainable infrastructure could even go beyond, becoming a design guide for sustainable behavior (Portman et al., 2019).

In addition, the BF award ensures equal services for everyone, reducing inequality among disabled people worldwide. This is certainly the case in the Dominican Republic, where in recent years the beaches have been made accessible to people with disabilities. On most Spanish beaches, anyone with disabilities can access both the water and the beach. Therefore, the BF program promotes a space that is accessible to all members of the public (Santana-Santana et al., 2021). In Greece, there is also another great example of how the BF program reduces inequalities through beach cleaning that took place in Limni (Attiki) where all participants had a disability (FEE, 2020).

5.2.5 The Blue Flag program contributes to sustainable cities (SDG 11) and responsible consumption and production (SDG 12)

BF beaches emphasize the importance of addressing environmental issues to improve the sustainability of urban planning, supporting alternatives such as green infrastructure and sustainable transport. Indeed, one of the criteria for awarding a

BF to beaches comprehends the promotion of sustainable means of transportation in the beach area. Besides this, the specific actions developed in the frame of BFs also contribute directly to the SDG of making cities resilient and sustainable. In Bulgaria, for instance, only sustainable means of transport are allowed in the parking lots of BF beaches (FEE, 2020).

BF initiatives also contribute to making human settlements inclusive and resilient by promoting environmental education activities and environmental awareness events for both local communities and tourists. In South Africa, all BF beach workers are trained in environmental education and their daily activities include raising awareness among beachgoers (FEE, 2020).

The BF program seeks to provide environmental education for people to encourage sustainable consumption and production patterns. Initiatives are promoted to support, among others, sustainable fishing and environmental protection, to enhance the efficient use of natural resources. Thus, people are encouraged to save energy and water, minimize their environmental footprint, and promote activities that reduce pollution. Following the guiding BF criteria, countries such as the Netherlands have implemented beachside water fountains to meet this objective. In the Virgin Islands, single-use plastics are forbidden (FEE, 2020). These actions promote responsible consumption to reduce the use of plastic on the beach, thus avoiding further pollution. However, as empirical evidence reveals, the main contribution of BFs to this SDG is the promotion of sustainable tourism, a key to ensuring sustainable consumption patterns (Castillo-Manzano et al., 2021; Merino & Prats, 2020).

5.2.6 The Blue Flag program contributes to climate action (SDG 13), life below water (SDG 14), and life on land (SDG 15)

BF beaches are known for raising awareness of climate change. Indeed, BF initiatives encourage the protection of green spaces, such as mangroves, which can reduce the effects of natural disasters. For instance, in Puerto Rico, strategies are in place to promote the development of climate and coastal resilience activities. After various hurricane seasons in which mangroves and other types of vegetation have been eliminated, beach reforestation was developed by using autochthonous plants. Furthermore, empirical evidence in Greece tends to show that BF sites are slightly more adapted to climate change effects (Tzoraki et al., 2018).

The BF program also promotes the sustainable development of marine and freshwater areas through criteria covering water quality and sensitive habitats monitoring. In this context, marine pollution is reduced, minimizing the environmental footprint of the oceans. It also supports coral reefs, sea turtles, and other endangered species. By undertaking specific case studies in countries such as the Dominican Republic, BF beaches promote the conservation of native flora and fauna such as mangroves and coral reefs, in addition to frequent activities related to turtle release and reforestation (FEE, 2020). Another example is Spanish beaches that promote the protection of seagrass and Posidonia meadows, which are endemic to the Mediterranean Sea. A code of conduct on how to navigate around seagrass meadows is also displayed in Spanish BF marinas, so they promote sustainable navigation tours, together with marine research.

Not only is the sustainable use of seas and marine resources encouraged by the BF program, but also the protection and restoration of terrestrial ecosystems. Seven out of thirty-three criteria for BF awarding cover in some way the protection and promotion of sustainable use of beach ecosystems. The compliance with the cleanliness standards of BF beaches and facilities, the presence of enough recyclable bins and toilets/restrooms, and the prohibition of unauthorized camping are examples of such criteria (FEE, 2020).

BF initiatives also contribute directly to the sustainable use of terrestrial ecosystems. For instance, in Italy, compliance with biodiversity conservation requirements is an additional criterion for the application to the BF program, together with biodiversity monitoring and education activities carried out to conserve endangered species. Denmark is another good example of *life on land* actions. Ocean containers are placed on the beach for the constant massive removal of waste, allowing the beaches to remain clean.

5.2.7 The Blue Flag program contributes to peace and justice (SDG 16) and partnership for the goals (SDG 17)

The BF program allows the engagement of society and institutions in sustainable development and ecotourism, promoting cooperation among people regardless of gender, age, or race. In particular, compliance with a code of conduct in BF sites, the establishment of a beach management committee, and the observance of local regulations are some of the established BF award criteria that directly contribute to the promotion of peaceful and inclusive societies for sustainable development. Cooperation between the public and private sectors has also been applied as a BF initiative to foster peace and social justice in countries such as Turkey and Slovenia (FEE, 2020).

In this sense, the BF program enables cooperation and partnerships among multiple actors from the public, private, and NGO sectors, at the local, national, and international levels. These linkages among actors from different sectors are key for the dissemination of experiences, knowledge, and financial resources to support the achievement of the SDGs. Thus, in some countries where cooperation is not always guaranteed, as is the case in Japan, BFs are seen as a solution to collaborate between governments and organizations in terms of accessibility. In Cyprus, the MELTEMI project aims to improve the legal framework and build the capacity of public authorities and decision-makers to reduce marine pollution (FEE, 2020). On the other hand, in New Zealand, cooperation is promoted with local research institutions to develop studies on the marine environment. Empirical evidence shows that the BF award increases cooperation among local stakeholders and raises political will in the medium and long term (Botero & Zielinski, 2020).

5.3 Key BF indicators for meeting the SDGs

Understanding the degree to which BF awards contribute to the accomplishment of SDGs is key. This is true not only for policymakers and stakeholders to guide their actions but also for the overall society's awareness of how social well-being relies on the sustainable management of natural resources – beaches in this case.

However, it becomes challenging if such contributions are not measured or objectified. Indicators arise therefore as a way to link BF actions and their respective contributions to the accomplishment of the SDGs, whose applicability lies for individual BF sites and also for intertemporal and across BF sites assessment. By using the revealed information from the actual direct and empirical evidenced indirect BF contributions, Table 5.2 proposes some key indicators for measuring the contribution of the BF program to meeting each SDG.

The proposed indicators should not be understood as a threshold to be pursued at any cost. Instead, they represent a guide for beach managers and stakeholders on how and where to focus their actions to improve the performance

Table 5.2 Proposal of key BF indicators for meeting each SDG

SDG	Key BF indicator
1. Ending poverty	Number of jobs created
2. Zero hunger	Volume of fish (offcuts) reincorporated into the value chain to feed the local population
	Proportion of local fisheries under productive and sustainable fishing
3. Well-being	Number of activities for the promotion of physical and mental health habits
4. Quality education	Number of environmental education activities
	Proportion of education activities other than environmental education ones
5. Gender equality	Proportion of women in BF jobs
6. Water quality	Proportion of wastewater safely treated
7. Clean energy	Presence of electric charging stations for vehicles in parking lots
8. Economic growth	Proportion of tourism income from BF beaches
9. Sustainable infrastructure	Number of environmentally friendly facilities
10. Reduce inequalities	Beach accessibility index (BAI)
11. Sustainable cities	Proportion of renewable energy transport vehicles
12. Responsible consumption/ production	Number of sustainable tourism strategies and implemented action plans
13. Climate action	Number of km of BF beaches under restoration programs for climate change mitigation and adaptation
14. Life below water	Presence of good ship navigation practices
15. Life on land	Number of species under biodiversity monitoring and conservation programs
16. Peace and justice	Number of incidents in the previous 12 months
17. Partnership for the goals	Number of cooperation networks

Note: All the indicators refer to BF beaches
Source: Own elaboration

of such indicators, and so the contributions of BFs to the accomplishment of the SDGs. Indeed, many of the indicators have been defined in an open-ended format, so the greater their value, the greater the contribution of BF beaches to the SDGs.

In such a context, the indicator "Beach Accessibility Index" (BAI) should be highlighted. This has been proposed by Santana-Santana et al. (2021) to measure the contribution of BFs to reducing inequalities. The BAI is a composed index that unites different accessible beach criteria according to three categories: (1) equipment and infrastructures, (2) services, and (3) management. Its score for each category ranges from 0 to 1, with 0 being not accessible and 1 highly accessible.

5.4 Recommendations and concluding remarks

This work has evinced the relationship between the BF and the SDGs, revising the direct and indirect contributions that the BF program may provide for the beaches and their surrounding areas where this eco-label is awarded. It gives examples of countries that are implementing activities that meet the SDGs. It has revealed how the BF is intended to combat inequality, unemployment, threats to health, depletion of natural resources, environmental threats, pollution, and environmental degradation. Thus, representative indicators for each SDG have been illustrated, which may serve as a guide for beach managers, policymakers, and BF operators in their commitment to supporting the accomplishment of the SDGs.

It has become clear that many developed countries such as Spain, England, Cyprus, and Greece are trying to meet targets related to the well-being of the population, bathing water quality, affordable and clean energy, and reducing inequalities, in the frame of BF beaches. This enables them to make significant contributions to the SDGs. However, the situation is not always the same in developing countries. Some efforts have been made by countries such as Puerto Rico, the Dominican Republic, and South Africa through actions to meet the goals related to fighting against climate change, ending poverty, and creating employment, although there is still a huge gap to be addressed. It will require not only commitment to the BF criteria but also more investment to fully deal with the challenges that meeting the SDGs in the BF beach environments may require.

Despite the progress made and the positive contributions to the SDGs achieved by the implementation of the BF program, there is still room for increasing the impact of BFs on the achievement of the SDGs. Some gaps have been found that policymakers, BF operators, and beach managers are encouraged to work on. In particular, more BF actions are recommended to cope with the zero-hunger goal, ensure gender equality while reducing overall inequalities, and deal with the expected impacts of climate change and the use of clean energy. Fishing resources in BF beaches might have a relevant role in fighting against hunger, so ensuring its sustainability and full use becomes a challenge for BF awards, especially in developing countries.

82 José A. Albaladejo-García and José A. Zabala

Gender equality needs more attention under the BF actions. Only a few initiatives in specific case studies have been revealed, so including gender equality as a full criterion for BF awarding may become a promising recommendation.

Climate change is a glaring fact. Actions to mitigate its expected effects become needed more than ever. Hence, it is expected that the BF program will also contribute directly to addressing this challenge. Some specific criteria for BF awarding could be included to cope with it, such as the inclusion of mandatory good management practices on beaches to mitigate the impact of climate change. Some of these practices could be the application of the "polluter pays" principle, the implementation of monitoring systems for clean-up operations, and the presence of restoration and conservation of natural vegetation and species, which will result in a good integration of the measures adopted for the improvement and care of the environment in light of climate change

Closely related to climate change, more efforts are also needed in the BF frame for ensuring affordable, sustainable, and clean energy. For instance, the installation of solar panels on BF beaches for obtaining all the clean energy required in the BF beaches could be proposed as a recommendation to increase the contribution to this SDG. This would encourage self-consumption of energy from lighting and beach businesses such as beach bars to reduce the carbon footprint. However, these measures should be supported by an adequate territorial planning to avoid undesired urban agglomerations.

Nevertheless, the contribution of BFs to sustainable development does not end with the SDGs. BFs are a widely used tool for the management of beaches and coasts following sustainable principles and policies. A BF award implies a deep commitment to sustainable management and the promotion of more environmentally friendly behaviour whose intrinsic value cannot always be measured by tangible indicators.

5.5 References

Blackman, A., Naranjo, M. A., Robalino, J., Alpízar, F., & Rivera, J. (2014). Does tourism eco-certification pay? Costa Rica's Blue Flag Program. *World Development*, 58, 41–52. https://doi.org/10.1016/j.worlddev.2013.12.002

Boluk, K. A., Cavaliere, C. T., & Higgins-Desbiolles, F. (2019). A critical framework for interrogating the United Nations Sustainable Development Goals 2030 Agenda in tourism. *Journal of Sustainable Tourism*, 27, 847–864.

Botero, C. M., & Zielinski, S. (2020). The implementation of a world-famous tourism ecolabel triggers political support for beach management. *Tourism Management Perspectives*, 35, 100691. https://doi.org/10.1016/j.tmp.2020.100691

Castillo-Manzano, J. I., Castro-Nuño, M., López-Valpuesta, L., & Zarzoso, Á. (2021). Measuring the role of Blue Flags in attracting sustainable "sun-and-sand" tourism. *Current Issues in Tourism*, 24(15), 2204–2222. https://doi.org/10.1080/13683500.2020. 1844642

Chamorro-Mera, A., Nobre de Oliveira, V., & García-Gallego, J. (2019). The Blue Flag Label as a Tool to Improve the Quality of Life in the Sun-and-Sand Tourist Destinations. In Campón-Cerro, A., Hernández-Mogollón, J., & Folgado-Fernández, J. (Eds),

Best Practices in Hospitality and Tourism Marketing and Management. Applying Quality of Life Research (pp. 255–274). Springer. https://doi.org/10.1007/978-3-319-91692-7_13

Dodds, R., & Holmes, M.R. (2018). Education and certification for beach management: Is there a difference between residents versus visitors? *Ocean & Coastal Management*, 160, 124–132. https://doi.org/10.1016/j.ocecoaman.2018.03.043

FEE. (2020). The SDGs and Blue Flag. 31 pp.

FEE. (2022). Guía de interpretación de los criterios bandera azul para playas. 99 pp.

Gissi, E., Maes, F., Kyriazi, Z., Ruiz-Frau, A., Santos, C. F., Neumann, B., & Unger, S. (2022). Contributions of marine area-based management tools to the UN Sustainable Development Goals. *Journal of Cleaner Production*, 330, 129910. https://doi.org/10.1016/j.jclepro.2021.129910

Guimarães, M. E., Mascarenhas, A., Sousa, C., Boski, T., & Ponce Dentinho, T. (2012). The impact of water quality changes on the socio-economic system of the Guadiana Estuary: An assessment of management options. *Ecology and Society*, 17(3), 38. http://dx.doi.org/10.5751/ES-05318-170338

Klein, L., & Dodds, R. (2018). Blue Flag beach certification: An environmental management tool or tourism promotional tool? *Tourism Recreation Research*, 43(1), 39–51. https://doi.org/10.1080/02508281.2017.1356984

Leonidou, L. C., Coudounaris, D. N., Kvasova, O., & Christodoulides, P. (2015). Drivers and outcomes of green tourist attitudes and behavior: Sociodemographic moderating effects. *Psychology & Marketing*, 32(6), 635–650. https://doi.org/10.1002/mar.20806

Loizidou, X. I., Loizides, M. I., & Orthodoxou, D. L. (2018). Persistent marine litter: Small plastics and cigarette butts remain on beaches after organized beach cleanups. *Environmental Monitoring and Assessment*, 190, 414. https://doi.org/10.1007/s10661-018-6798-9

Lucrezi, S., Saayman, M., & Van der Merwe, P. (2015). Managing beaches and beachgoers: Lessons from and for the Blue Flag award. *Tourism Management*, 48, 211–230. https://doi.org/10.1016/j.tourman.2014.11.010

Merino, F., & Prats, M. A. (2020). Sustainable beach management and promotion of the local tourist industry: Can Blue Flags be a good driver of this balance? *Ocean & Coastal Management*, 198, 105359. https://doi.org/10.1016/j.ocecoaman.2020.105359

Merino, F., & Prats, M. A. (2022). Are Blue Flags a good indicator of the quality of sea water on beaches? An empirical analysis of the Western Mediterranean basin. *Journal of Cleaner Production*, 330, 129865. https://doi.org/10.1016/j.jclepro.2021.129865

Nahman, A., & Rigby, D. (2008). Valuing Blue Flag status and estuarine water quality in Margate, South Africa. *South African Journal of Economics*, 76(4), 721–737. https://doi.org/10.1111/j.1813-6982.2008.00208.x

Portman, M. E., Pasternak, G., Yotam, Y., Nusbaum, R., & Bhar, D. (2019). Beachgoer participation in prevention of marine litter: Using design for behavior change. *Marine Pollution Bulletin*, 144, 1–10. https://doi.org/10.1016/j.marpolbul.2019.04.071

Ryan-Fogarty, Y., O'Carroll, D., O'Mahony, M. J., & O'Regan, B. (2016). Development of the Green-Campus Programme in Ireland: Ensuring Continuity of Environmental Education and Action for Sustainable Development Throughout the Irish Education System. In Leal Filho, W., & Pace, P. (Eds) *Teaching Education for Sustainable Development at University Level. World Sustainability Series* (pp. 269–284). Springer. https://doi.org/10.1007/978-3-319-32928-4_19

Santana-Santana, S. B., Peña-Alonso, C., & Pérez-Chacón Espino, E. (2021). Assessing universal accessibility in Spanish beaches. *Ocean & Coastal Management*, 201, 105486. https://doi.org/10.1016/j.ocecoaman.2020.105486

Sipic, T. (2017). Eco-labelling of marine recreation services: The case of Blue Flag price premium in Croatia. *Journal of Ecotourism*, 16(1), 1–23. https://doi.org/10.1080/147240 49.2016.1194848

Tzoraki, O., Monioudi, I. N., Velegrakis, A. F., Moutafis, N., Pavlogeorgatos, G., & Kitsiou D. (2018). Resilience of touristic island beaches under sea level rise: A methodological framework. *Coastal Management*, 46(2), 78–102. https://doi.org/10.1080/08920753. 2018.1426376

UN (United Nations). (2015). Transforming our world: The 2030 agenda for sustainable development: Preamble. United Nations Gen. Assem. Resolut.

Williams, A. T., & Micallef, E. (2009). *Beach management: Principles and practices*. Routledge.

6 Dive in Blue Flags

A historical evolution in Europe[1]

María Escrivá-Beltrán and Rosa Currás-Móstoles

6.1 Introduction

The motto of the European Union (EU) is "united in diversity", referring to the diversity of its cultures, traditions, and languages. It can also be applied to include the diversity of its seas and oceans. Of the 27 member states that make up the EU, 22 have a sea border. Only Czechia, Luxembourg, Hungary, Austria, and Slovakia are landlocked. The EU coastline is 68,000 km long, and the maritime area under the jurisdiction of the member states of the EU is larger than the total land area of the EU. The EU has the world's largest maritime territory, if we include its outlying regions (territories and entities in the Atlantic, Pacific, and Caribbean). There are six sea basins bordering the EU: Northern Sea, Atlantic Ocean, Mediterranean Sea, Black Sea, Baltic Sea, and the Outermost Regions, each of which has its own idiosyncrasy and personality (*European Environment Agency*, n.d.; *Glossary: Coastal Region*, 2022).

EU recognizes a total of 1,166 regions in the EU-27, 339 of which have been classified as Coastal Regions; 295 have a coastline, and 44 regions have more than half of their population within 50 km of the coastline (Eurostat, n.d.). In global figures, although only 30% of the EU regions are coastal, 40% of the population live within 50 km of the sea (*Coastal Zones – Copernicus Land Monitoring Service*, n.d.).

Since the Treaty of Rome in 1957, which set up the European Economic Community, oceans and seas have been a strategic issue of vital importance for the EU. From then on, different policies have been promoted in advocating for the sustainability of the seas, while at the same time starting from the idea that by coordinating its wide range of interlinked activities related to oceans, seas and coasts, the EU can draw higher returns from its maritime space with less impact on the environment (*Integrated Maritime Policy of the European Union | European Parliament*, n.d.).

Subsequently, the introduction of the Blue Growth Strategy (2012) supporting sustainable growth in the marine and maritime sectors (Eikeset et al., 2018) gave rise to the frequent use of the concept Blue Economy (BE hereafter) to refer all the economic activities related to oceans, seas, and coasts, covering a wide range of sectors, while other international organizations such as the World Bank or the Commonwealth of Nations started to embrace this same concept. Even the United

DOI: 10.4324/9781003323570-7

Nations incorporated the concept BE as a key point in achieving the 14 UN Sustainable Development Goal (SDG hereafter) "Life Below Water" (*Goal 14 | Department of Economic and Social Affairs*, 2022).

The Blue Growth strategy focuses on five sectors: aquaculture, mineral resources, renewable energy, biotechnology, and coastal and maritime tourism (*Sustainable Blue Economy*, 2022). Of these, coastal tourism has the greatest economic impact. In fact, Coastal tourism accounted for 63% of the jobs, 44% of the Gross Value Added and 38% of the profits in the EU Blue Economy in 2019 (European Comission, 2022). Tourism is included in the 2030 Agenda in Goal 8 – Inclusive and Sustainable Economic Growth; Goal 12 – Sustainable Consumption and Production, and Goal 14 – Sustainable Use of Oceans and Marine Resources, in the Agenda for Sustainable Development Goals (*Tourism in the 2030 Agenda | UN-WTO*, 2022).

Regarding Europe, it is the most visited continent in the world with over 68% (303 million) of the 446 million international arrivals in 2021. Prior to the Covid-19 pandemic, in 2019, the top three countries for inbound tourism were France, Spain, and Italy (*Global and Regional Tourism Performance*, n.d.). Tourism accounts for 10.3% of the EU's total GDP and 11.7% of total employment (Pernice, 2022).

In terms of accommodation, coastal areas received 47.4% of overnight stays in 2019, with the Mediterranean regions having the highest numbers. The Canary Islands (Spain) ranked first with 96.1 million nights, followed by Jadranska Hrvatska (Croatia), with 86.2 million. Only two non-coastal areas are included in the ranking of the top ten areas with the highest number of tourist overnight stays: Île-de-France (84.7 million, ranking third) and Rhône-Alpes (51.5 million, ranking fifth). Globally, coastal regions account for 1.4 million overnights stays (*Tourism in the 2030 Agenda | UNWTO*, 2022).

Most of the destinations in these coastal regions are fragile ecosystems, which are based on the well-known tourism of 3S (sea, sun, and sand) (Castillo-Manzano et al., 2021; Fayissa et al., 2008; Hall, 2019; Merino & Prats, 2020, 2022; Sequeira & Maçãs Nunes, 2008). Thus, the implementation of effective policies aimed at achieving coastal maritime sustainability must become a prime concern where preserving the natural environment and the cultural and natural heritage are of vital importance for tourism itself.

Maintaining the quality of beaches can be seen as an investment (Klein et al., 2004; Saayman & Saayman, 2017) to attract visitors. Thus, since the 1980s different ecolabels have appeared related to the quality of waters, beaches, and coastal areas, some of them in an award form. For the different countries and localities involved, the ecolabel offers them two different objectives: on the one hand, to preserve the coastal environment, and on the other hand, a positioning and competitiveness strategy at a tourist level (Botero et al., 2015; Capacci et al., 2015; Castillo-Manzano et al., 2021; Merino & Prats, 2022; Zielinski & Botero, 2019). Moreover, awards are useful management tools as they create a "willing framework'" and support the assessment and conservation of the beach environment (Mihalić, 2000).

This chapter shows the historical evolution of one of the most prestigious ecolabels in terms of coastline, the Blue Flags, with a focus on Europe. It is structured as follows: Section 6.2 focuses on coastal areas and quality certificates, Section 6.3 gives a historical overview of the Blue Flags obtained by European countries, and, finally, Section 6.4 presents the discussion and conclusions.

6.2 Coastal areas and quality certificates

The BF is a certificate of quality by the Foundation for Environmental Education that emerged in response to environmental awareness and education, together with the promotion of good practice among all stakeholders in the tourism sector. At its inception in 1987, the certificate was awarded to beaches and marinas, but boating tourism operators were added in 2016. From then on, it has evolved into an internationally trusted, world-renowned award. The BF involves some challenges for local authorities, site operators, and tourism boats, who must achieve standards in different categories: water quality, environmental management, environmental education and information, safety and services, social responsibility, and responsible operation around wildlife. Applying for the award is voluntary and must be made by the municipality of the locality where the beach or marina is located or by the private boat owner in the case of boats. Flags are awarded for every season (*Blue Flag*, 2022).

Cleanliness and water quality are among the most important BF indicators for bathers as it concerns sanitation issues. The fact that, in addition to the Blue Flag, the beach is guaranteed to have clean water is valuable additional information for bathers (Merino & Prats, 2022).The study conducted by these same authors on 5,000 coastal monitoring points in the three most important tourist destinations in the EU-27 (Spain, France, and Italy) revealed that the areas with the highest number of Blue Flags have significantly cleaner waters according the established EU criteria European Union Bathing Water Directive (Directive 2006/7/EC of the European Parliament and of the Council of 15 February 2006 Concerning the Management of Bathing Water Quality and Repealing Directive 76/160/EEC, 2006) (Merino & Prats, 2022).

The BF is considered to be a good starting point for the environmental management of beaches and a signal of quality, promotion, or local positioning in the touristic market, especially for small municipalities that have no experience or limited resources to invest in tourism, coastal and/or environmental management (Mir-Gual et al., 2015; Nahman & Rigby, 2008). However, the award of a Blue Flag does not in itself guarantee the sustainability of the coastal environment. This would need to be complemented with educational strategies for both beachgoers and locals in order to preserve the coastal ecosystem for future generations (Dodds & Holmes, 2020).

The accreditation of BF also has also received some criticism. Studies have highlighted that the BF program does not address all relevant aspects that are encompassed in beach ecosystem functions (Lucrezi, Saayman & Van der Merwe, 2015); or that it is more focused on the return in terms of destination image than on environmental concerns (Pencarelli et al., 2016). The Foundation for Environmental Education claims that the criteria for awarding BF are subject to permanent review processes and new criteria to safeguard their excellence are regularly developed (*Blue Flag*, 2022), but these criteria are still too standard and not easily adaptable to the different realities of the beaches, which continue to be overcrowded and at environmental risk. This has led countries such as Spain (the country with the highest number of Blue Flags) to seek other stricter awards or certifications distinctions related to higher environmental commitment (Fraguell et al., 2016), following the need to find new forms of equilibrium between sustainability, environment, and tourism.

On the other hand, the possession of the BF award has an unequal effect depending on the coastal destination. Some studies have shown that in countries such as Spain, for example, it is a contributing factor in the promotion of international tourism, but not a domestic one (Castillo-Manzano et al., 2021); while in other countries such as South Africa it has a greater impact on the local population's awareness (Saayman & Saayman, 2017).

6.3 EU and the Blue Flags – an historical evolution

At its inception in the late 1980s, the BF program encouraged beaches to comply with the EU Bathing Water Directive of 1976. Back then, the criteria for a BF award to beaches and marinas covered sewage treatment and bathing water quality, but also waste management and coastal and planning protection. Subsequently, the standards have become more holistic, changing with current research and technology, and have taken on an international perspective. But it was only in 1992 that the beach criteria were harmonized for all the European countries. Today, all participating countries follow the same international BF criteria for both beaches and marinas (FEE, 2022). Moreover, the BF program operates independently, as the award system cannot be influenced by local or financial interests.

This section presents an analysis of the historical evolution of BFs in European coasts. The data analyzed cover the period 1988–2022 and have been provided by the FEE. All these data correspond to the flags awarded, and there is no data available on applicant countries that did not receive an award.

In the year of its birth in 1987, it is known that 452 Blue Flags were awarded – 244 to beaches and 208 to marinas. For that year, no official data broken down by country are available – although the exact number of countries that received awards is not known, among them were Spain, France, Portugal, Denmark, and the Netherlands (*Blue Flag*, 2022).

6.3.1 Internationalization of Blue Flags

Table 6.1 shows the distribution of Blue Flags awarded by continent over the years. The first flag awarded outside the European continent was to the African continent, specifically to South Africa, which received five flags in 2001. It was not until 2004 that the first BF was awarded to the American continent, which went to the Caribbean countries: Puerto Rico, Bahamas, and Dominican Republic (13). The first flag for Russia (1) was awarded in 2007, and years later, in 2011, the first Asian countries received a flag – Jordan (3) and UAE (2). For Oceania, only New Zealand has applied. They obtained an award (in 2005), although they have not received any other during the last few years between 2020 and 2022.

The number of flags awarded per year and by continent grew from 452 in 1987 to 5,042 awarded 35 years later in 2022 (4,194 for beaches, 732 for marinas, and 116 for boats). The distribution by continent shows, year by year, the undisputed leadership of Europe. As an example, of the 5,042 flags awarded, the distribution was as follows: Africa 91, Americas 207, Asia (including Russia) 148, and Europe 4,596, of which 3,770 were EU-27, representing 74.77% of the flags, whereas non-EU-27 countries received 826.

Table 6.1 Evolution of BF awarded by year by continents

Year	Africa	Americas	Asia	EU-27	Non-EU-27	Oceania	Total BF
1988	0	0	0	474	21	0	495
1989	0	0	0	669	25	0	694
1990	0	0	0	832	35	0	867
1991	0	0	0	1,111	35	0	1,146
1992	0	0	0	1,234	19	0	1,253
1993	0	0	0	1,455	29	0	1,484
1994	0	0	0	1,752	40	0	1,792
1995	0	0	0	1,836	32	0	1,868
1996	0	0	0	1,979	53	0	2,032
1997	0	0	0	2,254	62	0	2,316
1998	0	0	0	2,391	106	0	2,497
1999	0	0	0	2,297	143	0	2,440
2000	0	0	0	2,349	178	0	2,527
2001	5	0	0	2,556	205	0	2,766
2002	8	0	0	2,560	266	0	2,834
2003	8	0	0	2,611	287	0	2,906
2004	14	16	0	2,600	320	0	2,950
2005	22	16	0	2,727	396	1	3,162
2006	27	15	0	2,829	388	1	3,260
2007	31	24	1	2,829	445	3	3,333
2008	33	30	2	2,742	450	3	3,260
2009	52	40	2	2,894	466	4	3,458
2010	58	58	2	2,979	506	5	3,608
2011	65	66	9	3,003	508	5	3,656
2012	76	64	18	3,118	567	5	3,848
2013	92	73	41	3,095	565	2	3,868
2014	99	89	61	3,224	576	2	4,051
2015	98	106	61	3,262	625	2	4,154
2016	113	123	48	3,313	667	2	4,266
2017	88	139	58	3,426	708	4	4,423
2018	88	152	74	3,520	720	4	4,558
2019	88	168	85	3,517	711	4	4,573
2020	87	203	115	3,544	727	0	4,676
2021	89	203	142	3,633	775	0	4,842
2022	91	207	148	3,770	826	0	5,042

Source: Own elaboration based on data provided by the Foundation for Environmental Education

90 *María Escrivá-Beltrán and Rosa Currás-Móstoles*

6.3.1.1. Non-EU-27 countries

Regarding the non-EU-27 countries involved with BF, England (20 BFs) and Wales (1) competed for their first flags in 1988, followed by Scotland (2) in 1995 and Northern Ireland (7) in 2001. By 2022, the total number of flags in the UK was 141. It should be noted that the UK left the EU at the end of January 2020.

Iceland obtained its first Blue Flag in 2003, Montenegro in 2004, Norway in 1999, Ukraine in 2010, and Serbia in 2012. Iceland and Norway were candidates to the EU and stalled negotiations, while Montenegro, Serbia, and recently Ukraine have been admitted as candidates.

As for Turkey, the eternal EU candidate country, it received its first BF (7) in 1993 and since then it has continued an exponential progression, reaching a total of 570 BFs in 2022, which accounts for 69% of the flags given to non-EU-27 countries. This is not surprising given that Turkey has 7,200 km of coastline and competes in the Mediterranean region as a tourist destination.

6.3.1.2 First BFs by EU-27 countries

In 1988 (the first year for which country-by-country data are available) all the coastal countries of what was the seed of the current EU-27 obtained a BF. The rest of the EU-27 countries have gradually obtained their first flags. Table 6.2 shows the EU-27 countries, the date of accession to the EU, together with their sea basin, the flags obtained in 2022, and the km of coastline of each country.

A total of 474 BFs were awarded in 1988: Spain (133), France (123), Portugal (72), Denmark (62), Germany (26), Ireland (22), Greece (15), Netherlands (11), and Italy (10). Of these, 54% were divided between France (26%) and Spain (28%). Since then, Spain has led in the number of BF awards, followed by France and Greece, which usually compete for a second-place year after year (see Graph 2). Neither of these countries has failed to apply for the award in the 35 years of the award's existence. All these countries together with Luxembourg (non-coastal country) and the UK formed the germ of today's EU-27.

Finland, member state since 1995, obtained its first flags in 1991 (9) and has continued participating regularly in the awarding of flags with the exception of the period 2010–2019, during which it did not obtain any. In 1994 Sweden (1) and Estonia (2) were awarded for the first time. Sweden, which joined the EU in 1995, shows a progressive increase in the number of flags obtained between 1994 and 2003 when it reached its peak (145). From then on, it experienced a downward trend until 2013, when it received the lowest number of awards (8). Since then, it has obtained an average of 20 flags per year. For its part, Estonia, which became a member state in 2004, has maintained a constant participation, except for the period between 2008 and 2013, when it did not obtain any flags. In 1995, Slovenia and Bulgaria were awarded for the first time, and have maintained their participation ever since. Slovenia joined the EU in 2004, while Bulgaria joined three years later. In 1996 Cyprus – which entered the EU in 2004 – was awarded 11 flags, and has been progressively increasing, reaching 76 BFs in 2022, which is its maximum thus far. In 1998 Croatia, another country on the Mediterranean coast where 3S tourism is vital for its economy, obtained its first flag, reaching its maximum number of flags (146) in 2008, and has maintained its participation since then. It should be noted that Croatia was the last country to join the EU in 2013. In 1999 it was Latvia that entered the game with one flag, and in 2002 it was Lithuania's turn (1). Both countries, together with Malta, joined the EU in 2004. Finally, 2009 was the year in which, with the incorporation of Malta (1), the participation of all the EU-27 countries was achieved. Except for the founding countries, all countries besides Malta obtained their first BF (on average 3–4 years before) prior to their accession, with the exception of Estonia, Bulgaria and Croatia, where there is a longer time lag between obtaining the first flag and their entry into the EU.

Table 6.2 Main data of Blue Flags in EU countries

Country	EU membership	First BF	BF 2022	Coastal km	Flags per 100 km
Belgium	1958	1989	37	67	55.22
France	1958	1988	536	3,427	15.64
Germany	1958	1988	137	2,789	4.91
Italy	1958	1988	509	7,900	6.44
Luxembourg	1958	Non-coastal		0	
Netherlands	1958	1988	189	451	41.91
Denmark	1973	1988	184	9,867	1.86
Ireland	1973	1988	95	5,874	1.62
Greece	1981	1988	602	13,676	4.40
Portugal	1986	1988	431	1,794	24.02
Spain	1986	1988	729	4,964	14.69
Austria	1995	Non-coastal		0	
Finland	1995	1991	2	1,250	0.16
Sweden	1995	1994	22	3,218	0.68
Cyprus	2004	1996	76	648	11.73
Czechia	2004	Non-coastal		0	
Estonia	2004	1994	5	3,724	0.13
Hungary	2004	Non-coastal		0	
Latvia	2004	1999	14	498	2.81
Lithuania	2004	2002	8	262	3.05
Malta	2004	2009	12	197	6.09
Poland	2004	1999	41	775	5.29
Slovakia	2004	Non-coastal		0	
Slovenia	2004	1995	15	47	31.91
Bulgaria	2007	1994	19	378	5.03
Romania	2007	2006	6	245	2.45
Croatia	2013	1998	101	5,835	1.73
TOTAL			3,770	67,886	5.55

Sources: Own elaboration based on Country Profiles (n.d.); Eurogeographics (n.d.); data provided by the Foundation for Environmental Education

6.3.2 Blue Flags by coastal kilometers

Although a country's coastal kilometers do not imply having accessible beaches due to the orography of the coasts, it is interesting to make a brief analysis taking this factor into account. Comparing the number of kilometers of coastline with the number of BFs, as shown in Table 6.2, there are five Blue Flags per 100 km of coastline in the EU-27. Obviously, the proportion of flags is higher in countries such as Belgium (55.22), the Netherlands (41.91), and Slovenia (31.91) as they have fewer kilometers of coastline. On the contrary, countries with more kilometers of coastline have proportionally fewer flags per 100 km. This is the case in Greece, the country with the most kilometers of coastline (13,676 km), or Denmark (9,867 km), which only has a ratio of 4 and 1.86 flags per 100 km, respectively. On the other hand, the third country with the longest coastline, Italy (7,900 km), has a ratio of 6.44 BF per 100 km.

6.3.2.1 BFs: Top 5 countries

Among the countries awarded during the 35 years of the BF's existence, the countries that lead the top 5 over the years are Spain, Greece, France, Italy, and Portugal. As it can be seen in Figure 6.1, Spain has led the ranking since 1988. This country made a key commitment to coastal tourism and the 3S as early as the mid-20th century.

The highest annual increase in the number of BF in Spain was between 1993 and 1994, from 236 BFs in 1993 to 356 BF in 1994. Except for small variations, the increase has been sustained over time.

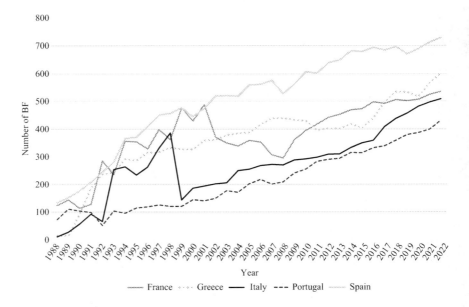

Figure 6.1 Evolution of the number of BFs obtained by the top 5 countries by year

With respect to France, there were three marked peaks: in 1992, when there was a 124.41% increase over the previous year; in 1994, when there was a 50% rise; and in 1999, when there was an increase from 362 to 476 BFs. In the remaining years, the annual increase compared to the previous year follows an upward trend with annual percentage increases of around 1%.

Greece, which is the country with the most kilometers of coastline, 13,676 km, is the country with the largest increases over the years. It started receiving few flags – considering its extensive coastline – rocketing to 186 BF in 1991, reaching 602 in 2022, thus taking the second place from France in the top 5.

As for Italy, the turning point came from 1992 to 1993, from 65 flags to 254, almost three times more flags than in the previous year. Except in 1999, when it lost 62% of its flags compared to the previous year, it has maintained a year-on-year growth of around 4%. These variations may have been affected by the change of direction taken by the EU in its relationship with the FEE and the suppression of the subsidy to the BF campaign (Prados, 1999).

Finally, Portugal, which had fluctuating beginnings, reached a turning point in 1993, doubling the number of BF of the previous year, and it has had an upward trend that continues to the present day, accumulating by 2022 a total of 24 BF per 100 km of coastline, being with 1,704 km the country with the shortest coastline.

6.4 Discussion and conclusions

Beaches are traditionally a place for leisure and recreation, so they bear a heavy burden for tourism. They have an enormous economic value for tourists and local inhabitants alike, so municipalities strive to obtain quality-related certificates to market their beaches.

The current growing concern for sustainability and the marine environment does not only come from institutions, but also from beachgoers, who have become sophisticated consumers when it comes to selecting their holiday destination. This has led to both institutions and tourists focusing their attention on beach quality certifications or ecolabels such as Blue Flags, which have become a hallmark that municipalities and beach managers capitalize on in two ways: to attract more tourists and/or as a tool for environmental protection.

Since the first Blue Flags were awarded to European countries, the trend has been spreading internationally, with the first flag being awarded to South Africa and later to countries in the Americas, Asia, and Oceania, respectively.

Europe is still the leader in obtaining Blue Flags, most of which have been given to Spain, France, Italy, Greece, and Portugal. This shows a clear commitment by these countries to position their beaches among the award winners. As for Spain, it is at the top of the ranking of Blue Flags obtained in Europe.

It should also be noted that all EU member countries with a coastal border have Blue Flags, which were awarded prior to joining the European Union.

EU-27, as a leading tourist-receiving region and with more than 45% of its accommodations in coastal areas, is clearly committed to sustainability and the quality of its waters. In fact, coastal tourism – the economic engine of the EU

94 María Escrivá-Beltrán and Rosa Currás-Móstoles

Blue Growth Strategy – struggles to maintain a balance between meeting tourism demand, its impact on coasts, and the maintenance of the marine environment, especially in the EU top five countries that are committed to 3S tourism.

Despite the fact that some studies suggest that they do not always imply environmental protection, the Blue Flag distinction does ensure minimum quality standards and shows a concern for the environment and the sustainability of its beaches. The study shows that over the years the interest in obtaining BF has not only diminished, but it has served as a first step towards the integration of the new member states, especially with regard to common strategies linked to coastal sustainability.

Note

1 This chapter is part of the Jean Monnet Chair funded by 612063-EPP-1–2019-1-ES-EPPJMO-CHAIR "Global Commons in the Global European Strategy: a specific revision of Human Rights, Security and Security and consideration the sea as an invaluable resource".

6.5 References

Blue Flag. (2022). Blue Flag. https://www.blueflag.global

Botero, C.-M., Williams, A. T., & Cabrera, J. A. (2015). Advances in Beach Management in Latin America: Overview from Certification Schemes. In C. W. Finkl & C. Makowski (Eds.), *Environmental Management and Governance: Advances in Coastal and Marine Resources* (pp. 33–63). Springer International Publishing. https://doi.org/10.1007/978-3-319-06305-8_2

Capacci, S., Scorcu, A. E., & Vici, L. (2015). Seaside tourism and eco-labels: The economic impact of Blue Flags. *Tourism Management, 47,* 88–96. https://doi.org/10.1016/j.tourman.2014.09.003

Castillo-Manzano, J. I., Castro-Nuño, M., López-Valpuesta, L., & Zarzoso, Á. (2021). Measuring the role of Blue Flags in attracting sustainable "sun-and-sand tourism". *Current Issues in Tourism, 24*(15), 2204–2222. https://doi.org/10.1080/13683500.2020.1844642

Coastal Zones – Copernicus Land Monitoring Service. (n.d.). [Land Section]. Retrieved August 29, 2022, from https://land.copernicus.eu/local/coastal-zones

Country profiles. Retrieved September 26, 2022, from https://european-union.europa.eu/principles-countries-history/country-profiles_en

Directive 2006/7/EC of the European Parliament and of the Council of 15 February 2006 concerning the management of bathing water quality and repealing Directive 76/160/EEC, CONSIL, EP, 064 OJ L (2006). http://data.europa.eu/eli/dir/2006/7/oj/eng

Dodds, R., & Holmes, M. R. (2020). Is Blue Flag certification a means of destination competitiveness? A Canadian context. *Ocean & Coastal Management, 192,* 105192. https://doi.org/10.1016/j.ocecoaman.2020.105192

Eikeset, A. M., Mazzarella, A. B., Davíðsdóttir, B., Klinger, D. H., Levin, S. A., Rovenskaya, E., & Stenseth, N. Chr. (2018). What is blue growth? The semantics of "Sustainable Development" of marine environments. *Marine Policy, 87,* 177–179. https://doi.org/10.1016/j.marpol.2017.10.019

Eurogeographics. (n.d.). EuroGeographics. Retrieved September 26, 2022, from https://eurogeographics.org/our-members/

Dive in Blue Flags: A historical evolution in Europe 95

European Comission. (2022). *The EU blue economy report 2022*. Publications Office of the European Union. Luxembourg.

European Environment Agency. (n.d.). [Page]. Retrieved August 11, 2022, from https://www.eea.europa.eu/themes/water/europes-seas-and-coasts/europes-seas-and-coasts

Eurostat. (n.d.). *Eurostat*. Retrieved September 16, 2022, from https://ec.europa.eu/eurostat/statistics-explained/index.php?title=Archive:Coastal_region_statistics

Fayissa, B., Nsiah, C., & Tadasse, B. (2008). Impact of tourism on economic growth and development in Africa. *Tourism Economics, 14*(4), 807–818.

Foundation for Environmental Education Foundation for Environmental Education. (2023, March 27). Foundation for Environmental Education. https://www.fee.global

Fraguell, R. M., Martí, C., Pintó, J., & Coenders, G. (2016). After over 25 years of accrediting beaches, has Blue Flag contributed to sustainable management? *Journal of Sustainable Tourism, 24*(6), 882–903.

Global and Regional Tourism Performance. (n.d.). Retrieved September 26, 2022, from https://www.unwto.org/tourism-data/global-and-regional-tourism-performance

Glossary: Coastal Region. (2022). https://ec.europa.eu/eurostat/statistics-explained/index.php?title=Glossary:Coastal_region

Goal 14 | Department of Economic and Social Affairs. (2022). https://sdgs.un.org/goals/goal14

Hall, C. M. (2019). Constructing sustainable tourism development: The 2030 agenda and the managerial ecology of sustainable tourism. *Journal of Sustainable Tourism, 27*(7), 1044–1060.

Integrated Maritime Policy of the European Union | European Parliament. (n.d.). Retrieved September 15, 2022, from https://www.europarl.europa.eu/factsheets/en/sheet/121/integrated-maritime-policy-of-the-european-union

Klein, L., Osleeb, J. P., & Viola, M. R. (2004). Tourism-generated earnings in the coastal zone: A regional analysis. *Journal of Coastal Research, 20*(4), 1080–1088.

Lucrezi, S., Saayman, M., & Van der Merwe, P. (2015). Managing beaches and beachgoers: Lessons from and for the Blue Flag award. *Tourism Management, 48*, 211–230.

Merino, F., & Prats, M. A. (2022). Are Blue Flags a good indicator of the quality of sea water on beaches? An empirical analysis of the Western Mediterranean basin. *Journal of Cleaner Production, 330*, 129865. https://doi.org/10.1016/j.jclepro.2021.129865

Merino, F., & Prats, M. A. (2020). Sustainable beach management and promotion of the local tourist industry: Can Blue Flags be a good driver of this balance? *Ocean & Coastal Management, 198*, 105359.

Mihalič, T. (2000). Environmental management of a tourist destination: A factor of tourism competitiveness. *Tourism management, 21*(1), 65–78.

Mir-Gual, M., Pons, G. X., Martín-Prieto, J. A., & Rodríguez-Perea, A. (2015). A critical view of the Blue Flag beaches in Spain using environmental variables. *Ocean & Coastal Management, 105*, 106–115.

Nahman, A., & Rigby, D. (2008). Valuing Blue Flag Status and Estuarine Water Quality in Margate, South Africa. *South African Journal of Economics, 76*(4), 721–737. https://doi.org/10.1111/j.1813-6982.2008.00208.x

Pencarelli, T., Splendiani, S., & Fraboni, C. (2016). Enhancement of the "Blue Flag" eco-label in Italy: An empirical analysis. *Anatolia, 27*(1), 28–37.

Pernice, D. (2022, March). *Tourism European Parliament*. https://www.europarl.europa.eu/factsheets/en/sheet/126/tourism

Prados, L. (1999, February 27). Bruselas retira su apoyo a las banderas azules. El País. https://elpais.com/diario/1999/02/28/sociedad/920156401_850215.html

Saayman, M., & Saayman, A. (2017). How important are Blue Flag awards in beach choice? *Journal of Coastal Research, 33*(6), 1436–1447.

Sequeira, T. N., & Maçãs Nunes, P. (2008). Does tourism influence economic growth? A dynamic panel data approach. *Applied economics, 40*(18), 2431–2441.

Sustainable Blue Economy. (2022). https://oceans-and-fisheries.ec.europa.eu/ocean/blue-economy/sustainable-blue-economy_en

Tourism in the 2030 Agenda | UNWTO. (2022). https://www.unwto.org/tourism-in-2030-agenda *Tourism statistics at regional level.* (2022). https://ec.europa.eu/eurostat/statistics-explained/index.php?title=Tourism_statistics_at_regional_level

Zielinski, S., & Botero, C. M. (2019). Myths, misconceptions and the true value of Blue Flag. *Ocean & Coastal Management, 174*, 15–24. https://doi.org/10.1016/j.ocecoaman.2019.03.012

7 The path of Blue Flag in Latin America and the Caribbean

History, challenges and learnings

Camilo M. Botero, Paloma Arias and Lourdes Diaz

7.1 Blue Flag's evolution in Latin America and the Caribbean

The development of Blue Flag (BF) in Latin America and the Caribbean (LAC) began in the early 2000s and has slowly but consistently grown ever since. The program has been recognized by the United Nations Environment Programme (UNEP), the World Tourism Organization (UNWTO), and the United Nations Educational, Scientific and Cultural Organization (UNESCO), and not only recognized but collaborated with the same organizations in the development and evaluation of sites (members of the international Jury) of BF. This is one of the reasons why many governments and other sectors have been eager to implement the program in their countries. Besides the environmental management aspect, there is an added value that tourism destinations, specifically those marketed as "sun, sea, and sand destinations" also identify BF as a marketing tool (Chamorro-Mera et al., 2019; Dodds & Holmes, 2019). Nevertheless, it is important to note that the continent has at least nine beach certification schemes, although Blue Flag has the highest number of awarded locations (Botero et al., 2015).

It is also important to state that the Blue Flag development in the Caribbean was not an easy ride. In the year 2000, when it was introduced in an agreement with the Caribbean Association for Sustainable Tourism (CAST), the Blue Flag criteria had to be revised and adapted to the geomorphology of the beaches in the region. This was done in collaboration with the knowledge of the experts in coastal environmental management and water quality of the region. It was only in 2003 that the first countries of the Caribbean could begin with the pilot phase. Four countries (Puerto Rico, Dominican Republic, Jamaica, and Barbados) engaged in the process, with only two going through.

In Puerto Rico's case, the Puerto Rico Tourism Company took the lead but engaged the Interagency Board for the Management of Beaches and the private sector through the PR Hotel and Tourism Association and environmental experts. As a result, the pilot phase began with four public beaches that reached certified status in 2004. It is important to state that the government has always been engaged with the program in a co-management model with the Organization for Sustainable Development[1] (OPAS by its name in Spanish), as the national operator and the official member of the Foundation of Environmental Education (FEE). Such engagement

DOI: 10.4324/9781003323570-8

98   Camilo M. Botero et al.

is validated as it is perhaps the only country in the world with legislation related to Blue Flag (Act No. 173 of August 12, 2000) stating that it is the only beach certification scheme that can have a presence in the Island – amended as Act No. 269 of August 13, 2008, to establish a co-management model between the Puerto Rico Tourism Company (representing the government) and the NGO responsible for the program's administration and recognized by FEE. With this legislation, the program has no cost for the participating beaches.

The program kept on growing until Hurricane Maria, a Category 5 hurricane, hit and devasted the entire Island in 2017. In the 2022 season, there was only one certified beach, with a second one submitted for the upcoming 2022–2023 season. Two new beaches were beginning to work towards Blue Flag, and the rest will not be up to the standards until the recovery efforts conclude. In the meantime, the focus has been on sustainable tourism boats and marinas, where there were two marinas and eleven sustainable boats with certified status in Puerto Rico (PR) in 2022.

At the same time, in the beginning, the Dominican Republic also began the process of raising their first flag, in 2004. Unlike Puerto Rico, the Institute of Environmental Rights of the Dominican Republic[2] (IDARD by its Spanish acronym), as national operator, focused on the tourism sector for the implementation of Blue Flag, selecting resort beaches to take part. This is because most of their visitors are from Spain (the leading country in Blue Flag) and the rest of Europe, where BF is quite well recognized. It is financed by the hotels – working towards the certification through administration fees.

These two countries adopted the program quickly because of their place on the Caribbean Sea, and one of the most popular beach regions in the world (perhaps the most). However, Blue Flag also turned south, and Brazil was the third country to adopt this international symbol in 2009, but the implementation process was difficult and slow. In Brazil, the program started in 2005 by the Environmental Institute of Ratones[3] (IAR by its Portuguese acronym) a Civil Society Organization of Public Interest (currently named as the *Environments in Network Institute*). After undergoing a complex technical and administrative capacity test process, IAR was chosen as representative of the FEE programs in Brazil. Its position as national operator was ratified during the General Assembly of the FEE, held in June 2005, in Antwerp (Belgium) (Scherer, 2006).

Brazil has had a slow but steady evolution. The first stage of the pilot, beach selection process, was held in Florianopolis at the First National Blue Flag Workshop in March 2006. The event was attended by representatives of NGOs from Bahia, Espirito Santo, São Paulo and Santa Catarina, the Ministry of the Environment, the Secretariat of Heritage of the Union, private companies, and collaborators (IAR, 2019). After three years of definitions, five officially registered beaches remained in the pilot phase. In July 2009 their request for Blue Flag certification was sent to the National Jury; only *Jurerê Internacional* received the award. In recent years, the award has been consolidated and in 2022 the number of winning beaches and marinas increased significantly, reaching a total of 40 flags. The role played by the government in Brazil has been institutional since the beginning, as members of the National Jury. Different ministries such as Economy, Environment, Tourism, and

The path of Blue Flag in Latin America and the Caribbean   99

Education, and the Coastal Agency, are part of the Jury. In addition, for a couple of years, the Ministry of Tourism has been publishing and giving national dissemination on its social networks to the list of award-winning beaches (IAR, 2019).

Following was the U.S. Virgin Islands (USVI) in 2009 when the Virgin Islands Hotel Association took on the challenge and supported a feasibility study to determine if the proper infrastructure was in place in the Virgin Islands to support such a rigorous project. That was when the Virgin Island Conservation Society[4] (VICS) became the national operator and was able to roll out four pilot beaches in 2010 and certify all four in 2011; during this year, they also began the pilot phase for marinas. The Department of Tourism, annual site dues, and private donations support Blue Flag in the USVI. Although in 2022 there were three certified beaches, for the past five years there have been environmental disasters (hurricanes and the pandemic) that have disrupted various services necessary to remain compliant – disruption in the water sampling schedule, waste management schedule, and the operation of the business that manages the program at each site (closed after hurricanes and during a pandemic). Because of this, some locations are no longer eligible or can no longer continue their participation in the program. Despite the situation, several new prospects are being considered for the 2022–2023 season as the recovery efforts come together.

In Mexico, a champion destination in several tourist products, with 3S (sun, sea, and sand) among the different tourist products, and even though it has its own beach certification scheme (called *White Flag*), the implementation of Blue Flag was easier and faster than it was for any other country in Latin America. It began with a feasibility study in 2012, including five pilot beaches that reached certified status in 2013 (and continue to be certified). In the same way, the government, mainly through the national secretaries of environment and tourism, had an important role to play in supporting the first national operator, *Pronatura Mexico*. Shortly afterward, this organization changed its focus of work and dropped the FEE programs, and it was then that *FEE Mexico*[5] took over, successfully becoming the national operator. Dues finance Blue Flag from the participating beaches where the establishment of adequate infrastructure, as well as the water quality testing cost, are the main challenges faced. Besides being an environmental management tool, it has meant a demonstration of global competitiveness in the tourism sector for the participating cities. Because of this, Mexico is the leading country in the Americas and Caribbean region with 64 certified beaches, two marinas, and 31 tourism-sustainable boats.

Trinidad and Tobago (T&T) also conducted its feasibility study in 2010 and began its pilot phase with two beaches in 2013. However, it was only in 2014 that only one of the two beaches met the Blue Flag criteria and was awarded. As in Puerto Rico, the Blue Flag program was financed by the government tourism department. For Trinidad, the Tourism Development Company received funding from the Ministry of Tourism (now referred to as the Ministry of Tourism, Culture, and the Arts). In Tobago, the Blue Flag program was financed by the Division of Tourism, Culture and Transportation (now referred to as the Ministry of Tourism, Culture, Antiquities, and Transportation). The national operator is the non-profit

100 *Camilo M. Botero et al.*

Table 7.1 Evolution and national operators of Blue Flag in Latin America and the Caribbean

Country	FEE member	First BF	National operator	Focus
Puerto Rico	2003	2004	Organization for Sustainable Development	Environmental education
Dominican Republic	2003	2004	Institute of Environmental Rights	Environmental law
Brazil	2005	2009	Environments in Network Institute	Environmental education
Virgin Islands	2009	2011	Virgin Island Conservation Society	Ecological conservation
Mexico	2012	2013	FEE Mexico (replacing Pronatura Mexico)	Environmental education
Trinidad and Tobago	2010	2014	Green T&T	Environmental education
Colombia	2017	2019	National Association of Sanitary and Environmental Engineering	Environmental engineering
Chile	2019	2021	Educarse Foundation	Accessibility and education
Argentina	2019	None	FEE Argentina – Alma Tierra	Environmental education
Ecuador	2022	None	Coastman Ecuador	Environmental consultancy

organization Green T&T[6], which has the FEE program at the core of its activities. Despite being considered an important product development initiative to attract international visitors, the high cost of water quality testing was and continues to be the main challenge for the development of the program.

Colombia was the seventh country in the continent to join the program, raising four flags in 2019, one on the Pacific coast. The feasibility study started in the year 2016 by an initiative of the Ministry of Trade, Industry, and Tourism, who contacted the FEE directly. The ministry created a temporary committee with the national authorities related to tourist beaches, environmental and tourist private organizations, and some recognized scholars of the country. During the first semester of 2017, the feasibility study was done and sent to FEE for revision and comments. Meanwhile, the ministry contacted the mayors of the 47 coastal municipalities of Colombia to invite them to propose the best beaches in their territories to join the pilot phase. In August 2017, ten pilot beaches were selected, covering all the coastal regions of Colombia. For eight months the ministry with the local authorities assessed the baseline of each of the ten beaches, according to the 33 Blue Flag criteria (Botero & Zielinski, 2020). The national operator was selected by FEE from a list of non-governmental organizations sent by the Ministry of Tourism because a public institution cannot occupy this role. In 2018 the National Association of Sanitary and Environmental Engineering[7] (ACODAL by its name in Spanish) was accepted as the national operator and started with the affiliation to FEE. Since this year the program has been managed by ACODAL, with the achievement of four beaches in the country's first season of Blue Flag. The main difficulties in

The path of Blue Flag in Latin America and the Caribbean   101

running the program in Colombia are related to the low technical capacity in many coastal municipalities to improve the aspects required by the Blue Flag criteria. In consequence, in 2021, the Ministry of Tourism gave a grant to ACODAL with the purpose of selecting at least five beaches and prepare them for the National Jury in June 2022. Lastly, the government chose ten beaches, and seven of them were assessed by the National Jury.

Chile, which had the approval of the feasibility study in 2019 prepared by the Educarse Foundation, [8] the national operator, began its pilot phase with five beaches. Unfortunately, because of the country's situation – its economic and political crisis at that time – and the pandemic, they were only able to work with one of the five beaches. Despite this, in 2021, the first flag was raised, starting its path to more awarded beaches. As in other countries in Latin America, water quality testing has been an issue not only because of its cost but because they did not have a history of testing the two chemical parameters (E-coli and Enterococci) required by Blue Flag or the necessary amount of certified laboratories to cover the entire coastline. Nonetheless, many sectors have recognized that the presence of BF could be beneficial for their coastline and beaches. In an interview with the senator for the Valparaíso Region, Kenneth Pugh states:

The benefits of having our coastline and beaches with this certification are multiple. From greater possibilities of tourism, since more and more tourists are looking for this type of certified beaches to go on vacation (especially those from developed countries); boost the economy of these localities; promote recycling, sustainable development, and sustainability on our beaches; improve the care of our marine resources such as fish, crustaceans, and shellfish; generate environmental awareness and education; among others.

(radiorecreo, May 12, 2020[9])

At the same time as Chile, Alma Tierra, [10] the national operator from Argentina, had its feasibility study approved in 2019 and began its pilot phase with five beaches. Like others, the implementation phase was stopped due to the COVID-19 pandemic. It was only in 2022 that they restarted the process with three pilot beaches hoping to be approved for the following BF season. Dues from each participating beach will support the program. The last country in Latin America to pursue BF is Ecuador. With Coastman Ecuador[11] as the national operator, they were finalizing the feasibility study to be sent for approval by the end of 2022, expecting to begin with three pilot beaches. Again, the lack of adequate infrastructure, the regulatory framework of the coastline, and the services required in BF are some of the main challenges. Regardless of the challenges, they see BF as the tool to reach beach planning and sustainability management to benefit the community and visitors.

Looking further north, the USA is the most recent country to join the Blue Flag network in the Americas through the American Shore & Beach Preservation Association[12] (ASBPA) as national operator. With the 2020 approval of its feasibility study, they have begun the pilot phase with three beaches hoping to receive the certification in 2023, as there is a presence of the infrastructure and services

102   *Camilo M. Botero et al.*

required. As for the challenges, besides the pandemic the biggest hurdle for the continental United States, Hawaii, and Alaska is the discrepancy in national water quality testing requirements and international standards. Besides donations and sponsorships, an administration fee will be established for participating sites.

Throughout these 20 years, other Caribbean countries have been part of the Blue Flag program and have been compelled to discontinue it for different reasons, such as lack of proper administration or meeting one or more of the criteria. On the other hand, other countries such as Uruguay, Curacao, and Turks and Caicos Islands have expressed intentions to join Blue Flag. They are either in the process of researching the program or submitting an application to FEE for approval.

7.2 Latin America's particularities from the European experience

As it was stated, the Blue Flag program came to Latin America with a high influence from European tourism. Therefore, for a better understanding of the implementation of BF in the continent, it is important to start pointing out the difference between both continents. The first difference is the geographical locations of the countries that make up Latin America and Europe. The first is mostly located in the tropics and the southern hemisphere, while the second is entirely in the northern hemisphere. Consequently, in European countries, the summer season will be only two or three months, while in almost all Latin American countries the bathing season extends throughout the year. Another existing difference is the political stability between both places. In Europe, there is political stability over decades, where it is possible to carry out long-term government policies. In Latin American countries, this stability is much lower, and it is very difficult to maintain long-term programs for municipalities, such as the Blue Flag program. Therefore, the certification processes should not depend on the existing government but should have continuity regardless of the existing partisan policies at any given time (Botero & Zielinski, 2020).

From the European perspective, some achievements were reached when BF was fully implemented. In Europe, one of the first advantages was the increase in the number of sampling points. From the start of the program until 2020, the number increased substantially as part of compliance with the Bathing Water Directive (1976/2013), which all Blue Flag beaches must comply with (EEA, 2020). In Europe, a beach can only be a Blue Flag candidate if it has been officially designated at the national level and reported to the European Commission as a bathing area with at least one sample point for analyzing its bathing waters. In addition, the name and physical limits of the beach must respond to those officially recognized. On the other hand, the Blue Flag sites have become a strong point of tourism promotion, once their visitors begin to demand the analysis of the quality of bathing water and the environment, as well as all the services and amenities necessary to enjoy a day at the beach. Despite the criticism given to the recognition of the program (McKenna et al., 2011; Mir-Gual et al., 2015), national operators consider that localities' incomes are improved as a consequence of visitors who choose a destination on the basis of the program (Bernardi & Pire, 2015).

During the 35 years of its existence, the BF program has evolved in order to adapt to the times and regions where it is present without jeopardizing its integrity or strict criteria. The application recently in Europe is digitized so the previously existing problems with postal services have been eliminated. Even so, each country usually establishes a period of consultations and doubts for identifying and submitting candidates. In general, the municipalities have a professional team in charge of managing the beaches, who are in contact with the national operator to solve any doubts. On the other hand, in Europe, the results of the bathing water quality carried out by each locality must be sent annually to the European Commission, an additional administrative procedure to verify the candidacy of each beach. The control visits made in the summer to each beach are also part of the final decision the National Jury must make. In short, the greatest difficulty is maintaining the 33 requirements each year, since the award must be renewed annually, which implies a constant budget and staff.

From the point of view of Latin America, the primary request for obtaining a Blue Flag is the change in behavior concerning the beach ecosystem, accompanied by a greater environmental awareness of public authorities, the private sector, and civil society. Even though there are few quantitative studies in this regard, in most Latin American countries, important improvements are required in the safety and security of visitors, from having a stable lifeguard service, to ensuring that there is sufficient surveillance to prevent theft and crime. Another of the difficulties of the Blue Flag program in Latin America is related to the lack of treatment of the discharges that flow into the beaches, affecting the quality of bathing water. Added to this is the limited collection and sampling of these bathing waters since in some countries this analysis is non-existent. In others, it is not carried out according to the European bathing water directive, which is the basis of the water quality criteria program, or only one microbiological parameter is analyzed, instead of the two mandatory ones.

The irregular occupations on the coast are another of the great difficulties for the progress of the program. In some countries there is no specific law for the management of beaches, or when there is it is not complied with due to lack of control. In addition, the lack of political willingness also affects the achievement of the award, since it is a program that is not a temporal goal, but rather it is continuous work that must be transversal for all the public and private entities of the municipalities. Lastly, the lack of dialogue between the authorities in charge on the beach is another of the greatest difficulties, because the Blue Flag requires consensus and joint work to obtain the award (Botero & Zielinski, 2020).

All these challenges to the management of beaches in LAC were not totally clear in majority of countries since the beginning of the century. Costa Rica was the first country to create its own beach certification scheme in 1996, but 20 years later the continent had at least eight other awards running in one or more countries, BF among them (Zielinski & Botero, 2015). Those certification schemes were mainly promoted by the International Standards Organization members of each country, which wanted to measure the beach through officially approved management systems; this was the case in Mexico, Colombia, Argentina, and Ecuador. In addition, the existence of the

104 *Camilo M. Botero et al.*

Proplayas Network for 15 years has reinforced the beach management and certification initiatives within the 17 countries it covers (Botero & Cabrera, 2019), which has also been beneficial for BF. In summary, the national certifications and the presence of a well-connected network of beach experts are two trends that mark an important difference to the European context in which BF was born.

7.3 Critical issues for a successful implementation of Blue Flag in Latin America and the Caribbean

More than evident differences between Europe and Latin America and the Caribbean countries, some critical issues can be evidenced after 20 years of Blue Flag implementation on the continent. The purpose of this last section is not to establish a final judgment, but to help the beach managers and national institutions in LAC to avoid or reduce the most common constraints experienced by the countries in which BF already exists. This analysis is done from the perspective of the field, where the challenges look more realistic and urgent than from the academic perspective. It does not mean that scientific literature cannot evidence the critical issues, but despite the almost 100 papers published about the topic, there are still some issues little studied.

As Table 7.1 shows, the first big challenge for a new country to implement BF is the leadership of an NGO that acts as a national operator. Except for Mexico, all countries in LAC have maintained the same organization as national operator since the beginning of the program in the country. However, this process has not been free of difficulties for an organization strong and stable enough to run the program. This is the example of Puerto Rico and Colombia, where national governments have supported economically the national operators, or at least some key activities that guarantee that the program will be active. The opposite is true in Mexico and Brazil, where the national operators depend on the fees paid by the applicants, and therefore require a huge effort to promote the certification within the public and private institutions in the country. Argentina and Ecuador seem to follow the same pattern.

In the same way, the pilot phase in new countries is a challenge that can delay or even cancel the implementation of BF. The case of Brazil is probably the clearest, where this pilot stage lasted four years, and only one beach could be certified in the first year. A similar situation was experienced in Trinidad and Tobago, which also needed four years to achieve its first flags, and with several struggles to maintain them during the years. In Colombia the Ministry of Tourism decided to select ten beaches instead of the five that FEE recommends and paid a technical consultant to accompany the process; even then, only two of them obtained the flag in 2019. In addition, the COVID-19 pandemic delayed this pilot phase in Chile and Argentina, which is an exception but important to consider. In sum, the pilot stage is a crucial period that must be carefully planned if the goal is to obtain the first flag; otherwise, it can be a challenge too big for the national operator.

Another critical issue in LAC is the cost to participate in the program for a candidate beach, which has two perspectives: costs for paying fees to the national operator and costs to prepare the beach conditions. The former is not the same in the whole continent, where some countries do not request payment (i.e., Puerto Rico), but the majority of them do. Although the amount varies from country to country, and year to year, it can be an obstacle for certain municipalities or hotels that cannot afford this payment. The second perspective is even more complicated to measure and to reach because it is associated with the status of the environmental and tourist quality of the beach. Considering that BF requires some minimum facilities to give the award (i.e., toilets, lifeguard station, signaling) and to accomplish several activities during the bathing season (i.e., sand cleaning, environmental education, pollution emergency simulation), an important budget should be guaranteed. Therefore, financing the investments to prepare the beach until BF levels could be an impossible goal if a strategic plan is not approved. Perhaps the solution is based on a governance process that creates a common space for collaborating between all the public and private stakeholders benefiting from the award. However, it is very difficult in the majority of Latin American countries, where beaches are public areas and government institutions can only act until the legislation allows them to.

Finally, but not less importantly, bathing water monitoring is still a hugely critical issue for applicants in LAC. Opposite to Europe, there is no continental program or agreement that promotes or requests a continental program or agreement that promotes or requests that countries to monitor their bathing waters. Therefore, each country has its own parameters and procedures based on several different regulations from diverse periods. In other words, when BF starts in a country, it also must confront the fact that the microbiological parameters (coliforms and enterococcus) are probably not in national regulation, or the technique of analysis (CUF) is not already implemented. This has been exactly the case in Colombia, where national regulation still uses the technique MPN. Later, several technical issues arise. First, the sampling process could be very challenging in remote tourist localities without accredited laboratories nearby and weak airline connections, mainly because samples must be analyzed within 24 hours. This situation is very common in LAC, where foreign tourists travel to remote destinations precisely because they want to stay far away from mass tourism. In brief, if a local destination such as Sayulita (Mexico), Cabo Frio (Brazil), or Buenaventura (Colombia) want to certify their beaches, first they must check that refrigerated samples can reach an accredited laboratory somewhere before 24 hours Critical.

Accredited laboratories are another of the issues related to this challenge of monitoring the bathing water. Each country has its accreditation structure and ways to access the list of accredited laboratories. This accreditation procedure used to be very expensive for the labs. Only a few of them can reach this high level of exigence, and they are usually located in the biggest cities. In addition, and to sum up the issue of national regulations, if the parameter or the technique is not legally approved in the country, the labs will not be encouraged to invest thousands of dollars and many months to reach the accreditation if the procedure already is approved in the country. In sum, the existence and location of accredited laboratories for the parameters and techniques requested by BF should be a critical point to approve the feasibility study for a new country; nowadays it is a nightmare for countries such as Colombia and Ecuador.

106 *Camilo M. Botero et al.*

In conclusion, the Blue Flag program has grown slowly but steadily in Latin America and the Caribbean. This program was originally created for the European countries within its political, economic, and environmental particularities. When BF was proposed to start in LAC, the expectation was that the process would be simple, but it was not. It was more challenging than expected. Although the first implementation was not too difficult in Puerto Rico and the Dominican Republic, the next steps were complicated. After almost 20 years, the program is more known on the continent, with several successes and learnings. The existence of other beach certification schemes in the continent, even if they have only local or national coverage, is another particularity. In sum, the program's future is still wide, with plenty of opportunities in LAC. Still, its advance will depend on strengthening the critical issues mentioned here, and the approach of FEE with the other beach certification schemes, which can be seen as partners or competitors. This chapter aims to contribute to making the best decisions in each country in LAC.

Notes

1 https://www.opaspr.org
2 https://idard.org.do/
3 https://iarbrasil.org.br/
4 https://viconservationsociety.org
5 http://www.feemexico.org/
6 https://green-tt.org/
7 https://www.acodal.org.co/
8 https://educarse.cl/
9 https://www.pugh.cl/pugh/sala-de-prensa/2020/playas-certificado-de-calidad
10 https://www.facebook.com/profile.php?id=100063655772435
11 https://coastmanecuador.com/
12 https://asbpa.org/

7.4 References

Bernardi, L. P., & Pire, P. (2015). O Programa Bandeira Azul de certificação para praias na percepção dos gestores nacionais dos países participantes. *Turismo – Visão e Ação*, 17(3), 542–568.

Botero, C. M., & Cabrera, J. A. (2019). Proplayas: la comunidad iberoamericana de gestión y certificación de playas. In M. Palacios & D. Soto (Eds.), *Pensar un Pacífico Latinoamericano: retos políticos, éticos y medioambientales* (pp. 135–152). Universidad del Pacífico.

Botero, C. M., Williams, A. T., & Cabrera, J. A. (2015). Advances in Beach Management in Latin America: Overview from Certification Schemes. In C. Finkl & C. Makowski (Eds.), *Environmental Management and Governance*. Coastal Research Library, vol 8, 33–63. Springer-Verlag. https://doi.org/10.1007/978-3-319-06305-8_2

Botero, C. M., & Zielinski, S. (2020). The implementation of a world-famous tourism ecolabel triggers political support for beach management. *Tourism Management Perspectives*, 35(April), 100691. https://doi.org/10.1016/j.tmp.2020.100691

Chamorro-Mera, A., Nobre de Oliveira, V., & García-Gallego, J. M. (2019). The Blue Flag Label as a Tool to Improve the Quality of Life in the Sun-and-Sand Tourist Destinations. In A. Campón-Cerro, J. Hernández-Mogollón, & J. Folgado-Fernández (Eds.), *Best*

The path of Blue Flag in Latin America and the Caribbean 107

Practices in Hospitality and Tourism Marketing and Management. Applying Quality of Life Research. Springer. https://doi.org/10.1007/978-3-319-91692-7_13

Dodds, R., & Holmes, M. R. (2019). Beach tourists: What factors satisfy them and drive them to return. *Ocean and Coastal Management*, 168, 158–166. https://doi.org/10.1016/j.ocecoaman.2018.10.034

EEA (2020). *Bathing water management in Europe: Successes and challenges.* EEA Report No 11/2020. European Environment Agency. Luxembourg: Publications Office of the European Union. ISBN 978–92–9480-261–3, ISSN 1977–8449.

IAR (2019). *Programa Bandeira Azul Praias-Brazil. Critérios e notas explicativas.* Instituto Ambientes Em Rede, Florianópolis. Available on: https://bandeiraazul.org.br

McKenna, J., Williams, A. T., & Cooper, J. A. G. (2011). Blue Flag or Red Herring: Do beach awards encourage the public to visit beaches? *Tourism Management*, 32(3), 576–588. https://doi.org/10.1016/j.tourman.2010.05.005

Mir-Gual, M., Pons, G. X., Martín-Prieto, J. A., Rodríguez-Perea, A. (2015). A critical view of the Blue Flag beaches in Spain using environmental variables. *Ocean and Coastal Management*, 105, 106–115. https://doi.org/10.1016/j.ocecoaman.2015.01.003

Scherer, M. (2006). Bandeira Azul: um programa de certificação ambiental de praias contribuindo para a política Brasileira de gerenciamento costeiro. *Revista de Gestão Costeira Integrada*, 5, 49–51. Available on: http://www.aprh.pt/rgci/pdf/RGCI_5.pdf

Zielinski, S., & Botero, C. M. (2015). Are eco-labels sustainable? Beach certification schemes in Latin America and the Caribbean. *Journal of Sustainable Tourism*, 23(10), 1550–1572. https://doi.org/10.1080/09669582.2015.1047376

8 Impact of Blue Flags on local economy in Spain

*Ana B. Ramón-Rodríguez, Teresa Torregrosa,
Luis Moreno-Izquierdo and José F. Perles-Ribes*

8.1 Introduction

Tourism is one of the primary sources of wealth in the Valencian Community, generating 17,883 million euros and 318,522 thousand jobs (15.9% of the total), according to the latest IMPACTUR Comunitat Valenciana study (2020). According to IMPACTUR (2019), the tourism sector closed 2019, the latest year of pre-pandemic data, with a contribution of 15.5% of the regional GDP. Occupancy surveys in tourist accommodation companies (EOAT) recorded 31.2 million overnight stays in 2021, 77.4% more than in 2020. Hence, the Valencian Community is the fifth most visited region in Spain by international tourists.

Valencian coastal municipalities are increasingly interested in improving the image and quality of their beaches, joining the concern to make mass tourism demand compatible with environmental protection and sustainability. This trend is growing worldwide (Kozak & Rimmington, 1999; Alegre & Garau, 2010; Torres-Bejarano et al., 2018; Goffi et al., 2019; Hall, 2019), with different quality accreditations emerging that assess the environmental commitment of the tourism industry (Zielinski & Botero, 2019; Castillo-Manzano et al., 2021). More than 100 eco-labels exist in tourism (Font, 2002), with Blue Flags (BFs) being one of the most important. The Valencian Community is the Spanish region with the highest number of BF on its beaches, representing 22.7% of all awarded to Spanish coasts.

Hence, in this chapter, we will analyze the economic impacts derived from the achievement of a BF on tourism activity and on the economic development of the tourist destinations analyzed, choosing the Valencian Community as a case study in Spain. The chapter is structured as follows. First, a review of the literature on the economic impact of BF is carried out, pointing out their direct and indirect effects and the criticisms of this certification system. Then, in the methodology section, the first subsection justifies the use of the Valencian Community as a case study and then explains the analysis methodology in the following subsections. Finally, the results obtained are analyzed, and the main conclusions of the chapter are drawn.

DOI: 10.4324/9781003323570-9

8.2 Economic impact of BFs in literature

8.2.1 Direct and indirect effects of BFs

Given its implementation, especially with the growing interest and need to make sustainability a competitive tourism element, the "Blue Flag program" has acquired an essential relevance in studying coastal tourist destinations. On an economic level, obtaining this recognition could positively affect the local population and the development of the tourist activity itself. According to the existing literature, this relationship seems to exist, although we can understand it from a threefold perspective.

The first of these perspectives results from the endogeneity between public and private investment in the tourism sector, which, though initially dependent on public activity, subsequently maintains a reciprocal relationship. In other words, public commitment to obtain recognition of the quality of a destination can naturally be accompanied by private investment. For example, Merino and Prats (2020) confirmed a positive impact by increasing the number of rooms and people working in tourism as Spanish destinations are awarded the BF distinction. This effect is also observed in the work of Blackman et al. (2014) on Costa Rica, concluding that investment by administrations to meet the BF recognition requirements attracts tour operators and boosts local economies. Consequently, this private investment will trigger the interest of administrations to maintain the BF status.

Second, we have a direct effect, as demand responds positively to destinations that obtain BF certification. The work of Capacci et al. (2015) reached this conclusion in their study of Italian coasts, although with two curiosities. The first curiosity is that the number of BF at a destination is irrelevant to demand, but this award exists on at least one beach. The second curiosity is that the demand reaction is not immediate but requires a year for a positive response. Chamorro-Mera et al. (2019) also stated that destination managers value BF certificates very positively, as it helps to attract tourists and maintain the residents' quality of life. As indicated in the work of Lucrezi et al. (2015), the existence of BF is generally well valued by tourists and destination businesses, which consider it an element of attraction. However, visitors are often unaware of the specific measures to be taken or the objectives to be met to obtain a BF award.

This lack of knowledge makes the third effect, which is the indirect effect, the most relevant to the literature. Merino and Prats (2022) mentioned that BF could be important for tourists in determining where to go. However, this factor is equally relevant that tourists unaware of their existence before traveling benefit from the commitment to sustainability and maintaining quality standards. These findings are shared by McKenna et al. (2011) for Ireland, Wales, Turkey, and the United States, and by Cabezas-Rabadán et al. (2019) for Spain. This result showed that BF awards are not motivating for traveling to a particular destination. However, the criteria required for such recognition (e.g., cleanliness or accessibility) are highly relevant

110 *Ana B. Ramón-Rodríguez et al.*

for tourists. Saayman and Saayman (2017) studied South African beaches. Their results also found that although tourists are unaware of whether or not a BF award exists, they value the attributes that are statistically most present at BF destinations, such as cleanliness, maintenance, infrastructure, location, accessibility, and popularity (Lucrezi and Saayman, 2015).

8.2.2 Criticism of BF policy

In the literature, we also find criticisms or ambiguous results on the effect of BF. The most decisive evidence is found when comparing BF beaches to other protected or undeveloped ones. For example, in the article by Dodds and Holmes (2019) carried out in Ontario, they observed that BF certification is not significant in bather satisfaction, but the fact that the beach is rural and not urban does have a positive effect on the final choice. This result is in line with Roig-Munar et al. (2018) and Mir-Gual et al. (2015), who found that obtaining BF recognition in Spain does not prevent the degradation of the natural landscape. Beaches with BF also tend to offer more activities and accommodation, access, and parking, which are detrimental to the peace that beaches far from urban centers have. Fraguell (2016) explained that this phenomenon is because the criteria for BF recognition "do not include essential characteristics of sustainable tourism, such as limiting the number of users or the preservation and restoration of sand ecosystems" (p. 882).

Klein and Dodds (2018) said that for municipalities in Canada and other countries, "the Blue Flag is not being used as a beach management tool for environmental protection [...], [they] are motivated to receive the Blue Flag for the tourism, promotion, and branding associated with the certification scheme" (p. 11). As highlighted in the work of Palazón et al. (2016) in the province of Alicante, natural beaches, that is, the most environmentally friendly ones, rarely have BF status.

In addition to this weakness in terms of nature protection, the relationship between BF and demand is mainly indirect and can increase the sustainability problems of destinations. Tourists are increasingly aware of the sustainability of the destinations they visit; therefore, environmentally friendly policies are useful and increasingly necessary (Iniesta-Bonillo et al., 2016; López-Sánchez & Pulido-Fernández, 2017). However, this factor is not yet decisive enough to correct market inefficiencies. Thus, public administrations need to act to reduce the diseconomies generated by the most polluting actions. For example, Karlsson and Dolnicar (2016) analyzed two boat trips in Iceland: with and without an eco-label. The results showed that only 19% of travelers' decisions are significantly affected by the pollution generated by boats, and 80% of travelers had not been informed of the existence of the eco-label on their trips. This type of "indifference" toward environmental sustainability in the choice of tourism demand has also been exposed in the study of Bernini et al. (2021) in the district of Rimini (Italy) or the research of Chamorro-Mera et al. (2019). These results indicated that tourists prefer not to pay additional tax for the conservation of the natural environment of the destinations they visit.

Impact of Blue Flags on local economy in Spain 111

However, not all tourists behave in the same way about environmental sustainability. For example, Castillo-Manzano et al. (2021) indicated that BF can be a "good indicator of quality and, therefore, of attracting foreign tourists" (p. 2214). However, domestic tourists tend to choose destinations for proximity and cultural reasons and not so much for the indicators that accredit beaches with sustainability labels. Raising the tourists' awareness of the importance of sustainability and respect for the environment should be a priority for destination managers.

In summary, the literature reviewed shows that BF exerts positive and negative effects on destinations. In general, the results suggest a direct link between a higher endowment of BF and the size of the tourism sector of destinations. However, no link exists when measuring the relationship between the destinations' BF and the well-being of their residents, a key aspect of their competitiveness.

8.3 Methodology

To analyze the economic impact of BF on the local economy we apply a two-step procedure on a case study: the Valencian Community. The first step, exploratory in nature, attempts to examine a broad set of relationships that may exist between the potential variables of interest, using the Structural Equation Modeling technique in the Partial Least Squares (PLS-SEM) version. The second step considers, through the analysis of dynamic panel data, the time dimension of the estimated model, overcoming the possible drawbacks derived from the static estimation of the first step and testing the robustness of the obtained results.

The advantages of analyzing a single tourism region help neutralize the effect of other possible variables or structural differences between destinations (product specialization, regional tourism policy, and so on), which can affect the conclusions linked to regional differences. This issue cold masks the phenomenon to be studied. The first subsection will justify using the Valencian Community as a case study. Then, in the second subsection, the two-step methodology will be explained in more detail.

8.3.1 BFs in Spain and Valencian Community as a case of study

Spain is fully committed to the recognition of its beaches with BF. As stated on the global BF website, Spain has the highest number of BF, that is, 615 in 2021, representing 45% of the total number of beaches in the country and more than 7 flags for every 100 km of coastline. In recent years, the Valencian Community has stood out as the region with the highest number of BF with more than 150, followed by Catalonia, Galicia, Andalusia, and the archipelagos (the Balearic Islands and the Canary Islands).

Considering the importance of BF in Spain, the study of their impact on Spanish tourist destinations has increased considerably in recent years. These studies analyze whether it has had an impact on tourist attractiveness or an increase in supply and whether it has had an impact on environment preservation. Table 8.1 summarizes some of these studies and the methodology used. To carry out this

112 Ana B. Ramón-Rodríguez et al.

Table 8.1 Literature review on studies of the impact of BF in Spain

Study	Methodology	Results
Rigall-i-Torrent (2011)	Ordinary Least Squares (OLS) using robust standard errors clustered by beach and time period. Data obtained from a sample of 197 coastal hotels in Costa Brava in 2002.	"Location close to a beach which has been awarded a Blue Flag increases hotel prices by 11.4–11.6%."
Mir-Gual et al. (2015)	Principal Component and Bray Curtis similarity analysis in 481 beaches of the Spanish coastline awarded with a Blue Flag. Period 2007–2012.	"Blue Flag award does not characterize an area for its natural conditions, the rewards only indicates that an areas includes a massive number of services fo their users. These kinds of awards should not be sold as eco-labels, but as quality labels of services offered to the bathers ir artificial and urban beaches."
Cabezas-Rabadán et al. (2019)	Descriptive analysis of 264 interviews in six beaches in Valencia, distinguished according to their degree of artificialization (urban or semi-natural)	"Users showed a significant lack of knowledge with regard to beaches' possession of Blue Flag"
Chamorro-Mera et al. (2019)	Conjoint analysis of 819 interviews in Spain and Portugal (District of Leiria and Region of Extremadura). Period: 2010.	"The Blue Flag can be considered as a good tool to manage the balance between the respect for the natural environment and the enjoyment of tourists and residents ot a sun-and-sand tourist destination."
Álvarez-Díaz et al. (2020)	Six models: gravity model, spatial autoregressive model (SAR), spatial error model (SE), spatial Durbin model (SD), spatial Durbin error model, and spatial lag X model (SLX). Data from domestic tourism trips in Spanish provinces. Period: 2011–2013.	"Blue Flags have positive and highly significant impacts on interprovincial trips." The estimated coefficient for the variable Blue Flags fluctuates between 0.02 (SE, SD, and SDE models) to 0.04 (gravity model).
Merino and Prats (2020)	Descriptive comparison of some variables that capture the economic development of the local tourism industry in the coastal municipalities of the Valencian Region. Period: 2003–2013	"Blue Flag recognition has a positive impact on the economic development of the tourism sector in those municipalities that have opted for more sustainable tourism, whereas municipalities that have not introduced any sustainable ecolabel schemes have had lesser development of tourism."
Castillo-Manzano et al. (2021)	Panel data for the 22 Spanish coastal provinces. Period: 2000–2019	"Blue Flags are effective at promoting international tourism but not domestic tourism"
Merino and Prats (2022)	Equality test and OLS, heteroskedasticity robust of 5,246 Mediterranean coastal monitoring points. Period: 2019.	"The results of the study have shown that along the bathing season, [...] Blue Flags areas have significantly cleaner waters than those monitoring points that are not in such areas. This difference is due to Spain and France, while in Italy there is no difference among the two areas."

Impact of Blue Flags on local economy in Spain 113

research, we select the Valencian Community as a case study for 2013–2019. This region has the highest number of BF in Spain, with almost 20% of the total BFs in Spain, while the coastline of this region barely represents 4% of the total coastline of Spain.

8.3.2 Models, estimation methods, and hypotheses

As described above, after a brief exploratory analysis, two different exercises are proposed to examine the effects of BF on the local economy. First, we estimate a PLS-SEM model. The PLS-SEM model is part of the family of structural equation models (SEM) which consist of a set of linear structural equations that allow to accommodate the relationship among the potential variables (observed and unobserved) of interest.

Variables in the equation system may be either directly observed variables – as is the case in this exercise – or unmeasured latent (theoretical) variables that are not observed but relate to observed variables. The measurement model and the structural equation model are the SEM model's two standard components. The measurement model describes the relationship between latent variables and the observed variables. It describes the reliability and validity of the observed variables' measurement qualities. On the other hand, the causal links between the latent (or the observed) variables are described in the structural equation model (showed as a figure with arrows and path coefficients) together with the causal effects and the variance's explained and unexplained components.

In this chapter, the method relates BF (the variable of interest in this chapter) to the main economic variables representative of the destination's tourism sector (Table 8.2), namely, its accommodation infrastructure (apartments and hotels) and the per capita income of the destination's inhabitants (the final endogenous variable of the model). Since all variables are observed, the measurement model is not estimated, and only the structure model will be showed.

According to Hair et al. (2017), PLS-SEM is a modality within SEM that makes no distributional assumptions (it is a non-parametric method), works with many data types (i.e., scale data, as is the case in this paper), easily incorporates reflective and formative measurement models, and achieves higher levels of statistical power with small sample sizes (as is also the case in this paper) than its covariance-based SEM counterpart method (CB-SEM). In PLS-SEM, the model is estimated using an algorithm that minimizes the amount of unexplained variance (i.e., maximizes the R^2 values) and suffers fewer convergence problems, even in complex model situations or with many datasets. However, one of the main disadvantages of the technique is that it lacks a general measure of the goodness-of-fit of the estimated model.

According to Hair et al. (2017), in contrast to the CB-SEM method, which is mainly used to confirm or reject theories, PLS-SEM is used to develop theories in exploratory research. The PLS-SEM model is static in nature. However, given the temporal stability or persistence of the per capita income variable in the destinations, researchers decided to incorporate the population of the destination and a

114　*Ana B. Ramón-Rodríguez et al.*

Table 8.2 PLS-SEM analysis on the impact of BF in Spain: Variables

Variable	Description	Source
Dependent variable:		
Income	Per capita income of residents at destinations	Spanish Tax Administration (Agencia Estatal de Administración Tribuataria)
Explanatory variables:		
Blue Flags	Number of Blue Flags in each destination	Fundación de Educación Ambiental
Apartaments	Number of bedplaces in apartments at destinations	Municipal and Regional Tourist Offer, Statistical Portal of the Generalitat Valenciana
Hotel	Number of bedplaces in hotels at destinations	Municipal and Regional Tourist Offer, Statistical Portal of the Generalitat Valenciana
Population	Registered population of tourist destinations	Spanish National Institute of Statistics

deterministic linear trend as control variables in this model. This first model aims to contrast the picture of relationships pointed out by the exploratory analysis.

In a second exercise, to consider the dynamic nature of the relationship between the variables and test the robustness of the results, the number of dynamic panel data models is estimated using various methods (e.g., pooled OLS, fixed effects, and generalized method of moments [GMM]) with various controls. The dependent variable used in these models is the per capita income of the inhabitants of the destination. The explanatory variables are a more or less extensive set that includes the supply of accommodation (apartments and hotel vacancies), the destination's population, and the destination's BF, which is the real variable of interest in the models.

In particular, a model of the form is estimated as follows:

$$Income_{it} = \delta Income_{i, t-1} + \beta Blue\ Flags_{it} + \gamma\ Controls_{it} + \mu_{it},$$

where $i = 1, ..., N; t = 1, ..., T$, and $\mu_{it} = \mu_i + v_{it}$, and the lagged values of the dependent variable attempt to control for all the relevant economic covariates not included in the equations (e.g., the labor productivity, development level of the destination, and an average level of education). These covariates are unobservable due to the lack of available data at the municipal level and would cause problems (mostly collinearity) in estimations.

The inclusion of the lagged dependent variable on the right-hand side is correlated with the error term, which makes the OLS estimator biased and inconsistent (Baltagi, 2021: p. 187), regardless of whether v_{it} is serially correlated or not. The bias is not solved using the Fixed effect (Within) estimator, which is still biased by $O(1/T)$ (Nickell, 1981). Given these drawbacks, the standard practice has been to estimate these models using instrumental variables and the GMM (Arellano & Bond, 1991), as well as the more efficient GMM-SYS method of Blundell and Bond (1998).

Impact of Blue Flags on local economy in Spain 115

The hypothesis tested in the estimated dynamic models is H_0: $\beta = 0$ versus H_1: $\beta \neq 0$. In the structural equation model, in addition to the coefficient relating the number of BF to income, the coefficients relating BF to the number of hotel and apartment vacancies representative of the highest degree of tourism development in the destination are also examined.

8.4 Results

8.4.1 Exploratory analysis

Table 8.3 shows the descriptive statistics, which indicate that the average number of BF for all destinations during the period is 2, with a significant dispersion with a maximum of 12. The sample consists of 58 destinations analyzed for 2013–2019 (a total of 348 observations), this period being the only one for which the per capita income is available. Regarding per capita income, the dependent variable in the estimated models, the average is 18,783 euros, although significant dispersion is observed between destinations with a maximum of 30,276 euros. The table also shows the majority nature of the extra hotels offered in the tourist destinations of the Valencian Community, with the average number of places in apartments considerably higher than in hotels. These destinations also vary significantly in size, as shown by the current dispersion and an average of 43,760 inhabitants.

Table 8.4 shows the correlations among various variables. Following the existing literature, the positive correlations between the number of flags a destination has and its tourism infrastructure measured by hotel and apartment vacancies are statistically significant. This variable also shows a statistically significant positive correlation with population. This result suggests that BF is concentrated in larger and more established tourist destinations. However, the table shows a negative correlation (although statistically insignificant) between the number of BF in the destination and the per capita income of the destination. This result suggests that a higher degree of tourism development does not always translate to greater well-being or better quality of life for the destination's residents.

8.4.2 Structural equation model PLS-SEM

The results of the exploratory analysis are reproduced in the PLS-SEM structural equation model shown in Figure 8.1. As mentioned above, the model relates BF

Table 8.3 PLS-SEM analysis on the impact of BF in Spain: Descriptive analysis

Variable	Mean	Std. dev	Minimum	Maximum
Blue Flags	2.32	2.30	0	12
Income	18,783.60	2,701.78	13,723	30,276
Apartment	4,197.16	6,222.70	0	31,750
Hotel	1,846.09	5,673.05	0	42,095
Population	43,760.32	111,696.10	472	794,288

116 *Ana B. Ramón-Rodríguez et al.*

Table 8.4 PLS-SEM analysis on the impact of BF in Spain: Correlation analysis

	Blue Flags	*Income*	*Apartment*	*Hotel*	*Population*
Blue Flags	1				
Income	−0.0197	1			
Apartment	0.4999	0.0254	1		
Hotel	0.2090	0.0723	0.6219	1	
Population	0.4213	0.2495	0.2613	0.3915	1

with hotel and apartment vacancies and per capita income of the destinations for 2013–2019 and the Valencia region. The model also controls for the population of the destinations and a linear trend that reflects the evolution of the per capita income of the destinations (it tries to reflect the dynamics of the model without being a dynamic model). The arrows indicate the direction of the estimated relationship, and the path coefficient is interpreted like a standardized regression coefficient.

As shown in the figure, the analysis of BF's influence on income shows that a direct path (has a negative coefficient) and two indirect paths have been estimated for each type of accommodation supply (hotels and apartments).

Table 8.5 shows the estimated coefficients and p-values obtained after performing a bootstrap process based on 500 replications. The original sample mean (O) reflects the original coefficient in Figure 8.1 and the sample mean (M) reflects the average coefficient over all bootstrapping runs. The small differences point out that no bias exists between original sample coefficient and sampling distribution. The table shows how positive and significant coefficients are again reproduced between the number of BF and the tourism development of the destinations (apartments and hotels). However, in this model, the direct coefficient relating BF to the per capita income of the destinations becomes negative and statistically significant (as occurs with apartments). This could imply that, even though obtaining Blue Flags could be an indicator of tourism competitiveness, destinations with greater specialization in the tourism sector have lower welfare than those with a more diversified industry.

On the other hand, the estimated model also points to a positive relationship between the hotel offer of the destination and its per capita income and a negative one for the case of the apartments offer. This could suggest, in principle, that destination managers should prioritize a tourism development model based on the hotel offer over the extra-hotel offer to improve the well-being of the destination's residents. However, given that no coefficient (neither that of apartments nor that of hotels) reaches statistical significance, the obtained results would point, with the data at hand, to the neutrality of the chosen tourism development model on the level of well-being of the destination's residents.

8.4.3 Dynamic panel data models

Finally, Table 8.6 reproduces the results of various dynamic models estimated using panel data analysis techniques. Columns (1) and (2) represent the basic model (without controls) and the extended model (adding the covariates of population,

Impact of Blue Flags on local economy in Spain 117

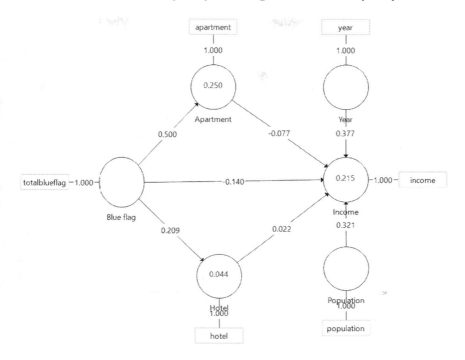

Figure 8.1 PLS-SEM: Results of the exploratory analysis in Spain

Table 8.5 PLS-SEM analysis on the impact of BF in Spain: Path coefficients and bootstrap p-values (basic bootstrapping 500 reps)

	Original sample (O)	Sample mean (M)	Standard deviation (STDEV)	t statistics (|O/STDEV|)	p-values
Apartment → Income	−0.077	−0.076	0.053	1.467	0.143
Blue Flags → Apartment	0.500	0.500	0.034	14.872	0.000
Blue Flags → Hotel	0.209	0.214	0.040	5.280	0.000
Blue Flags → Income	−0.140	−0.143	0.061	2.298	0.022
Hotel → Income	0.022	0.022	0.034	0.642	0.521
Population → Income	0.321	0.320	0.060	5.347	0.000
Trend → Income	0.377	0.375	0.038	10.027	0.000

apartments, and hotels) estimated by OLS, respectively. Neither of these estimates incorporates time dummies. Both estimates point to a negative and significant coefficient of BF on destination income, although the estimates obtained by this method are, in this context, biased and inconsistent.

Columns (3) and (4) are the estimates of the extended model with controls for population, apartments, and hotels estimated by fixed effect. The difference between the two estimates is that column (4) adds time dummies to column (3). The results still point to a negative coefficient, which is substantially larger than

118 *Ana B. Ramón-Rodríguez et al.*

that obtained by OLS but insignificant. As mentioned, the estimates obtained by these methods are still biased.

Column (5) reflects the estimation of the model by using the two-step SYS-GMM method of Blundell and Bond (1998). In this estimation, all variables (except time dummies) are considered endogenous and are therefore incorporated as GMM-type instruments. The diagnostic of the model is satisfactory. To reduce the proliferation of instruments, we use the collapse option, resulting in a total of 31 instruments less than the 348 observations and 58 destinations that make up the sample. This result is reflected in the fact that neither the Sargan nor Hansen test is significant. The Arellano–Bond test for AR(1) in first differences is statistically significant ($z = -1.69$, $p = 0.09$) but not the Arellano–Bond for AR(2) ($z = 1.13$, $p = 0.26$). Otherwise, this model agrees with the previous models in the negative coefficient of the BF variable, which is significant at 10% but not at 5%.

In summary, the estimated models point to negative coefficients between BF and the per capita income of the destinations, even after introducing control variables, such as population, flat vacancies, and hotel vacancies. However, in the correlation analysis and the estimated structural model, positive and logical correlations are observed between the number of BF of the destination and its degree of tourism development (measured by its number of hotel or flat vacancies). Therefore, the

Table 8.6 Dynamic panel data model on the impact of BF in Spain: Results

	Dependent variable: Income				
	(1)	*(2)*	*(3)*	*(4)*	*(5)*
	Pooled OLS	*Pooled OLS with controls*	*Within*	*Within time dummies*	*Two step SYS-GMM*
Constant	325.2	369.9	7,273**	19,005.6***	14,079.2***
	(515.4)	(584.7)	(3,207)	(2,442)	(2,998.88)
Income (−1)	1.010***	1.008***	0.7207***	−0.002530	0.1995
	(0.02831)	(0.03203)	(0.1581)	(0.1185)	(0.1712)
Blue Flags	−20.45*	−29.33*	−144.5	−136.3	−274.3*
	(11.04)	(16.50)	(135.3)	(110.9)	(141.9)
Population		0.0002443	−0.03615	0.03516	0.01110*
		(0.0003162)	(0.03514)	(0.03684)	(0.00575)
Hotel		−0.004135	−0.02562	0.1226	−0.05485
		(0.002751)	(0.2265)	(0.2149)	(0.07316)
Apartments		0.004229	0.08498**	−0.01069	0.00094**
		(0.003899)	(0.03923)	(0.01828)	(0.02421)
Number of observ.	348	348	348	348	348
Adjusted R^2	0.9072	0.9065	0.5032	0.7213	
lnL	−2831	−2831	−2805	−2704	

Notes: Standard errors in parentheses
* Significant at the 10% level ** significant at the 5% level *** significant at the 1% level;
(1) Pooled OLS without controls; (2) pooled OLS with controls; (3) One-way fixed-effects;
(4) Two-ways fixed effects; (5) Two-step System-GMM with time dummies.

Impact of Blue Flags on local economy in Spain 119

most likely conclusion from the results obtained is that although BF boosts tourism development or is associated with the most popular tourist destinations, it is not reflected in the per capita income of the destinations.

8.5 Conclusions

To analyze the effects of BF on the tourism sector and the economic growth of the destination, we use two exercises: a structural equation model with the PLS method. To consider the dynamics of the relationship, we use various dynamic panel data models (i.e., pooled OLS, fixed effects, and GMM). This study constitutes a considerable advance concerning similar studies such as Merino and Prats (2020) because it updates the number of years analyzed and adds a more detailed and complete methodological exercise. We use PLS-SEM structural equations and incorporate the income variable to measure the effect on tourism and the welfare of the residents of the destinations of the Valencian Community.

In line with the studies consulted, statistically, significant positive correlations are found between the number of BF a destination has and its tourism infrastructure measured by hotel and flat vacancies. The study also shows a concentration of the number of BF in consolidated and larger destinations. However, the results point to a negative correlation with per capita income. This result implies that better tourism development in a destination does not always translate into a better quality of life for its residents.

Meanwhile, the results suggest that the relationship between BF and the per capita income of the destination is conditioned by the tourism development model chosen by the destination. Thus, a greater supply of extra-hotel accommodation would be associated with lower per capita income levels. The majority of extra-hotel accommodation in the tourist destinations of the Valencian Community region is also extra-hotel, with the average number of beds in flats considerably higher than in hotels.

Thus, the results show that although BF boost tourism development, they do not automatically lead to an increase in per capita income in these destinations.

8.6 References

Alegre, J., & Garau, J. (2010). Tourist satisfaction and dissatisfaction. *Annals of Tourism Research*, 37(1), 52–73. doi:10.1016/j.annals.2009.07.001

Álvarez-Díaz, M., D'Hombres, B., Ghisetti, C., & Pontarollo, N. (2020). Analysing domestic tourism flows at the provincial level in Spain by using spatial gravity models. *International Journal of Tourism Research*, 22(4), 403–415.

Arellano, M. & Bond, S. (1991). Some test of specification for panel data: Monte Carlo evidence and application to employment equations. Review *of Economic Studies*, 58(2), 277–297.

Baltagi, B. H. (2021). *Econometric analysis of panel data* (6th ed). Wiley and Sons.

Bernini, C., Emili, S., & Vici, L. (2021). Are mass tourists sensitive to sustainability? *Tourism Economics*, 27(7), 1375–1397.

Blackman, A., Naranjo, M. A., Robalino, J., Alpízar, F., & Rivera, J. (2014). Does tourism eco-certification pay? Costa Rica's Blue Flag program. *World Development*, 58, 41–52.

120 *Ana B. Ramón-Rodríguez et al.*

Blundell, R., & Bond, S. (1998). Initial conditions and moment restrictions in dynamic panel data models. *Journal of Econometrics*, 87, 115–143.

Cabezas-Rabadán, C., Rodilla, M., Pardo-Pascual, J. E., & Herrera-Racionero, P. (2019). Assessing users' expectations and perceptions on different beach types and the need for diverse management frameworks along the Western Mediterranean. *Land Use Policy*, 81, 219–231.

Capacci, S., Scorcu, A. E., & Vici, L. (2015). Seaside tourism and eco-labels: The economic impact of Blue Flags. *Tourism Management*, 47, 88–96.

Castillo-Manzano, J. I., Castro-Nuño, M., López-Valpuesta, L., & Zarzoso, Á. (2021). Measuring the role of Blue Flags in attracting sustainable "sun-and-sand" tourism. *Current Issues in Tourism*, 24(15), 2204–2222.

Chamorro-Mera, A., Nobre de Oliveira, V., & García-Gallego, J. M. (2019). The Blue Flag label as a tool to improve the quality of life in the sun-and-sand tourist destinations. In *Best Practices in Hospitality and Tourism Marketing and Management* (pp. 255–274). Springer.

Dodds, R., & Holmes, M. R. (2019). Beach tourists; what factors satisfy them and drive them to return. *Ocean & Coastal Management*, 168, 158–166.

Font, X. (2002). Environmental certification in tourism and hospitality: Progress, process and prospects. *Tourism Management*, 23, 197–205. doi: 10.1016/S0261–5177(01)00084-X

Fraguell, R. M., Martí, C., Pintó, J., & Coenders, G. (2016). After over 25 years of accrediting beaches, has Blue Flag contributed to sustainable management? *Journal of Sustainable Tourism*, 24(6), 882–903.

Goffi, G., Cladera, M., & Pencarelli, T. (2019) Does sustainability matter to package tourists? The case of large-scale coastal tourism. *International Journal of Tourism Research*, 21, 544–559. https://doi.org/10.1002/jtr.2281

Hall, C. M. (2019). Constructing sustainable tourism development: The 2030 agenda and the managerial ecology of sustainable tourism. *Journal of Sustainable Tourism*, 27(7), 1044–1060.

Iniesta-Bonillo, M. A., Sánchez-Fernández, R., & Jiménez-Castillo, D. (2016). Sustainability, value, and satisfaction: Model testing and cross-validation in tourist destinations. *Journal of Business Research*, 69(11), 5002–5007.

Karlsson, L., & Dolnicar, S. (2016). Does eco certification sell tourism services? Evidence from a quasi-experimental observation study in Iceland. *Journal of Sustainable Tourism*, 24(5), 694–714.

Klein, L., & Dodds, R. (2018). Blue Flag beach certification: An environmental management tool or tourism promotional tool?. *Tourism Recreation Research*, 43(1), 39–51.

Kozak, M., & Rimmington, M. (1999). Measuring tourist destination competitiveness: Conceptual considerations and empirical findings. *International Journal of Hospitality Management*, 18, 273–283.

López-Sánchez, Y., & Pulido-Fernández, J. I. (2017). Factors influencing the willingness to pay for sustainable tourism: a case of mass tourism destinations. *International Journal of Sustainable Development & World Ecology*, 24(3), 262–275.

Lucrezi, S., & Saayman, M. (2015). Beachgoers' demands vs. Blue Flag aims in South Africa. *Journal of Coastal Research*, 31(6), 1478–1488.

Lucrezi, S., Saayman, M., & Van der Merwe, P. (2015). Managing beaches and beachgoers: Lessons from and for the Blue Flag award. *Tourism Management*, 48, 211–230.

McKenna, J., Williams, A. T., & Cooper, J. A. G. (2011). Blue Flag or Red Herring: Do beach awards encourage the public to visit beaches? *Tourism Management*, 32(3), 576–588.

Merino, F., & Prats, M. A. (2020). Sustainable beach management and promotion of the local tourist industry: Can Blue Flags be a good driver of this balance? *Ocean & Coastal Management*, 198, 105359.

Merino, F., & Prats, M. A. (2022). Are Blue Flags a good indicator of the quality of sea water on beaches? An empirical analysis of the Western Mediterranean basin. *Journal of Cleaner Production*, 330, 129865.

Mir-Gual, M., Pons, G. X., Martín-Prieto, J. A., & Rodríguez-Perea, A. (2015). A critical view of the Blue Flag beaches in Spain using environmental variables. *Ocean & Coastal Management*, 105, 106–115.

Nickell, S. (1981). Biases in dynamic models with fixed effects. *Econometrica*, 49, 1417–1426.

Palazón, A., Aragonés, L., & López, I. (2016). Evaluation of coastal management: Study case in the province of Alicante, Spain. *Science of the Total Environment*, 572, 1184–1194.

Rigall-i-Torrent, R., Fluvià, M., Ballester, R., Saló, A., Ariza, E., & Espinet, J. M. (2011). The effects of beach characteristics and location with respect to hotel prices. *Tourism Management*, 32(5), 1150–1158.

Roig-Munar, F. X., Fraile-Jurado, P., & Peña-Alonso, C. (2018). Analysis of Blue Flag beaches compared with natural beaches in the Balearic Islands and Canary Islands, Spain. In *Beach Management Tools-concepts, Methodologies and Case Studies* (pp. 545–559). Springer.

Saayman, M., & Saayman, A. (2017). How important are Blue Flag awards in beach choice? *Journal of Coastal Research*, 33(6), 1436–1447.

Torres-Bejarano, F., González-Márquez, L. C., Díaz-Solano, B., Torregroza-Espinosa, A. C., & Cantero-Rodelo, R. (2018). Effects of beach tourists on bathing water and sand quality at Puerto Velero, Colombia. *Environment, Development and Sustainability*, 20, 255–269. https://doi.org/10.1007/s10668-016-9880-x

Turisme Comunitat Valenciana/Exceltur. (2020). IMPACTUR Comunitat Valenciana, 2019, Valencia.

Zielinski, S., & Botero, C. M. (2019). Myths, misconceptions and the true value of Blue Flag. *Ocean & Coastal Management*, 147, 15–24, https://doi.org/10.1016/j.ocecoaman.2019.03.012

9 Blue Flag supporting implementation of environmental policies and nature conservation

The case of Greece

Nikos Petrou, Dareia-Nefeli Vourdoumpa and Chara Agaoglou

9.1 Introduction

Greece was one of the first ten countries to participate in the "Blue Flags of Europe", as the program was known when it started in 1987. The Hellenic Marine Environment Protection Association (HELMEPA) was the first National Operator; however, in 1991, it decided to withdraw due to increasing difficulties in implementing the program. At that time, the Ministry of the Environment, Urban Planning and Public Works was keen for the program to continue because it supported its efforts to implement the Bathing Water Directive (76/160/EEC), so it approached the Hellenic Society for the Protection of Nature (HSPN) to take over as National Operator. The proposal was enthusiastically supported by Peter Brussalis, then Vice President of the HSPN, was approved by its Board of Directors, and the HSPN became a member of FEEE in 1992. Aliki Vavouris was recruited as Blue Flag director, a position she successfully held for almost 15 years, playing a crucial role in the growth of the program.

The two main goals of HSPN, since its founding in 1951, are nature conservation and environmental education, and it implements a variety of relevant national and cross-border projects. Upon becoming the National Operator in Greece, it focused on addressing the challenges and ensuring growth of the program; the number of awarded sites grew rapidly and over the last 15 years Greece has consistently been in second place among the participating countries. Additionally, HSPN has used Blue Flag as a tool to support acceptance and application of environmental regulations and policies, and to leverage species and habitat conservation in the coastal environment, often engaging the international network as well.

9.2 Managing the early challenges

A significant challenge during the first years of running the Blue Flag was engaging the local authorities and gaining their acceptance and support, because they often perceived participation in the program, with its strict requirements, as an additional, unnecessary burden with little return. The entrenched bureaucracy and the cumbersome processes of government at all levels posed further obstacles, and

DOI: 10.4324/9781003323570-10

there was considerable mistrust of the control system and the transparency of the awards. Ensuring compliance with the criteria was, and still occasionally is, a contentious issue with local authorities, especially when flags are withdrawn. In the early years, there were numerous complaints, often accompanied by volatile criticism in local media, regarding control visits, especially the unannounced ones by international controllers. These obstacles were reflected in the number of awarded beaches and marinas in the early years: from a promising 51 at the start of the program in 1987, down to 15 in 1988 and 14 in 1989.

Participation increased in 1990 and reached 189 sites in 1991. When HSPN took over, the sites jumped to 240 and have been steadily growing ever since.

Winning over the local authorities and tackling bureaucracy required persistence and considerable effort – in fact for some areas it is still an ongoing process. Demonstrating the direct environmental benefits, but also the importance and strength of the Blue Flag as a promotional and marketing tool for a destination, and the resulting benefits for local stakeholders, is crucial in that respect. However, a consistent policy by the Ministry of Tourism to support ecolabels as valuable tools in promoting the country's touristic product, through incentives and/or direct assistance, is still lacking. This poses barriers in achieving the Blue Flag's full potential in Greece.

Despite improvements, bureaucratic procedures still occasionally prevent municipal authorities from complying with imperative criteria, leading to loss of the Blue Flag. A typical example is the seasonal contracting of lifeguards, which is frequently delayed until well into the bathing season, or even towards its end, because of the complicated tendering procedures.

Year after year, with continued support and encouragement from HSPN, the commitment and engagement of the beach managers to the program increased. Local authorities and site managers now strive to maintain the high standards of the program and improve their quality. The accumulated expertise also enabled HSPN to serve as a mentor for new members entering the program in the region, such as the Cyprus Marine Environment Protection Association and the Bulgarian Blue Flag Movement.

In 2022, Greece had a total of 602 Blue Flag awards – 581 beaches, 15 marinas and 6 Tourism Boats – thus ranking second among the 48 countries participating in the program globally.

9.3 Aiding national authorities to implement environmental policies

Greece is unique among Mediterranean countries for its diverse geomorphology and the complexity of its coastline. At the apex of the Balkan peninsula, it is surrounded by the Aegean Sea to the east of the mainland, the Ionian Sea to the west, and the Cretan, Libyan and Mediterranean Seas to the south. The seas are dotted with thousands of islands, and Greece has the longest coastline in the Mediterranean Basin, almost 16,000km; it is the second longest in Europe after Norway.

When the program started, compliance with the requirements of Directive 76/160/EEC regarding the frequency of the water sampling, the methodology and

124 *Nikos Petrou et al.*

the quality of results was difficult to achieve in a country with so many islands that created many transportation challenges, but also with a low number of certified laboratories.

During its first steps as National Operator, HSPN had to cope with all the difficulties regarding water quality assessment, as well as cooperate with the Ministry of the Environment to establish an effective system for the sampling. Its first year as National Operator, 1992, was very important because, at that time, all participating countries agreed to fulfil the same criteria from the start of the bathing season. Several years went by before a reliable, efficient policy was set in place, with the close cooperation and support of FEE. This is a textbook example of how a national NGO and an international organization can collaborate with central government to improve national policies and compliance to EU regulations, using the Blue Flag as a tool to achieve change.

Another example of how HSPN assists the administration in implementing EU and national environmental policy through the Blue Flag has to do with the management of protected areas. Many of the beaches applying for the Blue Flag in Greece fall within or are adjacent to NATURA 2000 sites. Under the current system, these sites are administered by local Management Units (MUs) under the overall control of the Natural Environment and Climate Change Agency connected to the Ministry of the Environment. The MUs monitor the areas, but, unfortunately, do not have any enforcing or policing jurisdiction, and depend on other competent authorities (e.g., police, coast guard) in cases of illegal activities, such as infringement on protected dune habitats, damage to Posidonia meadows, etc. In many cases, the MUs in cooperation with HSPN use the Blue Flag criteria to force site administrators (usually municipal authorities) to change their management practices. For instance, two years ago, the MU for the Protected Areas of Central Macedonia informed HSPN about the degradation of sand dunes, caused by illegal vehicle and foot traffic and vegetation trampling, within a protected area on the coastline of Thermaikos Gulf, next to a Blue Flag beach. HSPN intervened with the responsible municipality, and asked that measures be taken, otherwise the award would be withdrawn. Eventually, the municipality lost the Blue Flag for that beach and is now working closely with the MU on enforcing access restrictions and undertaking actions for the protection and restoration of the dunes. When these are completed, the beach will again be able to apply for the Blue Flag.

Moreover, several Blue Flag beaches in Greece are nesting areas for sea turtles. HSPN works closely with ARCHELON, the Sea Turtle Protection Society of Greece. ARCHELON is represented on the National Jury and has often brought up cases of non-compliance regarding activities detrimental to the sea turtles and their habitats. Along the coastline of northern Crete, Blue Flag beach managers comply with the management measures for the protection of the species, such as removing beach loungers and umbrellas at night, turning off lighting and reducing evening disturbance at the beaches. As of 2023, the loggerhead turtle population in that area is stable, but not showing signs of increase, due to dense coastal development and the high impact of tourism activities beyond the Blue Flag sites.

Blue Flag supporting environmental policies: The Greek case   125

9.4 Using the Blue Flag program to protect a unique Mediterranean natural resource

Coastal zones are among the most productive areas in the world, offering a wide variety of valuable habitats and ecosystems services, and have always attracted humans and their activities, becoming popular settlement areas and tourist destinations, major commercial zones and transit points.

Thus, they are subject to increasing pressures from a variety of sources, including industrial development, urban expansion, the exploitation of marine resources and tourism. They are also among the most vulnerable areas to natural hazards and climate change. Risks include flooding, erosion and sea level rise, all exacerbated by extreme weather events. These impacts are far-reaching and are already changing the lives and livelihoods of coastal communities.

In the Mediterranean basin, approximately 150 million people reside in coastal regions, about one-third of the population of the littoral countries in only 15% of their area (EEA-UNEP/MAP, 2014). This high concentration of population and the excessive exploitation of natural resources places enormous pressure on the coastal ecosystems, leading to biodiversity loss, habitat destruction, pollution, as well as conflicts between potential uses, and land use problems.

Tourism and recreation in the Mediterranean are connected with "sea and sun", and are recognized as significant contributors to economic growth. However, tourism has been shown to also have adverse impacts on the environment. During the summer season, the population in many of the region's popular destinations increases exponentially, and local governments struggle to provide the necessary resources. Demands of visitors and local users for "clean" beaches also often lead to management actions that damage sensitive coastal habitats or lead to increased erosion.

In the waters of the Mediterranean lives an endemic plant that is uniquely able to support biodiversity, improve water quality, enhance coastal structural integrity and habitat resilience, and contribute towards climate change adaptation by sequestering large quantities of carbon.

Posidonia oceanica, commonly known as Neptune grass, is a very selective species that requires clean, transparent waters and is very sensitive to pollution and other pressures. It forms remarkable underwater meadows, known as Posidonia meadows, beds or prairies, whose presence is an ideal indicator of ecosystem health and water quality.

Posidonia meadows are some of the richest and most valuable ecosystems in the Mediterranean. They provide food and shelter to marine life, serve as nurseries for countless species, and act as a natural water filtration system that traps particles and pathogenic microorganisms. They also reduce swell and wave strength, resulting in enhanced sand deposition and beach progradation, thus protecting the coastline from erosion. Because of their essential functions, but also because of the threats they face, Posidonia meadows are designated as a priority habitat type for conservation under the EU Habitats Directive (92/43/EEC).

This seagrass forms, in the lower part of the meadows, a structure called "matte", consisting of interlaced remnants of roots, rhizomes and entangled sediments.

It has been reported that some 50% of the carbon sequestered in marine sediments around the world is stored inside seagrass mattes. Their ability to remove carbon dioxide from the atmosphere means that mattes are excellent carbon sinks; therefore their conservation represents an effective strategy to combat climate change. In addition to abiotic factors, such as ocean acidification, Posidonia meadows are threatened by direct anthropogenic impacts, including pollution and mechanical damage by anchoring and improper use of fishing gear. Over the last decades, following increased coastal urbanization and industrialization, many meadows have disappeared or have been degraded. It is estimated that 46% of the underwater meadows in the Mediterranean have experienced some reduction in range, density and/or coverage, and 20% have severely regressed since the 1970s (Díaz-Almela & Duarte, 2008).

As a flowering plant, *Posidonia oceanica* regularly sheds its leaves and other parts, some of which are washed ashore according to local hydrodynamics. This material accumulates on the shoreline, mixed with sand, usually forming a strip that runs parallel to the water's edge. On sandy shores, these wrack deposits can vary from relatively thin and sparse sheets (beach-cast) to extensive wedge-shaped structures, up to several meters thick, commonly known as "banquettes". Posidonia banquettes are a vital contribution to the health and balance of the beach-dune system, as they protect the coasts from erosion, form and stabilize beaches and dunes, fertilize and moisten the coastal and dune vegetation, and create a unique habitat that supports biodiversity.

The assemblage of near-shore Posidonia meadows, beach with banquette formation and associated dunes, collectively referred to as the Posidonia littoral zone, is a valuable natural asset providing diverse ecosystem services. It is also a neglected and threatened ecological system, whose importance is, with rare exceptions, underappreciated.

Climate change is known to have adverse impacts on the beach-dune systems, including increasing susceptibility to erosion, shoreline regression, loss of habitats and saltwater intrusion. Human constructions have reduced natural wave buffering zones in many of these places, and interfere with longshore sediment transport, making urban beaches particularly vulnerable.

The Posidonia littoral zone plays a significant role in decreasing storm forces. Healthy meadows will supply cast material for beaches which, along with well-vegetated dunes, provide the best protection and adaptation against rising sea levels, coastal erosion, and storm surge occurrences, especially where coasts retreat in response to rising sea levels. However, Posidonia wrack and banquettes are often perceived as a deterrent for beach users and are removed by local administrators, frequently by using heavy machinery which causes significant damage to the shoreline and increases risk of erosion. Additionally, the lack of awareness regarding the threats that *Posidonia oceanica* faces, and the vital services it provides to the coastal landscape, causes substantial conservation concerns.

Clearly we are at a tipping point, at which prioritization for the conservation of species and habitat types will only be effective if accompanied by specific actions. Indeed, there is an increasing demand among many Mediterranean coastal

Blue Flag supporting environmental policies: The Greek case   127

municipalities and stakeholders for more sustainable and economically viable solutions for the long-term management of Posidonia banquettes. Thus, the adoption of conservation policies and management strategies that offer better ways of managing the Mediterranean coastal landscape and decreasing impacts, is essential.

Within this context, the HSPN joined forces with seven other institutions across six Mediterranean countries (Greece, France, Italy, Spain, Croatia and Cyprus) to implement the InterregMED projects PosBeMed (2016–2018) and POSBEMED2 (2019–2022). Blue Flag International was an associated partner in POSBEMED2.

These two projects stemmed from the controversy around the presence of *Posidonia oceanica* remnants on Mediterranean beaches, and aimed to develop an effective framework for the protection and sustainable management of the Posidonia littoral zone, balancing environmental, economic, social and recreational objectives. HSPN, as the only Blue Flag National Operator among the project partners, had the opportunity to disseminate the results to the international Blue Flag network, as well as propose new criteria to protect, sustainably manage and restore the Posidonia littoral zone.

During the PosBeMed project, HSPN utilized the Blue Flag network to send questionnaires to all beach managers and visitors in the Mediterranean countries to assess attitudes. These surveys showed that as much as 83% of coastal municipalities remove banquettes from beaches. In most cases, removal operations involve heavy (44%) or light (40%) machinery. At the same time, a large percentage of beachgoers (44%) are unaware of the ecological role of banquettes in the formation and maintenance of beaches, and in preventing beach erosion. Meanwhile, the concept of a Posidonia-free beach corresponds more to stakeholders' and decision-makers' perceptions of what beach users would expect, than to actual beach users' attitudes. Notably, 41% of the beach users want the banquettes removed; the rest either have a positive attitude (26%) towards the presence of banquettes or are indifferent (33%). Despite a 41% unfavorable attitude among beachgoers, only 38% ask for total removal and disposal either during the summer (28%) or throughout the year (10%). At the same time, 88% of decision-makers claim to plan beach operational procedures in response to visitor needs.

Since local administrations do not have a direct line of communication with tourists, it is reasonable to assume that their primary source of information about visitor preferences and perceptions is tourism operators. Indeed, the majority of operators believe that the most significant disadvantage of on-site preservation of Posidonia banquettes is that they are unpleasant for tourists: 65% of them ask for the most drastic management form, either during the summer (46%) or throughout the year (19%). Finally, although the beachgoers seem to have a negative perception of the banquettes and are unaware of their ecological importance, a great majority (74%) agreed that sufficient education and incentives might help change attitudes and shift mindsets.

For that reason, HSPN, in cooperation with the Hellenic Center of Marine Research, conducted online seminars for the Blue Flag Mediterranean network (beach managers, National Operators, relevant stakeholders). Furthermore, informative brochures were produced and posted each year to almost 600 Blue

128 *Nikos Petrou et al.*

Flag information boards on beaches around Greece, to educate the beach users and local communities. These brochures were updated and enriched during the POSBEMED2 project.

POSBEMED2 used the findings of PosBeMed to develop planning strategies that take into account the value of the Posidonia beach-dune environment and incorporate them into the overall Mediterranean coastal strategy, while addressing concerns and educating stakeholders. It also targeted knowledge gaps by providing information that can help beach managers make better decisions about adaptation, policy, planning and advocacy. The pilot management actions were implemented at seven sites, of which the two in Greece were on coastal sections with Blue Flag sites.

Both existing literature and the results of management measures implemented at the pilot sites project demonstrate that, in addition to protecting the meadows, on-site preservation of the banquettes plays a pivotal role in the sedimentary dynamics by enhancing the positive balance associated with their sediment retention ability, thus mitigating coast erosion. Despite these findings, engaging local stakeholders and beneficiaries in an alternative management approach may prove to be a challenging procedure.

The Blue Flag promotes sustainable development at beaches and has as major goals to improve understanding of the coastal environment and to encourage the inclusion of environmental issues in the decision-making processes of local authorities and stakeholders; therefore, it can play a key role in the management of the Posidonia littoral zone.

Environmental education is an essential element of the Blue Flag. Education includes themes such as conservation, sustainable practices, management systems, safety and environmental awareness, and targets decision-makers, beach users, managers, employees and local communities. An approach that respects the limits of natural resources and ecosystems, while enhancing the value of Posidonia beach-dune systems, can provide a significant contribution to the sustainable management of Mediterranean coastal areas.

9.5 Management recommendations for the Posidonia littoral zone

As mentioned before, coastal and marine areas are at immediate risk from stressors related to climate change, including sea level rise, increased storm intensity and frequency, altered hydroperiod or freshwater flows, prolonged drought, population shifts and other temperature-driven effects. Managers need a fundamental understanding of changing natural and social processes, as well as specialized knowledge of how these processes affect regional natural and cultural resources, and how they affect local communities, human activities and livelihoods.

The Mediterranean ICZM Protocol highlights the need for national and local institutions to develop appropriate plans tailored to local contexts, to employ adaptive management tools, and to prevent damage and restore it after it has occurred.

To that end, and by considering the benefits of management practices that incorporate the natural processes of the Posidonia beach-dune systems as nature-based solutions, it is recommended that a planning framework be put in place in

Blue Flag supporting environmental policies: The Greek case   129

Mediterranean coastal areas regarding the presence and management of Posidonia banquettes. Management should be responsive and adaptive, working with local interests in a way that builds support for conservation objectives, as it is already done with management of Blue Flag beaches. The plan should address endangering factors, and funding needs, follow relevant local and national regulations and include monitoring and evaluation indicators. All employees must be informed and educated about sustainable and conservation management practices wherever possible.

Depending on the beach status, it is recommended to consider the following:

- On beaches with low visitor numbers, especially ones with significant ecological value (like those that are part of designated protected areas) and/or having erosion problems, a non-removal strategy is recommended, to prevent further erosion. Only in exceptional cases (such as very high accumulation) may removal be considered; then it should be performed manually and with authorization.
- On beaches with high visitor numbers that are subject to erosion, a non-removal strategy is recommended in order to mitigate further erosion, with manual removal only in special circumstances (e.g. extreme events of very high accumulation) with appropriate permission.
- On beaches with high visitor numbers that are not subject to erosion, consideration could be given only during the summer season in clearing only small sections of beached material to form "clean zones" for the summer that would allow easier access from the top of the beach to the sea for the bathers.

In case of removal, if authorized by national legislation, it is recommended to consider the following:

- Removal operations should not take place between early autumn and late spring. As this variant is climate-dependent, an analysis of the wave patterns (long-term data of sea state parameters) in the surrounding area is recommended, to determine the individual temporal window in which banquettes might be managed in respect to lower beach morphological changes.
- Temporal displacement of banquettes to one side of the beach or to a non-recreational use area. After summer they should be returned to the beachfront line or in front of the dunes to help the sand build up.
- For minor accumulations, less than 10cm in height, consider on-site burial below the mean high-water line. Burial in the sand should be in the same place where the banquettes are found.
- Returning the material to the sea when wind/tide conditions are favorable. In case of an adverse weather forecast, removal operations should be canceled.

Regarding operational procedures, it is recommended to consider the following:

- Whenever beach cleaning must occur, the lowest impact techniques available should be used. The responsible authorities should use mechanical cleaning only as a last resort and only if local and national regulations allow it.

130   *Nikos Petrou et al.*

- Mechanical beach cleaning equipment should only be used in areas with a large number of visitors and its frequency should be kept to a minimum.
- During removal, machinery that uses top-down cleaning methods should be utilized to allow removal in layers, starting with the top layer.
- Sieving equipment shall not be introduced further than 10 to 15cm from the sand surface; sediments shall seep through the removed leaves. Posidonia seagrass should not be removed if mixed with high quantities of sand.
- Efforts should be made to remove as little sand as possible and to leave important substrate in place during the removal operations, in order to minimize impacts on beach morphology and sediment budget. A minimum thickness of seagrass deposits should be left on the beach (from 20 to 50cm), to avoid removing sand from the beach body itself as well as to function as a source of nutrients and as structural support for the beach and the dunes.
- Machinery should avoid scraping, gouging or scouring the beaches. Furthermore, machinery should not be used on the beach face, to avoid flattening or modifying the slope and thus encouraging potential shoreline retreat. Under no circumstances should any machine enter the sea nor remove Posidonia seagrass from the sea floor.
- All machinery should operate at least 3m seaward of dunes and avoid any vegetation to protect the stability and ecology of the area. Access to the beach for machinery should be via existing pathways.
- Seagrass wrack material should not be deposited on any dune area where it can smother live plants, leading to dune erosion and destabilization.
- Removal of anthropogenic litter found on Posidonia banquettes should be done manually.
- If the beach hosts nests of endangered species (such as sea turtles, birds, etc.), all actions must be suspended for the duration of the breeding period.

The management plan should stipulate communication and awareness activities as well as training operations:

- It is essential to promote the ecological importance of banquettes, coastal dunes and Posidonia meadows on the littoral ecosystem for both visitors and the local community, through various means, including use of information panels at appropriate locations so that the public can understand the beach management strategy, particularly if there is a change in beach cleaning methods.
- It is highly recommended that awareness raising and communication campaigns are developed at a local level.
- It is essential that time is invested in capacity building for the personnel involved in beach maintenance activities, in order to minimize stakeholder conflicts. Personnel should receive training each year on beach cleaning policies and characteristics of the beach-dune systems.

This recommended approach seeks to promote environmentally responsible tourism and prevent the degradation of Mediterranean coastal ecosystems and the loss of value associated with the diverse ecosystem services that they provide. As the Blue Flag program is a successful tool for coastal zone management by fostering the management of coastal areas in a holistic way and improving environmental quality, the inclusion of an approach that respects the limits, while enhancing the value of Posidonia beach-dune systems, can provide a significant contribution to the sustainable management of Mediterranean coastal areas.

The Foundation for Environmental Education is working on the update of the Blue Flag criteria. HSPN has already proposed changes to the clarifications of two criteria for beaches: 15 ("The beach must be clean"), namely that that the term "litter" be replaced with another term that distinguishes between man-made litter and marine vegetation; and 16 ("Algal vegetation or natural debris must be left on the beach"), namely that the term "algal" be replaced by "benthic", which refers to a variety of marine plants attached to the seabed or living within sediments in shallow depths. Additional clarifications about how and when to remove, or not, will ensure that proper management practices are in place for the protection of sensitive marine species (*Posidonia oceanica* in the Mediterranean but also other marine grasses and plants in different parts of the world) that can play crucial roles in addressing the biodiversity and climate crises through nature-based solutions. Additionally, further criteria about actions at sea, such as the anchoring of boats in relation to marine plant beds or sensitive areas, will be proposed for the Marina and Tourism Boats lists.

One of the main strategic goals of GAIA 20:30, the new strategy of FEE, is to protect global biodiversity. In this chapter coastal management practices that should be applied for the protection and preservation of natural resources were presented. The Blue Flag program is an ideal vehicle to disseminate these practices and ensure their application when needed.

Since its founding, the HSPN is working to protect habitats and threatened species of fauna and flora, and will continue its efforts to help preserving a safe planet for future generations.

9.6 References

Díaz-Almela E., & Duarte C.M. 2008. *Management of Natura 2000 habitats*. 1120 *Posidonia beds (Posidonion oceanicae). European Commission. Retrieved from https://ec.europa.eu/environment/nature/natura2000/management/habitats/pdf/1120_Posidonia_beds.pdf

EEA-UNEP/MAP (2014). *Horizon 2020 Mediterranean report. Toward shared environmental information systems*. Technical Report Nº6/2014.

HCMR, 2021. Geomorphological approaches to study Posidonia banquettes and their effects on the coastal front of Schinias-Marathon National Park. In the framework of Deliverable Report 3.3.2. Implementation of management measures, POSBEMED2- Governance and management of Posidonia beach - dune systems across the Mediterranean, HCMR Scientific Report (Salomidi M., Ed.), July 2021, 90 pp.

InterregMED PosBeMed project, Sustainable management of the systems Posidonia-beaches in the Mediterranean region, official website, https://posbemed.interreg-med.eu/

InterregMED POSBEMED2 project, Governance and management of Posidonia beach-dune systems across the Mediterranean, official website, https://posbemed2.interreg-med.eu/

Otero M.M., Simeone, S., Aljinovic, B., Salomidi, M., Mossone, P., Giunta Fornasin M.E., Gerakaris, V., Guala, I., Milano, P., Heurtefeux H., Issaris, Y., Guido, M., & Adamopoulou, M. (2018). *Governance and management of Posidonia beach-dune system.* POSBEMED Interreg Med Project. 66pp+ Annexes.

10 Blue Flag and tourism destination efficiency

The French case

Aurélie Corne, Olga Goncalves and Nicolas Peypoch

10.1 Introduction

Efficiency analysis is a topic of great interest in tourism research (Assaf & Tsionas, 2019) that is intimately linked to destination performance and competitiveness (Ritchie & Crouch, 2003). Tourism performance can be explained by several factors or determinants and, among these, environmental sustainability has been identified by Assaf & Josiassen (2012) as an important one.

In the case of coastal localities, tourism management presents a great and particular interest. Coastal authorities place tourism policies at the heart of their local development strategies as sandy beaches play an "important role as locations for recreation and as attractions" (Orams, 2003, p.74). However, beaches managers face two main concerns trying to improve their destinations' performance. First, beaches are unique environments that need to be protected against human activities like pollution, erosion, noise and waste (Nelson et al., 1999). Second, demand for high quality beaches is growing. Like many other organizations, beaches face important environmental challenges. However, their specificity relies on their offer being mainly related to natural surroundings and outdoor activities, which require a special attention. This situation questions the competitiveness of coastal tourism destinations where it is crucial for managers to develop sustainable practices in order to limit irreversible degradation (Defeo et al., 2009) and continue to develop beaches as a recreation and tourism location.

The growth of environmental awareness in society leads tourism managers to adapt their strategies, and the implementation of environmental strategies have become a major issue (Font, 2002; Dodds & Holmes, 2020). In this context, some coastal operators adopt the Blue Flag eco-label as a green strategy. This label certifies, in particular, the justification of a level of environmental quality for beaches. This chapter investigates whether or not "going green" pays off? To answer this question, an analysis of the impact of the Blue Flag quality system on French regional destination efficiency is provided.

The rest of this chapter is as follows. Section 2 proposes a literature review and identifies the research gap about Blue Flag and tourism efficiency analysis. The methodologies employed are presented in section 10.3. Section 10.4 is devoted to the empirical study on the French destinations at the regional level. Finally, section 10.5 concludes.

DOI: 10.4324/9781003323570-11

134   *Aurélie Corne et al.*

10.2 Literature review

10.2.1 Beaches' environmental challenges

Environmental challenges the tourism sector and coastal destinations are facing can be studied in different ways. On the one hand, the impact of recreational and tourism activities on beach environments is analysed (Hyman, 2014; Khan, 2017). On the other hand, the impact of the environmental context on coastal destinations is studied. Indeed, coastal zones have been identified as being particularly vulnerable to environmental evolution, such as climate change (Moreno & Amelung, 2009; Rosselló-Nadal, 2014; Toimil et al., 2018) impacting, for example, sea level rise (Alexandrakis et al., 2015; Thinh et al., 2019). Finally, there is the investigation of the impact of environmental strategies on coastal destination performance, which is the focus of this chapter.

In order to try to control the equilibrium between tourism demand and beaches' ecosystem conservation, coastal local authorities have to elaborate on sustainable strategies for beach management for a continuous development of tourism activities while preserving the coastal ecosystem from erosion and pollution (Koutrakis et al., 2011). To do this, the Blue Flag eco-label, one of the most recognized awards in the world, can be used. This international environmental quality award has been given in France since 1985 by the Foundation for Environmental Education (FEE) to coastal municipalities that leads, in a permanent way, to a policy of sustainable tourism development. This award guarantees that beaches and marinas are managed following several quality and environmental criteria. Concerning the beaches, the Blue Flag award provides 33 mandatory criteria of quality, which are grouped through four categories:[1] environmental education (6 criteria), water quality (5 criteria), environmental management (15 criteria) and safety (7 criteria) (Blue Flag, 2021). At the present time, 80% of the French municipalities awarded offer at least one environmental education activity on biodiversity (De la mer à la terre, 2022).

In general, with regard to the Blue Flag award, it's expected that a minimum of criteria of quality concerning information, signaling, water quality, cleanliness, waste management, safety and equipments/facilities are respected[2] by the local authority. The coastal municipalities that are interested in the Blue Flag award need to compete year after year to get it and, in a context of tourism competitiveness, this certification seems to be important to differentiate tourism destinations (Lucrezi et al., 2015). But, does this eco-label really impact destination efficiency?

10.2.2 Blue Flag and tourism efficiency: Current gap

Blue Flag certification is a topic investigated by a lot of researchers (Capacci et al., 2015; Lucrezi et al., 2015; Cerqua, 2017; Zielinski & Botero, 2019; Dodds & Holmes, 2020). Mir-Gual et al. (2015) and McKenna et al. (2011) proposed an extended literature review devoted to Blue Flag. It appears that Blue Flag can be identified as a "sign of prestige" (Font, 2002, cited by Mir-Gual et al., 2015) or "a measure of the quality and the effort of exhibiting a good image abroad"

(Medina et al., 2012: p.1249). However, the link between Blue Flag and destination performance is not clearly established in the literature and its real impact on the destination competitiveness can be mixed. As pointed out by Capacci et al. (2015, p.91):

evidence on their effectiveness in affecting tourism performances is unclear. Many attempts in assessing the effectiveness of tourist site labels can be found in the literature mainly with regard to environmental and cultural quality certifications, but heterogeneity in methods and scope make it difficult to draw reliable conclusions.

Among these, the inclusion in tourism efficiency analysis of the beaches labeled Blue Flag is particularly interesting. Indeed, from a methodological viewpoint, beaches can be treated either as an input of the production technology or a determinant of efficiency in second stage analysis (Assaf & Josiassen, 2016). For the French case, Botti et al. (2009) have used beaches as an input of the production technology, whereas Barros et al. (2011) kept this variable as an explanatory factor of the efficiency level in a second stage analysis. The same distinction has been implemented to analyze the efficiency of Spanish destinations, respectively by Fuentes Medina et al. (2012) and Benito et al. (2014).

In a more general way, this point has been investigated recently by Dong et al. (2021) about tourism attractions. By considering the Chinese case, they showed that tourism attractions could have an impact on the efficiency scores and rankings depending on whether they are included or not in the construction of the production technology. In this chapter, their recommended procedure is followed in order to check if beaches labeled Blue Flag should be considered as an input of the production technology.

10.3 Methodology

10.3.1 Data Envelopment Analysis

Data Envelopment Analysis (DEA) is a well-known method used to analyze the relative efficiency of a given sample of units. From a mathematical point of view, it is calculated using linear programming. In other words, it is part of the non-parametric methods. In the literature, the seminal work about DEA is from Charnes et al. (1978) who considered a production technology with constant returns to scale. Later, Banker et al. (1984) proposed a DEA version with variable returns to scale. The strengths of DEA rely on its flexibility from an operational viewpoint. Indeed, this technique permits to model a multi-output production technology and without assumption regarding its functional form is required.

In this chapter the destinations (French regions) are the units compared. The production technology is constructed as follows.[3] Each destinations uses inputs $x = (x_1, \cdots, x_N) \in R_+^N$ to produce outputs $y = (y_1, \cdots, y_M) \in R_+^M$. Hence, the

136 *Aurélie Corne et al.*

production technology, denoted by T, is $T = \{(x, y) \in R_+^{N+M} : x \text{ can produce } y\}$ and is defined by:

$$T = \left\{(x, y) : x \geq \sum_{i=1}^{k} \theta_i x^i, \ y \leq \sum_{i=1}^{k} \theta_i y^i, \ \theta_i \geq 0, \ i = 1, \cdots, k.\right\}$$

The efficiency scores of the destinations are calculated by using the following linear program:

$$\text{Max } \delta$$

$$\text{s.t. } x \geq \sum_{i=1}^{k} \theta_i x^i$$

$$\delta y \leq \sum_{i=1}^{k} \theta_i y^i$$

$$\theta_i \geq 0, \ i = 1, \cdots, k.$$

In the linear program, the estimation is output oriented in order to maximize the output for a given input quantity (Dong et al., 2020; Corne and Peypoch, 2020). Constant returns to scale (CRS) are assumed for the returns to scale of the production technology because of the relative homogeneity of the French regions in terms of size after the French territorial reform in 2015. This choice, instead of variable returns to scale (VRS), is confirmed later by a statistical test on returns to scale. Finally, this linear program is computed k times, where k are the 13 French tourism destinations.

10.3.2 Statistical tests

Several statistical tests are used in this chapter to check different assumptions about the data used and the results obtained. Regarding the construction of the production technology and the inclusion of an indicator about Blue Flag labels, both the statistical tests of Kruskal-Wallis and Kolmogorov-Smirnov are used by following the procedure described in Bogetoft and Otto (2011). The choice in terms of returns to scale for the production technology is also confirmed by following a procedure in the same vein.

Finally, the impact of group effect (location of the Blue Flag destinations: seaside vs. countryside) is checked by using the Mann-Whitney test (see Cooper et al., 2006). In this case, the following null hypothesis H_0 is tested against the alternative hypothesis H_1:

H_0: The efficiency of French Blue Flag destinations is independent to location
H_1: The efficiency of French Blue Flag destinations is dependent to location

Blue Flag and tourism destination efficiency: The French case   137

To avoid repetition about the presentation of these statistical tests commonly used in the tourism efficiency literature (Goncalves, 2013; Dong et al., 2020), we refer the reader to the above-mentioned references.

10.4 Empirical application to the French destinations

In this empirical section, similar data than the those used in Corne and Peypoch (2020) are considered. More precisely, two inputs related to number of employees and room capacity are considered as well as outputs about the number of tourist arrivals and the tourist tax (expressed in million €). These variables are standard in order to construct a tourism production technology from an economic viewpoint. Indeed, the inputs rely, respectively, on labor and capital factors. Concerning the outputs, tourist arrivals is a common indicator of tourism flows, whereas tourist tax represents the economic repercussion in the absence of available data for tourism receipts. These data come from the "Mémento du tourisme 2018" and are for the year 2017.

The production technology constructed in Corne and Peypoch (2020) is then expanded with specific data in order to consider the Blue Flag labeling for beaches. Beaches constitute a tourism attraction (Lew, 1987) based on a natural resource (Gunn, 1988) and have been considered in the tourism efficiency literature, especially as determinants of destination performance in two-stage DEA models (Corne & Peypoch, 2020). However, in the tourism efficiency literature, few contributions included directly an input related to Blue Flag labeling in the production technology. Botti et al. (2009) considered the number of beach kilometers as an input in order to assess the relative efficiency of French destinations at the regional level by using the directional distance function. Fuentes Medina et al. (2012) used the number of beaches labeled Blue Flag as an input and then they applied the three-stage DEA model proposed by Muñiz (2002) in order to disentangle the effect of specific inputs on the efficiency scores. In their study about Spanish destinations, they concluded that Blue Flag certification as an input influences the efficiency scores obtained. Doğanalp & Arslan (2021) included Blue Flag labels for both beaches and marinas as two inputs in the production technology they constructed in order to compare the relative efficiency of European destinations in the southern Mediterranean region. This study follows this stream of the literature by including an indicator about Blue Flag as an input of the production technology, as advocated by Dong et al. (2021) in the context of tourism attraction. Indicators for Blue Flag are aggregated at the regional level. These data are extracted from the journal *De la mer à la terre 2017* in order to retrieve the data for the same year.[4] Both number of beaches and number of cities labelled Blue Flag are considered.

Table 10.1 presents the descriptive statistics of the data used in this chapter for the inputs and outputs.

Several production technologies are considered in order to analyze the possible impact of Blue Flag labeling on the relative efficiency of French destinations.

138   Aurélie Corne et al.

Table 10.1 Analysis on the impact of BF in efficiency in the French touristic sector: Descriptive statistics

	Maximum	*Minimum*	*Mean*	*Standard dev.*
Inputs				
Employees	420,498	8,442	100,688	105,194
Rooms	156,405	12,517	49,328	39,280
BF beaches	104	1	29.1	33.7
BF cities	32	1	13.2	10.1
Outputs				
Arrivals	33,812	1,477	9,068	8,184
Tourist tax	100.3	1.05	17.8	27.3

On the one hand, a full production technology, denoted PT1, is constructed by including three inputs and two outputs:

• PT1: Inputs: employees, rooms, beaches labeled Blue Flag – termed BF beaches. Outputs: tourist arrivals, tourism tax

Efficiency scores are then calculated both under CRS and VRS assumption. By following the procedure described by Bogetoft & Otto (2011, p.161), a test on returns to scale is then implemented. The null hypothesis is a production technology assuming CRS and the alternative hypothesis is the one assuming VRS. Results from the tests of Kolmogorov-Smirnov and Kruskal-Wallis both indicate that the null hypothesis cannot be rejected and that CRS should be adopted for the production technology. This finding is in line with Corne & Peypoch (2020) and indicates that the inclusion of an indicator of Blue Flag labeling as an input of the tourism production technology doesn't affect the choice in terms of returns to scale. Indeed, it can be noted that the efficiency scores are similar to the ones obtained by Corne & Peypoch (2020) where there is no reference to Blue Flag certification in inputs. This finding could suggest that Blue Flag have no impact on tourism efficiency. However, it should be noted that, here, the production technology, denoted PT1, contained five variables (three inputs and two outputs). Without entering into the debate about the rule in the use of the DEA method between the number of units and the number of inputs and outputs where there is no consensus (Sarkis, 2007), but in order to increase the discriminatory power of the method and to identify the impact of Blue Flag labeling on the tourism efficiency in French regions, the following production technologies with three inputs and one output are used in a next step and are denoted, respectively, PT2 and PT3:

• PT2: Inputs: employees, rooms, BF beaches. Output: tourism tax
• PT3: Inputs: employees, rooms, BF beaches. Output: tourist arrivals

The findings for the three production technologies are reported in Table 10.2.

Blue Flag and tourism destination efficiency: The French case 139

Table 10.2 Analysis on the impact of BF in efficiency in the French touristic sector: Efficiency scores of French regions

	DMU[5]				*PT1*	
	Score[6]	Rank	Score	Rank	Score	Rank
ARA	0.76663	13	0.48009	5	0.73223	12
BFC	1	1	0.21873	11	1	1
Bretagne	0.84839	12	0.46364	6	0.80076	10
CVDL	0.97111	5	0.10329	13	0.97111	4
Corse	1	1	1	1	1	1
Grand Est	0.93348	6	0.10437	12	0.93348	5
HDF	0.92518	7	0.28109	9	0.92518	6
IDF	1	1	1	1	1	1
Normandie	0.89147	8	0.25299	10	0.89077	7
NAQ	0.86539	10	0.32161	8	0.84576	9
Occitanie	0.88595	9	0.74953	4	0.71206	13
PDLL	0.8484	11	0.44293	7	0.8484	8
PACA	1	1	1	1	0.73576	11

After computations using the DEA Solver software by Cooper et al. (2006), Table 10.2 provides efficiency scores and ranks for each French region. The efficiency scores equal to 1 specify that the related DMU is fully efficient and is a possible benchmark for the other inefficient units. Thus, there are four efficient regions (BFC, Corse, IDH and PACA) under PT1, whereas PT2 and PT3 have three efficient regions (without BFC and PACA respectively).

Corse and IDH are the regions efficient with the various configurations in terms of production technology. Results are interesting because Corse and IDH have, respectively, one and three BF beaches compared with Occitanie, for instance, which has 104 BF beaches and is relatively inefficient in each estimation.

For information, PACA is one of the French regions with the most BF beaches (i.e., 98) and BFC is one of those with the least (3 beaches labeled). PACA is also efficient with PT1 and PT2, but inefficient with PT3. In fact, this region is inefficient with a relative efficiency level of 73.57% and should improve tourist arrivals by 35.91%. From an ecological perspective, it's better to have a good tourism tax with less tourist arrivals. BFC is considered a benchmark in the first and the third technology. However, this region is very inefficient in terms of economic repercussions (tourism tax as output) with an efficiency level of only 21.87%.

Regarding the comparison between the different production technologies, efficiency scores of French regions with and without BF beaches reveal that the results and rankings are similar. It seems the case between PT1 and PT3 excepting a couple of destinations like the PACA region. This finding is confirmed by the statistical test of Kolmogorov-Smirnov, suggesting that Blue Flag doesn't have an impact on destination performance.

In a last step, the Mann-Whitney test is implemented to check if the location of the Blue Flag beaches (seaside vs countryside) could have an impact on

140   *Aurélie Corne et al.*

destination efficiency. For the three production technologies (the empirical values are, respectively, –0.88, 1.17 and –1.46 for PT1, PT2 and PT3), the null hypothesis cannot be rejected. Thus, the location of the Blue Flag beaches in the French territory doesn't have an impact on tourism efficiency.

Finally, to ensure the robustness of the findings obtained in this chapter, all the calculations have been reimplemented by using as an input the number of cities labeled Blue Flag instead of the number of beaches. It appears that the findings for the three production technologies are similar in terms of relative efficiency and the rankings of French regional destinations are not altered by this input change.

10.5 Concluding remarks

This chapter develops a methodological framework to evaluate the influence of environmental strategies on destinations' performance. More precisely, the impact of Blue Flag eco-label on the performance of 13 French destinations at the regional level is investigated.

A DEA approach is mobilized with different steps. On the one hand, several production technologies are considered in order to measure the efficiency of French destinations. On the other hand, the possible impact of the location of the regions labeled Blue Flag on destination efficiency is investigated. The results from this study don't reveal a significant link between the Blue flag distinction and the destination performance. These findings are in line with Capacci et al. (2015), showing that the debate about the impact of Blue Flag certification on destination performance is still open and very sensitive to case studies.

From a methodological perspective, this study investigates the use of a quantitative method based on DEA. Other methods available in the literature devoted to decision analysis could be mobilized like multi-criteria decision analysis (MCDA).

From an empirical point of view, this study is not directly comparable with alternative research because it focuses on French regions. However, other case studies reveal different insights regarding the importance of Blue Flag in the tourism production process (Fuentes Medina et al., 2012).

From the managerial perspective, this research confirms that the influence of Blue Flag strategies is not obvious in terms of efficiency and competitiveness. However, does this mean that it is not useful to be certified? No. This study can help regional operators deciding the most adequate eco-label strategy to enhance the competitive advantage and differentiation (Dodds & Holmes, 2020). More precisely, the results show that, at the regional level, quantity, in terms of number of beaches certified, seems to not be the most important characteristic, as some findings show that, in the most efficient destinations, some have a smaller number of certified beaches. According to Capacci et al. (2015), Blue Flag and certifications in general positively affect foreign tourist flows as this is a signal of quality. Furthermore, as highlighted by Mir-Gual et al. (2015), the Blue Flag award focuses on services offered and benefits to beach users, which can explain that Blue Flag certification is a factor of destination choice and helps to differentiate destinations and improve satisfaction (Dodds & Holmes, 2020). This certification "had a significant impact on a visitor's overall experience satisfaction, possibly demonstrating an indirect effect" (Dodds & Holmes,

Blue Flag and tourism destination efficiency: The French case   141

2020, p.191). Thus, the link between Blue Flag and satisfaction seems clearer in the literature compared to efficiency in the overall analysis of destination competitiveness. The satisfaction is higher for the tourists when beaches integrate the Blue Flag eco-label as an environmental concern (Dodds & Holmes, 2020). However, Klein & Dodds (2018, p.39) say about the Blue Flag label that "the certification system is perceived more as a tourism promotional tool rather than an environmental management or protection tool". That's why, as pointed out by Dodds & Holmes (2020), managers should convey more information about environmental rules and consider Blue Flag as an educational tool with, for example, natural awareness programs rather than using it as a marketing tool.

The study presented in this chapter also has some limitations. A first perspective is related to the data constraints. Indeed, it would be interesting to consider data over a more extended sample (different countries or different time periods for the same country) for comparative purposes. Furthermore, more detailed recommendations for managers could be derived from an analysis at a finer territorial scale by considering department or municipalities as decision-making units. Another possible future research is to include the environmental issue in the tourism production technology by considering undesirable outputs.

Notes

1 https://www.pavillonbleu.org/criteres/critere-commune.html
2 See the website devoted to Blue Flag for a detailed presentation of the criteria: https://www.pavillonbleu.org
3 The production technology satisfies axioms from production theory, especially convexity and free disposability of inputs and outputs; see, for instance, Cooper et al. (2006) for more details.
4 This information has been accessed from http://www.villesdefrance.fr/upload/PalmaresPavillonBleu2017.pdf
5 ARA for Auvergne-Rhône-Alpes, BFC for Bourgogne-Franche-Comté, CVDL for Centre-Val de Loire, HDF for Hauts-de-France, IDF for Ile-de-France, NAQ for Nouvelle Aquitaine, PDLL for Pays de la Loire and PACA for Provence-Alpes-Côte d'Azur.
6 The columns termed "score" indicate the percentage level of efficiency and are derived from 1/score because of the output orientation of the DEA model.

10.6 References

Alexandrakis, G., Manasakis, C., & Kampanis, N. A. (2015). Valuating the effects of beach erosion to tourism revenue. A management perspective. *Ocean & Coastal Management*, *111*, 1–11.

Assaf, A. G., & Josiassen, A. (2012). Identifying and ranking the determinants of tourism performance: A global investigation. *Journal of Travel Research*, *51*(4), 388–399.

Assaf, A. G., & Josiassen, A. (2016). Frontier analysis: A state-of-the-art review and meta-analysis. *Journal of Travel Research*, *55*(5), 612–627.

Assaf, A. G., & Tsionas, M. G. (2019). A review of research into performance modeling in tourism research – launching the Annals of Tourism Research curated collection on performance modeling in tourism research. *Annals of Tourism Research*, *76*, 266–277.

Banker, R. D., Charnes, A., & Cooper, W. W. (1984). Some models for estimating technical and scale inefficiencies in data envelopment analysis. *Management Science*, *30*(9), 1078–1092.

142 *Aurélie Corne et al.*

Barros, C. P., Botti, L., Peypoch, N., Robinot, E., & Solonandrasana, B. (2011). Performance of French destinations: Tourism attraction perspectives. *Tourism Management*, *32*(1), 141–146.

Benito, B., Solana, J., & López, P. (2014). Determinants of Spanish regions' tourism performance: A two-stage, double-bootstrap data envelopment analysis. *Tourism Economics*, *20*(5), 987–1012.

Blue Flag (2021). Blue Flag beach criteria and explanatory notes 2021. Retrieved August 31, 2022 from https://www.blueflag.global/criteria

Bogetoft, P., & Otto, L. (2011). *Benchmarking with DEA, SFA and R*. Springer.

Botti, L., Peypoch, N., Robinot, E., & Solonadrasana, B. (2009). Tourism destination competitiveness: The French regions case. *European Journal of Tourism Research*, *2*(1), 5–24.

Capacci, S., Scorcu, A. E., & Vici, L. (2015). Seaside tourism and eco-labels: The economic impact of Blue Flags. *Tourism Management*, *47*, 88–96.

Cerqua, A. (2017). The signalling effect of eco-labels in modern coastal tourism. *Journal of Sustainable Tourism*, *25*(8), 1159–1180.

Charnes, A., Cooper, W. W., & Rhodes, E. (1978). Measuring the efficiency of decision making units. *European Journal of Operational Research*, *2*(6), 429–444.

Cooper, W. W., Seiford, L. M., & Tone, K. (2006). Introduction to data envelopment analysis and its uses: With DEA-solver software and references. Springer.

Corne, A., & Peypoch, N. (2020). On the determinants of tourism performance. *Annals of Tourism Research*, *85*, 103057.

De la mer à la terre (2017). Printemps 2017, 16p., accessed from http://www.villesdefrance.fr/upload/PalmaresPavillonBleu2017.pdf

De la mer à la terre (2022). Saison 2022, 11p., accessed from https://www.pavillonbleu.org/

Defeo, O., McLachlan, A., Schoeman, D. S., Schlacher, T. A., Dugan, J., Jones, A., Lastra, M., & Scapini, F. (2009). Threats to sandy beach ecosystems: A review. *Estuarine, coastal and shelf science*, *81*(1), 1–12.

Dodds, R., & Holmes, M. R. (2020). Is Blue Flag certification a means of destination competitiveness? A Canadian context. *Ocean & Coastal Management*, *192*, 105192.

Doğanalp, N., & Arslan, A. (2021). Comparative Efficiency Analysis of Tourism Industry in the Southern Mediterranean Region. In *Contemporary Issues in Social Science* (Vol. 106, pp.49–66). Emerald Publishing Limited.

Dong, H., Liang, Q. B., & Peypoch, N. (2021). Tourist attractions in efficiency analysis. *Tourism Economics*, accessed from https://doi.org/10.1177/13548166211060190

Dong, H., Peypoch, N., & Zhang, L. (2020). Do contextual factors matter? Evidence from Chinese hotel productivity with heterogeneity. *Tourism Economics*, *26*, 257–275.

Font, X. (2002). Environmental certification in tourism and hospitality: Progress, process and prospects. *Tourism Management*, *23*(3), 197–205.

Fuentes Medina, L., Gonzalez Gomez, I., & Morini Marrero, S. (2012). Measuring efficiency of sun & beach tourism destinations. *Annals of Tourism Research*, *39*(2), 1248–1251.

Goncalves, O. (2013). Efficiency and productivity of French ski resorts. *Tourism Management*, *36*, 650–657.

Gunn, C. A. (1988). *Vacationscape: Designing tourist regions* (2nd ed.). Van Nostrand Reinhold.

Hyman, T. A. (2014). Assessing the vulnerability of beach tourism and non-beach tourism to climate change: A case study from Jamaica. *Journal of Sustainable Tourism*, *22*(8), 1197–1215.

Blue Flag and tourism destination efficiency: The French case 143

Khan, H. R. (2017). Impacts of tourism activities on environment and sustainability of Pattaya beach in Thailand. *Journal of Environmental Management & Tourism*, *8*(8, 24), 1469–1473.

Klein, L., & Dodds, R. (2018). Blue Flag beach certification: An environmental management tool or tourism promotional tool? *Tourism Recreation Research*, *43*(1), 39–51.

Koutrakis, E., Sapounidis, A., Marzetti, S., Marin, V., Roussel, S., Martino, S., Fabiano, M., Paoli, C., Rey-Valette, H., Povh, D., Malvárez, C.G. (2011). ICZM and coastal defence perception by beach users: Lessons from the Mediterranean coastal area, *Ocean & Coastal Management*, *54*(11), 821–830.

Lew, A. A. (1987). A framework of tourist attraction research. *Annals of Tourism Research*, *14*(4), 553–575.

Lucrezi, S., Saayman, M., & Van der Merwe, P. (2015). Managing beaches and beachgoers: Lessons from and for the Blue Flag Award. *Tourism Management*, *48*, 211–230.

McKenna, J., Williams, A. T., & Cooper, J. A. G. (2011). Blue Flag or Red Herring: Do beach awards encourage the public to visit beaches? *Tourism Management*, *32*(3), 576–588.

Mémento du tourisme 2018, Direction Générale des Entreprises, 146p., published in March 2019, available at https://www.entreprises.gouv.fr

Mir-Gual, M., Pons, G. X., Martín-Prieto, J. A., & Rodríguez-Perea, A. (2015). A critical view of the Blue Flag beaches in Spain using environmental variables. *Ocean & Coastal Management*, *105*, 106–115.

Moreno, A., & Amelung, B. (2009). Climate change and coastal & marine tourism: Review and analysis. *Journal of Coastal Research*, 1140–1144.

Muñiz, M. A. (2002). Separating managerial inefficiency and external conditions in data envelopment analysis. *European Journal of Operational Research*, 143(3), 625–643.

Nelson, C., Botterill, D., & Williams, A. (1999). The beach as leisure resource: Measuring user perceptions of beach debris pollution. *World Leisure & Recreation*, *42*(1), 38–43.

Orams, M. B. (2003). Sandy beaches as a tourism attraction: A management challenge for the 21 st century. *Journal of Coastal Research*, 74–84.

R Core Team (2019). R: A language and environment for statistical computing. R Foundation for Statistical Computing, Vienna, Austria, available from https://www.R-project.org/

Ritchie, J. B., & Crouch, G. I. (2003). The competitive destination: A sustainable tourism perspective. CABI.

Rosselló-Nadal, J. (2014). How to evaluate the effects of climate change on tourism. *Tourism Management*, *42*, 334–340.

Sarkis, J. (2007). Preparing your Data for DEA. In Zhu, J. & Cook, W. D. (eds), *Modeling Data Irregularities and Structural Complexities in Data Envelopment Analysis* (pp.305–320). Springer.

Thinh, N. A., Thanh, N. N., Tuyen, L. T., & Hens, L. (2019). Tourism and beach erosion: Valuing the damage of beach erosion for tourism in the Hoi An World Heritage site, Vietnam. *Environment, Development and Sustainability*, *21*(5), 2113–2124.

Toimil, A., Díaz-Simal, P., Losada, I. J., & Camus, P. (2018). Estimating the risk of loss of beach recreation value under climate change. *Tourism Management*, *68*, 387–400.

Zielinski, S., & Botero, C. M. (2019). Myths, misconceptions and the true value of Blue Flag. *Ocean & Coastal Management*, *174*, 15–24.

11 The challenge of sustainability in territorial development

The impact of Blue Flag on tourism – the Italian context

Francesco Manta, Giulio Fusco and Pierluigi Toma

11.1 Introduction

In recent years, sustainability has grown its impact throughout the world, radically changing the approach to many normal activities. Of course, this disruptive change occurred also in the economy, affecting many different sectors with different timings and modes. This concept has been excellently synthetized by Elkington (1997a, 1997b, 1998) with the expression of the triple bottom line of sustainability, clarifying a triple direction for a company's efforts in order to improve their impact on their stakeholders: "people, planet and profit" are the key to upgrade the ethics commitment of a firm to the purpose of achieving the creation of value.

So, the field of Corporate Social Responsibility, which over the years has gained a wider interest among academics and practitioners, booming in the '90s and evolving its definition in Corporate Sustainability, switched its role from a voluntary, ethically relevant behaviour, to – in some parts of the world – a mandatory regulated aspect of the economic activity.

This led to a totally new approach, as mentioned before, to the sustainable behaviour adopted by firms. Many of them started to understand that there was an opportunity to pursue a twofold objective by exploiting sustainable practices in production. The concept of Creating Shared Value, first described by Porter and Kramer (2006), which identified the opportunity of generating an interdependency between firms and the stakeholder environment. Although in the past many believed that firms and the surrounding environment were not communicating, and so they were disconnected, then many scholars understood that both entities could interact and build a common value. Subsequently, the triple bottom line approach has been updated by considering the fourth dimension of governance, including the role of institutional bodies in the concept of pursuing sustainability. The role of local governments, in some way, is proved to have a primary role in taking action for sustainability efforts (Brugmann, 1996; Saha, 2009; Zeemering, 2018).

All the above-mentioned points are of interest to this study, since, as the title suggests, the aim is to understand how sustainability issues of the market could boost local development. It will happen by considering some specific aspects, not just a broad approach, to understand if there are some interesting research paths to

DOI: 10.4324/9781003323570-12

focus on, by adopting some indicators that could signal, mark and assess the impact of sustainable practices on local development.

A synthetic, but often effective, indicator of sustainable behaviour adopted by firms, which may have multiple declinations in terms of best practices, product quality, social and environmental impact, is the eco-label.

Over the years the practice showed us the birth and the spread of an always growing eco-label "market", together with increased concern for sustainable consumption and the tightening of regulations by governments in the field of sustainability and environmental and social preservation.

Moreover, the coronavirus crisis that spread all over the world brought about a new debate on new issues on the economic impact of sanitary conditions. Normal activities such as work or leisure tourism became urgent themes of health security, generating a lack of trust among consumers, and a consequent considerable loss in revenues for public activities. The incumbent crisis, indeed, made it necessary to put order in the scenario, trying to find the right tools to boost a relaunch in consumption of goods and services, basing the strategy on some old, solid pillars, such as quality, genuineness, safety and sustainability.

The present work aims at establishing a relationship between sustainable tourism and income of coastal sites, by assessing the impact of eco-labels like Blue Flag, the percentage of recycling and tourists' attendance on the income per capita of those municipalities. An econometric model was built, in order to grasp the effect of such predictors on the chosen dependent variable. The remainder of the chapter is organized as follows: the next section focuses on the theoretical background on the interaction between eco-labels and tourism, and the previous studies on the impact of the Blue Flag award. A methodology section (11.3.) follows, section 11.4. includes the results of the empirical analysis; the chapter finishes with a discussion section and conclusions, including the paths for future research.

11.2 Theoretical background

11.2.1 Sustainable tourism certification

The UNWTO (United Nations World Tourism Organization) defines sustainable tourism as the "Tourism that takes full account of its current and future economic, social and environmental impacts, addressing the needs of visitors, the industry, the environment and host communities" (UNWTO, 2020). Sustainability principles refer to the environmental, economic and socio-cultural aspects of tourism development, and a suitable balance must be established between these three dimensions to guarantee its long-term sustainability. Thus, sustainable tourism should:

a) Make optimal use of environmental resources that constitute a key element in tourism development, maintaining essential ecological processes and helping to conserve natural heritage and biodiversity.
b) Respect the socio-cultural authenticity of host communities, conserve their built and living cultural heritage and traditional values, and contribute to intercultural understanding and tolerance.

146 *Francesco Manta et al.*

c) Ensure viable, long-term economic operations, providing socio-economic benefits to all stakeholders that are fairly distributed, including stable employment and income-earning opportunities and social services to host communities, and contributing to poverty alleviation.

Although sustainable tourism has many positive objectives, there must be a concrete measurement system that allows a company to determine its progress towards sustainability. In order to measure results and progress, some benchmarks are used. Benchmarking is "comparing the performance of a company in a given area with that of a similar company", which not only puts a company's activities into perspective with those of its competitors, but also contributes to many internal positive improvements. According to the extant literature, such strategies are the only way to make consumers aware of sustainable tourism programs. There is the need, in fact, to assess the quality and the stability of such programs via structured strategies and disclosure that can prove them to the consumer.

One of the most common strategies is to issue national and international standards, which implement fixed benchmarks and criteria to be accomplished, in order to validate the quality of programs, goods and services (Buckley, 2001). Of course, there must be at least two main points to be fixed in order to guarantee the effectiveness of a tourism label: first, the environmental concern of the consumer, which is essential and imperative; second, the ability and the sensitivity of the consumer to distinguish a product/service endowed with an eco-label from another one that is not.

Since 1992, UNWTO has developed and implemented sustainable tourism indicators on a destination-by-destination basis. The program has been very successful, and its aim is to help tourism managers prevent damage to their product and thus promote sustainable tourism on a specific scale by destinations.

Tourism eco-labels may be divided into two main groups: environmental quality labels for tourism destinations and environmental performance labels for tourism providers (Buckley, 2001). Only one or two labels do not fit these categories. Scholars argue that, given that an aware consumer pays attention to the provision of such certifications, these two kinds of labels can't be independent from each other, since there is a substantial difference in the establishment and recognition criteria that make them a reciprocal consequence of the issue of each of them.

Local authorities, and in particular sea municipalities, are gradually introducing sustainability as a key factor in order to boost the growth of the tourism industry, in an attempt to make the users of tourism services and the inhabitants themselves more responsible. In this regard, the adoption of initiatives like certifications, such as the "Blue Flag" program, is very important.

The Blue Flag is an international recognition, established in 1987: the European Year of the Environment, which is awarded every year in 49 countries, initially only in Europe, more recently also outside Europe, with the support and participation of the two UN agencies: UNEP (United Nations Environment Program) and UNWTO (World Tourism Organization) with which the Foundation for Environmental Education (FEE) has signed a global partnership protocol and recognized by UNESCO as a world leader in environmental education and development education.

Blue Flag is a voluntary eco-label assigned to seaside tourist locations that comply with criteria relating to sustainable land management. The Blue Flag program, an international eco-label for the certification of the environmental quality of coastal locations, has established itself and is currently recognized throughout the world, both by tourists and tour operators, as a valid eco-label in relation to sustainable tourism in marine and lake tourist sites.

By promoting a more respectful and sustainable use of a resource as fragile and scarce as the beach, the Blue Flag solves some of these shortcomings, thanks to the fact that it requires high standards in four basic areas: quality of bathing water, safety and services, environmental management, and information and education for sustainability (UNEP & UNWTO, 2006; UNWTO & FEE, 2006). Studies conducted on the economic impacts of the Blue Flag seem to suggest that there is considerable motivation for a municipality to seek Blue Flag status to increase municipal revenues (Blackman et al., 2014; Capacci et al., 2015; Dodds, 2014). The Blue Flag has become famous for its feasibility to act as a public marketing tool (Ariza et al., 2008). Font (2002) states that having a Blue Flag has a major impact on beach users' choice of destination. Creo and Fraboni (2011) conducted research that states that the Blue Flag program is a voluntary certification initiative that can be used as a tool to integrate environmental decision-making in municipalities. Some of the key results of this research were that over 84% of respondents said that there was an increase in recycling practices of municipal waste, over 63% of municipalities introduced new activities and in over 66% of cases general actions have been taken to improve environmental sustainability.

Blue Flag in Italy has had a significant increase in recent years. In 2017 there were 163 resorts, with 342 award-winning beaches. Liguria ranked first with 27 locations, followed by Tuscany (19) and Marche (17). In 2018, there were 175 resorts, with 368 awarded beaches (an increase of 26 compared to the previous year). The first and second places were once again occupied by Liguria (27) and Tuscany

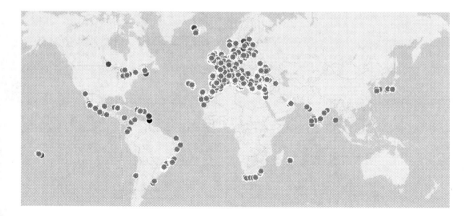

Figure 11.1 Blue Flag sites around the world
Source: Blueflag.global, 2019

(19), followed by Campania (18 – Bandierablu.org, 2020). Figure 11.2 displays the map of the situation.

In 2019 there were 183 places and 385 awarded beaches (an increase of 17 compared to 2018). The first places were always occupied by Liguria (30), Tuscany (19) and Campania (18). In 2020, this number grew further, awarding 22 more beaches, 407 in total, divided among 195 locations (Bandierablu.org, 2020).

Therefore, Italy is ranked in 5th place worldwide for the number of Blue Flags obtained (Blueflag.global, 2020). This number has been growing in recent years, together with the demand for tourism in the country. Indeed, the question around which the study has been conducted is the typology of relationship between the Blue Flag label and the average income of those sites that have been awarded.

What generates interest for the authors is the peculiarity of considering the relevance of the Blue Flag certification for this study, which is the opportunity to assess the role of local institutions as an active part of a process of territorial development. Indeed, as previously mentioned, the Blue Flag, as most of the destination quality labels, is a useful tool to boost, on the one hand, the governmental strategy to improve the environmental performance of local actors and, on the other hand, to push entrepreneurs in the tourism sector to enhance their sustainable business models in order to pursue a valuable sustainable tourism proposal. There is the need, actually, to assess the role of certifications and of local environmental concern in

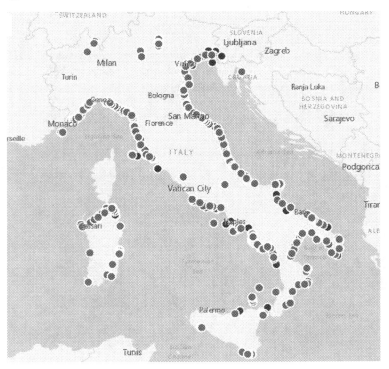

Figure 11.2 Blue Flag sites in Italy

Source: Blueflag.global, 2019

The challenge of sustainability: The Italian context **149**

order to understand how those variables are able to influence the increase of well-ness and richness of the communities endowed with such assets.

Some research showed that the quality certification issued to a province during the previous year has a positive effect on the current inflows. The time lag is probably explained by the fact that the public notice of the new certifications comes after the decisions have already been made for the current season, so the effect emerges during the following season (Capacci et al., 2015). From a political point of view, the results suggest that Blue Flag data are released too late in the year to influence the current decisions of foreign tourists. Furthermore, Capacci et al. (2015) state that quality certifications help bridge the information gap on destinations and positively influence the decisions made by foreign tourists.

We then formulated the following hypothesis, which ought to be confirmed or rejected:

H1: The Blue Flag label has a positive impact on the income per capita of the awarded site.

11.3 Methodology

The aim of the analysis is to assess the impact of the Blue Flag on the tourism industry of the coastal municipalities that in the five reference years (2014–2018) received the award of the Blue Flag.

Specifically, we wanted to understand how the income per capita (dependent variable) adjusts with the variation of tourist presences, Blue Flag award and recycling percentage.

We provided an empirical approach to follow up the hypotheses of the study. Specifically, we used the Generalized Moment Method Dynamic panel data (GMM/DPD), a suitable methodology to investigate the dynamic aspect of the phenomenon, such as the effects on economic policy, e.g., the effect of a Blue Flag in a specific place, to perform the analysis using the most recent version of the statistical software Stata. Previous studies (Yang, 2012; Li et al., 2017; Bernini & Cerqua, 2020) have attempted empirical approaches on this issue. In general, the elements of dynamics in the panel models can be introduced, including the delays of the dependent variable as regressors. In this case, the sample of the analysis is composed of 183 municipalities over the period 2014–2018. A possible advantage of using aggregate data is to remove the individual differences of macro samples, and at the same time maintain the common factor that justifies income per capita level. To assess the relationship between income per capita and the eco-label (Blue Fag), we built the following econometric model, with income per capita as the dependent variable, i.e., how the referenced phenomenon is influenced by the other variables.

$$IPC_{i,\,t} = \alpha + \beta IPC_{i,\,t-1} + \gamma WR_{i,\,t} + \delta BBI_{i,\,t} + \delta TA_{i,\,t} + \delta_i + \varepsilon_{i,\,t} \tag{1}$$

Where TA, WR, BBI and IPC respectively indicate tourist attendance, waste recycling, Blue Flag index and income per capita, δ_i indicates the effect of the ignored variables that correspond to individual difference and $\varepsilon_{i,\,t}$ is the stochastic error, which reflects the effect of the ignored variables.

150　*Francesco Manta et al.*

Moreover, as previously described, the inclusion of a lagged (delayed) dependent variable in the regression model provides a distortion in the parameter estimation that cannot be eliminated through the application of a fixed effect panel. Thus, in order to provide OLS robust and not distorted estimates, it is necessary for explanatory variables to be uncorrelated with the error vector.

The most common approach when dealing with non-stationary data is the application of the first order difference so as to achieve the dynamic specification in raw differences and eliminate the individual effect. According to Arellano and Bond (1991) and Arellano and Bover (1995), the new equation will be:

$$\Delta IPC_{i,\,t} = \alpha + \beta \Delta IPC_{i,\,t-1} + \gamma \Delta WR_{i,\,t} + \delta \Delta BBI_{i,\,t} + \vartheta \Delta TA_{i,\,t} + \delta_i + \varepsilon_{i,\,t} \quad (1)$$

The following step is to choose the instrumental variable, so they are correlated with $\Delta y_{i,\,t-1}$ but not with $\Delta \varepsilon_{i,\,t}$; usually, delayed dependent variables are effective instrumental variables, and so we obtained the instrumental variables like so.

Finally, according to Doornik et al. (2002), we built the optimum weighted matrix, and we followed the Arellano–Bond one-step estimation; pulling out the residual in one-step estimation and computing, a white period covariance matrix was obtained, and we replaced the weighted matrix with it. We used this matrix in a two-step Arellano–Bond estimation and to obtain the parameter estimators.

11.3.1 Variable definition

The variables on which the analysis was conducted were obtained as an average over the values of the years from 2014 to 2018. These were found and entered in the dataset as follows:

- The data on the Blue Flag index were obtained from the site Bandierablu.org. The data collected include a timespan from 2014 to 2018, for each Italian municipality (183) that received the award. It is a dummy variable where the value 1 is associated if the municipality in that year has a Blue Flag, and 0 is associated if it does not have a Blue Flag.
- The data on tourist attendance have been obtained from the ISTAT website (National Institute of Statistics), in the section customer movement in the accommodation venues. By tourist presences we mean the number of nights spent in the accommodation venues (hotel or complementary). The data available on the site range from 2014 to 2018 for each municipality that received the Blue Flag in those years (196).
- The data on income per capita (€/year) were obtained from the MEF (Ministry of Economy and Finance) website, calculated by comparing the taxable income and the number of taxpayers. This can be defined as the amount of gross domestic product that is hypothetically produced, over a certain period, by an individual. The data available on the site go from 2012 to 2017 for each municipality that in those years obtained the Blue Flag (196).

The challenge of sustainability: The Italian context   151

- The data on the percentage of recycling for each municipality that has obtained the Blue Flag (196) were obtained from the ISPRA (Higher Institute for Environmental Protection and Research) site, for a period ranging from 2010 to 2018. This variable has been taken into consideration, as the award of the Blue Flag prize is strongly influenced by this data, being one of the required criteria. Moreover, an additional point is assigned if the municipality carries out the door-to-door collection of waste.

11.3.2 Descriptive statistics

Table 11.1 shows the descriptive statistics of income per capita, the tourist presences and the percentage of recycled waste.

11.4 Results

After the description of the methodological approach, we ran the econometric model we built. The implementation of the econometric model resulted in the outcomes displayed in Table 11.2, including the three empirical techniques adopted to study the phenomenon, respectively OLS, SYS-GMM one step and SYS-GMM two step estimators.

In the first column we have used the OLS estimation; it estimates all three independent variables are statistically significant at the 0.001 level (p-value < 0.001). Unfortunately, the R^2 is very low and as explained in the methodology section the estimates could be distorted; in order to improve the robustness of the analysis, a dynamic panel model estimation has been used.

Columns labeled (2) and (3) report the results of panel dynamic estimation one step and two step with the application of SYM-GMM estimator. Findings show that for both regressions the relationship between IPC and BBI is positive and significant, at the 0.001 level for the column 2 and at 0.01 level for the dynamic panel regression with two step analysis.

In particular, we can interpret the effect of significant variables by concluding that:

- There is a significant and positive relationship between waste recycling and income per capita (Wang et al., 2020);

Table 11.1 Analysis on the impact of BF in Italy: Descriptive analysis

Variables	Mean	Standard deviation	Minimum	Maximum
IPC	16,953.62	3,139.68	9,367.81	27,328.56
WR	54.49	18.87	0.32	88.79
BBI	0.84	0.37	0.00	1.00
TA	616,957.70	1,257,835.19	4,176.00	12,118,298.00

152 *Francesco Manta et al.*

Table 11.2 Panel data model on the impact of BF in Italy: Results

	Ln *IPC (1)* **(OLS)**	**Ln *IPC* (2)** *(SYS-GMM one step)*	**Ln *IPC* (3)** *(SYS-GMM two step)*
Ln *IPC* $_{t-1}$		0.350612***	0.702968***
		(0.0750071)	(0.0984457)
WR	0.00177973***	0.000947902***	−0.000487896*
	(0.000607703)	(0.000165571)	(0.000293892)
BBI	0.0620285**	0.0353938***	0.0282351*
	(0.0274386)	(0.00641012)	(0.0145121)
Ln *TA*	0.0188044**	0.0125604***	0.00366486
	(0.00905122)	(0.00195963)	(0.00559759)
Constant	9.34073***	6.07927***	2.85177***
	(0.125995)	(0.700272)	(0.933984)
R^2	0.08		
Sargan over-identification test		183.952 [0.0000]	22.1548 [0.0046]
Wald test		629.444 [0.0000]	96.8881 [0.0000]

Notes: The values in the table are the coefficients, standard errors (in parentheses), their p-values and summary statistics, as can be seen in each row description
*, **, *** denote significance at the 10%, 5% and 1% levels, respectively

- In the presence of Blue Flag (eco-label certification), the log average income per capita increases, confirming that the presence of an eco-label certification fosters the local development (Crescenzi et al., 2022);
- When the log of average tourist attendance increases, the average per capita income log increases (Santos and Cincera, 2018).

By comparing the standardized betas, we can observe how, among the three significant variables, the one with the greatest impact (that is, the one with the highest standardized beta in absolute value) is Blue Flag.

11.5 Discussion

Through the model whose results we have reported, we tried to evaluate and quantify the impact of the Blue Flag in the municipalities on per capita income, by inserting the independent variables for tourist presences, recycling and Blue Flag index.

However, some relationships were found to be significant. In particular, for the second model, we observed that the Blue Flag has a positive, significant impact on the per capita income of the municipalities. The municipalities awarded with the Blue Flag in Italy still show much room to improve the necessary managerial actions. First, this could be achieved by developing coordinated communication strategies, trying to include the Blue Flag in every communication concept related to destination branding, so that certification can add value to the destination and act as a lever to differentiate the position from the competition, in order to obtain a

The challenge of sustainability: The Italian context 153

competitive advantage. Second, municipal administrations can use their Blue Flag as a springboard to implement territorial qualification strategies aimed at achieving greater sustainability, both on an environmental and socio-economic level. This point has a relevant implication for consumers as well. Indeed, as Buckley (2001) stated, the implementation of a solid and structured sustainable tourism program makes the labels recognizable, enhancing the reputation of the issuer and the appreciation for those locations which are awarded with certifications. This issue is a focal point for the topic, since the mechanism for municipalities to be awarded with the Blue Flag is absolutely voluntary. This implies considerable efforts for local administrations to encourage policies propaedeutic to accomplish the criteria of label endorsement. On the other hand, the monitoring by the international body that issues the Blue Flag requires strict respect of the criteria in order to increase and strengthen the reputation of the eco-label.

Another important implication is given by the role of environmental concern of local communities: although reporting a low coefficient, the impact of recycling on the income is positive and significant. This means that environmental concern has a role in the choice of the touristic destination, increasing the reputation of the site. On the other hand, this is a relevant signal of the ecological awareness of consumers on the site, who pay particular attention to environmental issues. Even if this indicator does not represent a central point of the analysis conducted, i.e., it is not studied in relationship with Blue Flag awarding, the presence of a variable that discloses the "green" behavior of the local community is a means to show off an attitude toward the ecology and respect for the environment and landscape (Claver et al., 2007), which has been proved to have a positive impact on economic performance, as also confirmed with our analysis.

11.6 Conclusions

Through the model's results that have been reported, we tried to assess and quantify the impact of the Blue Flag in the municipalities on per capita income, by including the independent variables for tourist presence, recycling and the Blue Flag index. The obtained results led us to conclude that the role of certifications in local development is significant and effective, meaning that consumers are revealing themselves to be more and more aware of environmental concerns, and of the attention paid by local stakeholders to sustainability issues.

We also understood that there is a strict need for stakeholders to cooperate in order to address useful and effective strategies to enhance the role of local governments and economic actors to improve the economic performance of the tourism locations. The role of institutions, in this sense, is essential and propaedeutic to the establishment of those criteria to make certifications recognizable and well-reputed by consumers and users in general.

Although implications and results turned out to be novel and significant, there were several limitations. First, the poor explanatory results may be due to the fact that the period of time considered is not long enough (four years). Hypothesis is, however, supported by a study conducted in Italy by Capacci et al. (2015), who

154 *Francesco Manta et al.*

stated that there is a significant link between a beach awarded with the Blue Flag and the increase in domestic and foreign tourism. This study showed that the quality certification issued to a province during the previous year has a positive effect on the current inflows. The time delay is probably explained by the fact that the public notice of the new certifications comes after the decisions have already been made for the current season, so the effect emerges during the following season. Consequently, more time is needed for the Blue Flag to have a really positive effect on the increase in tourist numbers for the municipalities that are granted it.

On the other hand, the period could not be extended since data for a longer period were not available for all variables. Future research could follow up the model by adding some variables regarding transport and logistical issues, and enlarge the dataset on a longer time interval. One more possible orientation could be the assessment of tourism income by applying a geographic criterion, understanding if a difference among Italian regions exists. A further inquiry could involve the cultural aspect, by assessing touristic attendance based on national culture dimensions.

11.7 References

Arellano, M., & Bond, S. (1991), Some tests of specification for panel data: Monte Carlo evidence and an application to employment equations. *The Review of Economic Studies*, 58(2), 277–297.

Arellano, M., & Bover, O. (1995), Another look at the instrumental variable estimation of error-components models. *Journal of Econometrics*, 68(1), 29–51.

Ariza, E., Sarda, R., Jimenez, J. A., Mora, J., & Avila, C. (2008). Beyond performance assessment measurements for beach management: Application to Spanish Mediterranean beaches. *Coastal Management*, 40(4).

Bandierablu.org (2021). *Programma Bandiera Blu*, available at http://www.bandierablu.org/common/blueflag.asp

Bernini, C., & Cerqua, A. (2020). Are eco-labels good for the local economy? *Papers in Regional Science*, 99(3), 645–661.

Blackman, A., Naranjo, M. A., Robalino, J., Alpizar, F., & Rivera, J. (2014). Does tourism eco-certification pay? Costa Rica's Blue Flag program. *World Development*, 58, 41–52.

Blueflag.global (2014). *Blue Flag Beach Criteria and Explanatory Notes 2014.*

Brugmann, J. (1996). Planning for sustainability at the local government level. *Environmental Impact Assessment Review*, 16(4–6), 363–379.

Buckley, R. (2001). Major issues in tourism ecolabelling. *Tourism Ecolabelling: Certification and Promotion of Sustainable Management*, 19–26.

Buckley, R. (2002). Tourism ecolabels. *Annals of Tourism Research*, 29(1), 183–208.

Capacci, S., Scorcu, A. E., & Vici, L. (2015). Seaside tourism and eco-labels: The economic impact of Blue Flags. *Tourism Management*, 47, 88–96.

Claver, E., Lopez, M. D., Molina, J. F., & Tari, J. J. (2007). Environmental management and firm performance: A case study. *Journal of Environmental Management*, 84(4), 606–619.

Creo, C., & Fraboni, C. (2011). Awards for the sustainable management of coastal tourism destinations: The example of the Blue Flag program. *Journal of Coastal Research*, 61, 378–381.

Crescenzi, R., De Filippis, F., Giua, M., & Vaquero-Piñeiro, C. (2022). Geographical Indications and local development: The strength of territorial embeddedness. *Regional Studies*, 56(3), 381–393.

The challenge of sustainability: The Italian context **155**

Cronin, J. J., Smith, J. S., Gleim, M. R., Ramirez, E., & Martinez, J. D. (2011). Green marketing strategies: An examination of stakeholders and the opportunities they present. *Journal of the Academy of Marketing Science*, 39, 158–174.

Dodds, R. (2014). *Determining the potential for environmentally sustainable recreation in the Lake Simcoe Watershed.* Ministry of the Environment and Climate Change.

Doornik, J. A., Arellano, M., & Bond, S. (2002). Panel data estimation using DPD for Ox. DPD Package for Ox manual.

Elkington, J. (1997a). *Cannibals with forks. The triple bottom line of 21st century.* Oxford (p. 73).

Elkington, J. (1997b). The triple bottom line. Environmental management: Readings and cases, 2.

Elkington, J. (1998). Partnerships from cannibals with forks: The triple bottom line of 21st-century business. *Environmental Quality Management*, 8(1), 37–51.

Font, X. (2002). Environmental certification in tourism and hospitality: Progress, process and prospects. *Tourism Management*, 23(3), 197–205.

Isprambiente.gov.it (2021). *Catasto rifiuti*, available at https://www.catasto-rifiuti.isprambiente.it/index.php?pg=nazione

Istat.it (2021). *Presenze turistiche medie giornaliere di vacanza in Italia per ripartizione geografica di destinazione e trimestre*, available at http://dati.istat.it/Index.aspx?QueryId=10071

Li, H., Song, H., & Li, L. (2017). A dynamic panel data analysis of climate and tourism demand: Additional evidence. *Journal of Travel Research*, 56(2), 158–171.

Mef.gov.it (2021), *Open Data dichiarazioni fiscali*, available at https://www1.finanze.gov.it/finanze/pagina_dichiarazioni/public/dichiarazioni.php

Saha, D. (2009). Empirical research on local government sustainability efforts in the USA: Gaps in the current literature. *Local Environment*, 14(1), 17–30.

Santos, A., & Cincera, M. (2018). Tourism demand, low cost carriers and European institutions: The case of Brussels. *Journal of Transport Geography*, 73, 163–171.

UNEP, & UNWTO (2006). *Making tourism more sustainable – a guide for policy makers.*

UNWTO (2005). *Indicators of sustainable development for tourism destinations. A guidebook.*

UNWTO (2020). *Tourism in the 2030 Agenda*, available at https://www.unwto.org/tourism-in-2030-agenda

UNWTO, & FEE (2006). *Awards for improving the coastal environment: The example of the Blue Flag.* UN Environmental Programme.

Wang, H., Liu, X., Wang, N., Zhang, K., Wang, F., Zhang, S.,.... & Matsushita, M. (2020). Key factors influencing public awareness of household solid waste recycling in urban areas of China: A case study. *Resources, Conservation and Recycling*, 158, 104813.

Yang, Y. (2012). Agglomeration density and tourism development in China: An empirical research based on dynamic panel data model. *Tourism Management*, 33(6), 1347–1359.

Zeemering, E. S. (2018). Sustainability management, strategy and reform in local government. *Public Management Review*, 20(1), 136–153.

12 Blue Flags on islands in the Republic of Croatia

Kristina Bučar, Izidora Marković Vukadin and Zvjezdana Hendija

12.1 Introduction

The international tourist market is dynamic, and trends have changed since the beginning of modern tourism. The 3S motive (sun, sea and sand) has been the most important motive for choosing tourist destinations over the last 70 years (Boniface & Cooper, 2001; Vukonić & Čavlek, 2001; UNWTO, 2022). Therefore, the tourist regions that have this type of tourism resource record the most tourist visits. In 2019, Europe was the most visited tourist region, recording a 51% share of international tourist arrivals, while the Mediterranean region had a 20.8% share of international tourist arrivals (UNWTO, 2022). To maintain such a position, the Mediterranean tourist region should find ways to preserve the environment and tourism resources (Bučar, 2017). However, a large number of tourist arrivals could lead to the saturation of tourist resources if a long-term planning process is not applied.

The idea of "sustainable development" in Europe started in 1973 when the Environmental Action Program for the first time presented minimum standards that should be respected and applied during long-term development (EC, 2022). After the concept of sustainable development emerged at the international level in 1987, Europe fully accepted and implemented this concept in its strategic documents, actions and businesses. Sustainable tourism development should provide a high-quality experience for tourists and bring long-term positive economic, sociocultural and environmental impacts (Inskeep, 1991). In 1993 a "European network of experts and organizations involved in tourism" (ECOTRANS) was founded, aimed at long-term and successful regional development and resulting from cooperation between "ecology" and "economy" and that the transfer of know-how to all stakeholders in tourism could increase their efficiency as well (ECOTRANS, 2022). At the level of the EU, in 2001 (subsequently renewed in 2006) a Sustainable Development Strategy (EU SDS) was brought, where the main objectives and goals to achieve sustainable development were defined (Eurostat, 2015). Later, in 2007, the European Commission (EC) issued an "Agenda for a sustainable and competitive European tourism", which pointed out that tourism in Europe should provide a balance between tourists' wishes, preserving tourist resources and providing a good environment/framework for doing business by applying a holistic, integrated approach to planning for the long term, and involving all stakeholders

DOI: 10.4324/9781003323570-13

in that process (EC, 2019). Withal, in 2013 the EC developed a "European Tourism Indications System" (ETIS) to encourage tourist destinations to adopt new approaches in tourism planning based on the analysis of collected data and applying a set of tools and indicators (EC, 2019). However, implementing sustainable tourism development into practice is a complex process because each tourist destination is different in its natural and social characteristics; thus it cannot be applied to a unique model of long-term sustainable tourism development (UNEP & UNWTO, 2012).

12.1.1 Emerging of ecolabels in sustainable tourism development

Every tourist destination should put together its development plan to ensure that tourism will take place in the long term. That is especially important for those located in narrow coastal areas and islands that are limited with space and often visited by numerous tourists in a short period of the year (Bučar & Vujević, 2020). The application of ecolabels can play a significant role in this process because their application focuses on identifying business practices based on sustainability principles (Bučar et al., 2022). Ecolabelling entered mainstream environmental policy-making in 1997 when the German government established the Blue Angel certification program (UNEP, 1998).

The first ecolabel for the tourism industry was established by Foundation for Environmental Education (FEE) – Blue Flag in France in 1985 to encourage sustainable tourism development by granting the ecolabel to beaches and marinas (UNEP et al., 1996; FEE, 2022). The ecolabel Blue Flag (BF) has been awarded to beaches and marinas that have clean water available to the local population and tourists in Europe since 1987 and outside Europe since 2001 (FEE, 2022). Since the BF appeared, the number of ecolabels and certificates in the international tourism market has rapidly increased (Bučar et al., 2019). UNEP states that in 1998 there were 28, and EC reports that in 2000 were approximately 60 different tourism ecolabels and certificates in the international tourism market (UNEP, 1998; EC, 2019). At the beginning of the 21st century, their number continued to increase rapidly. According to Totem Tourism, in 2013 there were 138 ecolabels in the tourism market (Totem Tourism, 2013). EC reported that there were 186 ecolabels and certificates in the field of tourism in 2017 (EC, 2019). According to Bučar et al., in 2019 203 ecolabels existed in the international tourism market, and 52% of them were on the international level; the rest were national ecolabels (Bučar, et al., 2019). In 2019 only 24 of them were for tourist destinations and only two were for beaches and marinas at the international level, while those on the national level did not exist (Bučar et al., 2019).

12.1.2 Structure and goal of the research

This chapter aims to show whether the BF ecolabel can encourage sustainable tourism development at the destination level, even though this ecolabel is awarded only for beaches and marinas. The research focuses on sustainable tourism development

158 *Kristina Bučar et al.*

and the role of the BFs ecolabel in this process on islands in Croatia. In addition, the island of Krk has been used for the case analysis since it is the largest island and the most visited by tourists in Croatia.

In the first part of the chapter, the research includes an overview of the scientific and professional literature aiming to emphasize the importance of implementation of the principles of sustainability in tourism development. The emphasis is on the role of applying the BF ecolabel in achieving the sustainable development of tourism.

In the second part of the chapter, the research focuses on investigating the role of the BF in sustainable tourism development on the islands. The focus of the research is on the analysis of natural-geographic and demographic characteristics and the tourism development of islands in Croatia. In this part of the chapter, the island of Krk is taken as an example. It is the largest Croatian island, has the most inhabitants of all Croatian islands, records the most tourist arrivals and overnight stays, and also has the most BFs of all islands in Croatia. Data on waste management, water supply, sanitation, transport infrastructure, sewage, traffic and other key challenges on this island are examined.

The research shows that although BF has been applied in Croatia for more than two decades, its positive impact is still limited only to beaches and marinas. The only exception is the island of Krk, which could serve as a good example for other islands.

12.2 Tourism on Croatian islands

The Mediterranean area is ecologically sensitive and tourism development was one of the reasons to start implementing environmental protection in the Mediterranean quite early. The first international protection started in 1975 when the Mediterranean Action Plan (MAP) was adopted by 16 European Mediterranean countries, and later more countries joined; 22 countries participated in this program in 2022 (UNEP, 2022). The MAP aims to help Mediterranean countries successfully respond to the increasing environmental degradation in the sea, islands and coastal areas and to develop their own national environmental protection strategies by implementing sustainable resource management (UNEP, 2022). This program as a part of UNEP has been created in order to protect the Mediterranean region and contribute to an improved quality of life for the local population (UNEP, 2022).

12.2.1 The importance of tourism development planning in the coastal area and islands in the Mediterranean

Tourism on the European coast of the Mediterranean began to develop at the end of the 19th century. In the beginning, health tourism was developing, and sun and sea tourism started to appear in the 1930s. A significant increase in tourist arrivals was recorded in the second half of the 20th century. In 2019 European countries in the Mediterranean tourist region had a 20.8% share of international tourist arrivals (UNWTO, 2022). Such a large number of tourist arrivals has numerous effects on

Blue Flags on islands in the Republic of Croatia 159

the environment in coastal areas and islands. In the area of the coastal Mediterranean and its islands, tourism has a high seasonality character, which in numerous cases causes problems in those areas. Small islands are limited by their natural resources (water, land, etc.); as a result supply problems in water and energy supply often appear during the peak season (UNWTO, 2004). Tourism development on the small islands significantly changed the way of living of the local population in all aspects of their lives (noise, crowds, etc.). Also, tourism has become an important – and often the only – source of income for many inhabitants, and they abandon their traditional economic activities, such as agriculture and fishing.

Thus, to reduce the negative effects and to increase the positive impacts of tourism development it is important to apply the process of long-term planning in tourist destinations. The application principles of sustainable tourism development at the destination level could be provided by destination management. UNWTO defines destination management as "the coordinated management of all the elements that make up a tourism destination (attractions, amenities, access, marketing and pricing)" (UNWTO, 2019). Destination tourism management (DMO) should harmonize the interests of different stakeholders in the tourism market to achieve optimal and long-term development, respecting economic, ecological and socio-cultural principles of sustainability (Čavlek et al., 2011). Harmonizing the interests of all involved potential stakeholders in tourism development, such as local government, the state and private sectors, non-government organizations, cultural organizations, media, local population and tourists, is a challenging and complex process (Swarbrooke, 2001; Petrić, 2011; Rudan, 2012; Hartman et al., 2019; Barišić et al., 2022). Therefore, for the successful implementation of all principles of sustainability, countries require the cooperation of all stakeholders, regardless of whether they participate in tourism development directly or indirectly (McComb et al., 2017; WWF, 2009; Paskova & Zelenka, 2019).

12.2.2 The role of islands in Croatian tourism

Croatia is located in southeastern Europe with a size of 56,536 km^2 (CBS, 2022a). Although its area is small, Croatia has three different regions in respect of their geography and climate features: (i) inland (continental climate), (ii) mountain region (mountain climate) and (iii) coastal region (Mediterranean climate), which records the most tourist arrivals and tourist overnight stays from all tourist regions in Croatia (Bilen & Bučar, 2004). Modern (organized) tourism in Croatia started in 1868 (Vukonić, 2005). The rapid development of mass tourism began after the 1950s mainly in the narrow coastal area and on the islands. Croatia recorded a constant increase in tourist arrivals until 1990 when, due to the Homeland war, a period of stagnation took place up until 1995 (Barišić et al., 2022). In the last 25 years, again, there has been a constant increase in tourist arrivals. In 2019, Croatia recorded 19.2 million tourist arrivals and 60 million overnight stays (CBS, 2022a). Tourism in Croatia has three main characteristics according to tourist arrivals and overnight stays: (i) 83.9% of all tourist arrivals and 88.6% of overnight stays are made up of foreign tourists; (ii) in the summer season – from June to the end of

160 *Kristina Bučar et al.*

August – Croatia recorded 73.7% of all tourist arrivals and 84.9% of all overnight stays; (iii) more than 85% of all tourist arrivals and overnight stays are recorded in the coastal Croatian region (CBS, 2022a).

The coastal region of Croatia is the most important tourist region in Croatia. The 6,278 km coastline stretches on the eastern coast of the Adriatic Sea, in the north-west from the Savudrija peninsula (the border with Slovenia), to the peninsula Prevlaka in the south-east border to Montenegro (CSB, 2022a). The coastline of the islands is 4,398 km long or 70.1% of the total coastline in Croatia (CSB, 2022a). There are 1,244 islands in Croatia, with the largest islands in Croatia being Krk and Cres, while only 20 islands are over 20 km². There are also 525 islets and 642 skeries i.e. which puts Croatian islands into the category of small islands (Table 1, CBS, 2022a; Duplančić Leder et al., 2004). Forty-seven islands in Croatia are populated and another 15 islands are considered temporarily populated during the summer season (CBS, 2022a).

The islands play an important role in Croatian tourism. In 2019 almost 16% of all tourist arrivals and about 30% of all tourist overnight stays in Croatia took place on 15 Croatian islands (Table 12.1).

The traditional way of living of the local population represents a significant, attractive factor for potential tourists. This tourist resource is slowly disappearing due to pronounced depopulation on the islands in recent decades. Out of the 15 most visited islands in Croatia, only islands Vir, Pag and Krk (all connected

Table 12.1 Most visited islands in Croatia (2019)

(ranked according to the number of tourist arrivals)

No.	Island	Size (km²)	Population in 1991	Population			Population growth 1991–2021 %	Tourist arrivals (in '000s) in 2019	Tourist overnight stays ('000s) 2019
				2001	2011	2021			
1	Krk	405.22	16,402	17,860	19,383	19,916	21.42	818	4,540
2	Pag	284.18	7,969	8,398	9,059	8,339	4.64	428	2,800
3	Hvar	297.38	11,459	11,103	11,077	10,678	−6.82	331	1,619
4	Lošinj	74.37	8,134	7,771	7,587	7,537	−7.34	316	2,364
5	Rab	86.12	9,205	9,480	9,328	8,268	−10.18	279	1,980
6	Korčula	271.47	17,038	16,182	15,522	14,594	−14.34	175	921
7	Brač	395.44	13,824	14,031	13,956	13,825	0.01	144	999
8	Cres	405.71	3,238	3,184	3,079	2,716	−16.12	135	1140
9	Murter	17.58	5,192	5,060	4,895	4,842	−6.74	123	890
10	Vir	22.08	860	1,608	3,000	3,045	254.07	95	718
11	Vis	89.72	4,338	3,617	3,445	3,312	−23.65	52	290
12	Mljet	98.02	1,237	1,111	1,088	1,062	−14.15	34	150
13	Pašman	60.11	3,349	2,711	2,845	2,884	−13.88	31	247
14	Ugljan	50.21	7,581	6,164	6,049	5,769	−23.90	27	22
15	Dugi Otok	113.31	2,873	1,772	1,655	1,746	−39.23	25	17

Sources: Islands' sizes: https://podaci.dzs.hr/media/wsdkedwa/sljh2018.pdf
Population: 2001 and 2011 – Lajić and Mišetić (2013); 2021: https://popis2021.hr/
Tourist arrivals and overnight stays: https://podaci.dzs.hr/hr/podaci/turizam/dolasci-i-nocenja-turista/

Blue Flags on islands in the Republic of Croatia 161

by bridge to the mainland) recorded an increase in population in the last 30 years (1991 to 2021) (Table 12.1). Although these islands record tourist arrivals, depopulation has not been arrested even by tourism development, which directly or indirectly provides a large number of workplaces on the islands in Croatia. However, tourism on islands in Croatia has a seasonal character because almost 90% of all tourist overnight stays are from June to September (CBS, 2022a). Such an annual distribution of realized tourist overnight stays encourages employment in tourism for only a few months, mainly during the summer season. Thus, the lack of apartments for workers has become a significant problem in recent years (Mustać, 2019; Vizek et al., 2022). That has lead to a constant increase in real estate prices in tourist destinations on the islands of Croatia in the last decade. This situation often encourages the local population to emigrate and also discourages positive migration trends through the permanent settlement of tourism employees (Mustać, 2019; Vizek et al., 2022). That demographic characteristic (depopulation) on the islands in Croatia could become one of their most prominent problems in future sustainable development.

12.3 The importance of Blue Flags in sustainable tourism development on the Croatian islands

12.3.1 Blue Flag on the islands in Croatia

The intensive tourism development on islands could cause numerous effects on the environment, such as population concentration in coastal areas, uncontrolled use of resources (drinking water, loss of soil and biodiversity due to large-scale construction), water pollution and generation of large amounts of waste (Bučar and Vujević; 2020). The same problems appeared on the islands of Croatia as a consequence of the relatively rapid tourism development in the last 70 years and also a large number of tourist arrivals, usually in a short summer period. The main threat to the environment on islands in Croatia is the state of the infrastructure. Almost no island in Croatia has an effective waste management system, so the large amount of waste generated through tourism in a short period of the year cannot be properly disposed of (Bučar et al., 2020). Also, the water supply and sewage (sanitation) systems are outdated on the islands in Croatia. Withal, their capacity is insufficient especially during the summer tourist season. The transport infrastructure is also in a bad state. Most of the islands in Croatia have only one main road that connects larger villages. Mainly the other roads on the islands are local and were built solely for the needs of the local population. The lack of parking spaces also increases the traffic jams on the islands. These traffic conditions in the summer peak tourist season disturb the everyday life of the local population and cause dissatisfaction and disappointment among tourists as well. Therefore, it is of utmost importance to implement different tools such as ecolabels, which can encourage the implementation of all sustainability principles to achieve long-term development at the level of a tourist destination (Bučar et al., 2022). BF, the oldest ecolabel in tourism, could be such an instrument because to obtain it, it is necessary to fulfill 29 criteria in four

162   *Kristina Bučar et al.*

categories (environmental education and information, environmental management, safety and services) (FEE, 2022).

BF for the first time was awarded in 1987 in Europe (FEE, 2022). In 2022, 4,932 BF certificates in 48 countries in Europe, the Americas, Asia, Africa and Oceania were awarded (FEE, 2022).

In Croatia, the first BF was awarded in 1997 for only one beach (Lijepa naša, 2022). After that year, the number of awarded BF ecolabels increased, so in 2003, 56 beaches and 16 marinas in Croatia were awarded it (Lijepa naša, 2022). In 2022, in Croatia, 70 beaches and 30 marinas were awarded the BF ecolabel (FEE, 2022).

In Croatia 185 nautical ports exist and 82 (44% of them) are marinas (CBS, 2022b). Of 82 marinas in Croatia, 30 marinas, or 36.5% of them, were awarded BF certificates in 2022 (FEE, 2022). Croatia has over 2,000 registered beaches and only 70 or 3.5% of them were awarded the BF ecolabel in 2022 (Kovačić & Magaš, 2014; FEE, 2022). However, out of the total number of 100 awarded BF ecolabels for beaches and marinas in Croatia, only 34 of them were on islands, of which 24 were for beaches and 10 were awarded to marinas.

The spatial distribution of the obtained BF ecolabels in 2022 on the islands in Croatia shows that 24 of them are located in the area of Istria and Kvarner (the northern part of the coastal region), by far the most developed Croatian tourist regions, while only 10 awarded BF ecolabels are located on the islands in the central and southern coastal tourist regions in Croatia (Figure 12.1; FEE, 2022).

12.3.2 The case of island Krk

The island of Krk has the most awarded BF ecolabels for beaches and marinas of all islands in Croatia (Figure 12.1). There are 15 of 34 awarded BF certificates on islands in Croatia (FEE, 2022). The island Krk is located in the northern part of the Croatian coastal tourist region and it is connected to the mainland by a bridge built in 1980 (Simović, 2000). Krk is the largest island in Croatia by size and population and according to tourist arrivals and overnight stays as well (Table 12.1; CBS, 2022a). This island has the largest number of weekend houses (Opačić & Mikačić, 2009). However, it is not the entire area of the island of Krk that is under equal pressure from economic and tourism development. The western (Malinska, Njivice) and south-western (Krk, Punat) parts of the island are under the most pressure from the population, tourist arrivals and the level of settlement construction, while the eastern (Vrbnik, Šilo) and southern coastal part of the island (Baška) are under much less intense pressure (Zovko et al., 2021).

On the island, efficient waste management has been established even though the island records a constant increase in tourist arrivals. During the summer tourist season, the share of municipal waste increases by up to 55% (MZOE, 2019). In 2005 authorities started the implementation of new waste management solutions on the island (Ponikve doo, 2022). Also, in 2014 a door-to-door collection system was implemented aiming to increase the separate collection of recyclable waste (Ponikve doo, 2022). In 2018, separated waste collection exceeded more than a 55% share of the total amount of municipal waste, with a big difference in the

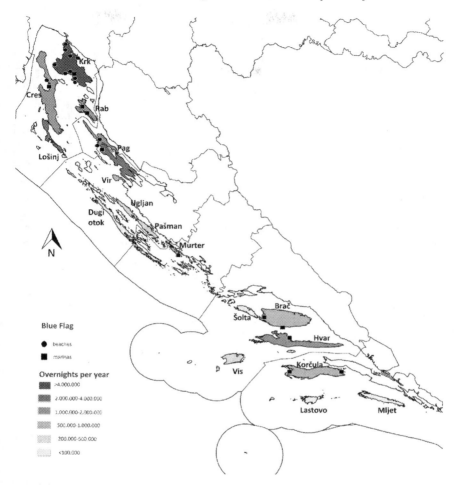

Figure 12.1 Spatial distribution of beaches and marinas with Blue Flag in Croatia

Source: Author's elaboration based on

https://podaci.dzs.hr/hr/podaci/turizam/dolasci-i-nocenja-turista/;

https://www.blueflag.global/;

https://www.lijepa-nasa.hr/wp-content/uploads/2022/06/popis_plaza_i_marina_nagradenih_plavom_zastavom_u_2022.pdf

amount of collected waste between the summer tourist season and the rest of the year (MZOE, 2019). Furthermore, a series of other environmental activities are applied, aimed at recycling, such as the installation of larger containers for biowaste, cardboard and paper, the installation of other containers such as waste textiles and the reconstruction of recycling yards, which leads to continuous progress in the waste management system, but also an increase in the level of awareness of the local community about possibilities of waste recovery (Zovko et al., 2021). This successful implementation of an efficient waste treatment system on the island of

164   *Kristina Bučar et al.*

Krk is a consequence of cooperation between stakeholders such as entrepreneurs, local government, NGOs and the local population.

The island of Krk has relatively efficient management of the water supply. In terms of water supply, the aim is to make the island independent of external sources (Ponikve doo, 2022). There are 500–700 new users per year in the system (mainly by building new swimming pools) and currently, almost 95% of 4-star accommodation facilities on the island of Krk have swimming pools (Ponikve doo, 2022). However, only 55% of households are plugged into seven pumping stations that provide them with purified wastewater to the primary level (Ponikve doo, 2022). Also, winter water consumption is six times lower (during the summer, the flow is 280 l/s) (Ponikve doo, 2022). Although the current number of households that are connected to a drainage system on the island is not satisfactory, it is significantly higher than on most Croatian islands.

The island has been highlighted as one of the ten best European eco-islands (EUKI, 2022). On the island of Krk, through various projects and community involvement actions they are implementing actions to improve the communal and energy infrastructure and services with the plan to become the first energy-independent green Mediterranean island with zero CO_2 emissions (EUKI, 2022).

However, such a number of awarded BFs on the island is not a simple indicator of the complete preservation of the beach or marine area. Nevertheless, the example of the island of Krk in Croatia provides insight into the synergy of sustainable management activities based on the implementation of BF into other aspects of tourist destination management.

12.4 Discussion

Tourists are mostly attracted to the tourist destination by tourist resources, which could not be found in the area of their permanent residence (Boniface & Cooper, 2001). However, tourists are increasingly specific in their demands and environmentally preserved resources become an important factor in choosing a tourist destination (Boniface & Cooper; 2001; King-Chan et al., 2021). The European Mediterranean tourist region records a large number of tourist arrivals and overnight stays, which mainly take place in the narrow coastal region and on the islands. This spatial distribution of tourist arrivals has many positive impacts on those destinations, but also many negative ones. In order to preserve these areas in the long term, it is necessary to apply development planning based on the principles of sustainability. Such tourism development could create the conditions for preserving the environment and the quality of life of the local population, and could also create the conditions for attracting tourists.

12.4.1 The importance of DMOs in sustainable tourism development on the small islands

To reach sustainable tourism development it is necessary to change the ways of management in these areas and all tourism stakeholders should act in a common direction. Ecolabels, if applied effectively, could be an efficient tool to achieve sustainability at the level of the whole tourist destination regardless of whether they relate only to certain parts of tourism (Bučar et al., 2022). In this process, local DMOs should have an important role, but also, they should receive support from the national level as well (UNWTO, 2021).

In Croatia, a new law was brought online in 2019 that determines DMOs as a crucial factor in tourism management at the level of the entire destination. However, this law has not been implemented in practice yet due to the Covid-19 pandemic. At the same time, the government should encourage the unification of a large number of small DMOs into one larger one, so it would be easier to design and implement the tourism development program. That would be especially important in the islands where are several DMOs in a small area.

The only exception among all the islands in Croatia is the island of Krk. Already in 1996, ten smaller DMOs joined together to form one big DMO for the whole island, which conceives and implements tourism development on the entire island (PGZ, 2011). Therefore, the government should make additional efforts to encourage the work of the DMOs in this direction. The first step is acceptance of the new Sustainable Tourism Development Strategy by the end of 2022 for the period up to 2030, while the old strategy ceased to be valid in 2020 (MINT, 2021). Also, it would be good if, in the new Tourism Development Strategy, the implementation of ecolabels is encouraged as one of the instruments that can induce the development of sustainable tourism development not only for individual tourist locations but for entire destination areas.

12.4.2 BF as a tool of sustainable development at the level of tourist destination

The application and number of ecolabels in the international tourist market has increased constantly over the last few decades. BF, as the oldest ecolabel in the field of tourism, is still the most widespread, and a large number of marinas and beaches all over the world apply for this ecolabel every year. One of the most important features is that BF enhances the recognition of sustainable management of coastal resources and may induce local economic growth (Sipic, 2017, Merino & Prats, 2020; Castillo-Manzano et al., 2021). Therefore, it should emphasize that BF is an instrument to improve beach management and not primarily a promotion tool. BFs direct visitors' attention to the fact that the resources of that beach or marina are used for desirable goals such as improving water quality, cleanliness and environmental education (Klein & Dodds, 2018). However, some authors emphasize that keeping maintenance of BF each year is expensive and also demands a lot of resources, and is often missing visible results in the form of additional tourist arrivals and unrealized income (McKenna et al., 2011, Zielinski and Botero, 2019).

Beaches should be considered as multidimensional natural systems where sustainable beach management could contribute not only to the environmental protection of the coast and the narrow coastal area but also to the entire tourist destination. Hence, BF could be one of the environmental management tools.

166   *Kristina Bučar et al.*

The example of the island of Krk shows that the islands face numerous challenges associated with developing tourism. This situation implies the importance of the synergy of all stakeholders involved in tourism development with the common goal of implementing sustainable environmental management at the level of the tourist destination. However, no other island in Croatia has so far tried to apply a similar management principle as did the island Krk. In most islands in Croatia, BF holders are either marinas or large hotel chains for beaches only; on the island of Krk most beaches received BF certificates supported by the local government. This situation shows the importance of the synergy of all stakeholders involved in tourism development with the common goal of implementing sustainable environmental management at the level of the tourist destination.

Thus, it cannot be concluded with certainty whether ecolabels for beaches and marinas (BF) encourage any other positive management activities at the level of the entire tourist destination. However, the goals are complementary and mutual. The quality of the sea is one of the essential prerequisites for granting BF but also for the development of summer tourism in other parts of the destination, so investments in drainage and sewerage at the level of tourist destination are directly related to this indicator.

The main limitation of this chapter lies in the fact that the research covers only one island in Croatia, which has been analyzed in detail. In future research, a detailed analysis should be carried out for the other islands where BF for beaches and marinas have also been awarded.

The contribution of this chapter is in the fact that for the first time it researched the impact of one ecolabel that is narrowly oriented – in this case, the Blue Flag ecolabel – as an instrument that can induce sustainable tourism development at the level of the tourist destination.

12.5 Conclusion

In the era of modern tourism, tourists expect environmentally preserved tourist destinations during their travels. Hence, ecolabels can provide such a guarantee to tourists. They could also stimulate the implementation of some environmental management practices such as the use of new ways and innovations in waste, water or energy management. Over the last three decades, the number of ecolabels and certificates in the international tourism market has significantly increased.

Although the activity of ecolabels is mostly narrowly oriented, they can become an important tool in sustainable tourism development. The Blue Flag is the oldest ecolabel in the tourism industry, and is also still the most widely used ecolabel in the tourism sector. The criteria for awarding the Blue Flag ecolabel are clearly defined. Even though Blue Flag is focused only on beaches and marinas, it could promote and induce the implementation of all principles of sustainability at the level of the whole tourism destination.

The first Blue Flag ecolabel in Croatia was awarded in 1997. However, the analysis of implementation on the Croatian islands shows that there are very few Blue Flag certificates and that their application has not spread beyond beaches and marinas. The only exception among all the islands in Croatia is the island of Krk, the Croatian island with the highest number of tourism arrivals and overnight stays, and the island with the most awarded BF certificates among all islands in Croatia. The island of Krk is also, compared to other islands in Croatia, the island where the biggest number of environmental management solutions have been implemented. That indicates that ecolabels like Blue Flag can contribute to management processes that could lead to greater environmental management efficiency at the level of the entire tourist destination. In addition to that, those positive changes in environmental management on the island of Krk are a result of the cooperation of numerous stakeholders in the last two decades. Therefore, the example of the island has showed that DMOs have a crucial role to play in tourism development, especially in small island areas where it is necessary to consider the whole island as one destination. Withal, this research has shown that for successful tourism development DMOs must take the main initiative and coordinate the work of all tourism stakeholders.

12.6 References

Barišić, P., & Bučar, K. (2022). The role of social media to increase social responsibility among sports tourists. In *International Perspectives on Sport for Sustainable Development* (Chapter 20, pp. 357–383), Springer Science and Business Media.

Bilen, M., & Bučar, K. (2004). *Osnove turističke geografije*. Mikrorad.

Boniface, B., & Cooper, C. (2001). *Worldwide destinations: The geography of travel and tourism*. Butterworth-Hainemann.

Bučar, K. (2017). Green orientation in tourism of Western Balkan countries. In *Green Economy in the Western Balkans: Towards a Sustainable Future* (pp. 175–209). Emerald Publishing.

Bučar, K., Hendija, Z., & Katić, I. (2022). Ecolabels as a tool of sustainable development in tourist destinations. *Sustainability*, 14(10), 6313. https://doi.org/10.3390/su14106313

Bučar, K., Van Rheenen, D., & Hendija, Z. (2019). Ecolabelling in tourism: The disconnect between theory and practice, *Tourism: An International Interdisciplinary Journal*. https://hrcak.srce.hr/file/335262

Bučar, K., & Vujević, S. (2020). ULOGA TURIZMA U STVARANJU OTPADA NA OTOCIMA // Conference Proceedings of the International Conference on the Economics of decoupling (ICED), Zagreb. https://drive.google.com/file/d/13SYU5M3O8_dCG6jmGTIXH6uMrpnK3mVO/view

Castillo-Manzano, J. I, Castro-Nuño, M., López-Valpuesta, L., & Zarzoso, A. (2021). Measuring the role of Blue Flags in attracting sustainable "sun-and-sand" tourism. *Current Issues in Tourism*, 24(15), 2204–2222. DOI: 10.1080/13683500.2020.1844642

Čavlek, N., Bartoluci, M., Prebežac, D., & Kesar, O. (2011). *Turizam – ekonomske osnove i organizacijski sustav*. Školska knjiga.

CBS (Croatian Bureau of Statistics – Republic of Croatia). (2022a). https://podaci.dzs.hr/media/wsdkedwa/sljh2018.pdf

168 *Kristina Bučar et al.*

CBS. (2022b). https://podaci.dzs.hr/media/fagflfgk/croinfig_2021.pdf

Duplančić Leder, T., Ujević, T., & Čala, M. (2004). Coastline lengths and areas of islands in the Croatian part of the Adriatic Sea determined from the topographic maps at the scale of 1:25 000. *Geoadria*, 9(1), 5–32. https://doi.org/10.15291/geoadria.127

EC. (2019). Facts and Figures: EU Ecolabel products/services keep growing. European Commission. http://ec.europa.eu/environment/ecolabel/facts-and-fi gures.html

EC. (2022). Programme of action (ECSC, Euratom, EEC) on the environment. 1973–1976. https://cordis.europa.eu/programme/id/ENV-ENVAP-1C

ECOTRANS. (2022). https://www.globalnature.org/35669/CooperatFions/Membership/ ECOTRANS/resindex.aspx

EUKI. (2022). Krk on the way to becoming a carbon-neutral and energy-autonomous island, European Climate Initiative EUKI. https://www.euki.de/en/euki-projects/ krk-carbon-neutral-island/

Eurostat. (2015). Sustainable development in the European Union: 2015 monitoring report of the EU Sustainable Development Strategy: 2015 edition. LU: Publications Office. https://data.europa.eu/doi/10.2785/999711

FEE. (2022). Blue Flag; The Foundation for Environmental Education. https://www. blueflag.global/all-bf-sites#

Hartman, S., Parra, C., & de Roo, G. (2019). Framing strategic storytelling in the context of transition management to stimulate tourism destination development. *Tourism Management*, 75, 90–98. DOI: 10.1016/j.tourman.2019.04.014

Inskeep, E. (1991). Tourism planning: An integrated and sustainable development approach. John Wiley & Sons.

King-Chan, M. S. E., Capistrano, R. C. G., & López, E. L. F. (2021). Tourists do behave responsibly toward the environment in Camiguin Province, Philippines. *Tourism Geographies*, 23(3), 573–598, DOI: 10.1080/14616688.2020.1833970

Klein, L., & Dodds, R. (2018). Blue Flag beach certification: An environmental management tool or tourism promotional tool? *Tourism Recreation Research*, 43(1), 39–51. DOI: 10.1080/02508281.2017.1356984

Kovačić M., & Magaš D. (2014). Beaches as a Croatian valuable resource and question are how to manage them? 7th World Conference for Graduate Research in Tourism, Hospitality and Leisure, Proceedings Book, Istanbul, Turkey, June 3–7, pp. 503–508.

Lajić, I., & Mišetić, R. (2013). Demografske promjene na hrvatskim otocima na početku 21. stoljeća. *Migracijske i etničke teme*, 29(2), 169–199, https://core.ac.uk/download/ pdf/18622167.pdf

Lijepa naša. (2022). https://www.lijepa-nasa.hr/plava-zastava/

McComb, E. J., Boyd, S., & Boluk, K. (2017). Stakeholder collaboration: A means to the success of rural tourism destinations? A critical evaluation of the existence of stakeholder collaboration within the Mournes, Northern Ireland. *Tourism and Hospitality Research*, 17(3), 286–297. DOI: 10.1177/1467358415583738

McKenna, J. W., Allan T., & Cooper, J. A. G. (2011). Blue Flag or Red Herring: Do beach awards encourage the public to visit beaches? *Tourism Management*, 32(3), 576–588.

Merino, F., & Prats, M. A. (2020). Are Blue Flags a good indicator of the quality of sea water on beaches? An empirical analysis of the Western Mediterranean basin. *Journal of Cleaner Production*, 330, 129865.

MINT. (2020). Pokrenuta Aktivnost Izrade Nove Strategije Razvoja Održivog Turizma do 2030. godine. https://mint.gov.hr/vijesti/pokrenuta-aktivnost-izrade-nove-strategije-razvoja-odrzivog-turizma-do-2030-godine/22088

Blue Flags on islands in the Republic of Croatia 169

Mustać, J. (2019). Real estate price bubble in the Republic of Croatia. *Oeconomica Jader-tina*, 9(1), 78–88.

MZOE. (2019). Izvješće o komunalnom otpadu za 2018. godinu, Ministarstvo zaštite okoliše i energetike Zagreb. https://mingor.gov.hr/UserDocsImages/Pristup%20informacijama/OTP_Izvje%C5%A1%C4%87e%20o%20komunalnom%20otpadu_2018.pdf

Opačić, V. T., & Mikačić, V. (2009). Second home phenomenon and tourism in the Croatian littoral – two pretenders for the same space? *Tourism: An International Interdisciplinary Journal*, 57(2). 155–175.

Paskova, M., & Zelenka, J., (2019). How crucial is the social responsibility for tourism sustainability? *Social Responsibility Journal*, 15(4) 534–552. DOI: 10.1108/SRJ-03–2018–0057

Petrić, L. (2011). Upravljanje turističkom destinacijom : načela i praksa, Udžbenici Sveučilišta u Splitu = Manualia Universitatis studiorum Spalatensis.

PGZ. (2011). Statut turističke zajednice otoka Krka, Primorsko-goranska županija, Službeno glasilo. http://www.sn.pgz.hr/default.asp?Link=odluke&id=21725

Ponikve doo. (2022). Working materials from interviews with Ponikve managers for the Regional TSSA.

Rudan, E. (2012). Uloga lokalnog stanovništva u razvoju turizma destinacije, *Tranzicija*, 14(29), 58–67. https://hrcak.srce.hr/86070

Simović, V. (2000). Dvadeseta obljetnica mosta kopno – otok Krk. *Građevinar*, 52(8), 431–442, https://hrcak.srce.hr/file/20029

Sipic, T. (2017). Eco-labelling of marine recreation services: The case of Blue Flag price premium in Croatia. *Journal of Ecotourism*, 16(1), 1–23. DOI: 10.1080/14724049.2016.1194848

Swarbrooke, J. (2001). Sustainable tourism management. CAB International.

Totem Tourism. (2013). Tourism & Greenwash Report. https://www.green-tourism.com/wpcontent/uploads/2016/03/Totem-Tourism-Greenwash-Report-2013.pdf

UNEP. (1998). The trade and environmental effects of ecolabels: Assessment and Response. https://unep.ch/etb/publications/Ecolabelpap141005f.pdf

UNEP. (2022). https://www.unep.org/unepmap/

UNEP, & UNWTO. (2012). Tourism in the green economy – background report, UNWTO, Madrid, Spain. http://staging.unep.org/greeneconomy/Portals/88/documents/ger/ger_final_dec_2011/To urism%20in%20the%20green_economy%20unwto_unep.pdf

UNEP, WTO, & FEE. (1996). Awards for improving the coastal environment: The example of the Blue Flag. https://wedocs.unep.org/bitstream/handle/20.500.11822/26310/Awards_coastal_environment.pdf?sequence=1&isAllowed=y

UNWTO. (2004). Indicators of sustainable development for tourism destinations, a guidebook, Madrid, Spain.

UNWTO. (2019). Practical guide to tourism destination management, Default Book Series. https://www.e-unwto.org/doi/book/10.18111/9789284412433

UNWTO. (2021). Launch of the global sustainable tourism criteria. https://www.unwto.org/archive/global/news/2011-08-16/launch-global-sustainable-tourism-criteria

UNWTO. (2022). Tourism highlights. https://www.e-unwto.org/doi/epdf/10.18111/9789284422456

Vizek, M., Stojčić, N., & Mikulić, J. (2022). Spatial spillovers of tourism activity on housing prices: The case of Croatia. *Tourism Economics*, 0(0). https://doi.org/10.1177/13548166221106442

Vukonić, B. (2005). Povijest hrvatskog turizma, Prometej, Zagreb, Croatia.

Vukonić, B., & Čavlek, N. (2001). Rječnik turizma, Masmedia, Zagreb, Croatia.

WWF. (2009). Towards sustainable tourism investment. https://assets.panda.org/downloads/towards_sustainable_tourism_investment.pdf

Zielinski, S., & Botero, C. (2019). Myths, misconceptions and the true value of Blue Flag. *Ocean & Coastal Management*, 174, 15–24. DOI: 10.1016/j.ocecoaman.2019.03.012

Zovko, M., Melkić, S., & Marković Vukadin, I. (2021). Primjena okvira DPSIR za procjenu ekoloških problema s naglaskom na gospodarenje otpadom izazvano stacionarnim turizmom u Jadranskoj Hrvatskoj. *Geoadria*, 26(1), 83–106. DOI: 10.15291/geoadria.3154

13 The impact on the local economy of having coastal areas with Blue Flag

The Turkish case

Zeliha Eser and Selay Ilgaz Sümer

13.1 Introduction

Tourism is one of the world's largest industries in terms of natural resources. This industry contributes significantly to the economies of developing countries by bringing in foreign exchange. However, uncontrolled and poorly planned tourism activities cause significant environmental damage. The diversity of such activities is growing in tandem with the increase in demand for tourism activities (FEE, 2006), which contribute to economic growth as an important component of national and international trade.

Tourism activities are intertwined with natural resources and are closely related to nature. A tourism approach that does not care about natural resources and nature cannot be successful in an environment where environmental awareness is developing and becoming widespread. According to this viewpoint, tourism businesses operating on a national and international scale, particularly by attracting the attention of their customers with innovative environmental awareness strategies, seek to gain a competitive advantage over their competitors and increase their revenues (Capacci et al., 2015; Fıskın et al., 2016).

In this context, there are economic instruments developed to implement environmental policies in the international arena. These tools, called eco-labels, raise awareness in the sector they are in, prevent environmental damage, support companies operating in this field in complying with national environmental regulations and at the same time contribute to their competitiveness (Kından, 2006). Various eco-label schemes emerged in Europe in the 1980s with the goal of introducing a distinction of quality assurance for beaches that provided economic, social, reputational and environmental benefits to a country, while also attempting to go further and strengthen European policy (Zielinski and Botero, 2019).

The Blue Flag as one of the eco-labels is an international environmental award given to qualifying beaches and marinas that meet certain criteria. "It represents a clean, well-equipped, safe, and thus civilized, sustainable environment. Aside from providing essentially clean sea water for beaches, it represents good environmental management with the necessary equipment, emphasizing environmental education and information." (Kindan, 2006)

DOI: 10.4324/9781003323570-14

Under the direction of the Ministry of Tourism, Turkey launched the Blue Flag program in 1993. The international Foundation for Environmental Education (FEE), based in Copenhagen, is in charge of the program's international coordination. This organization wants non-governmental organizations to represent countries that want to participate in the Blue Flag project. As a result, the Turkish Environmental Education Foundation has been carrying out the Blue Flag project since 1993.

Turkey benefits greatly from the Blue Flag's status as an eco-label. Turkey ranks third globally in the 2021 International Blue Flag Awards, with 519 Blue Flag beaches, and is predicted to win the World Championship in 2023. This merit might reflect Blue Flag's economic influence.

In this chapter, it is aimed to address the Blue Flag practices in Turkey and to examine the impacts of the Blue Flag on local economy from different perspectives. The rest of the chapter is organized as follows. Section 13.2 briefly introduces the Blue Flag practices in Turkey. Section 13.3 deals with the impact on the local economy of having coastal areas with Blue Flag in Turkey in macro and micro levels. The final part includes the concluding remarks.

13.2 Blue Flag practices in Turkey

Tourism has potential in the economic development of many countries. In terms of Turkey, tourism is one the sectors that generates significant income in the country. Tourism and travel services have a great contribution to GDP. In 2021, this contribution exceeded nearly 50 billion euros (Dierks, 2022).

Countries use various tools such as eco-labels to make tourism activities more attractive and provide a competitive advantage. Blue Angel, EarthCheck, Eco Hotels Certified, Green Key and Green Leaf Eco Standard are some of the eco-labels related to the tourism sector (Fıskın et al., 2016). The Blue Flag eco-label leads the way in this regard. Eco-label studies, which started with the Blue Flag campaign in 1985, gained momentum when it showed itself in practice in 1987 (Zielinski & Botero, 2019). Therefore, it plays a leading role in the development of eco-labeling activities.

When the number of international Blue Flag beaches in 2022 is examined, Spain (621), Greece (581), Turkey (531), Italy (427) and France (419) constitute the first five countries; the total number of international Blue Flag beaches is 4,194 (http://www.mavibayrak.org.tr/tr/icerikDetay.aspx?icerik_refno=1, n.d.).

By 2022, 45 countries had implemented the Blue Flag program. Turkey is one of these countries. According to the 2022 Blue Flag data, Turkey had 531 Blue Flag beaches, 24 Blue Flag marinas, 5 Blue Flag yachts and 15 Blue Flag tourism boats (http://www.mavibayrak.org.tr/en/Default.aspx, n.d.). Antalya is at the top of the list, followed by Muğla, İzmir, Aydın, Balıkesir and Samsun (Kobal, 2022). When the number of Blue Flags in the last five years in Turkey is examined, the numbers are on an increasing trend. The number of Blue Flag beaches was 459 in 2018, 463 in 2019, 486 in 2020, 519 in 2021 and 531 in 2022 (http://www.mavibayrak.org.tr/tr/icerikDetay.aspx?icerik_refno=1, n.d.).

13.3 The impacts of Blue Flag on the local economy

The growth of tourism has been the main driving force of economic growth in many countries, especially in those that have promoted mass tourism of "sea-sand-and-sun" (Gao & Zhang, 2019), and particularly in developing countries such as Turkey.

According to the United Nations Environment Program (UNEP, 2005), tourism is sustainable when there is public awareness of its present and potential economic, social and environmental effects and when it satisfies the needs of visitors, businesses, the environment and host communities. Combining a growing tourism industry with environmental sustainability is undoubtedly a major global challenge.

The impact of tourism on regional development can have both positive and negative effects. The benefits of tourism on the local economy and sociocultural development are among its advantages. In terms of the economy, tourist expenditures on things like lodging, transportation, food and shopping generate direct revenue for the area. Tourism also increases the demand for production and supplier firms to provide jobs and raw materials in that region. It has a positive sociocultural impact by fostering cross-cultural interaction and promoting harmony between residents and visitors. These factors support the notion that tourism is highly advantageous for local development.

It has been observed that the Blue Flag application, one of the eco-labels used in the tourism industry, has also contributed either directly or indirectly to the number of tourists, tourism revenue, employment and the economic and social development in the touristic settlements.

Contributions include the growth of tourism in the area, highlighting distinctive locally produced goods, protecting the region's historical and cultural richness, increasing societal awareness, increasing tolerance for visitors, developing and implementing sustainable tourism policies, generating new employment opportunities, raising income levels, etc.

In the following section, the effect of having Blue Flag coastal areas in Turkey on the local economy will be examined from different perspectives.

13.3.1 Promote the creation of new jobs and employment of local staff

Tourism, by creating new job opportunities in the country, has a positive impact on interregional income distribution and allows for balanced regional development. When tourism investments gain momentum in coastal regions, the new job opportunities created by these investments in the region raise working-class income and have a positive impact on the region's income distribution. Despite being a service sector, tourism has a close relationship with 33 other sectors due to its unique characteristics. In other words, developing tourism in a country or region entails developing 33 sectors (Çeken, 2008).

The tourism industry is an important economic tool for coastal regions, creating jobs and significantly increasing regional incomes with marinas and beaches having the greatest impact (Semeoshenkova & Newton, 2015; Fıskın et al., 2016;

Houston, 2013). The demand for beaches and marinas with the Blue Flag undoubtedly creates new business areas as well as jobs for local residents. Yacht textiles have become a new business area for yachts arriving at marinas on Turkey's Mediterranean and Aegean Coasts. Additionally, businesses offering yacht maintenance and repair services have created job opportunities for experienced individuals. In coastal areas, more than 1,000 lifeguards are on duty in approximately 600 touristic facilities located on 463 beaches, which received the Blue Flag Award in 2019. New luxury hotels are also being built on the coastal beaches and locals are employed in these hotels. Research showed that the Blue Flag practices have stimulated the construction of 12–19 additional hotels per year. This additional flow of tourists generates an increase in the hotel industry in the locality and, consequently, provides an additional stimulus for the local economy (Merino & Prats, 2020).

According to Blackman et al. (2014), the Blue Flag is an important factor in making investments in new luxury hotels, and it provides an opportunity to improve environmental performance by offering special opportunities to tourism operators in developing countries.

13.3.2 Favors sustainable tourism in coastal areas

Tourism eco-labels, like those for other industries, aim to reduce environmental impact. A well-executed Blue Flag enforcement program can influence both service providers and consumers. Because tourism businesses are environmentally conscious, they recognize the economic benefits of having the Blue Flag. To put it another way, the Blue Flag aids in the marketing of tourism services. Furthermore, tourists who value environmental sustainability consider Blue Flag facilities in their holiday preferences. Tourism eco-label programs frequently concentrate on facilities. The reason for this is that tourists spend the majority of their time in facilities (Fıskın et al., 2016).

The Blue Flag program has been publicized in the media in order to encourage the sustainable development of coastal areas through good environmental practices, fostering collaboration between the tourism industry and other sectors, and informing guests, managers and the general public through campaigns and a code of conduct (Fraguell et al., 2016). Favoring environmental values (such as clean and certified beaches) promotes a higher quality tourism sector that targets a higher-income segment of the population. This stimulates the local economy and ensures greater respect for natural resources and ecological values.

Blue Flag emphasizes the importance of addressing environmental issues in order to improve the sustainability of human settlement through planning and management through awareness-raising events and campaigns directed at local communities and tourists. Furthermore, it actively promotes local green transportation infrastructure alternatives (Kindan Cebbari, 2019).

In Turkey, visitors to Blue Flag–awarded areas personally witness the region's changes and improvements, and they demand that municipalities work toward receiving awards for places that did not receive the award. The TÜRÇEV Blue Flag program expressed its views in the Antalya Metropolitan Municipality Konyaalti

The impact of Blue Flag in Turkey   175

Beach Life Park Projects, and the municipality implemented a project that increased sustainable transportation, disabled facilities and green area texture.

Blue Flag's criteria encourage people to keep the water clean and save water, thereby reducing their environmental impact and promoting sustainable practices. Various training activities are organized to prevent and reduce waste, as well as to ensure waste reuse and recycling (Kindan Cebbari, 2019). Beaches in particularly sensitive areas are encouraged to provide special and additional information, and beaches, in general, are encouraged to provide information about the local ecosystem and support conservation efforts in accordance with environmental education criteria. The Ministry of Environment and Urbanization prepared the bathing water profile documents along the country because they were a requirement of the Blue Flag criteria in 2014. As an example, a hotel, located in Side, has made an effort to reduce the use of disposable plastic bottles by installing water dispensers in hotel areas. Similarly, by using paper straws instead of plastic straws in hotel areas, a hotel in Lara avoided the use of 142,600 PET bottles and 275,800 plastic straws in one year as a result of a decision made in 2018.

Hotels and beach businesses implementing these examples will help to reduce plastic waste pollution across the country. It would be misleading, however, to claim that this awareness is prevalent in all tourist attractions and small businesses.

13.3.3 Contribute to fighting poverty by supporting local economies

Tourism clearly has a significant impact in developing countries. The important question is how significant these effects are in countries with a high proportion of poor people. The data obtained reveal that tourism is important and growing in the majority of poor countries. As a result, tourism has the potential to become a source of income for the majority of the world (Özkök, 2006).

Tourism activity as a whole includes tourist transportation, accommodation, the service staff, the attitude of the local people and the overall quality of the region, which are all very important. In this regard, the municipality where the beach is located, as well as the marina and other touristic businesses in the area, bear a great deal of responsibility.

Tourism creates a broad field of activity for participation, opportunities that do not require large capital investments and products produced by hand labor that can be easily produced and sold. Because the consumer visits the location where the product is located, it creates the opportunity to sell various goods and services, as well as important opportunities for connections (Özkök, 2006).

Obviously, additional and indirect effects in the local economy can be generated outside of the tourism sector, as tourists consume goods and services from other sectors of the local economy that provide the inputs and the extra income generated. A lot of business is emerging, particularly in the yachting industry. Parallel to this, these business areas allow locals to earn a living as well as find work. Painting and varnishing, machinery and generators, electricity, electronics, plumbing, lathe, carpentry, hydraulics-based systems, safety tools, fire protection equipment, flooring, mechanical works, air conditioning and ventilation, diving services, jet

176 Zeliha Eser and Selay Ilgaz Sümer

ski services, fuel companies, sheet metal and fiber works, water making works, cleaning and spraying companies, winter boat personnel accommodation, rental houses, rental cars, taxi usage, supermarkets, hardware stores, shopping centers, restaurants and cafes generate economic income (Özatağ, 2022).

The Blue Flag encourages sustainable farming and boating practices, and supports local sustainable fishing communities. It also protects fisheries ponds and promotes sustainable fishing practices. Through awareness-raising activities for both adults and children, Blue Flag places a high priority on preventing food waste and the excessive use of natural resources, safeguarding ecosystems, and recycling water to reduce water consumption. These programs have positive outcomes, encouraging sustainable development, assisting local agriculture, boosting the economy and assisting in the fight against hunger and poverty (Kindan Cebbari, 2019). For example, in Antalya province in 2019, with the collaboration of the Turkish Environmental Education Foundation (TÜRÇEV), Antalya Agriculture and Forestry Directorate, Mediterranean Fishermen and Sports Club Association (AKBADER), Touristic Airline Transportation (Corendon Airlines), Belek Tourism Investors Joint Venture (BETUYAB), Mediterranean Fisheries Research Production and Training Institute (AKSAM), the project called "Let's Meet in the Blue" for Future Generation has been conducted to reach children aged 5–14. The project aimed to instill a love of nature and the sea in children and their parents by raising awareness about fish varieties, amateur fishing rules, sea creatures, sea pollution and its effects on sea creatures, and sustainable fisheries hunting (Antalya Provincial Agriculture and Forestry Directorate, 2019).

13.3.4 Attract potential visitors to that destination

Examining the literature on "Blue Flag" and "eco-label", it is clear that the academic community is divided on the importance and value of this practice. In their study, Kozak and Nield (2004) discovered that approximately 50% of German tourists prioritize environmental quality when planning their vacation and selecting a destination. According to Font (2002), the Blue Flag is an important reason for beach preference, and it is regarded as a sign of prestige. Similarly, Capacci et al. (2015) concluded in their study of the Italian coasts that foreign tourists prefer Blue Flag places. In addition, the findings of a survey conducted by Dodds (2010) with 500 tourists on the economic effects of beaches, the Blue Flag label encourages beach visitors to stay longer and be more satisfied, and also encourages tourists to return to these areas. The Blue Flag label would inevitably contribute significantly to the economic growth of these areas. Merli et al. (2019, p. 169) discovered that customers who stay in hotels that implement environmentally friendly practices are more satisfied and develop loyalty to those hotels (Zeydan & Gürbüz, 2021).

Consumer demand for tourism products frequently involves a complex decision-making process. Consumers have many decision stages, and these stages do not have to be in any particular order (Manap, 2006, p. 158). Blue Flags are signs that determine the environmental preference of a product within a specific product category and serve as a decision support mechanism for customer preferences

(Buckley, 2002). Research conducted by Nelson et al. (2000) reveals that it is critical to have a Blue Flag in order to meet the expectations and desires of customers. Respondents also believe that Blue Flag is a method of attracting customer attention and enhancing a company's marketing power. According to their findings, 72% of people believe that the Blue Flag is an important factor in choosing a beach. Buckley (2002) states that Blue Flag and other eco-labels are important in environmental management and tourism marketing. He also mentions how tour operators use it to market their services.

13.3.5 Encourage building new infrastructure in the region

Sun and beach tourism has thrived in coastal areas, typically in sand and beach-dune systems. Incompatibilities arose quickly as a result of the continued increase in visitor flows and the resulting increase in the supply of accommodation and services, particularly in relation to land development and the construction of housing for tourist use (Gual et. al, 2015). The growth of the infrastructure is equally important as this increase in supply.

Tourism development is dependent on well-prepared infrastructure. Prior to the 1990s, infrastructure and superstructure were classified separately; however, today, infrastructure and superstructure are considered together. Infrastructure includes sewerage, roads, water, electricity systems, communication, entertainment and park areas, resting places, museums, lodging businesses, restaurants and shopping centers (Akyurt, 2008). The region's physical infrastructure will be developed depending on the growth of tourism facilities. As a result of its tourist supply potential, the region will reduce the imbalance with other industrial regions with ready infrastructure (Çeken, 2008).

Blue Flag encourages environmental management innovation. The program promotes clean and environmentally friendly technologies while increasing resource efficiency. In addition to promoting sustainable infrastructure, the Blue Flag emphasizes accessibility for people with disabilities. The Blue Flag encourages the development and use of environmentally friendly transportation (Kindan Cebbari, 2019).

Luxury hotels, particularly in the Mediterranean and Aegean regions, help municipalities develop infrastructure opportunities. Not only tourists but also local people benefit from these infrastructure opportunities. Some practices in Turkey are as follows (Kindan Cebbari, 2019):

- There are devices that can charge mobile phones under solar-paneled umbrellas on some hotel beaches.
- Amphibious vehicles have been developed specifically for beach structure and have begun to be used to collect seaweed on Kocaeli's Blue Flag beaches.
- Alanya Municipality uses a marine garbage collection vehicle made of waste materials to clean up marine litter. (https://www.alanya.bel.tr/Haber/26858/ ALANYA-DA--DIP-TEMIZ-TERTEMIZ-ETKINLIGI-, 2019)

In 2018, approximately seven million euros in cultural and financial assistance was provided throughout Turkey for the Wastewater Treatment Plant, Sewage Collector

Line, Deep Sea Discharge, Storm Water Drainage and Road Construction. The requirements are based on the European Union Urban Wastewater Treatment Regulation, and in this context, each award-winning beach's sanitary facilities must be connected to a treatment plant with a sewage system. Many treatment plants have been built along Turkey solely for this criterion.

For its part, TÜRCEV has initiated the construction of many new treatment plants (Samsun Dou Advanced Biological Treatment Plant, Van Tusba Municipality Mollakasim Public Beach, etc.) with the Blue Flag program. Alanya-Antalya, Ölüdeniz-Fethiye has been instrumental in its renewal. In this regard, the Ministry of Culture and Tourism provided a total of 15.9 million euros in financial aid throughout Turkey in 2017 for infrastructure and environmental regulations (Wastewater Treatment Plant, Sewage Collector Line, Deep Sea Discharge, Storm Water Drainage, Road Construction). The amount allotted to the Turkish Blue Flag provinces is nearly 6 million euros.

13.3.6 Enhances international cooperation

Blue Flag's global profile is comprised of collaboration and partnerships at multiple levels between multiple stakeholders from the public, private and NGO sectors: at the local level, between establishments and tourists, suppliers and the local community, and at the national and international levels, between NGOs, corporate partners, public authorities and ministries, UN entities and other partners committed to sustainable tourism. Partnerships among these actors are critical for sharing knowledge, expertise, technology and financial resources to support the achievement of the Sustainable Development Goals (Kindan Cebbari, 2019).

Members of the international jury include the United Nations World Tourism Organization (UNWTO), the International Lifesaving Federation (ILS), the European Environment Agency, the European Network for Accessible Tourism (ENAT), the European Union for Coastal Conservation (EUCC), UNEP, UNESCO and the Responsible Whale Watching Project.

13.3.7 Promote active lifestyles and social well-being

The provision of supplementary services and complementary activities (such as diving, nature excursions, sailing, yachting or standard leisure activities) seems to be valuable as it is very likely that the types of visitors who value a sustainably managed environment will have different preferences for certain supplementary service (Merino & Prats, 2020).

Where people spend their money and time is related to their lifestyle. People can develop interests in the context of their lifestyles in an environment with a clean and sustainable ecosystem by considering the opportunities available to them. In this context, Blue Flag practices have an impact on people's lifestyles and social welfare. People in Turkey have begun to develop a lifestyle on the water as a result of Blue Flag practices. Every year, the number of people who choose to live on their boats grows, especially during the summer months. Furthermore,

The impact of Blue Flag in Turkey   179

it is observed that locals design various services for tourists who visit Turkey via cruise tourism, interacting with tourists and socializing with them. Furthermore, international marriages have been observed as a result of long-term visitors meeting the locals.

13.3.8 Promote the country in the world

Eco-labels are "tools used to inform consumers that certain levels of environmental performance have been met by products or services" (Lee, 2001, p. 317). Indeed, eco-labeling allows consumers to distinguish eco-friendly products from others. From this perspective, it is clear that eco-labeling aids in product differentiation among competitors. This is also applicable to countries in terms of Blue Flag.

Competition among seaside destinations occurs both nationally and internationally, and tourism companies are increasingly focused on gaining significant competitive advantages over competitors. Rejuvenation strategies are thus developed in order to gain or retain market power over domestic or international competitors and, as a result, increase revenues (Capacci et al., 2015).

The adoption of some kind of eco-label scheme is a way of introducing economic, social, reputational and environmental benefits to a country. Such schemes began around 1985 in Europe and they have spread worldwide, especially in developed countries. Among the best recognized are the Blue Flag and the Green Globe. Nowadays, eco-labeling schemes for tourist attractions are common among developed countries because they allow the development of sustainable tourism promotion strategies at local, national and international levels (Merino & Prats, 2020).

Mega yachts visiting Turkish coastal regions, in particular, play an important role in promoting the country. Mega yachts are closely followed in the countries they visit, so the country and location from which they originate are naturally advertised. Yacht owners visit Turkey because of the peace and security they find. These traveling yachts also bring other yachts, with each incoming yacht bringing three to four more yachts. Because these boats are world-renowned, the foreign press follow their arrival in the country. As a result of the media's coverage of these yachts, new yachtsmen are emerging. In a roundabout way, this situation demonstrates that Turkey is a trustworthy country (Özatağ, 2022).

13.3.9 Help to increase the profit of local establishments

Studies show that Blue Flag awards have an effect on the prices of accommodation businesses. Rigall-i-Torrent et al. (2011) examined the effects of beach characteristics and beach location on hotel accommodation fees, and as a result of the study, it was revealed that Blue Flag beaches increased hotel accommodation fees by 11.5%.

From another perspective, while the determination of product prices is dependent on many different factors and is not directly related to the Blue Flag, it can be said that the Blue Flag contributes to the product's price increase. It is well known that environmental information influences the consumer decision-making process as well as price, consumer perceived quality, promotion and the manufacturer's image, and so on.

Sipic (2010) investigated the Blue Flag label's effect on marina boatyard rental, weekly boat rental and hotel room rates. Blue Flag marinas earn 25% more annual revenue than other marinas, Blue Flag boats earn 14–20% more than others when weekly rental prices are considered and Blue Flag hotels earn 45% more than other hotels, according to a Croatian study. It is estimated that a hotel with Blue Flag status earns between 270% and 290% more. Capacci et al. (2015), on the other hand, examined the economic effects of the Blue Flag label using quantitative methods, taking into account the Blue Flag label's effectiveness in attracting foreign tourists to the region. Besides, according to Fıskın et al. (2016), the Blue Flag eco-label causes tourists to stay longer and raises the prices of hotels near Blue Flag beaches. Tourists who stay for an extended period of time increase their overnight stay and, as a result, their average length of stay.

Marinas and yachts, in addition to hotels, have high social and economic returns. According to reports, sea tourism accounts for 25% of total tourism revenue in Turkey. With its marinas, yacht building and boatyards, Turkey has established itself as an important yachting center in the Mediterranean basin. Istanbul, Antalya and Mugla are at the forefront of yacht distribution to Turkish ports. The majority of the revenue comes from mega yachts. The local and regional economic impact of yacht tourism can be divided into two categories: direct and indirect effects. The cash flow from cruise ship activity has a direct impact; these are direct expenditures on goods and services made by passengers, crew and the ship operator. Indirect effects, on the other hand, refer to the purchases of inputs required for local businesses to continue operating with cash flow generated by cruise activities. These are passenger expenses (airplane, tour and entertainment, accommodation, food and beverage, port expenses, other transportation expenses, duty-free expenses, souvenirs, shopping, sightseeing, etc.), operator expenses (port fees, agency service fees, ship repair, etc.) and ship personnel expenses (taxes, etc.) According to a study conducted on the cruise port of Kuşadasi, the largest contribution of cruise ships to the district was spent on carpets, jewelry, leather and souvenirs by ship passengers and ship personnel outside the port (Polat & Bitiktas, 2020).

The economic value left by mega yachts in marinas, as well as the provisions they receive, particularly fuel, make a significant contribution to the region's economy. Mega yacht maintenance and repairs are also profitable. Large shipyards can perform both scheduled and unscheduled maintenance. It makes a significant contribution to the country's economy. It is 20 times more cost effective than a sailboat. Mega yachts, due to their larger size and wealth of guests, provide economic value to marinas and the region. A yacht 100 meters long can leave an average of 2–3 million euros when it comes to maintenance (Özatağ, 2022).

The increased number of visiting yachtsmen during yacht races and festival periods boosts the incomes of local traders and entrepreneurs. During these times, the food and beverage and service sectors, in particular, increase their turnover. The total economic size of this sector's infrastructure is approximately $745 million (Polat & Bitiktas, 2020).

13.3.10. Provide health and recreational benefits to potential customers

The Blue Flag has a positive impact on health and quality of life. The program promotes healthy community development and well-being initiatives. Blue Flag areas encourage healthy living by organizing safety training activities and increasing public awareness. Blue Flag environmental quality standards help to create clean and healthy environments that reduce disease, infection, and communicable diseases. Beach activities encourage an active lifestyle as well as social well-being. Accidents are reduced at award-winning locations thanks to Blue Flag safety standards (Kindan Cebbari, 2019).

For example, in England, the Brighton State Health Service has set up a swimming group on Brighton Beach for those suffering from depression and mental illness. According to research, swimming in cold water is good for mental disorders and reduces drug use. Walking groups have been established on Blue Flag beaches in Scarborough to socialize older people.

A company that is a subsidiary of the Mersin Metropolitan Municipality has been organizing beach activity for the residents of a nursing home. In Turkey, people spend more time outdoors and they go to and benefit from the beaches in summer and winter thanks to the qualified facilities provided on the beaches.

13.4 Conclusion

The gradual expansion of the tourism market, as well as its importance in national economies, makes the Blue Flag application, which is a tourism eco-label, extremely important. Countries can use this program to demonstrate that their tourism activities are environmentally friendly and that they want to raise environmental awareness. Turkey is seen as having an important place among the countries implementing the Blue Flag program and as having shown the fastest development over the years. Turkey's third-place international ranking in terms of the number of Blue Flag beaches is thought to contribute significantly to the country's sea tourism.

On the other hand, Turkey, which has 22 Blue Flag marinas, is in the top ten in international rankings (for marinas). In terms of the number of Blue Flags awarded to provinces in Turkey, Antalya stands out from the rest. Antalya ranks first in the international arena in terms of the number of Blue Flag beaches, with more than any other province combined. Antalya, the province with the most Blue Flag beaches in the world, contributes significantly to the country's economy through tourism, and sets the standard.

The growing popularity and international acceptance of the Blue Flag program provides a competitive advantage. Geographically, Turkey, which is in a position to attract attention and demand in terms of tourism activities, will prioritize the Blue Flag application and gain an advantage over other Mediterranean countries with which it competes.

Blue Flag–awarded sites contribute to the enrichment of local economies in different aspects. At this point, it should be stated that the Blue Flag has a multiplier effect. It creates advantages for local establishments and new job opportunities in

182 *Zeliha Eser and Selay Ilgaz Sümer*

the related region. It also makes a great contribution to sustainable tourism activities. Furthermore, it can be used as a strong marketing tool. Facilities with Blue Flag have a remarkable feature among competing businesses and open new international collaborations. As a result, it is clear that the Blue Flag is an important marketing tool for businesses trying to maintain their existence in an intensely competitive environment.

13.5 References

Akyurt, H. (2008). Turizm Bölgesine Yönelik Talebi Etkileyen Faktörlerden İmaj Ve Çeşme Örneği, PhD Dissertation, 9 Eylul University Social Sciences Institute.

Antalya Provincial Agriculture and Forestry Directorate. (2019). Available from: https://antalya.tarimorman.gov.tr/Haber/967/Gelecek-Nesiller-Icin-Mavide-Bulusalim-Projesi-Imzalandi, retrieved August 14, 2022.

Blackman, A., Naranjo, M. A., Robalino, J., Alpizar, F., & Rivera, J. (2014). Does tourism eco-certification pay? Costa Rica's Blue Flag program. *World Development*, 58(8), 41–52.

Buckley, R. (2002). Tourism ecolabels. *Annals of Tourism Research*, 29(1), 183–208.

Cak, E., & Dirlik, S. (2021). Institutional influences in the diffusion of organizational practices: A research on the diffusion of the Blue Flag environmental award in Muğla, *Journal of Management and Labour*, 5(1), 1–14.

Capacci, S., Scorcu, A. E., & Vici, L. (2015). Seaside tourism and eco-labels: The economic impact of Blue Flags, *Tourism Management Journal*, 47(1), 88–96.

Çeken, H., (2008). A theoretical study into effect of tourism on regional development, Afyon Kocatepe Üniversitesi, İ.İ.B.F. Journal, 10(II), 293–306.

Dierks, Z. (2022). Travel and Tourism's Total Contribution to GDP in Turkey 2019–2021. Available from: https://www.statista.com/statistics/644846/travel-tourism-total-gdp-contribution-turkey/, retrieved September 27, 2022.

Dodds, R. (2010). Determining the economic impact of beaches: Lake Huron shoreline from Sarnia to Tobermory, report summary.

Dodds, R., & Holmes, M. R. (2020). Is Blue Flag certification a means of destination competitiveness? A Canadian context, *Ocean & Coastal Management*, 192, 05192.

Eser, Z., & Ilgaz Sümer, S. (2013). Managers' concerns to use Blue Flag as a marketing tool in tourism industry in Turkey, *Proceeding of ASBBS*, 20(1), 448–456.

Fıskın, R., Çakır, E., & Ozkan, E. D. (2016). The criteria and importance of Blue Flag implementation and the present situation analysis by countries, *Mehmet Akif Ersoy University Social Sciences Institute Journal*, 8(15), 224–247.

Font, X. (2002). Environmental certification in tourism and hospitality: Progress, process and prospects. *Tourism Management Journal*, 23(3), 197–205.

Foundation for Environmental Education (FEE). (2020). "Blue Flag". Available from: https://www. blueflag.global/, retrieved March 29, 2020.

Fraguell, R. M., Martí, C., Pintó, J., & Coenders, G. (2016). After over 25 years of accrediting beaches, has Blue Flag contributed to sustainable Management? *Journal of Sustainable Tourism*, 24(6), 882–903.

Gao, J., & Zhang, L., (2019). Exploring the dynamic linkages between tourism growth and environmental pollution: New evidence from the Mediterranean countries. *Current Issues in Tourism*, 1–17. Available from: https://doi.org/10.1080/13683500.2019.1688767

Gual, M., Pons G. X, Martín-Prieto, J. A., & Rodríguez-Perea, A. (2015). A critical view of the Blue Flag beaches in Spain using environmental variables. *Ocean & Coastal Management*, 105, 106–115.

https://www.alanya.bel.tr/Haber/26858/ALANYA-DA--DIP-TEMIZ-TERTEMIZ-ETKINLIGI. (2019), retrieved September 13, 2022.

http://www.mavibayrak.org.tr/en/Default.aspx. (n.d.), retrieved September 13, 2022.

http://www.mavibayrak.org.tr/tr/icerikDetay.aspx?icerik_refno=1. (n.d.), retrieved September 13, 2022.

Houston, J. R. (2013). The economic value of beaches – a 2013 update. *Shore & Beach*, 81(1), 3–11.

Kindan Cebbari, A., (2019). Küresel Bir Eko-Etiket Olarak Mavi Bayrak'ın Sürdürülebilir Kalkınma Amaçlarına Katkısı, 13. National Enviromental Engineering Conference Proceeding, 1–8.

Kindan, A. (2006). *Bir Eko-Etiket Olarak Mavi Bayrak'ın Türkiye Kıyı Turizminde Bir Pazarlama Unsuru Olabilirliğinin Araştırılması*, Unpublished Master's Thesis, Ankara Üniversitesi Sosyal Bilimler Enstitüsü, Ankara (Turkey).

Kobal, G. (2022). Number of Blue Flagged beaches rises in Turkey. Available from: https://www.hurriyetdailynews.com/number-of-blue-flagged-beaches-rises-in-turkey-174150, retrieved September 13, 2022.

Kozak, M., & Nield, K. (2004). The role of quality and eco-labelling systems in destination benchmarking. *Journal of Sustainable Tourism*, 12(2), 138–148.

Lee, K. F. (2001). Sustainable tourism destinations: The importance of cleaner production. *Journal of Cleaner Production*, 9, 313–323.

Manap, G. (2006). Analitik Hiyerarşi Yaklaşımı ile Turizm Merkezi Seçimi, *Ticaret ve Turizm Eğitim Fakültesi Dergisi*, 2, 157–170.

Merino, F., & Prats, M. (2020). Sustainable beach management and promotion of the local tourist industry: Can Blue Flags be a good driver of this balance? *Ocean and Coastal Management*, 198, 105359.

Merli, R., Preziosi, M., Acampora, A., & Ali, F. (2019). Why should hotels go green? Insights from guests experience in green hotels. *International Journal of Hospitality Management*, 81, 169–179.

Nelson, C., Morgan, R., Williams, A. T., & Wood, J. (2000). Beach awards and management, *Ocean & Coastal Management*, 43(1), 87–98.

Özatağ, E. (2022). Mega yatların ekonomiye katkıları da "mega", Dunya Gazetesi.

Özkök, F. (2006). Tourism – does it decrease poverty? *Electronic Social Sciences Journal*, 5(15), 85–98.

Polat, Ç., & Bitiktas, F., (2020) *Antalya İlinde Yat ve Kruvaziyer Turizminin Ekonomik Etkisi*. 5th National Sea Tourism Symposium Proceedings, İzmir, February 28–29, pp. 1–20.

Schumacher, I. (2010). Ecolabeling, consumers' preferences and taxation. *Ecological Economics*, 69, 2202–2212.

Semeoshenkova, V., & Newton, A. (2015). Overview of erosion and beach quality issues in three southern European countries: Portugal, Spain and Italy. *Ocean & Coastal Management*, 118, 12–21.

Sipic, T. (2010). Eco-Labeling of services: The Blue Flag. Available from: http://www.cwu.edu/~sipict/EcoLabelingBF.pdf, retrieved December 9, 2015.

Rigall-i-Torrent, R., Fluvià, M., Ballester, R., Saló, A., Ariza, E., & Espinet, J. M. (2011). The effects of beach characteristics and location with respect to hotel prices. *Tourism Management*, 32(5), 1150–1158.

Zeydan, İ., & Gürbüz, A. (2021). Turizmde Yeşil Pazarlama Uygulamaları: Mavi Bayrak Ve Yeşil Yıldızın Turistlerin Konaklama Tercihlerine Etkisi, *International Journal of Management Economics and Business*, 17(1), 224–235.

Zielinski, S., & Botero, C. M. (2019). Myths, misconceptions and the true value of Blue Flag. *Ocean & Coastal Management*, 174, 15–24.

14 Blue Flag South Africa

Reflections on a decade of progress

Serena Lucrezi and Peet van der Merwe

14.1 Introduction

South Africa has celebrated over 20 years of implementation of the Blue Flag award. The country was the first outside of Europe to adopt this beach management approach (in 2001) through the facilitation of CoastCARE (a program of the National Department of Environmental Affairs and Tourism), making it the forerunner of many other African countries. The Blue Flag in South Africa embraces 18 coastal municipalities and is run by the Wildlife and Environment Society of South Africa (WESSA), which is a non-governmental organization aiming to start and support environmental and conservation projects while promoting public participation in caring for the Earth (WESSA, 2022b). WESSA states that "Blue Flag is voluntary, which shows a very strong commitment to environmental sustainability from these municipalities, marinas and tourism boat operators that are awarded annually" (WESSA, 2022a). This commitment is reflected in the sustained growth in the number of coastal locations in the country applying for the Blue Flag, from only five in 2001 to 51 in 2022 (Figure 14.1), to have 100 beaches awarded by 2030 (Vivier, 2022; WESSA, 2022a).

Media reports and government releases have been depicting the Blue Flag award as a positive choice to meet different needs, namely improving beach management, enhancing tourism and revenue, uplifting communities, creating employment and engaging beach users in education and conservation activities. Despite the positive image surrounding the Blue Flag program, South Africa, just like other countries around the world, has been faced with challenges associated with the implementation and success of the award, often stemming from a lack of control of some parameters like water quality, and poor awareness and knowledge of the award by beach users, possibly compromising the role of Blue Flag in beach choice. These challenges have been thoroughly investigated and explained during studies conducted by tourism, economic and environmental scientists since 2001, including research conducted in 2013–2014 and published in 2015 which collated information from previous literature while also gathering new data on the Blue Flag (Lucrezi et al., 2015; Lucrezi & Saayman, 2015; Lucrezi & van der Merwe, 2015).

This chapter focuses on synthesizing this research and assessing the evolution of the Blue Flag in South Africa, especially over the last decade, with emphasis on whether any recommendations stemming from the research were addressed, and

DOI: 10.4324/9781003323570-15

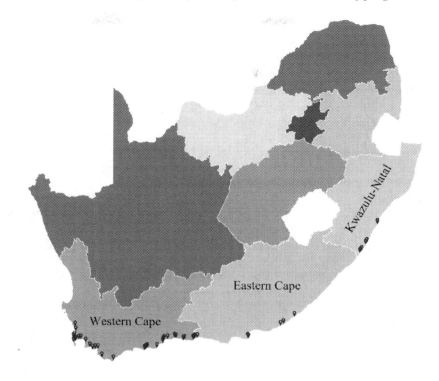

Figure 14.1 Map of Blue Flag beaches in South Africa in 2021–2022

on the actions taken by Blue Flag managers over recent years, including during the COVID-19 pandemic period. The method followes two specific approaches. The first one includes a study of scientific papers published on the Blue Flag in South Africa. These papers were sourced by conducting a scholarly search during June 2022, using search engines including Google Scholar (www.scholar.google.com), Scopus of Elsevier (www.scopus.com) and Web of Science of Clarivate Analytics (www.webofknowledge.com). The second one involves a study of relevant information sourced through the web. The web search was also conducted in June 2022, by visiting the search engine Google (www.google.com). The search began by visiting the Blue Flag and WESSA web pages, and then continued to include news articles, government documents and blog posts. Only web articles and documents published from 2015 were considered in the search. The assumption in this chapter is that, despite persisting challenges, the evolution of the Blue Flag in South Africa has been positive, and that the Blue Flag remains to this day a valuable tool to improve beach management while supporting tourism in the country.

14.2 The Blue Flag award before 2015

Over the years since its first implementation, the Blue Flag in South Africa was generally praised by the media for its purpose and actions, despite some challenges.

186 *Serena Lucrezi and Peet van der Merwe*

In 2008, the Department of Forestry, Fisheries and the Environment (DFFE, 2008) released a statement acknowledging the growth in the number of beaches applying for the award and attributing the supposed success of the program in the country to "the commitment of participating municipalities to provide beach-goers and holiday-makers with world class beaches offering safe, clean and well-managed facilities". DFFE pointed to research demonstrating the economic value of the Blue Flag, mentioning as an example Margate beach (KwaZulu-Natal), where the Blue Flag status was claimed to potentially generate tens of millions of South African rands (where ten million rand was equivalent to over half a million US dollars) annually. It was also mentioned that the program improved the environmental management of awarded beaches. Challenges, which included the necessity to manage damaged infrastructure as a result of climate change (including high seas and waves), had been successfully overcome through the allocation of resources to infrastructure rehabilitation (DFFE, 2008).

In 2010, South Africa celebrated the tenth anniversary of the Blue Flag, with proud announcements that the standards of beaches in the country had been significantly raised, paving the way for other countries outside of Europe to adopt the program (FEE, 2010). Additionally, it was declared that thanks to the award, local authorities had reported an increase in beach visitors, an improvement in their behavior, and an increase in property prices for homes near Blue Flag beaches (FEE, 2010).

In 2013, the Department of Tourism celebrated World Tourism Day, with the theme of Tourism and Water. The Minister explained the dependence of many tourism activities on water and the need to sustainably manage resources offering water-based tourism, including coastal areas and beaches, where leisure experiences represent one of the two pillars of tourism in South Africa together with "safari type" experiences (Media Update, 2013). The Blue Flag was described as epitomising a successful approach to sustainable planning and management around beaches in South Africa, necessary to optimize its domestic and international tourism potential and contribute to a green economy transition through investments leading to climate change mitigation, waste reduction, biodiversity conservation, and community engagement (South African Government, 2013). This view was shared by the United Nations World Tourism Organization (UNWTO), which stated that the Blue Flag is the best-known and oldest thriving eco-label of its kind. The Minister announced that 41 beaches and five marinas were awarded the Blue Flag in 2013, indicating continuous growth in South Africa despite the criteria for award accreditation becoming stricter (Media Update, 2013). He also pointed to research suggesting that both domestic and international tourists valued the quality assurance provided by Blue Flag beaches, making them "beaches of choice". This suggested that such value would contribute to "Brand South Africa" and give the country a competitive advantage as a world-class coastal tourism destination (South African Government, 2013). Ultimately, it was declared that the program's implementation in the country was shifting its focus from water quality alone to embracing the broader spectrum of categories, including safety, environmental education, conservation and management (Media Update, 2013). In 2013, marine protected areas were included as part of the Blue Flag criteria and South Africa was testing the possibility of wildlife tour boats joining the program, through a pilot whale-watching boat (Panorama, 2017).

14.3 Outcomes of research published in 2015

In 2013 and 2014, data were collected to evaluate the status of randomly selected Blue Flag beaches in South Africa, the level of beach visitors' awareness and knowledge of the award, as well as their attitude toward the program (Lucrezi et al., 2015; Lucrezi & Saayman, 2015; Lucrezi & van der Merwe, 2015). The research highlighted some issues as follows. Concerning environmental education and information (examples of education, information and regulation boards found on Blue Flag beaches in South Africa are displayed in Figures 14.2, 14.3 and 14.4), methods of imparting education may be inappropriate or insufficient. Examples include the neglect of target groups like tourists, poor maintenance of information and education boards at the beach, and limited interpretation at the beach. Concerning environmental management, some practices can be inconsistent or damaging to the ecosystem. Examples include the removal of natural debris from the beach, no enforcement of regulations, lack of recycling activities and limited monitoring and conservation activities on certain beaches. Concerning safety, some Blue Flag beaches deploy bather protection tools that are considered controversial, such as lethal shark control using shark nets and baited hooks or drumlines, as is the case along the coast of KwaZulu-Natal in South Africa (Lucrezi & Gennari, 2022). Last, concerning water quality, sampling can be questionable, and water quality too difficult to control to be guaranteed.

Lucrezi et al. (2015), Lucrezi and Saayman (2015) and Lucrezi and van der Merwe (2015) shed light on the understanding of and attitude towards the Blue Flag in South Africa. Based on a questionnaire survey run at 12 Blue Flag and non–Blue Flag beaches in two provinces (KwaZulu-Natal and Western Cape) and capturing data from 953 beach visitors, the authors found that people on Blue Flag beaches knew more about the Blue Flag compared with people on non–Blue Flag beaches. Beach visitors had heard of the Blue Flag at the beach or through the television, newspapers and word of mouth. Interestingly, visitors in KwaZulu-Natal were more aware of the Blue Flag than those in the Western Cape. Cleanliness (including water quality and beach cleanliness) and safety were the criteria most recognized by visitors. Between 60% and 95% of visitors on Blue Flag beaches did not select a specific beach because of the Blue Flag. Lastly, the development and commercialization of beaches were viewed negatively by beach visitors, with some associating these features with the Blue Flag award, potentially drawing too much tourism and resulting in greater pressure to urbanize and develop beaches. The authors concluded that these results potentially stemmed from issues related to management, promotion and education.

Concerning the first issue, poor management of the Blue Flag could lead to poor delivery and negative views of the award. Not enforcing beach etiquette could lead to beach users' misconduct. Lastly, beach managers do not have control over some aspects (like water quality) affecting users' views. In answer to these problems, the

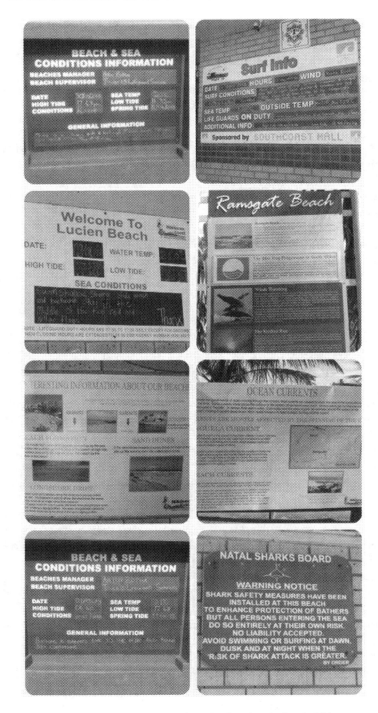

Figure 14.2 Information boards found on Blue Flag beaches in South Africa
Photo credit: S. Lucrezi.

Blue Flag South Africa: Reflections on a decade of progress 189

Figure 14.3 Education boards found on Blue Flag beaches in South Africa
Photo credit: S. Lucrezi.

authors recommended stricter control over the application of management actions on beaches, such as the introduction of beach wardens or stewards, and more inspections (e.g., of environmental quality parameters). Concerning the second issue, promotion may be inappropriate (i.e., focusing on some criteria more than others). It may not make use of all available resources, like tour operations and institutions, to reach target audiences. Lastly, it may not take advantage of the available collaborations with other organizations, like non-governmental ones. In response to these risks, the authors advised establishing a communication network between the Blue Flag program and conservation and environmental organizations, institutions and local businesses. Concerning the third issue, managers and authorities may not be as prepared as they should be, resulting in poor delivery of education. Education initiatives could be inconsistent or focus on some groups like residents and not others, like tourists (this may also explain the difference in knowledge of the Blue Flag between South African provinces, with Western Cape presenting lower levels

190 *Serena Lucrezi and Peet van der Merwe*

Figure 14.4 Regulation boards found on Blue Flag beaches in South Africa
Photo credit: S. Lucrezi.

of awareness due to a greater number of international visitors and tourists). Lastly, education may still be insufficient, calling for a radical change to be effective. In answer to these matters, the authors designed a brand new education framework for the Blue Flag award (see Lucrezi et al., 2015), recommending its implementation by the program on awarded beaches.

14.4 The Blue Flag after 2015

The Blue Flag in South Africa has undergone substantial changes in the last seven years, some of which are aligned with recommendations stemming from the research conducted before this period (Table 14.1). A commitment toward expanding the accreditation of the Blue Flag to areas beyond beaches, including marinas, remains strong (Barlow, 2021). Additionally, the National Department of Tourism declared its commitment to focusing spending over the medium term on creating employment opportunities through the Blue Flag program, based on its perceived aim to grow coastal tourism (Tibane, 2016). By the 2015/2016 bathing season, South Africa had 24 beaches that had been awarded the Blue Flag, receiving also special recognition for sustained commitment to marine and coastal conservation through its long-term and continuous participation in the program (Ugu South Coast Tourism, 2015). It was established that the award represented a critical way to build and maintain partnerships between stakeholders (including WESSA, municipalities, South African National Parks, beach guardians, private and public entities and individuals) who shared respect for natural resources and recognized the value of Blue Flag to the environment as well as tourism, economic development and job creation (Ugu South Coast Tourism, 2015). Blue Flag South Africa was also being promoted at international events like the Das Boot in Dusseldorf, Germany, where potential visitors, trade and media showed interest in the status of beaches in the country, reflecting the importance of the award as a criterion in beach selection among tourists (Ugu South Coast Tourism, 2015). Given the need to align coastal management programs with Operation Phakisa (a national initiative designed to fast-track the implementation of solutions on critical development issues), to support the ocean economy and job creation, the Minister of Tourism shared a vision for all South African beaches to receive the Blue Flag status and announced new initiatives that would be launched in support of this strategy.

One of the most notable initiatives has been the Tourism Blue Flag project. This long-term project, launched in 2016 in partnership with the NDT, espouses the need for capacity building, public engagement, education, community upliftment and monitoring of the award's impact on beaches and visitors (FEE, 2018; WESSA, 2022a, b). The project entails the recruitment and training of young people to become beach stewards and receive further employment in the Blue Economy. Since its launch, 300 beach stewards have completed their training and have been hosted by municipalities, non-governmental organizations and commercial tourism operators to fulfil their duties. Their role has included improving the experience of coastal visitors by monitoring their activity and trends and conducting visitor surveys; coordinating environmental education activities with school pupils; assisting lifeguards to improve safety at the beach and in the water; and assisting beach managers in maintaining Blue Flag beach standards (FEE, 2022b). An example of the successful training of beach stewards was reported by a whale-watching charter located in the Eastern Cape (Raggie Charters, 2022). The company hosted two stewards and provided them with a schedule of accredited and non-accredited training, Blue Flag events, and learning about operational management at the company. This collaboration resulted in the preparation of the WESSA Stewards Raggy Charters Training Manual (Raggie Charters, 2022).

Other projects have signified the branching of Blue Flag initiatives to include several environmental awareness and conservation activities coupled with community engagement. In 2017, a Fishing Line Recovery Program was established in Gansbaai, Western Cape, to raise public awareness of the negative impacts of fishing lines on the oceans, wildlife and people, and to promote the reduction and recycling of fishing lines (Panorama, 2017). The program secured funding and

Table 14.1 Assessment of the status quo related to Blue Flag in South Africa

Issues identified	Recommendations	Issue addressed?
Focus on and poor control over specific criteria (e.g., water quality).	Avoiding overemphasis on specific criteria, dedicating equal attention to all criteria through promotion and education campaigns. Educating and engaging stakeholders who are beyond beach management and affecting it indirectly, to integrate them into environmental education schemes.	☺ The Blue Flag South Africa is increasing its focus on promoting environmental education and public participation in management, conservation and safety activities. ☹ Control of water quality is still an issue.
Top-down and standardized management approach not addressing the diversity of users.	Long-term market segmentation research with a wide geographical spread. Bottom-up approach and collaborative decision-making for beaches considering the program. Engaging residents and tourists in education and environmental monitoring activities at the beach.	☺ The Blue Flag South Africa is collaborating with stakeholders on a national and local level, and engaging visitors, schools and the general public in several activities. The Blue Flag is now sided by the Tourism Green Coast project, targeting coastal areas with different characteristics compared with Blue Flag beaches. ☹ More longitudinal research at the national level is still required to monitor beach users' views and behavior.
Questionable or inconsistent environmental management, education and information practices. Poor enforcement of regulations.	Enforcing a high standard frame of reference to address criteria properly. Increasing the frequency of reporting to WESSA and FEE. Employing trained beach wardens with the legal power to enforce regulations and local by-laws. Launching workshops for beach managers. Balancing beach conservation and access to ecosystem services (e.g., recreation).	☺ Workshops for beach managers have been launched. The Tourism Blue Flag project has introduced beach stewards on Blue Flag beaches. The Blue Flag is aligning with achieving SDGs. ☹ Blue Flag beaches still implement some controversial management practices (e.g., lethal shark hazard mitigation).

Table 14.1 (Continued)

Issues identified	Recommendations	Issue addressed?
Limited public awareness and understanding of the program, also varying geographically.	Promotion of the award: In loco – using notice boards, beach guides, lifeguards, guest speakers at beach events, entertainment events at the beach, nearby businesses, and nearby accommodation facilities. Ex loco – using television, radio, newspapers, magazines, Blue Flag and WESSA websites, social media, travel and tourism websites, research outputs, school campaigns, workshops, events, tour operators and travel agencies. Promotion of all characteristics of the award in equal proportion (avoiding overemphasis on some criteria over others), with greater emphasis on education, information and active public engagement. Long-term research to assess whether awareness and knowledge of the program have improved over time.	☺ Beach stewards are actively involved in education and information on Blue Flag beaches. Promotion happens via various channels, including social networks, and collaborations with other stakeholders such as private companies, schools, organizations and event organizers. Several activities take place on Blue Flag beaches to engage visitors and raise awareness. ☹ More longitudinal research at the national level is still required to monitor beach users awareness, knowledge and attitudes.
Discrepancies between beach users' and Blue Flag managers' views concerning the effectiveness of the program.	Establishing a better dialogue between stakeholders. Including the human dimension in beach management. New education framework for the Blue Flag program (including communication and strategic interpretation at the beach, focus on beach ecosystems, interdisciplinary efforts, educating the educators and turning marine tourists into eco-tourists).	☺ Cooperation between stakeholders has resulted in the promotion of activities under the Blue Flag that have engaged visitors and the general public. Beach stewards collect data on beach users' preferences. Education efforts have increased, also through the promotion of active participation in activities like litter removal or rescue demonstrations. ☹ There is no evidence of the impact of new education efforts on visitors and the general public. More research would be required to evaluate the impact of education interventions.

(Continued)

Table 14.1 (Continued)

Issues identified	Recommendations	Issue addressed?
Deterring visitors (e.g., through development and crowding) or not necessarily representing a beach selection criterion	Long-term market segmentation research with a wide geographical spread to assess the diversity of users' profiles, behavior and attitude towards the beach and Blue Flag features. Investigating the needs of beach users to infer with confidence what beach factors influence destination choice and establish management priorities. Openly documenting differences made by the Blue Flag application to validate the claim that environmental management, safety, water quality and education are improved.	☺ Beach users' preferences tend to match the criteria of the Blue Flag award. ☹ Long-term research into the effects of Blue Flag promotion on users' behavioral intentions is still required.
Risks associated with investments and the loss of Blue Flag status.	Contingency plans in the event of award loss. Research assessing the changes in visitor behavior in case of award loss.	☺ Local authorities and the government continue to be willing to invest in the Blue Flag, signifying confidence in the program. Private investments allow the implementation of management strategies. ☹ Research into the economic impact of the Blue Flag (both being awarded and being lost) is still required.

Source: Based on issues and recommendations from Lucrezi et al. (2015), Lucrezi and Saayman (2015), and Lucrezi and van der Merwe (2015)

materials from a private association, which were used to make 100 bins, half of which were dedicated to the Blue Flag program (Panorama, 2017).

In 2020, WESSA initiated the Child Safe Beaches project funded by the World Childhood Foundation. The idea was to have the beach stewards integrate this project into the daily action plans of popular Blue Flag beaches where child safety issues have been recognized, also through awareness campaigns and training interventions for local stakeholders in the travel and tourism sector (FEE, 2022b). An example of the successful integration of safety initiatives into the Blue Flag program was a rescue exercise organized at Wilderness Beach, in partnership with the National Sea Rescue Institute (The Gremlin, 2017). The exercise was meant to raise awareness about the risks of rip currents and drowning, and educate the public on what to do in dangerous situations at sea. Children could also participate in the exercise and beach stewards used the opportunity to distribute brochures on environmental education activities (The Gremlin, 2017).

In conjunction with Tourism Blue Flag, the Tourism Green Coast project was launched in 2016 in partnership with NDT. This project was designed for a 300 km stretch of the Wild Coast of South Africa, which is less developed and urbanized compared with other recreational beaches in the country (Mclean, 2020). Currently targeting 20 sites, this project (awarded in the Bio-diversity category of the 2020 Eco-Logic Awards) aims to foster low-impact tourism and sustainable destination development while including local community members in tourism operations through a two-year job place mentorship (e.g., to become tourism guides). By 2020, 100 previously disadvantaged youth had been provided with placement at 30 private tourism operations (Mclean, 2020). Aside from tour guiding, these people were involved in activities like coordinating coastal clean-up events and supporting local schools with environmental education and action projects as part of an eco-schools program (Mclean, 2020). Tourism Green Coast intends to align with several Sustainable Development Goals, such as SDG1: no poverty; SDG13: climate action; and SDG14: life below water (Mclean, 2020). Similarly, the Blue Flag globally and in South Africa has recently been demonstrated to contribute to achieving SDGs (FEE, 2019). For instance, the Tourism Blue Flag project gave input to SDG1 by offering paid jobs in functions from lifeguarding to beach cleaning and environmental education. Being trained in environmental education, the beach stewards worked not only with tourists but also with local communities, providing tips on sustainability and promoting the healthy use of the beach space. This contributed toward achieving SDG11: sustainable cities and communities (FEE, 2019).

Slater and Mearns (2018) identified the Blue Flag as part of the toolbox of Sustainable Tourism and Integrated Environmental Management, offering an opportunity for the South African tourism industry to achieve SDGs, and facilitating the implementation of national agendas, policies and legislation. This takes place by providing operational guidelines to improve the performance of the tourism industry (in coastal areas) and offering a communication tool for consumers in identifying products and services that meet specific criteria. Using data from a survey conducted by beach stewards in 2016–2017, the same authors confirmed that beach visitors prioritize cleanliness (of water and the beach) and safety in

196 Serena Lucrezi and Peet van der Merwe

beach selection, and that understanding visitors' preferences remains essential to ensure an alignment between effective beach management and sustainable tourism development.

During the COVID-19 pandemic, South Africa did not desist from its commitment to the Blue Flag program. For example, the City of Cape Town successfully retained the status of its ten Blue Flag beaches during this difficult time, thanks to the dedication of environmental staff (Qukula, 2020). Despite the positive developments concerning the Blue Flag in South Africa, challenges remain, especially regarding bathing water quality assurance (keeping the values of fecal bacteria within acceptable limits). In 2020, it was reported that while the number of awarded beaches for the summer season had increased to 48, some beaches still struggled to control chronic water pollution and monitor and report water quality, especially in Cape Town where approximately half a million South African rands had been spent to apply for the award and comply with its requirements (Kretzmann, 2020). Some community members and scientists voiced concerns regarding the locations, frequency and rigor of water sampling and testing at Blue Flag beaches, implying that reported estimates of fecal bacteria would not be reliable for those beaches (Kretzmann, 2020). In the case of beaches where fecal bacteria parameters are unacceptable, Blue Flag beaches are still required to suspend their awarded status and lower their flag.

14.5 Conclusions

This chapter synthesized the evolution of Blue Flag South Africa, with a focus on the events of the last decade. The growing number of Blue Flag beaches, the implementation of the program by marinas and tour boats, spin-offs including Tourism Blue Flag and Tourism Green Coast and alignment with SDGs signify a commitment by the government, WESSA and stakeholders at the national, provincial and local level towards improving standards of environmental management, safety, education and water quality in coastal areas and the tourism sector, to promote sustainable coastal tourism growth in South Africa. Research published in 2015 on Blue Flag South Africa highlighted issues in need of addressing to support these objectives. While Blue Flag South Africa has been considering these issues and is in the process of tackling them, some gaps remain. The summary presented here offers an opportunity to focus on future strategies to fill these gaps, and one way to transversally do so is to research the human dimension of Blue Flag beaches, including nationwide long-term studies of beach users' profiles, needs, evaluations, awareness, knowledge, attitude and behavioral patterns. For example, the notion that Blue Flag accreditation offers a competitive advantage to South African beaches, contributing to "Brand South Africa", needs to be supported. There is a need to establish the current economic impact of the acquisition or loss of the Blue Flag. Finally, studies should measure the impact of education and participatory action interventions on beach users and other groups, to validate the educational effect of the Blue Flag program. In line with the objectives of the recently launched United Nations Ocean Decade, and the SDGs, the Blue Flag award ought to signify total alignment with conservation and eco-conscious coastal management practices. This would need to exclude actions that are considered inconsistent with conservation, such as the use of lethal shark hazard mitigation methods. Blue Flag South Africa remains a positive example of urban beach management in a developing country, creating an arena for different stakeholders to come together to improve the conditions of beaches, reduce environmental impacts, promote safety and educate the public.

Acknowledgment and disclaimer

Special thanks go to Melissa Muller for collating the panel figures. This work reflects only the authors' views. The North-West University accepts no liability whatsoever in this regard.

14.6 References

Barlow, G. (2021). *Keep the Blue Flag flying.* Retrieved June 20, 2022, from https://waterfrontcharters.co.za/keep-the-blue-flag-flying-143/?utm_source=rss&utm_medium=rss&utm_campaign=keep-the-blue-flag-flying-143

DFFE. (2008). *Blue Flag beaches announced.* Retrieved June 19, 2022, from https://www.dffe.gov.za/mediastatement/blueflag_programmesanlameer_marinebeach

FEE. (2010). *Blue Flag 10 year anniversary in South Africa.* Retrieved June 19, 2022, from https://www.blueflag.global/new-blog/2015/9/7/blue-flag-10-year-anniversary-in-south-africa#:~:text=For%20the%2010th%20anniversary%20year, Flag%20status%20for%20 2010%2F11

FEE. (2018). *Tourism Blue Flag project inspires youth in South Africa.* Retrieved June 18, 2022, from https://www.blueflag.global/new-blog/2018/12/11/tourism-blue-flag-program-by-wessa

FEE. (2019). *Blue Flag and the Sustainable Development Goals.* Retrieved June 21, 2022, from https://static1.squarespace.com/static/55371ebde4b0e49a1e2ee9f6/t/5f6b1706294e 19611c5fa55b/1600853816362/The+SDGs+and+Blue+Flag_FINAL.pdf

Kretzmann, S. (2020). *Blue Flag award no guarantee the water is clean.* Retrieved June 19, 2022, from https://www.dailymaverick.co.za/article/2020-12-21-blue-flag-award-no-guarantee-the-water-is-clean/

Lucrezi, S., & Gennari, E. (2022). Perceptions of shark hazard mitigation at beaches implementing lethal and nonlethal shark control programs. *Society & Animals, 30,* 646–667.

Lucrezi, S., & Saayman, M. (2015). Beachgoers' demands vs. Blue Flag aims in South Africa. *Journal of Coastal Research, 31*(6), 1478–1488.

Lucrezi, S., Saayman, M., & Van der Merwe, P. (2015). Managing beaches and beachgoers: Lessons from and for the Blue Flag award. *Tourism Management, 48,* 211–230.

Lucrezi, S., & Van der Merwe, P. (2015). Beachgoers' awareness and evaluation of the Blue Flag award in South Africa. *Journal of Coastal Research, 31*(5), 1129–1140.

Mclean, K. (2020). *Tourism Green Coast project summary report (2018–2020).* Retrieved June 18, 2022, from https://cld.bz/dFZ9wZo

Media Update. (2013). *International jury results place SA's Blue Flag programme on the map.* Retrieved June 20, 2022, from https://www.mediaupdate.co.za/publicity/56771/international-jury-results-place-sas-blue-flag-programme-on-the-map

198 Serena Lucrezi and Peet van der Merwe

Panorama. (2017). *Fishing Line Recovery Program and Blue Flag*. Retrieved June 20, 2022, from https://panorama.solutions/es/building-block/fishing-line-recovery-program-and-blue-flag

Qukula, Q. (2020). *10 Cape Town beaches keep Blue Flag status*. Retrieved June 20, 2022, from https://www.capetalk.co.za/articles/402822/10-cape-town-beaches-awarded-blue-flag-status#:~:text=Share%20This%3°, of%20South%20Africa%20(WESSA)

Raggie Charters. (2022). *WESSA*. Retrieved June 19, 2022, from https://www.raggycharters.co.za/page/wessa

Slater, R., & Mearns, K. (2018). Perceptions and activity profiles of Blue Flag beach users in South Africa. *African Journal of Hospitality, Tourism and Leisure*, *7*(4), 1–14.

South African Government. (2013). Media statement by the office of the Minister of Tourism, Mr Marthinus van Schalkwyk on the occasion of the launch of the Blue Flag season 2013/14 in Ramsgate, KwaZulu-Natal. Retrieved June 19, 2022, from https://www.gov.za/media-statement-office-minister-tourism-mr-marthinus-van-schalkwyk-occasion-launch-blue-flag-season

The Gremlin. (2017). *Successful sea rescue demonstration held at the Wilderness Blue Flag beach*. Retrieved June 21, 2022, from https://thegremlin.co.za/george-news/wordpress/2017/01/25/successful-sea-rescue-demonstration-held-at-the-wilderness-blue-flag-beach/

Tibane, E. (2016). *2016/2017 South Africa Yearbook*. Retrieved June 21, 2022, from https://www.gcis.gov.za/sites/default/files/docs/resourcecentre/yearbook/SAYearbook2016-17.pdf

Ugu South Coast Tourism. (2015). *Flying the Blue Flag. The KwaZulu-Natal South Coast boasts 7 Blue Flag beaches – the highest number in Africa*. Retrieved June 21, 2022, from https://www.zulu.org.za/files/images/files/Press%20release%20-%20Flying%20the%20Blue%20Flag.pdf

Vivier, T. L. (2022). *These are South Africa's Blue Flag beaches of 2022*. Retrieved June 18, 2022, from https://www.goodthingsguy.com/environment/these-are-south-africas-blue-flag-beaches-of-2022/

WESSA. (2022a). *Blue Flag South Africa*. Retrieved June 18, 2022, from https://wessa.org.za/our-work/sustainable-tourism/blue-flag-south-africa/

WESSA. (2022b). *Tourism Blue Flag*. Retrieved June 19, 2022, from https://wessa.org.za/our-work/sustainable-tourism/tourism-blue-flag/

15 Challenges and opportunities of the Blue Flag certification in Canada

Rachel Dodds and Mark Holmes

15.1 Introduction

If used responsibly and maintained in a sustainable manner, tourism based around beach areas can be a force for positive mental health and economic success (Klein & Osleeb, 2010; Ryan et al., 2010; Dodds, 2010a; Wesley & Pforr, 2010). Due to the wide use of beaches for recreational and leisure activities, tourism has great importance and economic impact on people and areas near oceans and lakes (Cicin-Sain & Knecht, 1999; Garcia & Servera, 2003; Dodds & Holmes, 2019, 2020a, 2020b). Beaches can also improve positive mood and relaxation (White et al., 2013) and for families, psychological and physical health (Ashbullby et al., 2013).

Apart from recreation, tourism has also become an important component of local economic development strategies in areas where other sectors such as manufacturing or agriculture have seen a decrease in employment levels (Koster & Lemelin, 2009). Tourists who select developed beach destinations go to participate in multiple water-based activities and excursions, such as snorkeling, fishing and boating, which engages them with their surroundings (De Ruyck et al., 1995; Cervantes et al., 2008). In some cases, such as in the United States and Australia, beaches even attract more visits than national parks (Houston, 2013; Blackwell, 2007).

One such way to manage the beach resource is through Blue Flag certification. This chapter will first outline the importance of beach and recreation tourism and then discuss their impact within the country of Canada and more specifically the province of Ontario. Blue Flag certification will then be discussed, followed by challenges and opportunities for beach management.

15.2 Who visits beaches?

Often people choose to vacation at a beach destination for relaxation, and to participate in beachfront recreation (Dodds & Holmes, 2020a; Lucrezi and Van der Walt, 2016). Botero et al. (2013) outline that water and sand quality, facilities, safety, relaxing atmosphere and family orientation are the key motivations for visitation. Geographic location, otherwise being rural or urban, was also found to play a role in attracting beachgoers. Dodds and Holmes (2020a) found that the beach was more likely a purpose of visit for those visiting a rural beach (83%), while

DOI: 10.4324/9781003323570-16

200   *Rachel Dodds and Mark Holmes*

only being the primary driver for just over one-third (69%) of those visiting an urban beach. Further, while Cai and Li (2009) found rural beaches to be a larger attractor for domestic tourists, Dodds and Holmes (2020a) found the opposite, with rural beaches attracting visitors more than residents. These differences suggest that beach tourists may differ by geography.

15.3 Beach, lake and recreational tourism in Canada

Within Canada, due to the country's size and the fact that the majority of the population live inland, a vast amount of lakes are used for recreation. Lake tourism is defined as a recreational activity (or activities) that involves travel away from one's place of residence and that has as its host or focus the water environment (Miller, 1990). Lake areas are one of the most valuable tourist attractions because of their vivid natural landscape, high-quality environment and cultural features (Zhou & Lin, 2003; Bahar & Kozak, 2008), and boating, swimming, relaxation and/or sunbathing have been identified as the main purposes of visits to beaches (Ontario Ministry of Tourism and Culture, 2007). For example, in some areas of the Great Lakes, recreation and tourism are becoming an increasingly important part of the economy, surpassing manufacturing and other activities (Environment Canada, 1995). Beaches are also prime recreational grounds that attract people to the water and therefore business to the surrounding area, which stimulates the local economy (Amyot and Grant, 2014). Dodds and Holmes (2019) found that overall beach satisfaction and experience satisfaction are positively correlated with intent to return, and that the key elements affecting satisfaction are facilities and beach and water cleanliness.

15.4 Blue Flag development in Canada

In terms of rating water quality in lakes, there are various systems with various labels denoting water quality; however, one of the most popular labels denoting high water quality is the Blue Flag label. Operated originally by the independent non-profit organization Foundation for Environmental Education (FEE) and more recently Swim Drink Fish (https://www.swimdrinkfish.ca/blue-flag), the Blue Flag is a well-known international eco-certification that certifies and assesses beaches based on 32 criteria in four main areas: (1) environmental education and information; (2) water quality; (3) environmental management; and (4) water safety (Blue Flag Canada, n.d.). Certifications are only awarded for one year at a time. Blue Flag began its operations in Europe in 1987, but has expanded and gained popularity internationally (Honey, 2002; McKenna et al., 2011). There are now 4,831 beaches (and marinas and boats) in 50 countries that have obtained the status. Although the program remains the most popular in Europe (with over 90% of the certified beaches being located in this continent, and over 500 certifications in Spain alone), Blue Flags are only slowly growing in popularity in North America, and there are now flags flying at 22 beaches in Canada (Swimdrinkfish, n.d.), down from 30 previously, mainly in the province of Ontario.

Challenges and opportunities of the Blue Flag certification in Canada 201

Looking at four Ontario beaches specifically, Dodds and Holmes (2020b) investigated the influence that Blue Flag certification had on beachgoers. Their findings also showed that those who visited Blue Flag beaches were more satisfied with the environmental education provided, garbage/recycling available, designated swimming areas, beach water quality, water cleanliness, water clarity and algae present than those at the non–Blue flag beaches (Dodds & Holmes, 2020a, 2020b). While they did not find the Blue Flag beach certification to directly influence return intention, the greater satisfaction levels with facilities and beaches did influence both overall experience satisfaction and return intention (Dodds & Holmes, 2019). Dodds and Holmes (2018) also examined the use of Blue Flag beaches by residents and visitors, finding that residents were more interested in utilizing environmental education provided by the beach, as well as being more likely to support the Blue Flag certification; however, they did believe that the cost should be borne by the visitor and not the locals/municipality.

15.5 Challenges for Blue Flag

There are a number of challenges for the Blue Flag: inclusion, scope, critical mass, awareness, consumer confusion and beach management consistency.

15.5.1 Inclusion

From an inclusion standpoint, according to Lucrezi et al. (2014), Blue Flag certification can create environmental awareness while being a management tool for ensuring waste management and cleanliness. Other studies, however, have criticized beach managers globally for inappropriate beach management strategies that disregard the beach environment or don't include proper conservation measures (Lucrezi et al., 2016). Often beach management is limited to monitoring elements such as water quality, climate, scenery, safety and sometimes accommodations (Alegre & Cladera, 2006; Yoon & Uysal, 2005), yet beach recreation and tourism are often a primary contributor to the economy; and dissatisfaction of the state of a beach can sometimes result in tourism downturn and therefore economic loss. As Frampton (2010) and Klein and Dodds (2017b) argue, amenities and recreation should also be considered in order to achieve holistic beach management. Part of this issue is that, historically, destinations have a marketing organization and "DMOs have positioned themselves as marketing and promotion organizations, acting also as catalysts for private sector initiatives" (Guerreiro, 2021), which has not afforded the option to engage in community and environmental well-being. Within the Canadian context, Klein and Dodds (2017b) outline that management strategies often do not include conservation measures and that amenities and recreation need to be considered to maintain a holistic approach.

15.5.2 Scope

Scope is another issue. There are many factors that lead to beach and water quality degradation that stem from much larger issues than just beach management and certification. For example, algal bloom affects water quality in Canada, such as in Lake Erie (Vollmer-Sanders et al., 2016). Algal bloom affecting this lake (and others) is connected to a multitude of sources including sewer overflows, water treatment plants, subsurface farm field loss, rainfall intensity, aquatic invasive species as well as recreation and tourism industries of boating and birding (Smith et al., 2015). It is one thing to have your beach certified but entirely another to be able to control factors outside of your control.

15.5.3 Critical mass

Critical mass is also an issue. Even though beaches can be major economic generators for the economy (Blackwell, 2007; Houston, 2013), protection of these resources is still minor. As stated by Houston (2018), voluntary programs are only as successful as the rate of implementation. Within Canada, there are only 22 Blue Flag beaches and almost all are located in just one province (Ontario). Additionally, the number of Blue Flag–certified beaches has dropped. As there are thousands of lakes, and even greater numbers of coastal beaches in Canada, and 563 lakes larger than 100 sq. km (Government of Canada, n.d.), this number is microscopic. This issue extends beyond Canada to the rest of North America as there are no Blue Flag–certified beaches in the USA and only 60 in Mexico (Blue Flag Mexico, n.d.) despite the attraction of beaches for tourism. One possible reason that no Blue Flag beaches exist in the US may be the issue of funding, as beach restoration funding in Florida, for example, is only 0.5% of the budget for the U.S. National Parks (Houston, 2013).

15.5.4 Awareness

Awareness of the Blue Flag program has also been identified as an issue. Within the Canadian context, Dodds (2014) found that less than a quarter of Ontario beach visitors they surveyed were familiar with Blue Flag. While beachgoers may be familiar with Blue Flag certifications, awareness of this certification does not tend to translate into return intention. Geldenhuys and Van der Merwe (2014) and Lucrezi et al. (2015) examined the influence that Blue Flag beach certification has on visitor beach selection, finding that it had no difference on beach visitation in South Africa. While there does not appear to be research supporting the idea that awareness of Blue Flag certification translates into repeat intention, research in Canada by Dodds and Holmes (2018) found that once they educated beachgoers as to the benefits derived from the Blue Flag program, they were more likely to indicate that this would influence their future beach selection.

15.5.5 Consumer confusion

The Blue Flag award suffers from a lack of knowledge of the certification itself as well as what the certification means. In a 2015 study of South African beachgoers, Lucrezi et al. (2015) found that only 20% of in-season Blue Flag beachgoers were familiar with beach awards. Further, they found that when asked what the Blue

Challenges and opportunities of the Blue Flag certification in Canada   203

Flag criteria entailed, only half of the survey respondents attempted to answer, and only 10% identified the correct criteria. These results confirmed the findings by Marin et al. (2009), who found that 81% proposed that they knew what Blue Flag was, but only 8% could correctly define the program. Within Canada, Dodds (2014) found similar results in the province of Ontario, with only 23% of Ontarians interviewed being aware of the Blue Flag certification. This suggests that work needs to be done to not only market the Blue Flag award but also to make it clear to beachgoers what the award is meant to do. Beyond the specific confusion pertaining to Blue Flag certification, the consumer also suffers from certification overload with the proliferation of such programs that exist (Font, 2002).

15.5.6 Beach management consistency

Klein and Dodds (2017b) found there to be an issue with consistency in applying the Blue Flag certification in Ontario, Canada. This issue was further broken down into beach committee, water testing and mechanical grooming. The interviews with 14 beach managers across the province of Ontario revealed that some of the managers believed that there was no guidance as to when the beach committee should meet, the purpose of the committee and who should be a member; however, the following guidance is provided:

> The beach management committee is a means of ensuring that these personnel continue working together throughout the years to maintain Blue Flag standards. The committee should also include representatives of community groups, clubs, non-profits and conservation authorities. The committee should meet at least twice a year to discuss the management of the beach and ensure that all criteria are being met. Committee members may also take a hands-on approach, such as providing support to the beach manager, facilitating environmental education activities and promoting the program.
>
> (Environmental Defence, n.d., p. 10)

This lack of understanding may contribute to each of the beaches having different forms and participation in the workings of each beach.

In terms of water quality, although the criteria require water testing five times per year, some beaches interpret the requirement to mean that they can send in their best five per year, omitting their worst samples (Klein and Dodds, 2017b). While this is not the acceptable practice of the Blue Flag certification program, there is a lack of follow-up enforcement to ensure this type of practice is eliminated. There was a similar finding regarding mechanical grooming, with there being differences in when beaches thought that they should groom the beach. One beach might propose that mechanical raking should be done every once in a while, while another might say that it should be done every day. Again, this demonstrates that there is a lack of clear messaging from Blue Flag in Canada as to when these tasks should take place. These types of issues have the potential to degrade and bring into question the quality/reliability of the Blue Flag certification.

15.6 Opportunities for Blue Flag

Opportunities exist for both the management of beaches as well as the management of destinations across Canada and potentially globally. First is destination management. Destination marketing organizations (DMOs) have been slowly making the shift to become destination management organizations or destination marketing and management organizations (DMMOs) (Dodds, 2010b). Dodds and Holmes (2019), using Canada as a case study, suggest that better understanding the factors that influence overall satisfaction will help destinations be better equipped to manage the visitor experience. By better managing their visitor experience, destinations will be able to more effectively attract and retain their customers (Dodds & Holmes, 2019).

Another opportunity for Canada is better beach management. Currently, the Blue Flag program is being used primarily as a marketing and promotion tool in Canada, even though it was designed as a simplified breach management certification tool (Klein & Dodds, 2017b). Beaches should look to use the Blue Flag certification program as a beach management tool, which may require beaches to more closely follow the Blue Flag guidelines and for the Blue Flag certification body to institute more regular follow-up site visits and conformance evaluations. While the Blue Flag certification may not be a perfect tool, it provides clear and manageable guidelines that are "achievable to reach by a non-scientific group of managers with some expertise from environmental authorities, which in turn provide the visitor with some guarantees of cleanliness, safety and basic facilities they would expect from a tourist beach" (Zielinski & Botero, 2019, p. 21; Klein and Dodds, 2018).

To maximize the Blue Flag opportunities for destinations, the benefits of using such a program need to be more clearly articulated to both destinations and their beach visitors (Geldenhuys and Van der Merwe, 2014). By better informing the beachgoer of the benefits of the program, destinations can utilize the certification as a beach differentiator (Lucrezi et al., 2014). Further, education programs in Canada increase awareness of the benefits for the beachgoer, which may result in increased intent to return (Dodds & Holmes, 2020a). Better communication of the benefits of the program to destinations is a means of not only monitoring and standard-setting but also creating strategic alliances both locally and nationally, helping destinations to maximize the results they can derive from the program (Geldenhuys and Van der Merwe, 2014; Lucrezi et al., 2014). When used properly, the Blue Flag certification can spur local economic development through such investments as new hotel investments (Blackman et al., 2014).

15.7 Conclusion

One thing is clear. If beaches or beach destinations and the communities and tourists which depend on them wish to thrive, the interests of tourism and other community interests must be compatible, not conflicting (Udiyana et al., 2018). Post-Covid, there is a growing transition toward the net zero climate, green economy and adherence to commitments such as the Sustainable Development Goals

Challenges and opportunities of the Blue Flag certification in Canada **205**

and Paris Agreement. The key is pressuring the tourism industry to align its practices with these very demanding challenges (Guerreiro 2021). The solutions are threefold. First, destinations such as Canada must take on more of a management role. Second, environmental agencies across the country, as well as certifications, must consider economics and community well-being in their measurement. Third, Canadian policies and governance must focus on long-term solutions that will be measured and implemented (Dodds & Butler, 2019; Butler & Dodds, 2022a).

Blue Flag, in its current state, is only focusing on part of the problem. A systematic regenerative approach must be the future if we are going to protect beaches, conserve the environment, include communities and also offer a good tourism experience. One thing is clear: a good place to live is often a good place to visit.

15.8 References

Amyot, J., & Grant, J. (2014). Environmental Function Analysis: A decision support tool for integrated sandy beach planning. *Ocean & Coastal Management*, 102, 317–327.

Alegre, J., & Cladera, M. (2006). Repeat visitation in mature sun and sand holiday destinations. *Journal of Travel Research*, 44(3), 288–297.

Ashbullby, K. J., Pahl, S., Webley, P., & White, M. P. (2013) The beach as a setting for families' health promotion: A qualitative study with parents and children living in coastal regions in Southwest England. *Health & Place*, 23, 138–147.

Bahar O., & Kozak, M. (2008). *Tourism economics: Concepts and practices*. Nova Science Publishers Inc.

Billington, R., Carter, N., & Kayamba, L. (2008). The practical application of sustainable tourism development principle: A case study of creating innovative place-making tourism strategies. *Tourism and Hospitality Research suppl. Special Issue: Innovation for Sustainable Tourism*, 8(1), 37–43.

Blackman, A., Naranjo, M. A., Robalino, J., Alpizar, F., & Rivera, J. (2014). Does tourism eco-certification pay? Costa Rica's Blue Flag program. *World Development*, 58, 41–52. https://doi.org/10.1016/j.worlddev.2013.12.002

Blackwell, B. (2007). The value of a recreational beach visit: An application to Mooloolaba Beach and comparisons with other outdoor recreation sites. *Economic Analysis and Policy*, 37(1), 77–98.

Blue Flag Canada. (n.d.). Last accessed May 2022 from https://www.swimdrinkfish.ca/blue-flag

Blue Flag Mexico. (n.d.). Last accessed May 2022 from http://www.blueflagmexico.org/

Botero, C., Anfuso, G., Williams, A. T., Zielinski, S., Silva, C. P., Cervantes, O., Cabrera, & J. A., (2013). Reasons for beach choice: European and Caribbean perspectives. *Journal of Coastal Research*, 1(65), 880.

Butler, R. W., & Dodds, R. (2022a). Overcoming overtourism: A review of failure. *Tourism Review*, 77(1), 35–53. https://doi.org/10.1108/TR-04-2021-0215

Butler, R., & Dodds, R. (2022b) Island tourism: Vulnerable or resistant to overtourism? *Highlights of Sustainability*, 1, 54–64. https://doi.org/10.54175/hsustain1020005

Cai, L. A., & Li, M. (2009). Distance-segmented rural tourists. *Journal of Travel and Tourism Marketing*, 26(8), 751–761.

Cervantes, O., Espejel, I., Arellano, E., Delhumeau, S. (2008). Users' perception as a tool to improve urban beach planning and management. *Environmental Management*, 42(2), 249–264.

206 Rachel Dodds and Mark Holmes

Choi, C. & Sirakaya, E. (2006). Sustainability indicators for managing community tourism. *Tourism Management*, 27, 1274–1289.

Cicin-Sain, B., & Knecht, R. W. (1999). Coastal tourism and recreation: The driver of coastal development. *Industry Driven Changes and Policy Responses*, 73–75.

De Ruyck, A. M. C., Soares, A. G., & Mclachlan, A. (1995). Factors influencing human beach choice on three South African beaches: A multivariate analysis. *Geojournal*, 36(4), 345–352.

Dodds, R. (2010a). Determining the economic impact of beaches: Lake Huron shoreline from Sarnia to Tobermory. *Report Summary*. Ryerson University and Ausable Bayfield Conservation Authority, Toronto, 2010, 15 pages. https://doi.org/10.13140/2.1.3702.0483

Dodds, R. (2010b). Destination marketing organizations and climate change: The need for leadership and education. *Sustainability*, 2, 3449–3464.

Dodds, R. (2014). Determining the potential for environmentally sustainable recreation in the Lake Simcoe Watershed. Toronto, ON: Ministry of the Environment and Climate Change.

Dodds, R., & Butler, R. (Eds.). (2019). *Overtourism: Issues, realities and solutions* (Vol. 1). Walter de Gruyter GmbH & Co KG.

Dodds, R., & Holmes, M. (2017). Lake watershed tourists: Who they are and how to attract them. *Journal of Tourism & Hospitality*, 6(6), 1–8. https://doi.org/10.4172/2167-0269.1000331

Dodds, R., & Holmes, M. (2018). Education and certification for beach management: Is there a difference between residents versus visitors? *Ocean & Coastal Management*, 160, 124–132. https://doi.org/10.1016/j.ocecoaman.2018.03.043

Dodds, R., & Holmes, M. R. (2019). Beach tourists; what factors satisfy them and drive them to return. *Ocean & Coastal Management*, 168, 158–166.

Dodds, R. & Holmes, M. R. (2020a) Preferences at city and rural beaches: Are the tourists different? *Journal of Coastal Research*, 36(2), 393–402. https://doi.org/10.2112/JCOASTRES-D-19-00048.1

Dodds, R., & Holmes, M. R. (2020b) Is Blue Flag certification a means of destination competitiveness? A Canadian context. *Ocean and Coastal Management*, *192*, 1–8. https://doi.org/10.1016/j.ocecoaman.2020.105192

Environmental Defence. (n.d.). Criteria for beaches: Blue Flag Canada criteria for beaches. Retrieved from http://environmentaldefence.ca/report/guide-blue-flag-criteria-for-beaches/

Environment Canada. (1995). The Great Lakes: An environmental atlas and resource book. Retrieved from https://publications.gc.ca/site/eng/9.858440/publication.html

Font, X. (2002). Environmental certification in tourism and hospitality: Progress, process and prospects. *Tourism Management*, 23(3), 197–205.

Frampton, A. P. (2010). A review of amenity beach management. *Journal of Coastal Research*, 26(6), 1112–1122.

Garcia, C., & Servera, J. (2003). Impacts of tourism development on water demand and beach degradation on the island of Mallorca (Spain). *Geografiska Annaler: Series A, Physical Geography*, 85(3–4), 287–300.

Geldenhuys, L. L., & Van der Merwe, P. (2014). The impact of Blue Flag status on tourist decision-making when selecting a beach. *African Journal of Hospitality, Tourism and Leisure*, 3(2), 1–16.

Government of Canada. (n.d.). Water sources. Last accessed May 2022 from https://www.canada.ca/en/environment-climate-change/services/water-overview/sources/lakes.html

Guerreiro, S. (2021). Destination management in a post-covid environment. *Worldwide Hospitality and Tourism Themes*, 14(1), 48–55. https://doi.org/10.1108/WHATT-10-2021-0137

Honey, M. (2002). *Ecotourism and certifications: Setting standards in practice.* Island Press.

Challenges and opportunities of the Blue Flag certification in Canada 207

Houston, J. R. (2013). The value of Florida beaches. *Shore and Beach*, 81(4), 4–11.

Houston, J. R. (2018). The economic value of America's beaches – a 2018 update. *Shore & Beach*, 86(2), 3–13.

Klein, L., & Dodds, R. (2017a). Perceived effectiveness of Blue Flag certification as an environmental management tool along Ontario's Great Lakes beaches. *Ocean and Coastal Management*, 141(1), 107–117. https://doi.org/10.1016/j.ocecoaman.2017.03.001

Klein, L., & Dodds, R. (2017b). Blue Flag beach certification: An environmental management tool or tourism promotional tool? *Tourism Recreation Research*, 43(1), 39–51. https://doi.org/10.1080/02508281.2017.1356984

Klein, Y., & Osleeb, J. (2010) Determinants of Coastal Tourism: A Case Study of Florida Beach Counties. *Journal of Coastal Research*, 26(6), 1149–1156.

Koster, R., & Lemelin, R. (2009). Appreciative inquiry and rural tourism: A case study from Canada. *Tourism Geographies*, 11(2), 256–269.

Lucrezi, S., Saayman, M., & Van der Merwe, P. (2014). Influence of infrastructure development on the vegetation community structure of coastal dunes: Jeffreys Bay, South Africa. *Journal of Coastal Conservation*, 18, 193–211.

Lucrezi, S., Saayman, M., & Van der Merwe, P. (2015). Managing beaches and beachgoers: Lessons from and for the Blue Flag award. *Tourism Management*, 48, 211–230.

Lucrezi, S., Saayman, M., & Van der Merwe, P. (2016). An assessment tool for sandy beaches: A case study for integrating beach description, human dimension, and economic factors to identify priority management issues. *Ocean & Coastal Management*, 121, 1–22.

Lucrezi, S., & Van der Walt, M. F. (2016). Beachgoers' perceptions of sandy beach conditions: Demographic and attitudinal influences, and the implications for beach ecosystem management. *Journal of Coastal Conservation*, 20, 81–96.

Marin, V., Palmisani, F., Ivaldi, R., Dursi, R., & Fabiano, M. (2009). Users' perception analysis for sustainable beach management in Italy. *Ocean & Coastal Management*, 52, 268–277.

McKenna, J., Williams, A. T., & Cooper, J. A. G. (2011). Blue Flag or Red Herring: Do beach awards encourage the public to visit beaches? *Tourism Management*, 32(3), 576–588.

Midwood, J., & Chow-Fraser, P. (2012). Changes in aquatic vegetation and fish communities following 5 years of sustained low water levels in coastal marshes of eastern Georgian Bay, Lake Huron. *Global Change Biology*, 18, 93–105.

Miller, M. L. (1990). Tourism in coastal zones: Portents, problems, and possibilities. In M. L. Miller & J. Auyong (Eds), *Proceedings of the 1990 Congress on Coastal and Marine Tourism*, Vol. 1. National Coastal Resources Research Institute.

Ontario Ministry of Tourism and Culture. (2007). Canadian travel market: Swimming & boating while on trips. Retrieved from http://www.mtc.gov.on.ca/en/research/travel_activities/CDN_TAMS_2006_Swimming_and_Boating_Oct2007.pdf

Ryan, C., Huimin, G., & Chon, K. (2010). Tourism to polluted lakes: Issues for tourists and the industry. An empirical analysis of four Chinese lakes. *Journal of Sustainable Tourism*, 18(5), 595–614.

Smith, D. R., King, K. W., & Williams, M. R. (2015). What is causing the harmful algal blooms in Lake Erie? *Journal of Soil and Water Conservation*, 70(2), 27A–29A.

Swimdrinkfish. (n.d.). Last accessed August 2022 from https://www.swimdrinkfish.ca/blue-flag

Yoon, Y., & Uysal, M. (2005). An examination of the effects of motivation and satisfaction on destination loyalty: A structural model. *Tourism Management*, 26(1), 45–56.

Udiyana, I. B. G., Suastama, I. B. R., Astini, N. N. S., Mahanavami, G. A., Karwini, N. K., & Maretta, Y. A. (2018). Innovation strategy the development of competitifeness of eco-based coastal tourism destination, management organization and quality of services. *Journal of Environmental Management & Tourism*, 9(4), 851–860.

U.S. Department of Agriculture, Natural Resources Conservation Service. (2016). Effects of Conservation Practice Adoption on Cultivated Cropland Acres in Western Lake Erie Basin, 2003–06 and 2012.

Vollmer-Sanders, C., Allman, A., Busdeker, D., Moody, L. B., & Stanley, W. G. (2016). Building partnerships to scale up conservation: 4R Nutrient Stewardship Certification Program in the Lake Erie watershed. *Journal of Great Lakes Research*, 42(6), 1395–1402.

Wesley, A., & Pforr, C. (2010). The governance of coastal tourism: Unravelling the layers of complexity at Smiths Beach, Western Australia. *Journal of Sustainable Tourism*, 18(6), 773–792.

White, M. P., Pahl, S. Ashbullby, K., Herbert, S., & Depledge, M. H. (2013). Feelings of restoration from recent nature visits. *Journal of Environmental Psychology*, 35, 40–51.

Zhou, L. Q., & Lin, Q. (2003). On lake tourism development: Modules and tendencies in the 21st century. *Economic Geography*, 1, 234–248.

Zielinski, S., & Botero, C. M. (2019). Myths, misconceptions and the true value of Blue Flag. *Ocean & Coastal Management*, 174, 15–24.

16 Managing paradise

Reflections on the management of Mexican beaches with the Blue Flag label

Omar Cervantes, Aramis Olivos-Ortiz, Jerónimo Ramos Sáenz Pardo, Dora María Castro-Linares and Itzel Sosa-Argáez

16.1 Introduction

The beach is a place where the ocean and land converge; it is a key ecosystem that provides several benefits to the society, such as coastal protection and infrastructure, known as environmental services. It is a scarce, complex, and irreproducible good that can be called an *environmental asset*, being the support of an economic sector made up of hotels, real estate, services, and supply with effects on labor and its associated social welfare. This complex socio-ecological system, known as "the Paradise", results from the interaction of its elements, giving rise to emerging properties such as the *beach landscape*, whose appeal resides in its types, shapes, and associated attributes, highlighting the color of its sand and the condition of sea water and their coastal marine biophysical elements represented by mollusks, birds, fish, and dunes and vegetation cover, whose variety competes with the biodiversity of plants and animals.

This economic, social, environmental, political, and institutional territory sustains multiple uses and activities in the exposed (sandy intertidal area) and submerged (immersed, swash, or scrolling) zones. In this strip, visitor flows range from hundreds over a few hours throughout the day, to thousands seasonally, on top of its intrinsic ecosystem dynamics. All of these make environmental management a major challenge (Cervantes, 2019).

It is worth mentioning that cultural aspects, such as gastronomy, are part of a beach landscape resulting from a complex system of interrelations between biodiversity, coastal territory, and the background of the actors who live and work in this particular ecological context. Through observation, they have become acquainted with the reproductive seasons and cycles of the flora and fauna, and the best time for collection, hunting, or consumption; the perception, production, acquisition, preparation, consumption, and disposal of food, as well as the technology that develops around all these processes. For the above, food is considered a complex identity element intrinsically linked to the beach. It is a clear example of the nature–society–culture interplay that evidences the historical memory and its traditions inherited from generation to generation, which remain in the taste of the local community, travelers, and tourists looking for unique local features.

DOI: 10.4324/9781003323570-17

210 *Omar Cervantes et al.*

This work outlines a dissertation on the Blue Flag scheme from the perspective of socio-environmental and cultural complexities in a country characterized by five coastlines. It describes the scope, benefits, issues, and pending evolutionary topics of this renowned eco-label in the context of recreational and tourist beaches.

16.2 Coasts and beaches in Mexico

Mexico has the third-largest coastline in America; it has 159 municipalities in 17 states with access to the sea. Its geographic location is privileged, as it confers a tropical climate. Besides, its east coast covers 3,294 km between the Gulf of Mexico and the Caribbean Sea, across the states of Tamaulipas, Veracruz, Tabasco, Campeche, Yucatan, and Quintana Roo. Its west coast faces the Pacific Ocean and the Gulf of California along 7,828 km in the states of Baja California, Baja California Sur, Sonora, Sinaloa, Nayarit, Jalisco, Colima, Michoacan, Guerrero, Oaxaca, and Chiapas; this coastal strip is also called the Mexican Riviera (Azuz et al., 2018).

In the beach tourist destinations of Mexico, the coastal zone and beaches have been occupied mainly by tourist and residential facilities, involving a series of mostly permanent works and activities (Cervantes et al., 2020). Beach facilities and infrastructure include public accesses, parking lots, showers, and toilets administered by municipalities, as well as private hotels, beach clubs, and on-beach restaurants that provide services to tourists and local inhabitants, such as shades, awnings, and bars (Cervantes, 2018).

These facilities and their associated uses produce effects and impacts, including solid wastes, pet feces, emissions of gases and particles, and discharges of fats and oils, among others, which affect the local environmental conditions and, thus, their quality and appeal. Therefore, the need arises to develop beach certification strategies, along with standards and regulations, addressing beach management and the spatial distribution of recreational activities in the emerged (dry sand) and submerged area of the beach (limit of the wet area and, toward the sea, the swash zone or the buoys installed to delimit the bathing area and ensure the safety of users). These promote an efficient and organized use, with no competition for the space, which brings along effects on the beach itself and the recreational experiences of users.

The coastal gastronomic landscape is a cultural phenomenon in which the original peoples, mestizo communities, or migrants have developed hybrid uses and customs combined in a socio-cultural process to generate new structures, objects, and practices (García-Canclini, 2011). Thus, the Regional Food Heritage (PAR, in Spanish) involves not only artistic objects, historical spaces, and the landscapes of a territory, but also the living, immaterial, and popular culture, the ways of life, and traditional knowledge (Lejavitzer & Ruz, 2020). This intangible socio-cultural dimension of beaches – a complex socio-environmental system (Cervantes, 2019) – is not included in their evaluation, but would supplement and strengthen, in community terms, their certification process within an inclusive and participatory context.

Given its physical-geographic characteristics, Mexico has developed port infrastructure and promoted tourism through cruise ships since the 1970s. Acapulco was the first tourist port, and by 1985 this activity expanded to Puerto Vallarta, Cabo San Lucas, and Cozumel, which together hosted 70% of the 1,482 cruise arrivals to the country (Martínez, 2011). By the year 2010, the coastal cities receiving tourist cruises in the Pacific coast were Ensenada, Cabo San Lucas, Loreto, Pichilingue - La Paz, Guaymas, Topolobampo, Mazatlan, Puerto Vallarta, Manzanillo, Ixtapa-Zihuatanejo, Acapulco, Huatulco and Puerto Chiapas; in the Gulf of Mexico and the Caribbean, Dos Bocas, Progreso, Playa del Carmen, Punta Venado, Cozumel, and Costa Maya. Between January and August 2022, 1,660 cruise ships with 4,117,000 passengers were recorded. The ports that received the largest number of cruise passengers were Cozumel, Costa Maya, Cabo San Lucas, Puerto Vallarta, Mazatlan, and Ensenada, which accounted for 95.4% of all passengers (Datatur, 2022).

According to figures from the Secretaría de Turismo (Datatur, 2022), between January and August 2022, the percentage of hotel occupancy in 70 of the most representative tourist centers in Mexico was 58.2%, a figure 16.8% higher than the level in the same period of 2021. The beach centers of Akumal, Playacar, Cancun, Playa del Carmen, Tijuana Cabo San Lucas, San Jose del Cabo, Mazatlan, Nuevo Vallarta, and Puerto Vallarta accounted for 66.6% as of August 2022, a figure 18.7% higher than the one observed in August 2021. Considering the main tourist ports that captured 95.4% of foreign passengers arriving on cruise ships, each had an estimated average expenditure of US $1,113.4 according to INEGI y Banco de México (2022). This figure translates into an estimated economic revenue in excess of US $4.583 million in this tourism cruise sector.

It is worth mentioning that this recovery corresponds to the transition and/or recovery of tourist flows, especially to the coasts and their beaches, and the withdrawal of mechanisms that limited and restricted mobility due to the COVID-19 pandemic. The increase in flows is explained by the search for open spaces and contact with nature, given the enclosure, by the population and travelers. And specifically, those sites where healthy spaces are ensured in terms of public health and with management actions, management and preventive infrastructure of COVID-19; highlighting the coasts and certified beaches (Perillo et al., 2021).

16.3 Coastal tourism policy

The Mexican coast is characterized by a physiognomy, morphology, and conditions that produce a diversity of landscapes associated with different climates, flora, and fauna attractive for the development of productive activities such as tourism and real estate associated with the sun-and-beach product in the Pacific Ocean, Gulf of Mexico, Caribbean Sea, and Sea of Cortez. Based on the amount, quality, and diversity of beaches, this sector has been growing over six decades from the increasing demand of domestic and foreign tourists. The above is reflected in the accommodation sector, which by 2019 totaled 22,560 hotels with 808,139 rooms, including those with one to five stars and non-classified hotels in 70 tourist centers. In the period 2015–2019, the total room availability increased by 3.5% in Mexico and 4.3% in beach destinations, representing 46.7% of the rooms available in the country. In 2019, hotel occupancy in beach destinations was 69.1% in the four

212   *Omar Cervantes et al.*

integrally planned beach centers (CIP, in Spanish), 56.1% in traditional destinations, and up to 72.1% in other beach destinations like Nuevo Vallarta and Riviera Maya. On the other hand, from a total hotel occupancy of 65.9%, domestic tourists contributed with 24.6% and foreign tourists with 41.3%. For this same period, big cities reported 64% hotel occupancy, highlighting the dynamism of beach destinations (SECTUR, 2019).

The above is reflected in the account of accommodation, food, and beverage services, which represent approximately 35% of expenditure (OECD, 2020, p. 25). Therefore, it is imperative that tourism supply evolves toward a sustainable scheme in agreement with the Sustainable Development Goals (SDGs) in the area of Sustainable Cities, Submarine Life, and Terrestrial Ecosystems, also considering the inclusion and perspective of the local communities.

That is why the tourism sector becomes a priority of the Mexican state, developing its strengths and leveraging opportunities along with the analysis and attention of its weaknesses and threats. The goal is consolidating tourist destinations and diversifying their products, taking advantage of Mexico's huge potential in terms of natural and cultural resources.

One strategy issued by SECTUR to manage this variety of beach destinations is through the Beach Center Program, which groups the so-called Traditional Beach Centers, i.e., those whose development is linked to historical aspects, such as Acapulco, Mazatlan, and Veracruz. On the other hand, the development of modern beach destinations, called Integrally Planned Centers (CIP, in Spanish), started in 1974. These are located in seven states on the Pacific coast and five between the Gulf of Mexico and the Caribbean Sea (Riviera Maya). Altogether, there are 263 recreational beaches registered, with internationally renowned destinations such as Cabo San Lucas, Riviera Nayarita, Huatulco, Cancun, and Cozumel (Azuz et al., 2018). These centers concentrate the tourist recreational beaches that have been awarded the Blue Flag label in Mexico. For the 2022–2023 season, these are distributed as follows: Mexican Riviera, 25 beaches for Los Cabos, Baja California Sur; five (5) in Zihuatanejo, Guerrero; four (4) in Puerto Vallarta, Jalisco; one (1) in Bahía Banderas, Nayarit; two (2) in Huatulco, Oaxaca; and one (1) in Sonora, in the Gulf of California. Additionally, there are 22 CIP beaches in the Riviera Maya (Mexican Caribbean), one (1) in Tamaulipas, and two (2) in Yucatan, in the Gulf of Mexico.

In this sense, Mexico's tourism policy has established that environmental and social management systems should be performed in planning products (plans, programs, laws, standards, certifications, and good practices) with the participation of all stakeholders: entrepreneurs, civil organizations, local communities, and governments. A precedent is the 2013–2018 Program for the Tourism Sector, seeking to strengthen the competitive advantages of tourism, the generation of information, research, and knowledge on tourism destinations and product lines, by encouraging innovation, diversification, and consolidation of tourism by region and destination, promoting high-quality standards in tourism services and a comprehensive safety policy to provide a fulfilling leisure and recreational experience to visitors. Accordingly, the period 2013–2018 is a new era toward the certification of the three sectors – industry, trade, and services – where the Secretaría de Turismo (SECTUR, in Spanish), responsible for addressing public policies, develops the design, structure, promotion, and application of *certification models* tailored to micro-, small-, and medium-sized businesses in the tourism sector.

The tourism policy has focused on establishing sustainability programs through certifications and awards such as S, Punto Limpio, Moderniza, Tesoros de México, and Playas Blue Flag. These certifications are endorsed by organizations such as Earth Check, Rain Forest, Green Key, and NOM 171 green hotels. Besides, large hotel chains have participated by establishing sustainability departments, certificates such as Green Globe and Green Key, and good management practices as in the sargassum case. All these follow the criteria set out by the Global Sustainable Tourism Council (GSTC) and the World Tourism Organization (UNWTO). In this sense, the General Law of Tourism (LGT, in Spanish) was published in 2009, directing the concurrence of attributions for the participation of the states and municipalities in various aspects, highlighting the need for land-use planning in the tourist sector. On August 5, 2019, the General Land-Use Planning of Tourism (POTGT, in Spanish), aiming to *promote land use for the organized and sustainable use of tourism resources*, was published in the *Official Journal of the Federation*. The POTGT established Sustainable Tourism Development Zones (ZDTS, in Spanish), which are essential for land-use planning of tourism in beach destinations. In line with the above and in response to the Climate Change agenda, the federal government conducted several studies for 16 beach tourist destinations to determine the degree of vulnerability to climate change, set actions aimed at restoring the water cycle, and build an inventory of greenhouse gases from activities associated with the tourism sector. It should be mentioned that these are considered cases of good practice for promoting sustainable development in America by the World Tourism Organization (SECTUR, 2018).

16.4 Beach certification

The vision of beach management in developed countries is embedded within integrated management schemes for coastal zones, which have set environmental, economic, and social objectives to achieve sustainability for the coastal strip (Zielinski & Botero, 2015). The appeal of sun-and-beach destinations largely depends on the maintenance of the natural conditions of their main resource: sandy beaches. However, the common scenarios observed are crowded spaces with a disorganized spatial distribution and inadequate disposal and management of solid and sanitary wastes. In addition, competition for space between uses and activities has brought with it changes and alterations in the landscape and its functionality as an ecotone, threatening the permanence of sandy areas. Thus, beach certification appears as a management scheme where both society and suppliers of tourist services seek to homogenize technical criteria for environmental and recreational quality. At the international level, this certification scheme includes the Blue Flag program (Cervantes et al., 2017).

214 *Omar Cervantes et al.*

16.5 Certification context

Certified recreational beaches with environmental awards have implemented environmental practices that seek the satisfaction of users that utilize a space considered a product. Some have implemented environmental management systems (SGA, in Spanish) that supplement awards like Blue Flag at the international level. In Mexico, there is a certification called *Bandera Blanca* (White Flag) or *Playa Limpia Sustentable* (Sustainable Clean Beach); beaches are assessed for compliance with these certifications as per the Mexican Standard NMX-AA-120-SCFI-2016, which, unlike the mandatory Official Standards, is non-binding. The certification or award assessment process evaluates, monitors, and endorses that the beach meets a series of standards, attributes, and sustainability measures related to three strategic aspects: *economic*, characterized by proposed investment ideas aiming to produce high profitability rates; *social*, involving the need to include social and community benefits in projects, as well as the attitudes, behaviors, and preferences of users, given that besides being a scheme that provides leisure and recreation, it supports emotional health; *and environmental*, addressing the commitment with space from an integrated perspective as a unique and essential ecosystem (Cervantes & Alafita, 2015). Certifications are competitiveness and marketing elements, in addition to demonstrating political and social relevance and will. Today, the most competitive destinations are those that guarantee their schemes, processes, and services, that is, the social sustainability of environmental zones according to international standards. In other countries, it has been demonstrated that certification processes not only incorporate those destinations that hold them on important reference lists, but also place them in positions of financial competitiveness of great importance. Certification and acknowledgment of good practices through compliance assessments allow for establishing sustainable financial, social, and ecological schemes, in addition to operationally maintaining and potentially obtaining other environmental beach awards. Nevertheless, evaluation criteria generalize and consider all beaches equal, which becomes a challenge in Mexico, a country with a diversity of beach shapes, traits, conditions, and compositions. There are beaches with different tidal ranges (macro and micro) that are also socially and culturally heterogeneous, reflected as differentiated environmental perceptions and attitudes among local users and visitors of sandy areas.

16.6 Blue Flag

The Blue Flag (BF) label seeks to promote, among other things, the installation of leisure infrastructure and services without differentiating by beach types, thus homogenizing the application of the evaluation criteria, as all beaches are different from one another. To note, one of the key steps in integral beach management is the classification and typology as the basis for any management strategy or action. Its structure includes: a) the quality of bathing water; b) educational and environmental information; c) safety and services; and d) environmental management. Currently, Mexico has 64 beaches, 2 marinas, and 31 ships certified with the BF label in 9 states of the country (Figure 16.1).

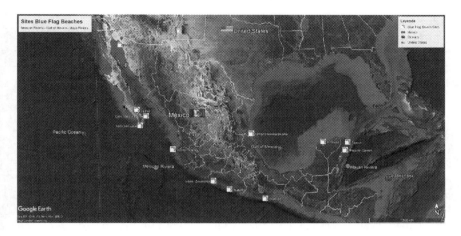

Figure 16.1 Blue Flag beaches in Mexico (2022–2023 season)

The selection process of BF sites is carried out by a national board composed of several government secretariats related to tourism, trade, and the environment, which in turn interact with an international jury chaired by the Foundation for Environmental Education (FEE). In 2012, FEE initially selected PRONATURA A.C. as a national operator with 11 beaches; this organization was later replaced by FEE México (http://www.blueflagmexico.org/index.php), which has 47 certified beaches to date (2022–2023 season). It is worth mentioning that the hotel sector plays a relevant role in the occupation of land, the maintenance and protection of beaches and coastal resources, and the impact on the local communities from investments and the generation of employment. Hence its natural relationship with Blue Flag's momentum and growth in Mexico.

Improving the environmental and recreational quality of beaches is an added value that contributes to the competitiveness of sun-and-beach tourist destinations. Besides, it is always important for the authorities responsible for beach management to achieve the goals of certifying all beaches for recreational and tourist use. Once awarded, beach certification is valid for a given period of time (Blue Flag is granted for one year and NMX for two years) and is renewed provided the conditions that supported the original certification are either maintained or improved. In this sense, the continuous improvement levels include aspects such as dune conservation, estimates of load capacity to maximize the recreational experience, sand conservation (color, texture), and scenic value. Also, loss of human life must be prevented through risk minimization strategies, such as the continuous monitoring of return currents – a relevant aspect that is gaining increasing international attention in beach management given its social, economic, ecological, and environmental impacts.

16.7 Knowledge, flavors, and tourism

The climate, the locations, and their elements in an environment of nature, culture, flavors, and knowledge are an attraction in destinations that involve and promote

216 *Omar Cervantes et al.*

different aspects within an alternative tourism context. Coastal destinations stand out because the availability and type of resources promote the development of topics such as gastronomy, a privileged field of study for the in-depth analysis of the relationship between nature (ecological environment) and culture (Secretaría de Turismo, 2020; Ugaz Cruz, 2017). This tourism segment has a huge potential to boost local, regional, and national economies and promote sustainability and inclusion (WTO, 2017).

Tourism and gastronomy are an indissociable binomial or ensemble that contributes to the diversification of Mexico's tourist offering (SECTUR, 2013). Over the past few years, this relationship has become closer since international organizations such as the World Tourism Organization (WTO) promote strategies for the development of the gastronomic tourism segment as a sustainable activity. Consequently, it has become a driving factor to energize, innovate, or expand markets for more sustainable development (Gómez Nieves, 2018). Thus, at the country level, gastronomic tourism is also considered a segment with the potential to promote tourist development in Mexico. This option, besides beach certificates, contributes to the attractions for travelers and tourists seeking intangible experiences to take back home.

Regional traditional cuisines as an element of local identity or "grandmother's" cuisine are those that are transmitted from generation to generation and are modified with the passing of time. They are made up of the ingredients, technique, and flavors of the regions and includes drinks, grains, red meats, white meats, seafood, spices, and fruits and vegetables (Sosa-Argáez & Silvestre-Campos, 2018). The traditional profile is oriented toward features gained by the cuisines from the influences of other states and/or countries, the socio ecological environment and historical contexts in which they arise and are being transformed with the passing of time these cuisines. Regional characteristics are determined by the customs and lifestyles of the population of each coastal area, their usual celebration practices and their own ingredients, endemic and/or introduced, which are the flavors, colors, shapes, and textures that the inhabitants relate to and identify as their own. Some examples that could be mentioned are the forms and variations of fish and/ or seafood *ceviches* of each beach and coastal area. It changes its title depending on the community and region, with the addition of ingredients for the adobo and fish species, without altering the principal cooking technique, which is cooking in firewood, giving it a characteristic flavor that creates a peculiar taste. This is mixed with the adobo that each cook creates through the coastal flavors and the knowledge that has been passed from generation to generation, as does the use of a grill, which presses the fish on both sides, called *zaranda*, so that the traditional knowledge and flavors are something to be taken into account for tourism and beach certifications, promoting the uses, traditions, histories, and identities of these beaches and locations (Sosa Argáez & Pérez-Magaña, 2020).

16.8 Concluding remarks

In Mexico, the *Bandera Blanca* or *Playa Limpia Sustentable* certification processes, as part of the social strategic perspective, consider the local population in projects

Reflections on the management of Mexican beaches 217

through the attitudes, behaviors, and preferences of users that entail social and community benefits. For its part, Blue Flag contemplates integrated coastal zone management schemes oriented to the sustainability of the coastal strip without considering the social and cultural heritage of beaches and coasts. The vast Mexican territory is multicultural and biodiverse, including coastal cultural landscapes that are holders of knowledge and whose population play key roles in the construction of guidelines and charters in beach acknowledgment and certification processes. Recognized as unique and essential socio-ecological systems, beaches are the starting point for the construction of acknowledgment or certification that contributes to strengthening territorial development with cultural identity and land management (DTIC), enhancing tangible and intangible local cultural aspects (festivals, and tourist and ethno-gastronomical tours, among others) to promote development highlighting the interrelation between products, ecosystems, and territory (Fonte & Ranaboldo, 2007). In this sense, it is necessary to speak of coastal territories with cultural identity and the opportunity they represent for areas of Mexico and Latin America and include them as parameters for evaluation in certification processes to the benefit of coastal communities, reflected in the economy of the population, seeking the balance between large certification bodies and the benefit of the local community.

16.9 References

Azuz, I., Cervantes, O., Espinoza-Tenorio, A., & Santander-Monsalvo, J. (2018). Númeralia de las Costa Mexicana. Red Temática CONACYT/RICOMAR. 10 pp. México.

Cervantes, O. (2018). Modelo de Capacidad de Carga y Ordenación de las playas. Informe Técnico Final. Proyecto SECTUR 2015-C01–26456. 114 pp. México.

Cervantes, O. (2019). Las playas mexicanas; retos y desafíos. Centro Tepoztlán Victor L. Urquidi, A.C. El Colegio de México. CDMX. DF.16 P. (available from www.centrotepoztlan.org)

Cervantes, O., & Alafita, H. (2015). Las playas certificadas de recreación y los sistemas de gestión ambiental (SGA) en México. In: Sosa-Avalos, R., Verduzco-Zapata, M. G. (Eds.), *Estudios acuícolas y marinos en el Pacífico mexicano*. Universidad de Colima, México.

Cervantes, O., Chávez-Comparan, J. C., Botero, C., Martínez-Díaz, E. (2017). Certificación de Playas en Bahía Banderas. Cap. 9: 199–224. In: Chávez Dagostino, R. M. (Ed.), *Investigaciones costeras en turismo: dos estados una región*. Universidad de Guadalajara.

Cervantes, O., Urrea-Mariño, U., López-Urbán, A., Cortina Segovia, S., Ventura-Díaz, Y., & Quiroz-Villanueva, E. (2020). Las dunas costeras y ZOFEMAT: un vínculo necesario para fortalecer la gestión de las costas. In Rivera-Arriaga, E., Azuz-Adeath, I., Cervantes, O., Espinoza-Tenorio, A., Silva-Casarín, R., Ortega-Rubio, A., Botello, A.V., & Vega-Serratos, B. E. (Eds.), *Gobernanza y Manejo de las Costas y Mares ante la Incertidumbre. Una Guía para tomadores de decisiones*. Universidad Autónoma de Campeche. 878 pp. (p. 24). Campeche, México. https://www.redicomar.com/banco-de-datos-y-repositorio/

Datatur. (2022). Resultados de la Actividad Turística. Agosto 2022. Secretaría de Turismo, México. https://datatur.sectur.gob.mx/SitePages/Actividades%20En%20Crucero.aspx

Fonte, M., & Ranaboldo, C. (2007). Desarrollo rural, territorios e identidades. Perspectivas desde América latina y la Unión Europea. *Revista Opera*, 7, 9–32.

García-Canclini, N. (2011). *La sociedad sin relato: antropología y estética de la inminencia*. Katz.

218　*Omar Cervantes et al.*

Gómez Nieves, S. (2018). *Reflexiones sobre una nueva formación universitaria en el campo de la gastronomía* (1st ed.). Universidad de Guadalajara, México.

INEGI y Banco de México. (2022). *Cuenta de Viajeros Internacionales.* https://www.datatur.sectur.gob.mx/SitePages/VisitantesInternacionales.aspx

Lejavitzer, A., & Ruz, M. (2020). *Paisajes sensoriales: un patrimonio cultural de los sentidos (México – Uruguay).* Universidad Católica del Uruguay, México: Universidad Nacional Autónoma de México.

Martínez, C. I. (2011). Organización espacial del turismo de cruceros en México. Études Caribéennes, 18. Last viewed October 26, 2022. https://journals.openedition.org/etudescaribeennes/5077

OECD. (2020). *Tourism Trends and Policies 2020,* OECD Publishing. https://doi.org/10.1787/6b47b985-en

Perillo, G., Botero, C., Milanes, C., Elliff, C., Cervantes, O., Zielinski, S., Bombana, B., & Glavovic, B. (2021). Integrated coastal zone management in the context of COVID-19, *Ocean & Coastal Management,* 210, 105687. https://doi.org/10.1016/j.ocecoaman.2021.105687

Secretaría de Turismo. (2020). *Programa Sectorial de Turismo 2020–2024* (pp. 29–30). https://www.gob.mx/sectur/acciones-y-programas/mensaje-del-secretario-programa-sectorial-de-turismo-2020-2024

SECTUR (Secretaría de Turismo). (2013). *Programa Sectorial de Turismo 2013–2018.* México.

SECTUR (Secretaría de Turismo). (2018). *Programa de Ordenamiento Turístico General del Territorio (POTGT). Zonas de Desarrollo Turístico Sustentable (ZDTS) México.* http://sistemas.sectur.gob.mx/dgots/08-programa-ordenamiento-turistico-general-territorio.pdf

SECTUR (Secretaría de Turismo). (2019). DATATUR. *Análisis Integral Del Turismo. Resultados del Monitoreo Hotelero 2019* (70 Centros Turísticos). 15 pp. https://www.datatur.sectur.gob.mx/Documentos%20compartidos/Reporte70CentrosCierre2019.pdf

Sosa-Argáez, L. I., & Pérez-Magaña, A. (2020). Las mujeres de las ramadas de playa La Boquita. *GénEros,* 27(27), 381–388.

Sosa-Argáez, L. I., & Silvestre-Campos, M. A. (2018). Evaluación de la Calidad de los Servicios Turísticos Gastronómicos en los Establecimientos de Alimentos y Bebidas de comida tradicional regional Colimota en Manzanillo, Colima. *El Periplo Sustentable,* 35, 151–179.

Ugaz Cruz, J. (2017). *Patrimonio Alimentario Regional de Bolivia, Marco conceptual y metodológico para el registro y aplicación de estrategias de desarrollo* (1st ed.). Paz Fernanda Carvajal López.

World Tourism Organization (WTO). (2017). *Second Global Report on Gastronomy Tourism.* https://www.e-unwto.org/doi/pdf/10.18111/9789284418701

Zielinski, S., & Botero, C. (2015). Are eco-labels sustainable? Beach certification schemes in Latin America and the Caribbean. *Journal of Sustainable Tourism,* 23(10), 1550–1572, https://doi.org/10.1080/09669582.2015.1047376

17 Blue Flag in Brazil

Beginning and growth

Marinez Scherer, Leana Bernardi, Isabela Keren Gregorio Kerber and Alessandra Pfuetzenreuter

17.1 Introduction

The coastal zone houses almost 23% of the world's population and tourism and recreation are the basis for socioeconomic development in many coastal cities, as well as fishing and port activities, among others (Manjarres Bovea et al., 2020). In addition to supporting these activities, the coastal zone plays a key role in protecting the coastline, preserving ecosystems and biodiversity, and contributing to human well-being (Rocha et al., 2013). The increase in activities in the coastal zone intensifies problems such as coastal erosion, solid waste deposition, water pollution, loss of habitat, decreasing the value of the landscape scenery, reducing safety and accessibility and providing risk to human health (Semeoshenkova et al., 2017).

Brazil has around 10,800 km of coastline (MMA, 2010) comprising 443 coastal municipalities (MMA, 2021) distributed accross 17 states. Beaches cover around 83,000 hectares along the Brazilian coast (MMA, 2010) and are considered a public asset, with a guarantee of free access to all. On the coastline, there are terrestrial environments and marine environments with overlapping uses and activities, as well as institutions responsible for their management and supervision.

Thus, the management of these spaces is a complex task, but extremely necessary (ME, 2022) and must ensure compliance with national, state and municipal legislation. To help these processes the Blue Flag Programme was brought to Brazil by the Instituto Ambientes em Rede – a non-governmental environmental organization based in Florianópolis, Santa Catarina state, in the southern region of the country.

17.2 Blue Flag in Brazil

Feeling the need for more proactive and practical actions in the coastal zone, the Instituto Ambientes em Rede team decided to start the Blue Flag Programme in Brazil. As a result, Instituto Ambientes em Rede became an FEE (Foundation for Environmental Education) member in 2005 and Brazil was the 49th country to receive the certificate of full membership of FEE. The Blue Flag Programme was brought into Brazil in 2006 (Figure 17.1) and was established just a few years after the legal establishment of the Orla Project, a Brazilian coastal management initiative aiming to plan and manage the land and sea interface.

DOI: 10.4324/9781003323570-18

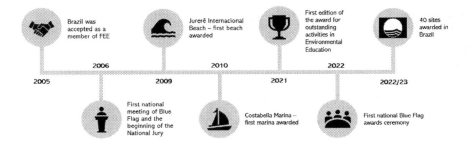

Figure 17.1 Blue Flag Programme timeline in Brazil
Source: Based on Blue Flag Programme Brazil – Instituto Ambientes em Rede (2022)

Blue Flag aims to raise awareness among citizens and decision-makers about the need for protecting the coastal and marine environment. It encourages actions that lead to the resolution of conflicts, improves environmental management and help managers to achieve the desired improvements in the social and environmental quality of beaches. The pilot phase of the programme started with ten beaches, previously selected through a public call for proposals and analysis by a national commission, during the 1st National Meeting of the Blue Flag Programme in March 2006. These ten beaches were located in the States of Bahia (three beaches), Espirito Santo (two beaches), Rio de Janeiro (one beach), São Paulo (one beach) and Santa Catarina (three beaches). The national commission that selected the beaches became the embryo for the programme's National Jury in Brazil.

The criteria, either for beaches, marinas or boats, are similar for the 50 participating countries. They are basic criteria and refer to compliance with the pre-existing legislation of each country. The adaptation of criteria for the Blue Flag Programme in Brazil was also discussed at the 1st National Meeting of the Blue Flag Programme. And, following the international trend, the criteria are continuously analyzed and debated. The debate takes place within the FEE, National Jury and National Workshops.

At the end of two years (2008), the progress of improvements and changes in the management of the ten pilot beaches was analyzed. However, none of them was able to apply for the Blue Flag at that time, and another year was granted to those beaches that had started their adaptation work. Thus, of the initial ten beaches, seven remained in the programme. In 2009 five beaches presented the documentation in order to be awarded but only one was approved. This became the first Blue Flag beach in South America and is located in Florianópolis, in the state of Santa Catarina.

The following year, 2010, the first awarded beach had its certification renewed and one more beach received the Blue Flag, this time in the state of São Paulo, totalling two beaches with the Blue Flag international award in Brazil. However, during 2011, the summer season, [1] one of the beaches failed to meet a series of criteria necessary to maintain the environmental quality and lost the flag. Most of the non-compliances on this particular beach were related to litter management and access safety. Along the Blue Flag history in Brazil other beaches also lost the award either for a few days, for one season or permanently (Figure 17.4). The problems were mostly related to beach safety, water quality issues, litter management and unauthorized trade.

When it comes to marinas, the first one was awarded in 2010 and is located in the state of Rio de Janeiro. The marinas' Blue Flag growth is much lower than the beaches due to the lack of documentation. These days it is most unlikely that a marina will be implemented without all permits. It was not like that in the past. So, we have a few traditional marinas participating in the programme and a bigger perspective of growth on the new marinas being implemented in the next few years.

The programme experienced slow growth in its first ten years but for the last six years Blue Flag increased by an average of five new sites per year and it is expected to increase by at least 10–15 new sites next season. Currently (2022), Brazil has 29 beaches and 11 award-winning marinas (Figures 17.2, 17.3 and 17.4), plus another 15 beaches and 2 marinas in the pilot phase preparing to apply next season.

The municipalities of the beaches that have the Blue Flag strive to maintain the high standard of environmental quality of the award, having beaches and marinas that have already had the Blue Flag for more than ten years (e.g., Tombo Beach and Marina Nacionais, Guarujá, in the São Paulo State and Marina Costabella, Angra dos Reis, in Rio de Janeiro State). Municipalities are slowly understanding that it

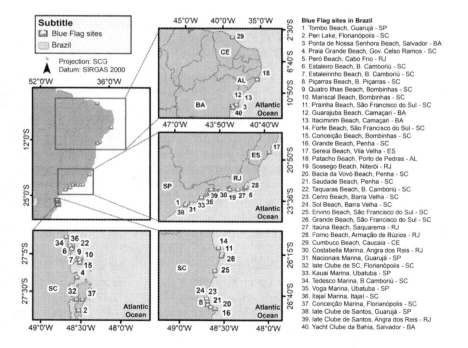

Figure 17.2 Blue Flag sites in Brazil for 2022/2023

Source: Based on Blue Flag Programme Brazil – Instituto Ambientes em Rede (2022)

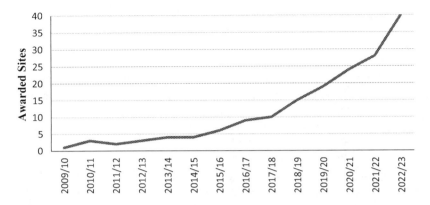

Figure 17.3 Blue Flag's growth in Brazil since its implementation

Source: Based on Blue Flag Programme Brazil – Instituto Ambientes em Rede (2022)

does not take too much to plan environmental educational activities and the results are impressive in respect of behaviour change towards the natural environment and on maintaining public infrastructure.

In 2020, the government tourism agency of Santa Catarina state (SANTUR/SC) asked Instituto Ambientes em Rede to evaluate and indicate 40 beaches in the state to verify which ones have the best chances of earning the Blue Flag. With more than 560 km of coastline and several essential water courses in the interior, Santa Catarina is a state with great potential for nautical and beach tourism. Thus, starting the field visits, the team ended up inspecting 67 beaches in 21 municipalities. Out of those, 25 received the recommendation to start the pilot phase right away and the others will start the work for an eventual application in the future. This is why there is a good perspective for the programme to grow in this state, which already has the largest number of Blue Flag beaches since the 2018/2019 season. Also in 2020, the Blue Flag National Jury felt the need to give some kind of distinction to the sites that proved to be putting great effort into their environmental education activities. So, the award for outstanding activities in environmental education was planned, communicated to the municipalities and organized to have its first edition in 2021. The award was created to recognize the ongoing effort of the Blue Flag site managers regarding the implementation of innovative and effective educational activities, and also to highlight the importance of this criterion within the programme's principles.

As a result, in 2021 four trophies were given to the most outstanding environmental education activities, in which candidates were evaluated and voted on by the Jury members. The candidates were divided into beaches and marinas, and the highest voted group of activities of a site as well as a single exceptional activity were rewarded.

The 2022 edition of the award will feature a new category: best educational video. The National Coordination proposed as a common activity for all beaches and marinas the creation of a video presenting content on the causes and consequences of

Blue Flag in Brazil 223

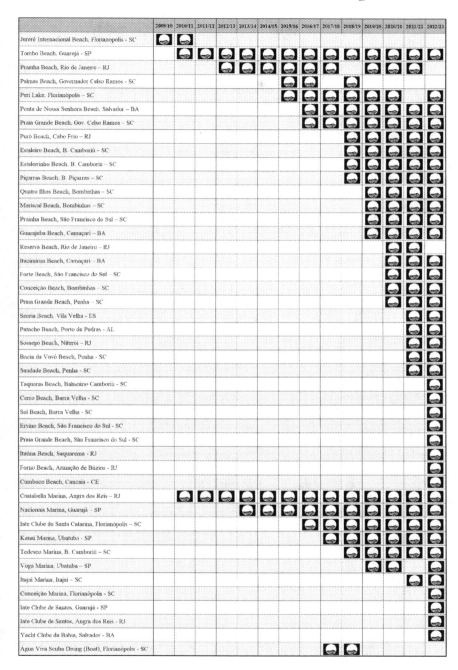

Figure 17.4 Blue Flag certified sites across the years 2006–2022 in Brazil
Source: Based on Blue Flag Programme Brazil – Instituto Ambientes em Rede (2022)

224 *Marinez Scherer et al.*

climate change. The most-voted video will be awarded together with the other four categories presented in previous years. The prizes will be handed to the winners in the first national awards ceremony, an event that will gather representatives of municipalities and members of the National Jury among other entities for the delivery of the Blue Flag to the awarded sites and to mark the beginning of the new season.

In previous years, the flags were delivered to each site in their own city. However, due to the increased number of awarded beaches and marinas in 2022, a national event was necessary to deliver all the flags in time for the beginning of the season. But more than a necessity, the national Blue Flag awards ceremony also provides an opportunity to connect site managers with others involved in the programme, resulting in an exchange of experiences and also the chance of celebrating together another year of progress for the Blue Flag Programme in Brazil.

It is important to note that Brazil has a well-represented National Jury. Therefore, the National Jury of the Brazilian Blue Flag Programme is composed of the Ministry of Tourism (MTur), the Ministry of Economy, the National Heritage Secretary (SPU), the Ministry of the Environment (MMA), the Ministry of Education (MEC), the Instituto Ambientes em Rede, the Brazilian Nautical Association (ACATMAR), the Brazilian Coastal Management Agency (Agência Costeira), the SOS Mata Atlântica Foundation, the Brazilian Society for Water Rescue (SOBRASA), the National Association of Municipal Environmental Agencies (ANAMMA) and the Brazilian Association of State Environmental Entities (ABEMA).

17.3 Blue Flag and Projeto Orla – managing the Brazilian beaches

Brazil has had a Coastal Management National Programme since 1988 when Federal Law no. 7661 instituted the National Coastal Management Plan. Ever since, the Brazilian federal government has been looking for alternatives to organize uses and activities, guarantee environmental conservation and protect the national heritage sites in the coastal areas. Several tools and strategies were established, such as ecological-economic zoning, management plans and coastal monitoring, among others.

In particular, discussions regarding how to better manage the beaches and shoreline were held in the late 1990s. Based on that, the Shoreline Integrated Management Project, known as the Orla Project, was created and later formalized by Federal Decree 5300 in 2004. The Orla Project aims to articulate different public policies affecting the shoreline with effective measures balancing economic development and environmental and heritage protection, considering aspects of the urban occupation, conservation and leisure activities, among others (ME, 2022). Orla Project aims to not just manage the beaches, but also the nearshore, planning and ordering activities such as aquaculture, surf, bathing and artisanal fisheries. In addition, the Orla Project has the potential to be responsible for enhancing erosion control and nature-based solutions (NBS) to climate change effects, being an important tool for the management of land and sea interaction (LSI).

The Blue Flag Programme started in Brazil (2006) soon after the establishment of the Orla Project, and has been developed hand in hand. It can be considered that

Blue Flag in Brazil 225

there is a relationship between the growth in the number of Blue Flags and the evolution of the Orla Project. The Orla Project has also been growing in recent years after a period of stagnation, mainly due to Federal Law no. 13240/2015, which transfers the beach management responsibility from the federal government to local councils, as long as the Orla Project is developed.

Taking into account the nature of the beach award initiative, there is a great opportunity for an even stronger relationship between the Blue Flag Programme and the formal coastal and management initiatives in Brazil, especially considering the Orla Project.

Considering that the Blue Flag Programme is a non-governmental and voluntary initiative, and it is not possible for the programme alone to tackle structural problems existing in the coastal zone of Brazil, the Orla Project presents an important strategy for resolving conflicts, ordering the shoreline and beaches, and paving the way for the beach to receive the Blue Flag (Pfuetzenreuter, 2021). On the other hand, municipalities that want recognition regarding their efforts in coastal management can develop the Orla Project and apply for a reward through Blue Flag.

In order to make this even stronger relationship a reality, the Blue Flag Programme criteria could also focus a bit more on ocean uses and activities and on climate change effects in coastal zones. A reward should be considered for those municipalities that apply nature-based solutions to mitigate erosion and flooding issues, restore ecosystems, preserve biodiversity and prevent ocean pollution.

17.4 Threats and opportunities for the Blue Flag Programme in Brazil

Along with the implementation of the Blue Flag Programme in Brazil, several difficulties were identified by the Blue Flag National Coordinators.[2] The main vulnerabilities found were the following:

- *Conflict of competencies:* Despite the law that makes possible the transfer of the management of the beaches from the federal to the local government, there are still conflicts of management. It is sometimes observed on the beaches a series of activities that are not authorized, such as street vendors, sports courts, kiosks, bars, concerts, boat rental services, etc. This situation can lead to difficulties in identifying misuse of public space (Lima et al., 2018; Scherer, 2013; Scherer et al., 2020).
- *Lack of enforcement of environmental norms*: Most coastal municipalities lack a capacitated team to monitor and enforce environmental norms. In addition, beach users, in general, are unaware of the rules or do not feel compelled to comply with them (Oliveira et al., 2016; Scherer et al., 2020).
- *Lack of management processes in the administrative structure of municipalities:* In general, municipalities do not have a sufficiently organized administrative structure to carry out management processes in their various phases. There is a failure in the diagnosis of problems, in the planning of actions to solve these problems, in the implementation of these actions, and practically no monitoring (Lima et al., 2018; Scherer et al., 2020).

226   *Marinez Scherer et al.*

- *Irregular occupation of the sand dunes area and/or the sand strip on the beaches:* this characteristic is present on many Brazilian beaches. The lack of law enforcement and the growing urbanization on the beachfront had led to a disorderly occupation of this narrow strip, not only by buildings but also by unauthorized equipment. In addition to the resulting environmental impacts, this kind of occupation impacts the coastline and its capacity to minimize climate change effects, such as coastal erosion and flooding (Lima et al., 2022).
- *Lack of appropriate water quality:* Environmental management and award programmes such as Blue Flag demand excellent bathing quality, and the current situation of basic sanitation in Brazil, especially in the coastal zone, does not allow for this. The lack of basic sanitation throughout Brazil, especially in areas of high concentration of people, such as the coastal area in the summer months, leads to contamination of the waterways and the sea, impairing the quality of water for bathing or recreational use (Instituto Brasileiro de Geografia e Estatística, 2002; Instituto Brasileiro de Geografia e Estatística, 2010; Pfuetzenreuter, 2021).
- *Poor solid waste management:* For a decade, Brazil has been discussing regulations to control solid waste, at the federal, state and municipal levels. However, there is still a lack of awareness among the population and tourists about the management of the waste produced during their visits to the beaches, resulting in the presence of garbage in the sand and in the sea. Also, taking pets to the beach can damage the health, of humans and pets alike (De Araújo, 2003; Pfuetzenreuter, 2022)
- *Lack of educational activities:* Educational programmes for sustainability are not very widespread among beach users. Local councils promote very few environmental education activities; most of the activities are created and developed by local associations or NGOs (Kerber, 2020).
- *Little financial support:* There is little investment in adequate infrastructure and services in most coastal tourism destinations. Beach infrastructure bears the minimum, either in basic sanitation or in safety equipment and services at the beach (Scherer, 2013).

On the other hand, the Blue Flag Programme brought to Brazil the discussion on beach management and compliance with Brazilian legislation for beaches and marinas. For instance, the possibility of receiving the Blue Flag is a great incentive for municipalities to adhere to the Orla Project as a way of planning and ordering the uses and activities on the shoreline.

The synergies observed between the Blue Flag Program and the Orla Project are the formation of a management council responsible for the activities carried out in the coastal zone, the growth of entities and institutions involved in the discussions, and the strengthening of the presence of civil society, including academy and businesses, in the management group. Also, the elaboration of a diagnosis of coastal ecosystems, enabling the ordering of the strip of sand and promoting the mediation of conflicts, is a relevant synergy between the Blue Flag Programme and the Orla Project.

Besides the synergy with the federal government initiatives, the Blue Flag Programme in Brazil has the potential to increasingly contribute to the

Blue Flag in Brazil   227

socio-environmental quality of our beaches and marinas. Improvements have been observed in the certified beaches, such as:

- Improvement of coastal ecosystems' health.
- Rise of environmental awareness due to educational activities (e.g., understanding the importance of correct waste disposal, the need for pet-free beaches, the reduction of single-use plastic, among others).
- Improvement of water quality.
- Improvement of the accessibility to the beach.
- Better services for tourists and the local community.
- A greater number of public bathrooms.
- The presence of lifeguards, which improves safety for beachgoers.
- Strength of the local council management measures.
- Improvement in quality of life.
- Improvement in the sense of belonging to the public space.
- Real estate valuation.
- Job and income generation, encouraging better training for the local workforce.

Therefore, we strongly believe the Blue Flag Programme has a true potential to leverage sustainable coastal management in Brazil, especially if it incorporates criteria aiming to help local councils to protect the coastline against climate change effects, restore ecosystems and protect biodiversity.

Notes

1 Blue Flag season in Brazil may vary, depending on the region. In South Brazil, the season comprises the months of December to March, while in the rest of Brazil it is considered BF season all year round.
2 The first author of this chapter was the Blue Flag National Coordinator from 2006 to 2010, while the second author has been the National Coordinator since then.

17.5 References

Alves, B., Rigall-I-Torrent, R., Ballester, R., Benavente, J. & Ferreira, O. (2015). Coastal erosion perception and willingness to pay for beach management (Cadiz, Spain). *Journal of Coastal Conservation*, 19(3), 269–280. https://doi.org/10.1007/s11852-015-0388-6

BRASIL. Lei Federal no 7.661, de 16 de maio de 1988. Institui o Plano Nacional de Gerenciamento Costeiro. 1988.

BRASIL. Decreto no 5.300 de 07 de dezembro de 2004. Regulamenta a Lei no 7.661, de 16 de maio de 1988, que institui o Plano Nacional de Gerenciamento Costeiro – PNGC, dispõe sobre regras de uso e ocupação da zona costeira e estabelece critérios de gestão da orla marítima, e dá outras providências. 2004.

BRASIL. Lei Federal no 13.240 de 30 de dezembro de 2015. Dispõe sobre a administração, a alienação, a transferência de gestão de imóveis da União e seu uso para a constituição de fundos; altera a Lei no 9.636, de 15 de maio de 1998, e os Decretos-Lei no s 3.438, de 17 de julho de 1941, 9.760, de 5 de setembro de 2015.

228 *Marinez Scherer et al.*

De Araújo, M. C. B. (2003). Resíduos sólidos em praias do litoral sul de Pernambuco: origens e consequências. *Global Garbage, [S. l.]*.

Instituto Ambientes em Rede. (2022). Blue Flag Program in Brazil. https://bandeiraazul.org.br/

Instituto Brasileiro de Geografia e Estatística. (2002). Pesquisa Nacional de Saneamento Básico – PNSB 2000. Departamento de População e Indicadores Sociais, Rio de Janeiro.

Instituto Brasileiro de Geografia e Estatística. (2010). Pesquisa Nacional de Saneamento Básico – PNSB 2008. Departamento de População e Indicadores Sociais., Rio de Janeiro.

Kerber, I. K. G. (2020). Análise das estratégias de Educação Ambiental propostas pelo Projeto Orla em praias marítimas. Trabalho de Conclusão de Curso. Graduação em Oceanografia, Universidade Federal de Santa Catarina. Orientadora: Marinez Scherer.

Lima, A. S., Figueiroa, A. C., Coelho, V. G. Z. G., Vieira, C. V., Veiga-Lima, F. A., & Scherer, M. E. G. (2018). Diagnóstico da gestão costeira e das políticas públicas do município de São Francisco do Sul, SC, Brasil. *Revista Brasileira de Geografia, 63*(2), 139–153. https://doi.org/10.21579/issn.2526-0375_2018_n2_141-155

Lima, A. S., Gandra, T. B. R., Bonetti, J., & Scherer, M. E. G. (2022). Exploring the contribution of climate change policies to integrated coastal zone management in Brazil. *Marine Policy, 143*, 105180. https://doi.org/10.1016/j.marpol.2022.105180

Manjarres Bovea, C. P., Botero Saltaren, C. M., & Pereira Pomarico, C. I. (2020). Design of a method of evaluation of the beach tourist potential from an integrated management approach: Case of the Magdalena Department, Colombia. *Revista Costas, 2*(1), 1–24. https://doi.org/10.26359/costas.0102

ME. (2022). Ministério da Economia. Manual Projeto Orla. Ministério da Economia. Secretaria de Coordenação e Governança do Patrimônio da União – Brasília: Ministério da Economia, 324 p. 1. Plano de Gestão Integrada; 2. PGI; 3. Gestão Costeira Integrada; 4. Gerenciamento Costeiro; 5. Gestão ambiental; 6. Gestão patrimonial; 7. Gestão de Praias. Brasil. Ministério da Economia. Secretaria de Coordenação e Governança do Patrimônio da União. Brasil. ISBN 978-65-997520-0-1

MMA. (2010). Ministério do Meio Ambiente. Programa Nacional para Conservação da Linha de Costa – PROCOSTA. 2010 [s.n.].

MMA. (2021). Ministério do Meio Ambiente. Portaria MMA no 34, de 2 de fevereiro de 2021. (MMA. Ministério do Meio Ambiente, Ed.) Aprova a listagem atualizada dos municípios abrangidos pela faixa terrestre da zona costeira brasileira.

Oliveira, T. C. R., Scherer, M. E. G., Anfuso, G., Almeida, F. B., Diederichsen, S. D., & Williams, A. (2016). Classificação dos cenários costeiros de praias da Ilha de Santa Catarina, Florianópolis – Brasil. *Desenvolvimento e Meio Ambiente* (UFPR, v. 39, 217–229). https://dx.doi.org/10.5380/dma.v39i0.46171

Pfuetzenreuter, A. (2020). Revisão Sobre o Saneamento Básico Dos Municípios do Entorno da Baía Babitonga. *Revista Costas, 2*(2), 201–210. https://doi.org/10.26359/costas.1702

Pfuetzenreuter, A. (2021). Análise do Projeto Orla sob a ótica dos Novos Paradigmas da Gestão de Praias no Brasil. Dissertação apresentada ao Programa de Pós-Graduação em Oceanografia, da Universidade Federal de Santa Catarina. Orientadora: Marinez Scherer.

Pfuetzenreuter, A., & Vieira, C. V. (2022). Avaliação do lixo marinho nas praias do norte da ilha de São Francisco do Sul, SC. *Revista Geama – Ciências Ambientais e Biotecnologia, 8*(1), 4–13.

Rocha, T. B., Fernandes, G. B., & Nascimento, L. C. (2013). Avaliação dos critérios morfodinâmicos para a fase de diagnóstico do Projeto Orla: um estudo de caso em praias arenosas com desembocaduras fluviais. *Sociedade & Natureza, 25*(2), 333–348. https://doi.org/10.1590/S1982-45132013000200010

Semeoshenkova, V., Newton, A., Contin, A., & Greggio, N. (2017). Development and application of an integrated beach quality index (BQI). *Ocean & Coastal Management, 143*, 74–86. https://doi.org/10.1016/j.ocecoaman.2016.08.013

Scherer, M. E. G. (2013). Gestão de Praias no Brasil: Subsídios para uma Reflexão. *Journal of Integrated Coastal Zone Management, 13*(1), 3–13. https://doi.org/10.5894/rgci358

Scherer, M. E. G., Nicolodi, J. L., Costa, M., Corraini, N. R., Goncalves, R., Cristiano, S., Ramos, B., Camargo, J. M., Souza, V. A., Fischer, L., Sardinha, G. D., Mattos, M., & Pfuetzenreuter, A. (2020). Under new management. *Journal of Coastal Research, 95*, 945–952. https://doi.org/10.2112/SI95-184.[1]

18 Blue Flag in India
Beacons for sustainable coastal management

Sujeetkumar M. Dongre, Shriji Kurup and Sanskriti Menon

18.1 Introduction

India's coastline of about 7,500 km along the mainland and oceanic islands has unique ecosystems and habitats: sandy beaches, dunes, seagrass meadows, mangroves, coral reefs, rocky shores, lagoons (Nazneen et al., 2022), etc. About 15% of the Indian population live along the coast or on islands in nine coastal states and four union territories, each with its own unique cultural and social identity and dependence on coastal resources and opportunities. This combination of beaches, people, culture and amenities makes some of these areas attractive tourism destinations.

Some Indian states like Goa, Kerala and Karnataka have developed policies and infrastructure for responsible tourism and beach destination management, some even mentioning "commitment for sustainable tourism development in coastal areas", and committing to "supporting relevant state agencies in obtaining Blue Flag certification" (Government of Goa, 2020; Government of Karnataka, Dept of Tourism, 2020; Government of Kerala, Responsible Tourism, n.d.). However, tourism pressure, often overwhelming the carrying capacity of many of these destinations, inadequate coastal zone planning and multi-stakeholder conflicts have resulted in damage to the coastal landscape, especially beaches. The problems range from inadequate waste management, biodiversity loss, pollution and significant land use change.

The Government of India, Ministry of Environment, Forests and Climate Change (MoEFCC), as part of its mandate for integrated coastal zone management, has developed related policy and legislation, institutional mechanisms and technical capacity for beach conservation and tourism development. The Society of Integrated Coastal Management (SICOM) and the National Centre for Sustainable Coastal Management (NCSCM) have been constituted for technical and scientific support and operationalization of policies and plans. SICOM has four core thematic areas: (i) Conservation of coastal ecosystems and resources; (ii) Pollution abatement; (iii) Livelihood security; and (iv) Capacity building. SICOM initiated the Beach Environment & Aesthetic Management Services (BEAMS) program for sustainable beach tourism development. BEAMS strives for and seeks to maintain high standards of eco-tourism. The program aims to address gaps in facilities at selected beaches for local authorities and stakeholders by providing required beach

DOI: 10.4324/9781003323570-19

facilities, pollution abatement services, and safety services with prime consideration of environmental norms and regulations (SICOM, n.d.).

The BEAMS program envisioned developing internationally recognized and quality benchmarked beaches across all the coastal and island states in India. Implementation was initiated at 13 locations with support from the World Bank under the Integrated Coastal Zone Management project. Centre for Environment Education (CEE), a member of the Foundation for Environment Education (FEE), saw the opportunity to introduce the international Blue Flag Beach program as a best practice and sustainable model for beach tourism in India. Subsequently, CEE took up the role of the National Operator Blue Flag India as the official country member of FEE. The CEE–Blue Flag India team (hereinafter referred to as the Blue Flag team) undertook site visits and primary discussions with different stakeholders to visualize and identify the scope and challenges of rolling out the Blue Flag program in India. A national workshop with participation from the government of India, state governments, FEE International and experts deliberated on the strategy and road map for implementation. Thus, the commitment and in-principle agreement of the government of India paved the way for several institutions and states to come on board. The state governments identified suitable beaches where BEAMS could be implemented. These were considered pilot sites and the experience of developing the beach amenities and management systems helped all stakeholders in the development of the Blue Flag program in India.

The Blue Flag India National Operator team conducted gap analyses at each pilot site, which included beach visits and assessments of the ecological, social, economic, cultural and legal implications of the development of facilities and amenities at the sites. This study across different beach locations in India also helped to address the concerns of multiple stakeholders, particularly the coastal community. This was also useful to provide specific inputs to the infrastructure designs and spatial site plans developed under BEAMs, enabling the incorporation of eco-friendly and sustainability features. The significant input was to view the beaches as educational sites and use the Blue Flag criteria to infuse a sustainability ethos as the key driver amongst the beach operators, local administrations and visitors. CEE also identified diverse expert members from government, academia, civil society, research institutions, etc. to constitute a Blue Flag National Jury. They also provided overall guidance, technical support, and scientific advice to the government of India to integrate the Blue Flag program into their coastal and beach development initiatives.

Initially, the SICOM had identified specific beaches across the country that include Shivrajpur (Gujarat), Ghoghla (Diu), Miramar (Goa), Bhogwe (Maharashtra), Padubidiri (Karnataka), Kappad (Kerala), Mahabalipuram (Tamil Nadu), Emerald beach (Puducherry), Radhanagar (Andaman island), Bangaram (Lakshawadeep), Rushikonda (Andhra Pradesh) and Chandrabhaga (Odisha) to roll out the BEAMS program. Blue Flag India conducted due diligence processes and gap analyses for these sites and provided critical inputs as to the feasibility of pursuing beach development for the possibility of a Blue Flag award. Some sites had to be reconsidered due to safety risks related to the beach profile, prevalence of rip

232 Sujeetkumar M. Dongre et al.

tides, disturbance to the local communities' needs of using the beach space for their livelihoods, especially fishing, drying and mending nets, or the need for more time for the development of facilities for waste management or wastewater treatment. The processes for preparing the pilot sites yielded the learning that it would be beneficial to kick-start the Blue Flag program by prioritizing sites where there was already appropriate environmental management infrastructure available, cooperation of the local panchayats (village councils), community and other stakeholders, interest in the conservation of beach habitats like dunes, flora and fauna, the scope for involving local communities and enhancement of livelihood opportunities.

Hence, SICOM dedicated its efforts and focused on specific beaches and closely worked with the district administration, local panchayats and the tourism and forest departments. The Blue Flag India team guided the formation of a beach management committee at each site, which helped to bring about decentralized planning and supervision of beach development. A key feature is that the local community and women members were prioritized for employment in the management operations and service provision at the beaches. Today, local women comprise over 90% of the staff at almost all Blue Flag beaches in India. Their contribution to overall beach management, sand dune, sand binder conservation and cleanliness has been the hallmark of the program.

Blue Flag India subsequently has been providing offline and online orientation, training of beach managers and operators, nodal officers on the Blue Flag mission, customizing localized plans, educational focus, evolving implementation strategies, reporting mechanisms and troubleshooting issues across beach sites. Thus, Blue Flag India along with SICOM created the foundations for a robust structural, operational and administrative framework for implementation focused on sustainability, education and Blue Flag criteria.

18.2 Challenges, opportunities and interventions

From among several challenges of sustainable beach tourism, we present those related to the key areas of sustainability and eco-friendly practices that were addressed through the Blue Flag India program: biodiversity conservation, infrastructure for waste management and water quality, energy efficiency, environmental education and instituting a revenue model and decentralized management approach.

18.2.1 Conservation of biodiversity, sand dunes and sand binders

The sites proposed under the BEAMS program had several challenges, such as erosion, habitat disturbance and beach littering, including instances of damage to the dunes and native flora, particularly the sand binder vegetation. Further, there was a notion that these sand binders were a hindrance to the "clean beach" status and needed to be removed. The Blue Flag team provided on-site orientation to beach managers and local staff about the role and importance of sand binders and native vegetation in the beach ecosystem. The educational approach and sensitization enabled the capacity building of the beach team and instituting conservation measures, including sand dune rejuvenation. A unique approach was allocating small patches of sand binder areas to specific beach staff and encouragement to nurture them over three to four months in friendly competition. Their efforts, experiences, challenges and progress were periodically shared with other beach teams in different locations, thus enabling peer learning and action for the conservation of dunes and sand binders. The overall impact was that all beaches retained the sand dunes, and over time, sustained healthy growth of sand binders. The protection of sand binders eventually led to a significant noticeable presence of other beach flora and fauna over time, including butterflies, reptiles, insects, mollusks and crustaceans that were otherwise rarely found on the beach.

This habitat conservation approach with a seemingly simple yet effective sand dune and sand binder conservation effort, instilled tremendous motivation, skilling, and aspiration to develop Blue Flag beaches that are not only aesthetically appealing but also healthier ecosystems.

Shivrajpur, Gujarat

The site identified at Shivrajpur, Gujarat had pristine sand dunes and beach. However, the sand dunes were completely covered with *Prosopis juliflora*, which is an alien invasive species. As the program rolled out, the beach team puzzled over how the infrastructure and beach facilities could be developed without disturbing the sand dune and beach habitat. The Blue Flag team conducted on-site assessments and oriented the beach development team, including the cleaning staff, beach managers and contractors to sensitively handle the constructions done at Shivrajpur. The National Jury members were apprised of the situation and their advice was sought for appropriate measures to conserve the sand dunes. A National Jury member, who is an expert in coastal conservation, conducted a sand dune assessment and prepared guidance to develop and restore native vegetation while conserving the natural sand dune habitat (Selvam, 2019). This step has led to a dune management plan and monitoring system to promote appropriate sand dune conservation measures at Shivrajpur. The result is a restored sand dune habitat with more than eight different species of sand dune vegetation and sand binders like *Ipomea spp.* and *Spinifex* at the beach. Invasive species remain prevalent on dunes and other coastal stretches in proximity of the awarded site, and encouraging adoption of conservation measures is expected to be part of future environment education initiatives by the beach managers. The Blue Flag awarded beach at Shivrajpur demonstrated sustainable tourism, sensitive area management, and biodiversity conservation. The beach management team continues to protect the sand dunes and sand binders and explains their benefits to tourists as part of the educational activities.

The Blue Flag team also used the field visits to study the beach profile and habitats. They conducted nature walks along the beach with the local Panchayat Sarpanch (elected village head), beach managers, officials and visitors. The walks helped evoke a sense of wonder and responsibility towards the natural treasures of the site, such as rock pools, coral detritus, sand dunes, local vegetation, marine life, etc.

Ghogla, Diu

At Ghogla, Diu, too, the conservation of sand binders was a significant component of site improvement. This beach had patches of sand binder vegetation, often ignored, and not conserved. There was very little awareness of beach biodiversity. While visiting the Ghogla beach, the Blue Flag team saw this as an opportunity to orient and engage the beach manager and staff towards sand dune conservation. They suggested that staff members be assigned patches of sand binders to be nurtured over three months. The beach manager created innovative team-building activities for sand binder conservation. He organized competitions and awarded prizes for the team members who took their best efforts in managing the sand dune patches and made efforts to know about it. Further, their efforts were shared with other beach managers across India. This led to the Ghogla team initiating a simple yet powerful way of demonstrating that sand binders can be conserved even in small beaches and even where dunes do not exist. The learnings and experiences of the staff members were shared with several officials and team members and the effort was much appreciated. This specific effort triggered similar conservation efforts for sand binders across Blue Flag sites.

Today, each Blue Flag awarded site has a healthy growth of sand binders, associated biodiversity and specific zoning for their protection. Visitors are also encouraged to know about this vegetation, and sign boards and information boards further inform them about its importance. The beach staff and beach managers have a deep sense of ownership and feel proud to have contributed to beach biodiversity conservation.

Kappad, Kerala

Kappad beach in Kerala is unique in the sense that it is one of the rare beaches along the coastal stretch that is protected by groynes (rock boulders) to prevent erosion. Before the Blue Flag program, this beach was usually subject to heavy erosion, especially during the monsoon, and then sand retention after a few months. The Blue Flag team through its educational and technical support encouraged the beach management and local administration to take up sand binder conservation and protection as a priority. This led to proactive measures by the beach manager and staff to cordon off the sand binder patches and guide visitors away to avoid their walking and trampling on the vegetation patches. They also used the compost material from the solid waste management plant to nourish the sand binder areas. Supervision and regular maintenance led to profuse growth of sand binders, which may not occur in the wild or in non-conserved conditions. The beach team also propagated sand binders in the proximity of the rock boulders, creating a bio-fence preventing the unsafe and unsupervised presence of visitors near the groynes. The site design at Kappad innovated in using sand binders as a natural landscaping element to prevent crowding and to guide visitor access with distinct pathways defined by the sand binder beds. Observations over the last three years show that the presence of sand binders retained a significant amount of sand even during the monsoon and post-monsoon periods. Feedback from visitors elicited by the Blue Flag India team during monitoring visits indicates that this distinct observable feature at the Kappad beach makes them feel safe since they are now able to see and experience a more stabilized beachfront.

Golden, Odisha

The Golden beach in Puri (Odisha) is one of the highest footfall beaches, particularly since it is very close to the Lord Jagannath Temple, which is among India's most visited pilgrimage sites, with over 13 million visitors annually in the years before the Covid-19 pandemic (Government of Odisha, Department of Tourism, 2021). The Blue Flag team oriented the beach managers and officials to use the sand binder vegetation for beach habitat conservation and natural landscaping to guide visitor movement. Golden beach in Odisha, located along the east coast of India, annually faces cyclones and depressions arising in the Bay of Bengal. The sand binder vegetation helps protect the beachfront from erosion and creates buffer space and protection for the facilities and infrastructure. This benefit of sand binders as coastal bio shields and as an important element of disaster risk reduction is now evident and known to the officials and beach managers.

18.2.2 Waste management

The sites identified under the BEAMS program were in a precarious situation with large quantities of litter at the beach and in the water. The major constituents were plastics, glass bottles, fishnets, clothes, decomposing food waste, consumer items, etc. The Blue Flag team embarked upon an educational approach orienting the beach management teams towards identifying the root causes of littering and litter management. This prompted the beach managers to look closely at waste generation and management practices in and around the beach, and the local panchayat. Holistic waste management plans were prepared, including rules to avoid single-use plastics, managing disposables and littering. A code of conduct has been enforced both for visitors and local community residences around the beach. To facilitate the collection of the waste and scope for recycling, the beach management teams have set up appropriate waste bins based on segregated waste collection and a solid waste management plant with periodic monitoring and maintenance of the facilities and services.

The Blue Flag team oriented the beach management team towards applying the Blue Flag environment management criteria to build systems for sustainable waste management and maintenance of clean beaches, "cleanliness rating" for beaches and systematically documenting the presence of bulk and fine litter. The beach managers were able to visualize the impact of their efforts and the gravity of the situation. Subsequent interactions of Blue Flag India with nodal officers, beach managers and maintenance teams during site visits reveal their recognition of the interconnections of beach biodiversity, water quality and visitors' experience of a beach with appropriate waste management.

Before the BEAMS program intervention, Ghoghla beach saw very high levels of littering. Once the site was recognized as a potential pilot site, the beach was raked and the sand was sifted to remove the trash accumulated over the years, especially plastic and broken glass. A regular waste management system was instituted with cleaning

236 *Sujeetkumar M. Dongre et al.*

done multiple times a day and on-site waste separation and composting facilities. The beach ambiance and cleanliness scenario brought about a change in visitor perception and conduct while accessing the beach and its facilities. The beach is now known for being family-friendly and offering peaceful and enjoyable experiences – a unique experience only found at Ghogla beach in the entire Diu union territory.

At beaches along the east coast, particularly at Rushikonda and Golden beach, a lot of sea-based debris accumulates on the beachfront whenever cyclones or low-pressure events occur. The beach management teams are well prepared and put in extra effort and resources to manage the beach after such events. At all awarded beaches, the waste management system includes regular removal of litter, waste bins and waste segregation. Organic wastes are composted and used for the local vegetation, while plastic and other recyclable materials are collected by recyclers. The effort made for keeping the beach clean also influences visitor behavior, resulting in reduced or no littering. It can be said that this is the situation and visitor experience at all the Blue Flag awarded beaches in India. The primary feedback by visitors, elicited through personal interactions and observed in the feedback registers at all sites, has been that they haven't experienced any comparable clean, safe beach with proper waste management and visitor-friendly facilities elsewhere in the country.

18.2.3 Water quality monitoring

Compliance with beach bathing water quality standards and standards for the quality of drinking water supplied at the beach is mandatory for the Blue Flag award. Generally, beaches in India are not periodically tested for water quality. Due to the Blue Flag program, this has become a regular feature of beach monitoring. Given the waste management challenges, ensuring proper water quality was an issue. However, the Blue Flag team encouraged beach management and concerned officials at the different sites to take samples frequently from multiple locations to better detect pollutants, observe monthly trends and take appropriate action for stopping or controlling the pollution sources and pathways to the beach waters. In some cases, district officials redesigned and relaid stormwater drains, prohibited open water discharges, and regulated the nearby hotel and restaurant establishments so that they also took up appropriate wastewater treatment. The local pollution control boards were also involved in water quality monitoring, thereby providing officials with direct observations, checking the effectiveness of pollution abatement schemes and regulations, and taking timely corrective management decisions.

This new feature of water quality monitoring and results being publicly available instilled greater confidence in beach operations and facilities, and transparency in management. Visitors, therefore, have a sense of security and safety and are willing to pay a small fee for the enhanced experience at the beach, the waters and the facilities. Usually, visitors in India only wade into beach waters and seldom take a dip or bathe in them. However, the water quality monitoring and public information of the results, and the visible waste management efforts, encouraged visitors to bathe, often resulting in a higher number of visitors in the safe waters and more time spent on the beach.[1]

A key feature of the Blue Flag beaches is the setting up of grey water treatment plants – by which the treated shower water is used for watering the vegetation and landscape maintenance. The output from the grey water plant is periodically checked and the entire facility has been useful to conserve water and ensure good water quality and overall waste management. India was also awarded a prize for best international practices on pollution abatement by the International Jury.

18.2.4 Public safety

Beaches in India generally have lifeguards as a basic public safety provision. The Blue Flag program has enlarged the scope of "safety" at the beach to cover visitor first aid, accessibility, a safe environment and safe facilities. Beach lifeguards were selected from the local fishing community and trained and licensed to operate through validation from the internationally recognized Rashtriya Life Saving Society (RLSS). This brought standardization of safety operations, provision of standard safety and rescue equipment, and availability of watch towers, including CCTV facilities, a first aid centre and first aid attendant – all available and easily accessible on the beach. The enhanced safety services provide visitors with a deep sense of security and freedom to enjoy themselves on the beach with their families, including women and children. The facilities are designed for universal access.

A significant outcome of the safety features is that numerous lives have been saved at the beach sites, preventing drowning cases and better visitor management, especially during festival days. The safety audits also extend to other service providers who operate water-based sports, speed boats, kayaking, surfing, etc. Thus, the Blue Flag program has helped to prioritize safety and access as key features of beach tourism facilities.

18.2.4 Environmental education

Beaches in India are generally not associated as spaces for learning about the environment or sustainability aspects. The Blue Flag team, therefore, took the opportunity and initiative to use the Blue Flag criteria on Environmental Education to develop, design and implement a planned set of environmental activities on the beach. The beach managers and officials were oriented toward various environmental educational activities, including hands-on exposure on the beach. This instilled a keen sense of curiosity and encouragement to invest in converting beaches into learning spaces for visitors. Each beach team, therefore, began planning and rolling out a distinct set of activities to be carried out over the season and involving experts, volunteers and key leaders from the community to be part of several public environmental awareness events.

As the Covid-19 pandemic restricted tourism, the Blue Flag team took the opportunity to initiate online meetings and orientation for all beach managers on various beach management aspects, ecology, conservation and sustainable tourism. National Jury members were also invited to interact with the beach teams and officials. The scientists and officials from the NCSCM and SICOM also played

238   Sujeetkumar M. Dongre et al.

an important role in facilitating technical sessions with the beach managers. This phase saw a month-long interaction, sharing of learnings and team building, paving the way for implementing Covid-19-appropriate protocols for beach management. The cross-learning and interaction among the beach managers helped to identify various challenges of visitor management, dune conservation, facility maintenance and scope for conducting online educational campaigns.

The MoEFCC's Environmental Education Cell has integrated its National Green Corp (NGC) program with Blue Flag educational activities. NGC is a national-level program of school-based eco-clubs supported by the MoEFCC. Through the NGC, the Blue Flag beach in the state was introduced to students, teachers and district coordinators in the coastal states. The educational activities conducted were hands-on, collaborative, involved the local experts and used the beach space, with a focus on local biodiversity, water quality and waste management to inculcate responsible behavior and sensitization for beach ecosystem conservation. Several events, such as beach walks, campaigns and rallies, are conducted, enhancing people's perception of the Blue Flag beach being a learning space. Due to the educational activities, visitors were able to observe significant improvements in the beach environment and services and had a richer recreational experience. Visitors' perception and ownership of the beach have improved, and they are conscious of contributing to actions that help retain the Blue Flag status.

Visitors often capture their experiences on mobile devices and post commentary, photographs and videos on social media platforms, bringing about an indirect multiplier effect of disseminating the good and positive aspects of Blue Flag beaches, especially to their immediate relations and families. The Blue Flag team and beach managers have received positive feedback from beach visitors, highlighting the proactive engagement of visitors with beach facilities and services. The system of being able to give feedback and see actions taken on it was also a trust-building feature that has been cultivated by the Blue Flag team and the beach managers.

Efforts are underway to deepen environmental education at Blue Flag awarded sites for training local authorities in beach management, promoting solid waste management and wastewater treatment in nearby areas and initiating FEE's other programs (Eco-Schools and Young Reporters for the Environment) in schools and colleges close to awarded sites.

18.2.5 Revenue

To maintain the infrastructure and services at Blue Flag sites, beach management committees (BMC) generate revenue based on user fees. This includes fees for parking vehicles and usage of toilet and shower facilities. This income generated is mostly used to support the salaries of beach management staff and the improvement of facilities. The district administration continues to support the BMC by investing in allied infrastructure like better roads, stormwater management, traffic management, connectivity, promoting electric vehicles, patrolling and ensuring compliance with waste management by nearby hotels, restaurants and enterprises.

This in turn has, overall, seen higher footfalls on the Blue Flag beach. The autorickshaw drivers and local vendors have also benefited from improved income sources. Shivrajpur, Golden and Padubidiri beaches have shown promising results.

18.3 Learnings from the Blue Flag program – potential for sustainable coastal development

The experience of implementing Blue Flag in India since 2018 has highlighted and demonstrated key aspects of beach management for consideration towards a sustainable future. A key element is to design and evolve coastal interventions, programs and activities with the spirit of people's engagement, participatory approach, nurturing of local partnerships and scope for multiple stakeholders to contribute positively to the development process. The role of women and providing opportunities for their proactive participation and decision-making is an important aspect of beach management and operations. Blue Flag beaches have showcased how women from local communities may be oriented and employed in various beach operations, including visitor hospitality, maintenance of facilities and safety and security services. This is a tremendous opportunity for women empowerment, benefiting local communities, and particularly women. Coastal management in India, therefore, requires inclusive participation across various levels to ensure sustainable approaches and practices for beach and coastal area development.

Most coastal states are now identifying beaches across their coastline for redesigning management systems and amenities at beaches in line with the Blue Flag criteria and approach. The World Bank-supported project Enhancing Coastal and Ocean Resource Efficiency (ENCORE) through the ongoing ICZM program aims to "protect coastal resources by focusing on the rehabilitation of coastal beaches and mangroves; address pollution from untreated waste streams including plastics; and support sustainable tourism to boost vulnerable coastal communities" (The World Bank, 2020). Thus far, the identification and development of sites have been led by the SICOM, which then seeks participation from state and local governments. With the benefits of site management and compliance with Blue Flag criteria now evident, there is an emerging demand from public representatives for more sites to be included in the program. In the future, it would be helpful to evolve new models of eco-tourism that are community-based and community-led with greater benefits accruing to the villages and towns close to awarded sites.

All awarded beaches have made beach conservation, such as dune and sand binder maintenance, a part of beach management and operations. This nature-based conservation approach to beach management brings in a deeper connection with economical, social and cultural aspects rather than banking on mere infrastructure building and development in the name of tourism development. The Blue Flag program has helped integrate a conservation-oriented and precautionary principle approach towards beach development as a critical element to sustain and enable responsible eco-friendly tourism in India.

240 *Sujeetkumar M. Dongre et al.*

Note

1 Beach managers' observations and feedback, personal communications, August 2022.

18.4 References

Government of Goa. (2020). Goa Tourism Policy 2020.

Government of Karnataka, Dept of Tourism. (2020). Karnataka Tourism Policy 2020–25. Government of Karnataka. https://www.karnatakatourism.org/documents/karnataka-tourismpolicy-englsih.pdf

Government of Kerala, Responsible Tourism. (n.d.). Responsible Tourism Mission, Kerala. Responsible Tourism. Retrieved October 1, 2022, from https://www.keralatourism.org/responsible-tourism/

Government of Odisha, Department of Tourism. (2021). Statistical Bulletin 2020. Government of Odisha. https://dot.odishatourism.gov.in/sites/default/files/Statistical%20Bulletin%202020.pdf

Nazneen, S., Madhav, S., Priya, A., & Singh, P. (2022). Coastal Ecosystems of India and Their Conservation and Management Policies: A Review. In S. Madhav, S. Nazneen, & P. Singh (Eds.), *Coastal Ecosystems: Environmental importance, current challenges and conservation measures* (pp. 1–21). Springer International Publishing. https://doi.org/10.1007/978-3-030-84255-0_1

Selvam, V. (2019). Shivrajpur Beach: Report on ecological status of dune ecosystem with reference to plantation on dune [Unpublished internal report]. Blue Flag India.

SICOM. (n.d.). Beach Environment & Aesthetic Management Services (BEAMS). SICOM. https://sicom.nic.in/projects/beach-environment-aesthetic-management-services-beams

The World Bank. (2020, April 28). New World Bank Program to Strengthen Integrated Coastal Zone Management in India [Press Release] [Text/HTML]. World Bank. https://www.worldbank.org/en/news/press-release/2020/04/28/india-integrated-coastal-zone-management

19 The status of Blue Flag in Japan
Can Blue Flag be used for beach community development as a sustainable tourist destination?

Norie Hirata and Susumu Kawahara

19.1 Introduction

19.1.1 Purpose and research methods

In this chapter, we discuss the circumstances surrounding Blue Flag beaches in Japan. The history of the Blue Flag (BF) program in Japan is still short, and there have only been a few successful cases. Due to the rise of the COVID-19 pandemic in 2020, assessing the economic impact of BF is difficult. However, we can hypothesize that through activities involving area organizations and neighboring residents, the BF program can have an effect on the community.

Therefore, through research and analysis of beach-related policy records and beach area activities before and after BF certification, we clarify the societal effects of sustainable community development in the BF-certified beach area, as well as the outlook for the future.

Research methods include literature, Internet searches, and stakeholder interview surveys. We will conduct a comparative analysis on the differences obtained from the surveys in the history, environmental conservation, and tourism policies of Japanese beaches, as well as in the activities before and after the certification of BF, etc., depending on its motivation and circumstances in the area. We also conducted interviews with the domestic BF certification group called JARTA (Japan Alliance of Responsible Travel Agencies), and a BF acquisition support group – the "Japan BF Association" – to gather information regarding the current state of Japan's BF beaches.

19.1.2 Current seven BF sites in Japan: Six beaches and one marina

In April 2016, two beaches received the first BF beach certifications in Japan, which were also the first in Asia. They are both located near famous Japanese tourist cities: Yuigahama Beach near Tokyo and Wakasa-Wada Beach near Kyoto. Suma and Motosuka Beaches, which obtained certifications in 2019, are also accessible from major cities, Osaka and Tokyo. The 2021-certified Katasenishihama/Kugenuma Beach have the highest number of visitors in Japan and were the first in Asia to obtain BF certification by a private group (such as beach business cooperative associations). All the beaches mentioned above have passed qualification exams every year (Kaizu et al., 2022). Additionally, a beach and a marina were added

DOI: 10.4324/9781003323570-20

242 *Norie Hirata and Susumu Kawahara*

to the group in April 2022. Riviera Zushi, which obtained BF certification along with Zushi Beach, became the first BF marina in Asia. Note that in this chapter we describe the six beaches (Table 19.1) only.

19.1.3 BF-related research in Japan

Outside Japan, there have been much research on BF (Hirata & Kawahara, 2020), but in Japan, the first literature released on BF was back in 2001, a guidebook entitled "The Blue Flag", a joint publication by UNEP, WTO, and FEEE. The translation was supervised by Ishii (2001). It was the first to introduce the concept of BF to Japan. Following this publication, there was no study of the BF system or the certified sites until our research began in 2018.

First, we analyzed the contents of the 33 criteria required to be certified as a BF beach. We compared this with the four aspects and 12 issues required to become sustainable tourist destinations (UNWTO, 2004) and investigated which categories the 33 BF criteria focused on. We found that no criteria corresponded to economic issues and that more than half were related to social issues (Hirata & Kawahara, 2020).

19.2 History and environment of bathing beaches in Japan and the beach policies

First, we will discuss the country's measures for the bathing beaches and the history, opening periods, and surrounding environment.

19.2.1 Bathing beaches' history, surrounding environment, and opening periods

Bathing beaches have been tourist attractions in Japan since the beginning of the Meiji era (1868–1912) when the Ministry of Home Affairs began to designate them across Japan (Kubo & Sugawara, 2008). At first, the beaches were used for medical

Table 19.1 Basic information on six BF Beaches in Japan

BF beaches in Japan	Date certified	Location	Length[a]	Approx. number of annual visitors[b]
Yuigahama	April 2016	Kamakura city, Kanagawa	890m	587,700
Wakasa-Wada	April 2016	Takahama town, Fukui	590m	146,700
Suma	April 2019	Kobe city, Hyugo	1,800m	648,700
Motosuka	April 2019	Sanmu city, Chiba	500m	43,700
Katasenisihama /Kugenuma	April 2021	Fujisawa city, Kanagawa	1,006m	1,268,300
Zushi	April 2022	Zushi city, Kanagawa	630m	329,000

Sources:
Authors' elaboration based on information provided by the Japan Blue Flag Association (Length) and article in DIAMOND online (August 11, 2020): https://diamond.jp/articles/-/245273 (Approx. number of annual visitors).
[a] From the BF application documents
[b] Average value of 2017–2019

practice, but they gradually became destinations for entertainment and relaxation. The transportation network of roads and trains also helped to make beaches tourist attractions. One of the first bathing beaches introduced was the "Kugenuma Beach" in 1886. In 1887, Fujisawa Station was built near the beach, and then several Japanese traditional inns were built (Sumitomo Mitsui Trust Real Estate HP). Eventually, an area next to the beach with inns/resort houses was also developed as a residential area.

After World War II, Japan experienced rapid economic growth, and leisure spots used solely for entertainment began to emerge. Guesthouses emerged throughout the coastal area, and restaurants and shops opened along the beach in summer. After the 1987 Act on Development of Comprehensive Resort Areas, the diversity of leisure areas increased and the development of theme parks and resort facilities thrived.

In 1985, domestic bathing beaches reached their peak of visitors with about 37.9 million people annually. However, in 2015, the number decreased to about 7.6 million, which was about one-fifth the number of that peak (Nikkei Newspaper, August 26, 2017).

As Japan is a long island country spreading from north to south, the season for its beach opening period (when lifeguards are assigned for safety and accident prevention) differs by location. For example, the opening periods for 2022 were the following: Yuigahama is from July 1 to August 31, and Wakasa-Wada is from July 9 to August 21. Most beaches are open for one to two months during the summer season. Many people visit the beaches during this period as it occurs during the summer break of most schools and companies. As shown in Figure 19.1 (Yuigahama Beach), the area behind the beach across the road is a residential area, and the beach is very close to the local residential life area.

19.2.2 Maintenance and awards of bathing beaches in Japan

A bathing beach is a location that has passed a water quality inspection and is approved by the prefecture ordinance. Since 1973, the Ministry of the Environment

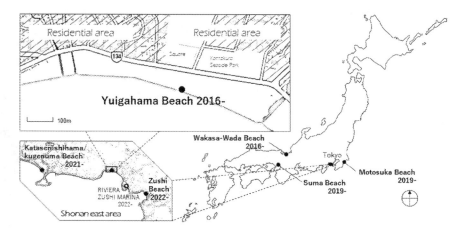

Figure 19.1 Maps of Japan's BF beach location and around Yuigahama Beach

Source: Prepared by the authors based on http://www.blueflag.global

244 Norie Hirata and Susumu Kawahara

(at that time, the Environment Agency) has implemented yearly water quality inspections for the main beaches. In 1985, 100 springs and rivers across Japan were designated as the "Top 100 Waters" (Ministry of the Environment, n.d.). The purpose of this was to enlighten people regarding the purity of the country's water, to boost water preservation awareness, and to develop positive protective measures to ensure a high-quality water environment.

Later, the top bathing beaches (including seaside and riverside) were selected: "Top 55 Japanese Beaches" (1998), "Top 88 Japanese Beaches" (2001), and "Top 100 Comfortable Beaches" (2006). The "Top 10 Comfortable Beaches" were strongly valued for their unique waterfront that people could interact with directly. They were selected by evaluating their beauty, purity, tranquility, and richness. However, unlike the BF, this recognition does not have any criteria for beach maintenance or renewal obligations.

19.2.3 Tourist-related beach policies

The Ministry of Land, Infrastructure, Transport and Tourism (MLIT) and the Fisheries Agency had been promoting the "Blue Tourism" action, which provides various leisure activities for urban residents to visit fishing villages, take advantage of local resources and beautiful scenery, and explore traditional cultures. With this at the core, they proposed measures to revitalize fishing communities in islands and coastal areas. One of the measures was the creation of two booklets (Ministry of Land, Infrastructure, Transport and Tourism and Fisheries Agency, n.d.) to promote Blue Tourism.

In 2003, Japan declared itself to be a tourism-oriented country for inbound tourism. In 2006, the Basic Act for Promoting a Tourism-Oriented Country was founded, and in 2008, the Japan Tourism Agency was established inside the MLIT.

After the certifications of Japan's first two BF beaches, the Japan Tourism Agency introduced the BF beach certification as one of its revitalization strategies in the "Knowledge Collection for the Revitalization of Beaches as Tourism Resources" (Japan Tourism Agency, 2019). Furthermore, they launched the "Blue Tourism Promotion Support Project" (Japan Tourism Agency, 2022). This project supports the development of environment for visitors to beaches and other locations, the facilitation of an enjoyable beach experience, the enhancement of promotions focusing on beaches, and the data needed to acquire BF certification. As a measure to avoid negative publicity regarding nuclear radiation caused by ocean discharge of treated water with radioactive materials removed to low concentrations, this project aims to enhance the appeal of the ocean as a method to attract visitors from inside and outside of Japan and promote a steady influx of tourists. Organizations to promote Blue Tourism were recruited from the municipalities of the four Tohoku region prefectures, including Fukushima, tourism associations, and registered destination management organizations (DMOs).

19.3 Acquisition motives and activities of BF beaches

Here we discuss the BF acquisition motives by region in Japan, as well as their later activities, especially focusing on the two beaches that received BF certification in

The status of Blue Flag in Japan 245

2016. We investigated and organized information from Hirata & Kawahara (2020) and Blue Flag Japan Summit Reports (2019/2021).

19.3.1 *Yuigamaha Beach, Kamakura City, Kanagawa Prefecture*

Kamakura City's bathing beach history goes back to the Meiji era, when it was a thriving villa community. Visitation peaked at 4.15 million people in 1964 with 200 shops on the beach. Yuigahama is the main beach among the three beaches in the city, and in 1990, manufacturers and media came together to transform it into a diverse beach resort. However, its visitors gradually decreased to approximately 520,000 by 2015.

During this situation, Kiyohiro Katayama, a surfer and municipal staff member (Chief Director, Policy Department) who was born in Kugenuma, Fujisawa City, learned about BF from the Ishii (2001) paper when researching the coastal litter challenges of his daily beach-cleaning experience. He then established the "Shonan Vision Institute" with a mission of "community development that takes advantage of the sea" (Figure 19.2) in 2011. He aimed to receive Asia's first BF certification, and, in order to promote BF activities in the entire area, felt the need to promote an area-wide "community development vision" that went beyond individual munici-palities. He organized the "Shonan City Plan 2022" to engage with 1,200 citizens through 80 meetings (including non-BF community issues). He also proposed the promotion of BF certification to the chiefs of eight municipalities in Shonan in 2013. Katayama presented proposals to municipalities and beach business asso-ciations, but the only person to agree was Masuda, the leader of the Yuigahama association. Masuda anticipated benefiting from the advertising effects of leading efforts for Asia's first BF-certified beach.

In 2013, in neighboring Fujisawa City, regulations were put in place regard-ing the playing of music on public beaches. These led Kamakura City to enact the "Regulations Regarding the Improvement of Beach Manners" in 2014. At that time, Masuda and the city came into conflict when he opposed the enactment of this regulation in Yuigahama.

The primary motives for obtaining BF certification for Yuigahama were Katay-ama's strong interest in Shonan Beach, Masuda's expectations of improving the im-age through BF branding, and Kamakura city's goal to resolve the conflict between Yuigahama and the city by supporting the citizens' proposal for BF certification.

After the BF beach certificate acquisition in 2016, in 2018, Katayama estab-lished the "Shonan Vision University", a community college specializing in marine environment, as one of his measures to expand BF activities to citizens. In three years of holding 95 lectures, approximately 3,400 citizens attended. This contrib-utes toward the expansion of BF pursuits; for example, citizens who attended the lectures could become operational staff members or lecturers by becoming familiar with the approach. Each lecture is associated with the 17 SDGs and constructs specific actions to promote these SDGs. Kaizu et al. (2021) show that to encour-age the diverse participation of citizens, Katayama set a precise goal to "acquire BF certification" and define the tasks required of residents who want to contrib-ute to the community. By constructing opportunities to gather and educate people,

Figure 19.2 Community development that takes advantage of the sea

Source: Prepared by the authors based on the mission diagram of Shonan Vision Institute: https://shonan-vision.org/about/

giving each person a sense of accomplishment and assigning a role to each, he successfully created a system that worked toward his goals. Moreover, this will be a model of diverse solutions to certification problems and demonstrates how to involve citizens.

After this, the Shonan Vision Institute and related organizations (Bunkyo University Shonan Institute and FEE Japan) held the "Blue Flag Japan Summit" in December 2019, which was the first gathering of BF beach personnel in the four areas in Japan. The second and third summits were held online in February and November 2021. During the second summit, an activity introduction and a discussion by the personnel of the six beaches, including four BF beaches and two sites aiming for certification, were conducted (Blue Flag Japan Summit Report, 2019/2021).

19.3.2 Wakasa-Wada Beach, Takahama Town, Fukui Prefecture

Beach maintenance in Takahama Town started in 1921. Wakasa-Wada was recognized as a summer tourism spot with beach visitors rising to 1.2 million and inhabited villas increasing to 400 during the summer in the 1980s. In 1998, it was selected as one of the "Top 55 Japanese Beaches" mentioned in section 19.2.2. After that, the number of guests declined, starting in 200, due to the ongoing predicaments faced by the tourist destination (a reduction of travel agents and an increase in low-quality guests). The first "Jet Ski Strategy Conference" was held in October 2013 to discuss countermeasures with the local communities regarding jet skis and illegal fishing.

In October 2013, FEE Japan conducted a survey of the local governments of the "Top 100 Comfortable Beaches" about BF. Takahama Town was also included. This brought BF to the attention of Takahama Town and movements toward the adoption began. In 2014, it was decided that, among the eight town beaches, Wakasa-Wada would aim to acquire the certification. They launched the "BF Promotion Subcommittee" in 2015, which has been held almost every month since then.

From these actions by the town, we can say that the BF acquiring activities are led by the town office in Wakasa-Wada and the main motive for acquiring the BF is to obtain BF as an indicator of the beach's environmental management by the region.

Hirata and Kawahara (2020) discuss the activities of the Wakasa-Wada Beach, which obtained the first BF beach certifications in Asia along with Yuigahama.

In Wakasa-Wada, discussions regarding beach maintenance have taken place among concerned staff since 2013, and these meetings are currently functioning as the "BF Beach Criterion 12 Management Board". In Wakasa-Wada, there is a tradition of cleaning the beach periodically, by tourist companies and the local communities, four times a year (spring, summer, and New Year holidays). Due to this unique tradition, Wakasa-Wada was chosen out of the eight beaches in town for certification. Moreover, they also created working opportunities for personnel with disabilities using "Criterion 18 Trash Separation".

From 2018, in order to provide consistent management of various activities in case the officials in charge are transferred to a different division, they passed the BF activities initiative role to the Tourism Association. Furthermore, they adopted an advanced trash measurement system from the General Incorporated Association "JEAN" throughout the year, which resulted in raising awareness among the local communities.

According to the "BF Japan Summit Report 2019", an increase in foreign tourism was seen due to the BF certification in Takahama Town (population of about 10,000): 1,242 visitors in 2018, and 2,250 people in 2019. In addition, the number of lodgers also increased. Guesthouses and restaurants catering to foreigners opened, and instructors for activities such as yoga and stand up paddleboarding (SUP) came to live there. Restaurants that stayed open year-round also appeared, and the atmosphere of private companies became more energetic.

With the establishment of appealing local activities due to the acquisition of the international BF certification, it was evident there was a rise in pride and connection toward the regional sea area. We can also state that it is linked to the increase in year-round community activities, the improvement in their quality, and an increase in their frequency.

19.3.3. Summary of the later four beaches' BF certification acquisitions

After BF certification of two beaches in 2016, four beaches were added. We describe below whether the BF certification activities are mainly led by local authorities or private groups. The BF acquisitions for the two beaches, Suma and Motosuka, which succeeded in 2019, were both led by the local authorities.

Suma Beach, which is located in Kobe City, enacted an ordinance in 2008 due to the beach's deterioration of public safety, and changed the beach management department from economy/tourism to harbor/coast management. Kobe City's Coast Disaster Prevention Division Manager stated that there are three reasons why they aimed for acquiring BF certification: to promote the restoration of the Suma coast/beach, improve the coast's environmental conservation and safety measures, and increase tourism. After certification of BF, in order to continue the efforts to protect and develop the Suma Coast, it is expected that the certifications activities switch from government-led to cooperation between administrators and locals.

Motosuka Beach is almost at the center of Kujukuri Beach, located in Sanmu City, Chiba Prefecture. Acquiring BF certification was an idea initiated by the mayor, who was inaugurated in 2018. Since he was a member of the Chiba

Prefecture assembly, the mayor stated that he hoped to pass on the beautiful Kujukuri Beach to the next generation. Due to the mayor's proposal in 2018 and led by the government, the beach obtained BF certification within only a year. After certification, they continued to plan to increase BF awareness in the area.

In addition, the two beaches detailed below obtained BF certification in 2021/2022, which was organized by private groups.

Since about the year 2000, **Katasenishihama/Kugenuma Beach** has been receiving complaints from local residents regarding the deterioration of the beach's condition and safety, such as alcohol and smoking issues and music/noise throughout the night. The beach responded with self-regulatory measures, such as music regulation and the early closing of shops, but this led to the number of visitors decreasing to one million, down from 3.5 million people at its peak.

Kugenuma-born Morii became the head of the beach business association for this area in 2018 and collaborated with Katayama since they were graduates of the same local junior high school. In January 2020, they started BF acquisition actions under the cooperation of the beach business association, the Shonan Vision Institute, and the city's tourism promotion team in its economic department. Though the majority of the beach's development is accomplished by the local government in Japan, this beach was established through the beach business association, and the BF acquisition activities were controlled by the civilians. They continued their activities and cooperated with a variety of other groups and became the first private group to obtain BF certification in Asia in 2021.

Zushi Beach is visited by many people year-round for the citizen's everyday walk, the spring movie festival, and winter marine sports. The Zushi Beach's cleaning team's activities have been held once a month for more than 30 years. They fully revised the beach ordinance in 2014 and established several prohibitions such as alcohol (see Hirata & Kawahara [2020] for details). Visitation decreased immediately following the change, but currently the number of visitors has increased to more than 300,000 people per year.

Aiming to acquire BF certification first started with a request from the beach business association, but Zushi City concluded that the PR activity of a world-certified beach in and outside the city would enhance its image and increase civic pride. One of their unique activities is led by university student volunteers from Tokyo, who call on people to sort trash and end littering. Through this activity, the city encourages participants to get involved in the community and potentially make the city their home in the future. Zushi Beach asked the beach business association to pay the application fee and obtained BF certification in 2022.

From this, we understood that for local governments to accomplish BF acquisition activities, it is necessary for residents to understand BF measures and participate in the required steps to achieve certification. The examples of BF certification that were led by private groups accounted for three out of six beaches, and these three beaches are all located in the Shonan area.

We assessed that these accomplishments were achieved with the support of the Shonan Vision Institute's BF promotional activities, as well as the Shonan Vision University's actions mentioned in 19.3.1.

The status of Blue Flag in Japan 249

19.4 Blue Flag certification's new system in Japan

Since April 2022, the General Incorporated Association JARTA (Japan Alliance of Responsible Travel Agencies) has been the BF certification authority in Japan. Its background and future prospects are explained below.

19.4.1 Change of BF certification system in Japan

BF certification in Japan had been held by FEE Japan. FEE Japan started this movement in 2007 and established the General Incorporated Association FEE Japan to operate/conduct the FEE programs in Japan after obtaining permission from the FEE headquarters in 2009. As mentioned in 19.3.1, FEE Japan was BF's certification authority in Japan, but the program had not been initiated when Katayama started BF certification activities in 2011. Coordinating with the FEE headquarters, FEE Japan applied for BF certification in 2015 with Katayama's assistance. In Japan's early years of BF acquisition, FEE Japan was responsible for all necessary work: the proposal conception for application preparation, consulting work (research of locations, coordination with the FEE headquarters, and application), and the creation of approximately 300 pages of application forms and requests for screenings.

JARTA (https://jarta.org/), which took over as the BF domestic certification authority, was established in 2018 and began the operation as the point of contact in Japan by forming an alliance with "Travelife" (www.travelife.info) in 2019. Travelife is an international certification authority that conducts screenings for the sustainability of tour companies and travel agencies.

JARTA has been supporting the sustainability of travel agencies and their international certificate acquisition. To expand this support to accommodation facilities, they reached out to FEE headquarters for approval from the Green Key (hereinafter GK) certification groups, since FEE Japan had returned that responsibility to FEE headquarters. GK complies with the strict rules of FEE and is an international ecolabel that evaluates/determines the environmental policies and sustainable operations of various accommodation facilities, such as hotels and campgrounds. After agreement with FEE headquarters, JARTA became the domestic certification authority on BF measures, following GK.

Out of the five programs developed by the FEE headquarters in Japan, three programs on environmental education will be carried out by FEE Japan, and two programs on environmental certifications regarding tourism will be carried out by JARTA.

The activities of JARTA, the domestic certification authority that is an international ecolabel, not only function as a support to travel agencies and accommodation facilities that are "points", but they also provide support for the fields of environmental conservation and education, focusing on work with children as well as adults, which are also significant "aspects" of BF.

It can be expected that new collaborations with businesses concerned with the development of BF beaches into sustainable tourism spots, such as travel agencies and accommodation facilities, will be made in the future.

250 *Norie Hirata and Susumu Kawahara*

19.4.2 Certification support consulting organization

When JARTA became a BF certification authority, the FEE headquarters decided to divide the certification inspection department and the acquisition support consulting department.

Therefore, Katayama, who made efforts to spread awareness of BF, established a General Incorporated Association, the "Japan BF Association", specializing in BF acquisition support, separate from the office and the inspection department for certification. As previously mentioned, Katayama is the BF pioneer who took action within the Shonan area in 2011. BF acquisition support consulting organizations must register with the FEE headquarters, but only one organization is currently registered in Japan.

Katayama will be in charge of BF acquisition support consultation for the "Japan BF Association", separate from the NPO Shonan Vision Institute's "community development that takes advantage of the sea". Unlike the volunteered guidance he has offered so far, this will be a paid contract as a business. The first certification support consultation business in Japan was born, and Katayama has accumulated achievements and competencies from his ten years of experience. Specialized support and BF promotional activities will become possible by establishing expert BF acquisition support, and improvement of BF reliability and recognition can be expected. Through his consulting business, Katayama focuses on cooperating with local companies and the government, as well as developing local brands and enlivening the local economy.

As we mentioned in 19.2.4, the Japan Tourism Agency started the "Blue Tourism Promotion Support Project" in 2022. The Japan Tourism Agency informed its participants of the "Japan BF Association", the BF acquisition support consultation organization.

To ensure fairness, a clear separation between the inspection and consulting departments was created. This movement establishes the reliability of the international ecolabel. Moreover, having the "Japan BF Association" acknowledged by the Japan Tourism Agency is a significant step. Japanese BF has entered the next phase of its development.

The establishment of a BF acquisition consulting business will lead to its recognition in society regarding the importance of comprehensive area management for the coexistence of the environment and tourism. There is a possibility of a regional economic circulation effect resulting from the far-reaching effects of future regional revitalization.

19.5. Conclusion: Community development from BF certification

To conclude, BF is bringing social benefits to Japan. In this chapter, section 2 explained the beaches' histories, characteristics of coastal areas' usage, management, awards, and tourist policies. Section 19.3 explained the summaries, acquisition motives, and activities following the acquisition of the six BF beaches. Japanese BF began with a promotional activity carried out by one individual, a former local official who loved the ocean. After this, BF acquisition activities were held in the Shonan area by private groups. The Shonan Vision Institute is working toward "Human Resource Development" (Figure 19.2) as mentioned in 19.3.1. The attendance of lectures linked with SDGs (As mentioned in 19.3.1.) by several thousand people is connected with the improvement of BF acknowledgment and the community's expansion of BF activities. This is the indication of "sustainable community development" taking advantage of the sea. Katayama's contribution toward Japanese BF development is very significant.

Section 19.4 introduced the new BF domestic system. We can expect the new certification organization to cooperate with tourism-related businesses surrounding the beach, as well as new developments. In 2022, the BF program was utilized as the country's tourism policy for improving the attractiveness of the beach and the "Japan BF Association" was recognized by the Japan Tourism Agency. We hope that the number of BF beaches will increase, such as in the Tohoku region, and that the acknowledgment of BF will improve during the second stage of BF in the future.

Finally, we expect regional branding impacts from the international certificate brand and PR benefits since BF has easily understandable goals. Also, BF appeals well to educators and increases the chances of providing environmental education to children of the next generation. By aiming for BF to function as a brand concept using regional branding within the beach area, we can expect improvements in the frequency and quality of comprehensive beach management activities by regional communities, and we can strive to foster connections to these areas. Therefore, it can be utilized for beach areas as tourism community development.

We are unable to directly identify the economic issues in the 33 BF beach criteria. However, the commitment to BF activities by the local communities to two of the three SDG fields (environment/social) will continue. Although the economic field is not currently included, we expect that there will be regional economic effects in the future.

Acknowledgment

This work was supported by JSPS KAKENHI Grant Numbers JP18K18276, JP17H00901.

19.6 References

Hirata, N., & Kawahara, S. (2020). Can Blue Flag award contribute to develop sustainable tourism destinations? *AIJ Journal of Technology and Design*, 26(63), 719–724. http://doi.org/10.3130/aijt.26.719

Hirata, N. (2015). *Development of a place branding method which involves various local stakeholders focusing on environmental and human interactions*. Tokyo Metropolitan University, Doctoral dissertation. http://hdl.handle.net/10748/00008623

Ishii, A. (2001). Awards for improving the coastal environment: The example of the Blue Flag. *Rikkyo University Bulletin of Studies in Tourism*, 3, 101–128.

Japan Tourism Agency. (March 2019). *Knowledge collection for revitalization of beaches as tourism resources*. https://www.mlit.go.jp/common/001279559.pdf

252 *Norie Hirata and Susumu Kawahara*

Japan Tourism Agency. (March 24, 2022). Blue Tourism promotion support project. Retrieved July 12, 2022, from http://www.mlit.go.jp/kankocho/topics04_000163.html

Kaizu, Y., Katayama, K., & Sugawara, S. (2021). Toward the Realization of SDGs through Citizen Networks in Bay Side City. *Shonan Forum: Journal of the Shonan Research Institute Bunkyo University*, 25, 91–107.

Kaizu, Y., Katayama, K., & Sugawara, S. (2022). Environmental conservation movement and citizen networks at Bay Area in Japan. *Shonan Forum: Journal of the Shonan Research Institute Bunkyo University*, 26, 27–45.

Kubo, H., & Sugawara, Y. (2008). A study on birth and development of beach sightseeing spots in the Modern times. *Proceedings of Tokai Chapter Architectural Research Meeting*, 46, 757–760.

Ministry of the Environment. (n.d.). *Top 100 waters*. Retrieved July 30, 2022, from http://www.env.go.jp/water/meisui/

Ministry of the Environment. (2006). *Top 100 comfortable beaches*. https://water-pub.env.go.jp/water-pub/mizu-site/suiyoku2006/

Ministry of Land, Infrastructure, Transport and Tourism and Fisheries Agency (n.d.). *Charm of blue tourism*. Retrieved July 30, 2022, from http:/www.mlit.go.jp/crd/chirit/blue-t/blue_index.html

Nikkei Newspaper (August 26, 2017). Sea bathers 20% of peak. https://www.nikkei.com/article/dgkkasdg21h2t_w7a820c1cc0000/

NPO Shonan Vision Institute, Bunkyo University Shonan Institute & FEE Japan. (2019/2021). *Blue Flag Japan Summit Report: Shonan Vision* Vol. 28 & 53. https://shonan-vision.org/socialmagazine_shonan-vision/

Shimizu, M. (August 11, 2020). DIAMOND online. https://diamond.jp/articles/-/245273

Sumitomo Mitsui Trust Real Estate, Town-archives3, Japan's first planned villa "Development of Kugenuma". (n.d.). Retrieved July 12, 2022, from https://smtrc.jp/town-archives/city/fujisawa/p03.html

UNWTO. (2004). Indicators of Sustainable Development for Tourism Destinations – a Guidebook.

General conclusions

María A. Prats and Fernando Merino

Blue Flags are awards given by the Foundation of Environmental Education to beaches, marinas and tourism boats that meet certain criteria related to how they are managed. Since the program's inception, one of its main aims has been to promote the sustainable management of these important resources for the tourism industry: beaches and coasts. To do so, it establishes requirements linked to environmental education and the management practices. The value and effectiveness of this strategy is linked to the public acknowledgment of the award and its capacity to establish the goals of managers towards those ends. So, on behalf of the Foundation of Environmental Education, different actions to make the award valued by the society and the local communities have been implemented.

As societies have evolved, and the concern for a sustainable use of natural resources has increased, a symbol like the Blue Flag may become a source of differentiation between localities, as it provides a clear signal on the management of these areas. Besides the requirements to mitigate environmental impact of the use and management of these areas, some of them also include references linked to the quality or availability of services for the user. Therefore, we can say that the Blue Flag is a reference of certain characteristics linked to how the impact on the signaled site is managed, the services it provides, etc.

A reference like this one may have important effects on the tourism industry in the participant locations. As was indicated in the introduction, the existing research on this subject is scarce and disorganized. Even more, the history on how the program was designed and launched, the challenges it faces in the future and the main related study topics have not previously been presented as one joint study. With the aim of filling this void, this book has presented, across a series of chapters, a revision on the history of the program, some of its main characteristics and a set of research works where details on implementation, the challenges it faces and its consequences are deeply studied by its managers and specialized scholars. Although there are Blue Flags for beaches, marinas and tourism boats, the focus of this book has been on beaches since it is by far where Blue Flags have the most impact, as the expansion opportunities and user numbers are greater.

It must be noted that the effects of participating in the Blue Flag program are not solely relevant to the tourism industry. For instance, the program promotes cleaner waters, and forces them to be monitored, which in exchange will have a long-term

DOI: 10.4324/9781003323570-21

254 *María A. Prats and Fernando Merino*

positive effect on public health; the requirement to have lifeguard services and first aid teams will contribute to reduce beachgoers' accidents, and even reduce public expenditures in the health system. The support for greater sustainable policies will have a positive impact on the environment and biodiversity that, in many cases, would not otherwise have been adopted.

As presented in the first chapter, the Blue Flag was created in Europe and spread quickly to other continents across countries with different economic levels, cultural backgrounds and traditions on their use of the beaches and coastal areas. So as to validate the consequences of Blue Flags, a diverse set of case studies are included. Twelve countries across four continents, all with very different economic situations (from Japan or Canada to India or Brazil), where the beach tourism has differing importance (from France, Spain or Greece to South Africa or Mexico) have been studied, thus allowing us to endorse the following set of conclusions:

- For different goods and services there are certifications aimed to provide information on its characteristics to the consumer. Certifications for an ecological/ environment-conscious management of beaches and coastal areas also exist. Among these, the Blue Flag is, by far, the most recognized beach certification scheme in the world. It is widely known in its participating countries, and it has received increasing attention in the academic literature; however, the number of scholarly contributions in this field needs to increase, and clearly there are important and interesting topics that will generate further future research.
- One interesting characteristic of this program is that it was promoted and managed by an agent (initially the Foundation for European Environmental Education, later the Foundation for Environmental Education), which was not one of the providers of the service (beach tourism) nor a government agency. Other certifications stem from the firms in the industry as a way to differentiate themselves from competitors or assess their characteristics, or by the government to encourage compliance of requirements beyond established laws and regulations. Although cooperation and fluid communication with beach managers and the tourism industry exist, the fact that the program, its requirements and awards are externally managed supposes an additional guarantee of independence and, therefore, increases its recognition.
- The Blue Flag program is well established in Europe, where it continues to grow in a number of countries and awarded beaches but also, and very significantly, in the rest of the continents, especially in the Americas, as well as in some African, Oceanic and Asian countries. This growth validates the broad international consensus around Blue Flags as a beach eco-labeling scheme despite its limitations and the particularities of each continent.
- Blue Flags contribute positively to most of the Sustainable Development Goals established by United Nations, although there is scope to enhance the actions developed at Blue Flag–awarded beaches to improve mainly their socioeconomic impact. While developed countries have made notable contributions to the SDGs, under the Blue Flag program, the situation is far from the same in developing countries where there is a significant gap to be closed that will

require further investment to fully address the challenges that compliance with the SDGs may require in Blue Flag beach environments.

- The Blue Flag program becomes a public warning for beach managers and local governments responsible for the implementation and maintenance of the necessary measures to get the award. Then, it can be used (and in some countries, it is) as a political tool to encourage to meet and/or exceed environmental and safety standards, while also providing environmental education activities to citizens. The fear of public criticism if a beach does not get the Blue Flag in the following year supposes a push for managers to continue meeting the requirements, as well as a support on the demands they must place on other agents. This effect is especially important in the case of public beaches, where the responsible agents are local authorities and for politicians it becomes a type of public auditing of their activity. The fact that to obtain a Blue Flag for a beach is the result of an external evaluation encourages all involved groups to observe them, knowing that the decision is outside the remit of government officials. Besides, in the case of many developing economies this is perceived as an additional value of the program.
- From the perspective of an emerging economy, the development of the tourism sector can go hand in hand with its incorporation into the Blue Flag program. This allows both an increased recognition of the beaches, and provides a signal that they meet exigent requirements of their quality and sustainable management. Examples on how important this strategy has become on the development of coastal tourism in the country can be found especially in Turkey or India.
- The analyses presented for countries such as Croatia, Mexico or Canada have highlighted the importance that the program's development incorporates elements of the local context (in different dimensions such as cultural traits and the institutions in charge of its management) to exploit all the potential it has.
- Using different methodologies (as DEA or Structural Equations Models), and in countries whose beach tourism industry presents important differences (as Spain or Japan), departing from different economic levels (as South Africa) or whose beaches present different characteristics (as Italy or a variety of examples in India), or the seas have different characteristics (from the Mediterranean to the Caribbean or the Pacific Ocean), it is observed that there is a direct and positive relationship between the number of Blue Flags and the development of the tourism industry, the income it generates, even socio-political factors (such as population maintenance).
- Although some challenges remain, the impact of the Blue Flag program on the environment has been observed to be positive in cases such as Greece, and with the capacity to generate internal forces in the communities for greener behaviors as in the case of Italy.
- The revision of the application of the Blue Flag program in different contexts, such as Mexico, Canada or Brazil, highlights some of its challenges. Some of them are country-specific, that is they are dependent on specific characteristics of the country where it is going to be applied, whether because of geographic characteristics, the availability of skilled staff to manage, develop or enforce

the necessary measures or the current valuation of the Blue Flag by beachgoers. Meanwhile, others stem for the proper aims or design of the program for its limited goals in terms of the preservation of the natural values of beaches.

These conclusions inspire future research avenues in this field. As indicated in the book's literature review, there remain important areas where academic research can provide valuable results, both for scholars as well as practitioners and agents with responsibilities in beach management. To highlight a few, we can point to the search for the best strategies that local stakeholders can use to exploit the benefits of Blue Flag status on local beaches, to the design of the policies that encourage all local agents to achieve or maintain the quality levels that Blue Flags suppose, or the establishment of the Blue Flag criteria that, while promoting sustainability and the quality of the beach services, foster the development of the tourism industry in the locality.

Index

administration 7, 16, 25–7, 98, 102, 109–10, 114, 124, 127, 153, 231–2, 234, 238

Africa 3, 6–7, 88–9, 95, 162, 184, 198, 254

America 3, 6, 88–9, 93, 101, 106, 162, 200, 202, 207, 210, 213, 220, 254

Asia 3, 6, 88–9, 93, 162, 241–2, 245–6, 248, 254

Asociacion de Educacion Ambiental y del Consumidor (ADEAC) 10, 18

Atlantic Ocean 85, 224

bathing water directive (76/160/EEC) 12–13, 87–8, 102, 122–3

bathing water quality 24, 33, 71, 81, 87–8, 94, 103, 196, 236

beach certification 3, 33, 46, 57–61, 63, 65, 67, 83, 120, 143, 168, 201–2, 207, 210, 213, 215, 244

beach certification schemes (BCS) 2, 7, 58, 61, 67–8, 97, 106–7, 218

beach-dune system 126, 128, 130–2

beach ecosystem 61, 79, 87, 103, 142, 193, 207, 232, 238

beachgoer 7, 29, 46, 57–8, 61–2, 67, 69, 71, 75–6, 78, 83, 87, 93, 95, 120, 127, 143, 197, 199, 201–4, 207, 227, 254, 256

beach tourism 1, 7, 68, 142, 177, 222, 230–2, 237, 254–5

benefit 3, 4, 6–8. 17–18, 20, 28, 33, 58–60, 62–5, 67, 69, 70, 75, 77, 101, 105, 109, 123, 128, 140, 146, 171–4, 177, 179, 181, 202, 204, 209–10, 214, 217, 233, 235, 239, 245, 250–1, 256

Blue Flag certification, BF certification *see* beach certification

Blue Flag criteria 6, 32, 65, 69–70, 78, 81, 88, 97, 99–101, 124, 131, 175, 186, 206, 231–2, 237, 239, 242, 256

bibliometric 5, 43–5, 47, 49–51, 53, 55, 57

biodiversity 21–2, 27, 30–1, 46, 56, 74, 79–80, 125–6, 131, 134, 145, 161, 186, 209, 219, 225, 227, 230, 232–5, 238, 254

Brazil 5, 7, 66–7, 98, 100, 104–5, 107, 228, 254–55; Bahia (State of) 98, 212, 217, 220; Blue Flag 219–25, 229; Cabo Frio 105; Espirito Santo 98, 220; Rio de Janeiro 27, 220–1, 228; Santa Catarina 98, 219–20, 222, 228; São Paulo 98, 220–1; *see also* Orla Project

Canada 7, 29, 63, 71–2, 76, 110, 199, 200–7, 254, 255; Great Lakes (Canada) 47, 57, 200, 206, 207; Ontario (Canada) 7, 47, 57, 63, 110, 199–203, 207

carbon footprint 22, 82

Caribbean 5, 68, 85, 88, 97–107, 205, 210–2, 218, 255

certification 2–5, 7, 15, 17, 29, 32–3, 40–1, 43, 46–7, 53–56, 59–63, 65–8, 76, 82–3, 94, 97–9, 101–4, 106–10, 119–20, 134, 137–8, 140–3, 145, 147–9, 152, 154–5, 157, 168, 182, 199–208, 210, 213–18, 220, 230, 241–2, 244–51, 254

Chile 5, 100–1, 104

circular economy 22

city council *see* local government

clean beach 66, 214, 232

climate change 22, 27, 54, 73, 78, 80–2, 124–6, 128, 134, 142–3, 155, 186, 206, 213, 224–8, 230

258 *Index*

CO_2 emissions 15, 22, 164
coast 7, 11, 13, 27, 46, 53–4, 57, 66, 68, 91, 100, 103, 124, 128, 158, 160, 165, 187, 191–2, 195–8, 210–2, 217, 219, 228, 230, 235–6, 247
coastal: areas 6–8, 14, 27–8, 32, 63–4, 69–70, 86–7, 93, 128–9, 131, 157–9, 161, 171–4, 177, 186, 192, 195–6, 224, 230, 244, 250, 254; ecosystem 87, 125, 130, 134, 226–7, 230, 240; destination 29, 68, 88, 134, 216; management 2, 8, 63–4, 68, 121, 131, 191, 197, 219, 224–5, 227, 230, 239; tourism 7–8, 46, 56, 66, 70, 86, 92–3, 120, 133, 142, 154, 186, 191, 196, 206–8, 211, 226, 255; zones (*see* Integrated Coastal Zone Management (ICZM))
Coastal and Marine Union (EUCC) 25, 178
coastline 8, 15, 22, 85–6, 90, 92–3, 101, 111–13, 123–5, 160, 168, 210, 219, 222, 226–7, 230, 239
Colombia 5, 63, 74, 100–1, 103–5, 121, 228; Buenaventura 105
contamination *see* pollution
continent 86, 88–9, 97, 100, 102–6, 200, 254
coral: detritus 233; reef 34, 62, 73, 78, 230
corporate social responsibililty 31, 36, 144
Council of Europe 10
COVID 7, 86, 101, 104, 165, 185, 196, 204, 206, 211, 218, 235, 237–8, 241
credibility 13, 18, 20, 28–9
Croatia 72, 84, 86, 91, 127, 158–65, 167, 169, 255; islands 158–62, 165–7; Krk (Croatia) 158, 160, 162, 164–9
cultural 1–2, 7, 23, 26–7, 59, 71, 75, 86, 111, 128, 135, 145, 154, 156, 159, 173, 177, 200, 209–10, 212, 217–18, 230–1, 239, 254–5
customer 150, 176–7

Data Envelopment Analysis (DEA) 6, 135, 137–43, 255
defibrillator 18
Denmark 11, 74, 79, 88, 90–2
depopulation 1, 160–1
diving 31, 40–1, 175, 178
dolphin 42
Dominican Republic 5, 71, 73, 75, 77–8, 81, 88, 97–8, 100, 106
dune 51, 62, 124, 126, 128–32, 177, 207, 209, 215, 226, 230, 232–4, 238–40; conservation 215, 233–4, 238

ecolabel 2–3, 7–8, 12, 15, 46, 53–56, 58, 64, 66, 68, 69, 82, 86, 93, 95, 106, 112, 123, 154, 157–8, 161–2, 165–9; Bandera Blanca 214, 216; Good Beach Guide 2, 47; Playa Ambiental (award) 2; Playa Limpia Sustentable 214, 216; Playa Natural (award) 2; Seaside Award 2; Tesoros de México 213
economic: development 2–3, 6–7, 14, 58, 108, 112, 172, 191, 199, 204, 224; growth 1, 3–4, 6, 8, 72, 77, 80, 86, 95–6, 119, 125, 165, 171, 173, 176, 243; GDP 1, 86, 108, 172, 182
ecosystem 1–2, 22, 27, 46, 51–2, 57, 86, 110, 126, 128, 131, 175–6, 178, 187, 192, 209, 212, 214, 217, 219, 225, 230, 233
employment 1, 4, 8, 71, 75, 77, 81, 86, 119, 146, 154, 161, 173, 184, 191, 199, 215, 232; job creation 3, 191
enterprise 3, 29, 238
environment 1–3, 7, 12–15, 17, 24–6, 28–30, 32, 35, 37, 51–2, 61–2, 64, 68, 79, 82, 85–8, 93–4, 99, 102, 110–2, 121, 123, 125, 128, 131, 143–6, 153, 156, 159, 161, 164, 168–9, 171, 173, 178, 182, 184, 186, 191, 198, 200–1, 205, 215–16, 220, 222, 231, 233, 235, 237–8, 240, 242, 245, 250–1, 254–5
environmental: education 10, 15, 21, 26–7, 29–31, 33–7, 45, 60–2, 65, 71, 73, 75–6, 78, 80, 83, 87, 100, 105, 122, 128, 134, 146, 162, 165, 171, 175–6, 186–7, 191–2, 195, 200–1, 203, 222, 226, 232, 237–8, 249, 251, 253, 255; information 14, 69, 131, 179, 214; performance 2, 28, 146, 148, 174, 179; policy 14, 35–7, 124, 157
Escherichia coli 33, 54, 61, 66, 72
Europe 2–3, 5–7, 13, 24, 60, 86–7, 89, 91, 93, 95, 98, 102–5, 107, 122–3, 146, 156–7, 159, 162, 171, 179, 184, 186, 200, 254
European Commission 2, 4, 12, 15, 102–3, 131, 156, 168
European Directive on Bathing Waters *see* bathing water directive (76/160/EEC)
European Environment Agency (EEA) 25, 85, 95, 102, 107, 125, 131, 178
European Network for Accessible Tourism (ENAT) 25, 178

Index 259

European Union (EU) 14, 17, 85, 87, 93, 95, 107, 168, 178

European Union for Coastal Conservation *see* Coastal and Marine Union (EUCC)

fishing 27, 31, 41, 75, 78, 80–1, 126, 159, 176, 191, 198–9, 219, 232, 237, 244, 246

flora and fauna 22, 78, 209, 211, 232, 233

Foundation for Environmental Education (FEE) 3–4, 9–10, 12, 15, 20, 22, 24–6, 30–3, 35, 61–2, 67, 69, 74–9, 83, 87–9, 91, 93, 95, 97–100, 102, 104, 106, 124, 131, 134, 146–7, 155, 157, 162, 168–9, 171–2, 182, 186, 191–2, 195, 197, 200, 215, 219–20, 231, 246, 249–50, 252, 254

Foundation for Environmental Education in Europe (FEEE) 9–11, 122, 242

founder (co-founder) 4, 9–11

France 2, 86–8, 90–3, 112, 127, 134, 157, 172, 254

GAIA 20:30 4, 21–2, 26, 30, 32, 131

government 8, 13, 28, 53, 60, 62, 64–5, 74, 79, 97–9, 101–2, 105, 122, 145, 148, 157, 165, 172, 184–6, 189, 191, 194, 196, 198, 202, 206, 212, 213, 215, 219, 222, 224, 226, 230–1, 235, 240, 247, 250, 254–5; central government 124; federal government 213, 224–6; national governments 104; state government 231

Greece 6, 46, 57, 73, 77–8, 81, 90–3, 122–4, 127–8, 254–5; Crete 124; Thermaikos gulf 124

Gulf of Mexico 210–2

health 10, 12–14, 17–18, 20–3, 25, 27, 35–6, 47, 51–2, 57, 61, 64, 66, 68–9, 71, 75, 80–1, 125–6, 145, 158, 181, 195, 199, 211, 214, 219, 226–7, 233–4, 254

Hellenic Society for the Protection of Nature (HSPN) 4, 6, 122–4, 127, 131

history 4, 27, 94, 97, 101, 221, 241–2, 245, 253

holiday 13, 28, 93, 174, 186, 205, 247

human rights 17, 36, 94

India 8, 32, 230–7, 239–40, 254–5; Goa (India) 230–1, 240; Gujarat (India)

231, 233; Karnataka 230–1, 240; Kerala 230–1, 234, 240; Odisha (India) 231, 238, 240

inhabitant 7, 93, 113–5, 146, 158–9, 210, 216

Instituto Ambientes em Rede 107, 219–24, 228

Integrated Coastal Zone Management (ICZM) 2, 27–8, 32, 128, 143, 217–18, 228–31, 239–40

international 2–6, 10–11, 13–15, 17, 24–33, 35, 37, 39, 41, 51, 58, 66, 79, 85–8, 93, 98, 100, 102–3, 108, 112, 122–4, 127, 134, 146–7, 153, 156–8, 165–7, 171–2, 178–9, 181–2, 186, 190–1, 200, 212–16, 220, 231, 237, 247, 249–51, 254; consensus 2, 254; policy 2, 14, 27, 28, 35–7, 51–2, 56, 58, 64–5, 80–1, 85, 94–5, 110–1, 120, 123–4, 128, 134, 149, 155, 157, 171, 205–6, 211–13, 228, 230, 240–1, 245, 251

International Council of Marine Industry Associations (ICOMIA) 25

International Lifesaving Federation (ILS) 25, 178

International Life Saving Federation of Europe (ILSE) 15

International Union for Conservation of Nature (IUCN) 15

Ipomea spp. 233

island 5–7, 32, 67–8, 73, 76, 78, 84, 86, 98–100, 102, 111, 121, 123–4, 157–68, 205–6, 230–1, 243–4

Italy 28, 45–46, 55, 57–8, 68, 72, 74, 76, 79, 86–7, 90–3, 95, 110, 112, 127, 147–8, 151–3, 172, 183, 207, 255

Japan 8, 74, 79, 241–52, 254–5; Katasenishihama/Kugenuma Beach 241, 248; Motosuka Beach 241–2, 247; Suma Beach 241–2, 247; Yuigahama Beach 241, 243; Zushi Beach 242, 248; Wakasa-Wada Beach 241, 246

Japan Alliance of Responsible Travel Agencies (JARTA) 241, 249–50

jury 16, 25, 61, 97–9, 101, 103, 124, 178, 197, 215, 220, 222, 224, 231, 233, 237

labor 17, 36, 39, 114, 137, 175, 209

lake 30, 147, 199–200, 202, 206, 207–8

260 *Index*

landscape 1, 77, 110, 126, 127, 153, 200, 209–10, 213, 217, 219, 230, 237
land use 17, 51–2, 125, 213, 230
Latin America (LAC) 2, 5, 60, 66–8, 94, 97, 99–7, 217–8
law 3, 33, 35, 74, 76, 100, 103, 165, 192, 212–13, 224–6, 254
legal framework 2, 32, 79; legality 17
lifeguard 10, 18, 61, 75–6, 103, 105, 123, 174, 191, 193, 195, 227, 237, 243; services 14, 254
local: community 1, 25–8, 31, 37, 39, 61–2, 69, 73–5, 78, 128, 130, 153, 163, 174, 178, 195, 209, 212, 215, 217, 227, 232, 235, 239, 246–7, 251, 253; development 133, 144–5, 152–4, 173; economy 5, 7–8, 39, 108–9, 111, 113, 115, 117, 119, 121, 154, 171–5, 200, 250; ecosystem 37, 41, 71, 75; government 53, 60–1, 65, 125, 144, 153–5, 159, 164, 166, 225, 232, 239, 246, 248, 255
locality 3, 5, 87, 103, 174, 256; *see also* municipality

mangrove 78, 230, 239
marina 6, 12, 15–16, 24–5, 30–1, 34–5, 37, 67, 75, 77, 79, 87–9, 98–9, 123, 131, 134, 137, 157–8, 162–3, 165–7, 171–5, 180–1, 184, 186, 190, 196, 200, 214, 220–2, 224, 226–7, 241–2, 253
marine: environment 2, 79, 93–4, 219–20, 245; litter 46, 57, 66–7, 74, 78–79, 83, 131, 177; protected areas 41, 47, 57, 73, 186; resources 15, 70, 79, 101, 125
mass tourism 1, 105, 108, 120, 159, 173
Mediterranean beaches 46, 56, 66, 127, 128; countries 123, 127, 158, 182; sea 79, 85, 123
Mexico 5, 7, 72, 76, 99–100, 103–5, 202, 205, 210–18, 254–5; Riviera Maya 212; Sayulita 105
municipality 8, 23, 25, 31, 34, 53, 58, 60, 74, 87, 93, 100–3, 105, 108, 110, 112, 124, 127, 134, 141, 145–7, 149–54, 174–5, 177–8, 181, 184, 186, 191, 201, 210, 213, 219, 221–2, 224–6, 244–5; *see also* locality

national park 17, 131, 191, 199, 202
Netherlands 11, 73, 78, 88, 90–2

non-government organization (NGO) 11, 61, 74, 79, 98, 100, 104, 123–4, 159, 164, 172, 178, 184, 189, 191, 219, 226, 246

Oceania 3, 88, 93, 162
Orla Project 7, 8, 219, 224–6

Pacific Ocean 67, 85, 100, 106, 210–2, 217, 255
Paris Agreement 7, 31, 205
planning 1, 4, 19, 27, 77, 82, 101, 128, 154, 156–9, 164, 174, 176, 186, 205, 212, 224–6, 232, 237; coastal 14, 88, 230; land-use 17, 213; tourism 1, 157–8, 168, 213; urban 77, 122
plastic 35, 38, 46, 57, 73, 78, 83, 175, 227, 235–6, 239
policy maker 2, 155
pollution 21–2, 27, 30, 34–6, 38, 50–6, 61, 67, 69, 71, 78–9, 81, 105, 110, 125–6, 133–4, 143, 161, 175–6, 182, 196, 219, 225–6, 230–1, 236–7, 239; noise 39; pollutants 22, 236
port 10–11, 15, 162, 180, 210–1, 219
Posidonia oceanica 6, 78, 124–32
Pronatura Mexico 99, 100, 215
Prosopis juliflora 233
protection: coast 88, 126, 209, 215, 235; environment & natural elements 1, 7, 28, 76, 78–9, 93–4, 108, 124, 131, 141, 158, 165, 202, 224; heritage 7, 224; social 27, 69
publication (scientific) 4, 15, 43–5, 47–50, 53, 55–6, 242
Puerto Rico 5, 73, 78, 81, 88, 97–100, 104–6

quality certification 2, 93, 135, 149, 154

river 68, 244
rule 13, 23, 25, 37, 138, 141, 176, 225, 235, 249
Russia 88–9

safety 15, 24, 26–7, 30–2, 34–7, 39, 60–2, 64–5, 69, 71, 75, 87, 103, 128, 134, 145, 147, 162, 175, 181, 186–7, 191–2, 194–7, 199–201, 204, 210, 212, 214, 219, 221, 226–7, 231, 236–7, 239, 243, 247–8, 255
sand 18, 61, 6–8, 86, 105, 110, 121, 124–6, 129–30, 133, 142–3, 156, 177, 199,

202, 205, 207, 209–10, 213–15, 226, 230, 232–5; binder 232, 233, 234, 235, 239; sand dune 232–4
sargassum 213
sea grass 6, 34, 62, 73, 78–9, 125–6, 130, 230
seaweed 61, 73, 77, 177
sewage 5, 33–6, 38, 72, 88, 158, 161, 177–8
signs of identity 9, 13, 18–20
social: benefit 3, 18, 59, 62, 69–70, 171, 179, 214, 217, 250; consideration 18, 60; dimension 1, 69; impact 8, 11, 27, 62, 145, 215; objectives 9, 27, 60, 127, 213; perspective 7, 58–59, 61, 167, 216; responsibility 24, 39, 87, 167, 169; support 13–14, 76; usefulness 2, 9, 18; value 9, 60
South Africa 7, 46–7, 57, 59, 66–8, 71–3, 75, 78, 81, 83, 87–8, 93, 95, 110, 120, 184–8, 190–3, 195–8, 202, 206, 207, 254–5
Spain 6, 10, 11, 46, 57, 66–88, 71–3, 75–6, 81, 86–8, 90–3, 95, 98, 107–13, 115–19, 121, 127, 143, 169, 172, 182–3, 200, 206, 227, 254–5; Valencian Community (Spain) 6, 108, 111, 113, 115, 119
Spinifex 233
sports 167, 176, 225, 237, 248
stakeholder 5, 8, 14, 22, 25, 28–9, 31–2, 59–60, 64–5, 69, 74, 80, 87, 105, 123, 127–8, 130, 144, 146, 153, 155–6, 159, 164, 166–8, 178, 191–2, 195–7, 212, 230–2, 239, 241, 251, 256; cooperation 27–8, 70, 74, 79, 153, 159, 164, 167, 193
strategy 2–3, 86, 140, 145–6, 155, 171, 179, 201, 207, 215–16, 232, 244, 256; beach management 3, 53, 129–30, 201, 205, 207, 210, 214; Blue Growth 85–6, 94; coast management 8, 64, 127–128, 225; action, policies 28, 53, 61, 78, 87, 128, 133–4, 140, 148, 152–3, 158, 165, 168, 191, 194, 224, 231, 246, 253, 255; sustainability 2–3, 6–8, 80, 94, 126, 133–4, 146, 155, 179, 196; tourism planning 1–3, 7, 80, 179
structural equation model (SEM) 6, 111, 113–17, 119
sun-and-sand tourism 66, 82, 94, 97, 99, 106, 112, 120, 167, 173, 205

sustainability: aim 6, 20, 26, 29, 63, 69, 88, 93, 109–10, 143–4, 146, 153, 165–6, 214, 216, 232; environmental 4, 63, 81, 85–7, 93–4, 101, 110–1, 133, 147, 153, 159, 173–4, 184, 213, 217; perspective 8, 25, 37; principles 2, 22, 32, 35, 69, 88, 145, 158–9, 164, 174, 237; promotion 5, 23, 29, 33, 231–2, 256; social 16, 59–60, 63, 153, 159, 214; standards 22, 31, 41, 58, 60, 63, 69, 77, 111, 144–6, 154–5, 157, 161. 195, 206, 213, 226, 231, 237; tourism 5, 15, 59, 63, 75, 108–9, 119–20, 146, 158, 165–6, 169; *see also* strategy
Sustainable Development Goals (SDG) 4–5, 7, 9, 21–22, 26–7, 69–72, 74–8, 80–3, 86, 178, 192, 195–7, 204, 212, 245, 251–2, 254–5; SDG Agenda 21, 69

territory 1, 6–7, 27, 75, 85, 140, 209–10, 217, 236
tourism: demand 1, 94, 108, 110, 134, 155; industry 2, 3, 6, 8, 28, 30, 64, 67–8, 83, 95, 108, 112, 121, 142, 146, 149, 157, 166, 173–4, 182–3, 195, 205, 253–6; policy 111, 211, 212, 213, 251; sector 1, 3, 4, 6–8, 22, 24, 26, 28, 58, 69, 70, 75, 77, 87, 98–9, 108–9, 111–13, 116, 119, 134, 138–9, 148, 166, 172, 174–5, 195–6, 212–13, 255
tourism boat 24–5, 30–1, 37, 39, 41–2, 76, 87, 98–9, 123, 131, 172, 180, 184, 200, 220, 253
Trinidad and Tobago 5, 99–100, 104
TÜRÇEV 174, 176, 178
Turkey 7, 74, 79, 90, 109, 168, 172–6, 177–83, 255

UNESCO 25, 97, 146, 178
United Kingdom (UK) 2, 46, 57, 68, 90, 164, 168
United Nations Conference on Environment and Development (UNCED) 2
United Nations Environmental Programme (UNEP) 15, 25, 97, 125, 146–7, 157–8, 173, 178
urban beach 60, 112, 126, 197, 200, 205
urbanization 1, 126, 175, 226; pressure 15

village council *see* local government
Virgin Islands 5, 73, 78, 99–100
vision and mission 17, 20
visitor 1, 16, 20, 26–9, 46, 56, 58–9, 61–2,
64–5, 67, 83, 86, 98, 100–3, 109,
125, 127, 129, 130, 140, 145, 165,
173–4, 176–9, 186–7, 190–6, 200–
2, 204, 206, 209, 212, 214, 231,
233–9, 241–8

waste disposal 34, 74, 227; management
65, 88, 99, 134, 158, 161–3, 201,
226, 230, 232, 234–8

water quality 7, 11, 15, 26, 29–31, 33, 36, 47,
56, 61–2, 68–72, 75–8, 80–1, 83, 87,
95, 97, 99, 100–3, 124–5, 134, 165,
184, 186–7, 192, 194, 196, 200–3,
221, 226–7, 232, 235–8, 243–4
whale 31, 42, 178, 187, 191
Wildlife and Environment Society of South
Africa (WESSA) 184–5, 191–3,
195–6
World Cetacean Alliance (WEA) 25 World
Tourism Organization (WTO,
UNWTO) 4, 15–16, 25, 97, 145–6,
159, 178, 186, 213, 216

Printed in the United States
by Baker & Taylor Publisher Services